Andy Warhol

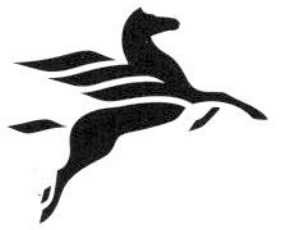

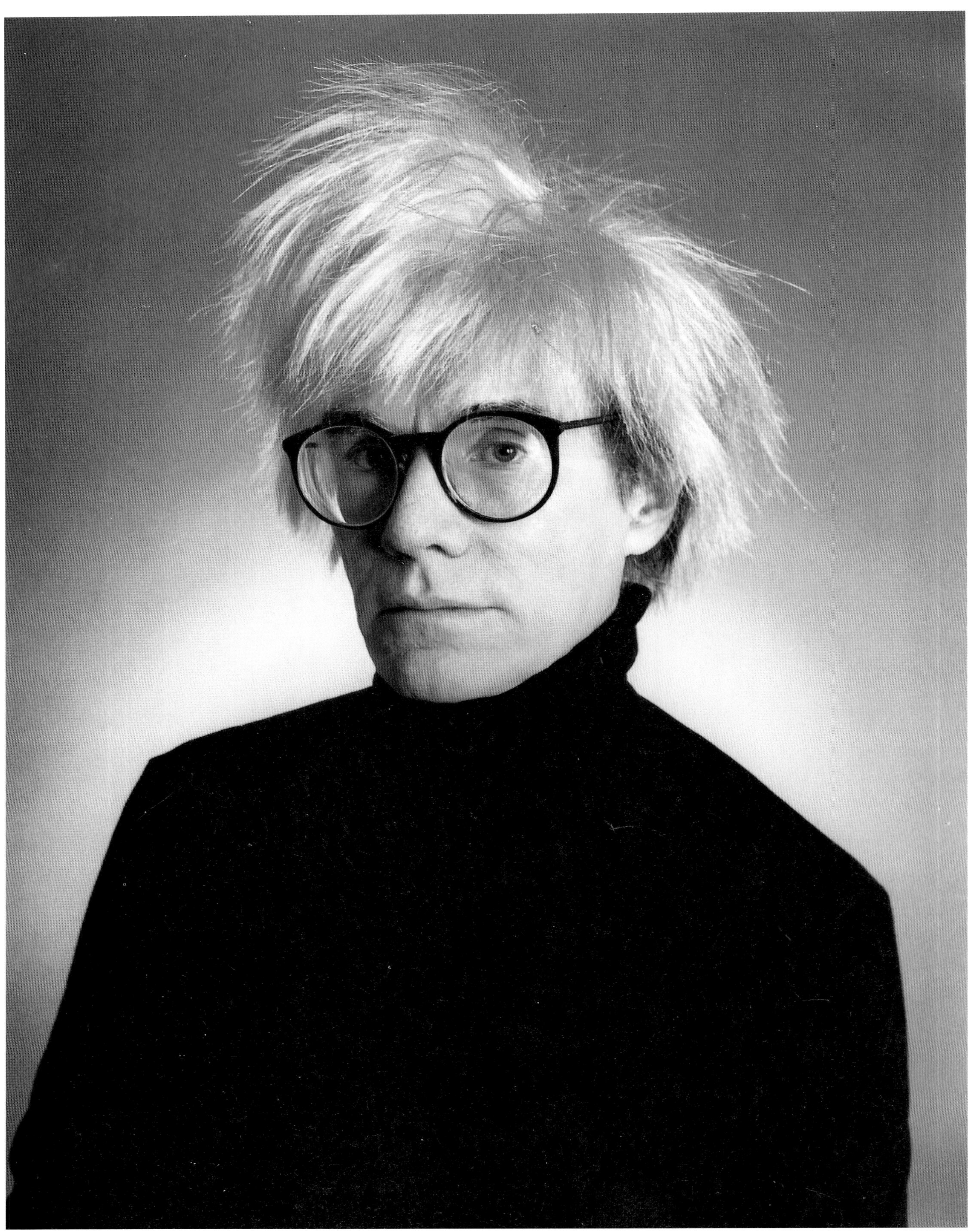

Andy Warhol
1928-1987

Works from the Collections of José Mugrabi and an Isle of Man Company

Edited by
Jacob Baal-Teshuva

With contributions by
David Bourdon, Pierre Restany,
Jacob Baal-Teshuva, Gene R. Swenson,
and Paul Taylor

Prestel

This book is the English edition of the German publication *Andy Warhol: 1928-1987* published to accompany the exhibition held at the KunstHausWien, Austria, from February 23 to May 31, 1993.

Further venues:
Orlando Museum of Art, Orlando, Florida
(October 9 – December 12, 1993)
Museum of Art, Fort Lauderdale, Florida
(January 13 – March 13, 1994)
Curator of the exhibition: Jacob Baal-Teshuva

Photo Acknowledgments, see p. 144

Front cover: *Nine Multicolored Marilyns*, 1986, plate 100 (detail); *Panda Bear* (No. 100), 1983, plate 81; *Campbell's Tomato Soup Can*, 1968, plate 39; *Flowers*, 1964, plate 17; back cover: *Self-Portrait*, 1966, plate 33; quotes by Andy Warhol from *Andy Warhol* (Stockholm: Moderna Museet), 1968
Frontispiece: Andy Warhol, 1986. Photo: Christopher Makos

Prestel-Verlag, Mandlstrasse 26, D-8000 Munich 40, Germany, Tel. (89) 38 17 09 0; Fax: (89) 38 17 09 35

Distributed in continental Europe by Prestel-Verlag
Verlegerdienst München GmbH & Co. KG
Gutenbergstrasse 1, D-8031 Gilching, Germany
Tel. (81 05) 38 81 17; Fax (81 05) 38 81 00

Distributed in the USA and Canada on behalf of Prestel by te Neues Publishing Company, 15 East 76th Street, New York, NY 10021, USA
Tel. (212) 288 0265; Fax (212) 570 2373

Distributed in Japan on behalf of Prestel by YOHAN-Western Publications Distribution Agency, 14-9 Okubo 3-chome, Shinjuku-ku, J-Tokyo 169
Tel. (3) 32 08 01 81; Fax (3) 32 09 02 88

Distributed in the United Kingdom, Ireland and all remaining countries on behalf of Prestel by Thames & Hudson Limited, 30-34 Bloomsbury Street, London WC1B 3 QP, England
Tel. (71) 636 5488; Fax (71) 636 1659

Copyedited by Michael Robertson, Augsburg
Designed by Rainald Schwarz, Munich
Color separations by RCS, Stadtlohn, und Krammer, Munich
Typesetting by Vornehm, Munich
Printed and bound by Neue Stalling, Oldenburg

Printed in Germany

ISBN 3-7913-1277-4 (English edition)
ISBN 3-7913-1284-7 (German edition)

Contents

Foreword

Even during his own lifetime, Andy Warhol's fame was legendary. The work of this "superstar of art history" is covered in this book not only through essays by his major biographer, David Bourdon, and by the art critic, Pierre Restany, but also through quotations from, and interviews with, Warhol himself. Above all, the body of work speaks for itself, and proves that Warhol's place in the history of American art, and the art of the twentieth century, is secure. His work spans a period from the early 1950s to the year of his death, 1987. An unusual, and as yet almost unknown, aspect of it lies in the "Paintings for Children," published here for the first time. The paintings show a series of toy motifs, and were produced by Warhol in 1983 for a children's exhibition in Zurich, where they were shown at child's-eye height.

Some eighty percent of the works illustrated in the plates here belong to the collection of José Mugrabi, and the remainder are held in the collection of an Isle of Man company. José Mugrabi is a passionate collector and admirer of the work of Andy Warhol, and we are grateful to him for allowing his collection to be reproduced in this publication, thereby making it accessible to a wider public.

Special thanks are due to my colleague, David Bourdon, for his essay, and to my close friend and mentor, art historian and critic Pierre Restany, for his memoir of Warhol, which first appeared in the April/May issue of *Galeries Magazine* in Paris, 1987. Milton Estrow kindly gave permission to reprint from *ARTnews* the first important Warhol interview (1963), by the late G.R. Swenson. We are also grateful to the magazine *Flash Art*, Milan, for permission to reprint the last interview given by Andy Warhol, in April 1987, to Paul Taylor, the Australian critic and author. It was with great sorrow that I recently learned of his untimely death at the age of 35 from Aids.

Thanks are also due to Bruno Bischofberger, a close friend of Warhol, for his help and permission to use several photos and transparencies; to Andrea Caratsch at the Bischofberger Gallery for his kind support; to the Leo Castelli Gallery, New York, and to Vincent Fremont of the Warhol Foundation for kind and prompt assistance; to the Ronald Feldman Gallery for their cooperation and Esti Neuman, for her tireless help; to Josie Lerch, for her cooperation; to my wife, Aviva Baal-Teshuva, for her help, advice, and tenacity in researching Warhol's extensive biography and bibliography; to photographer Billy Name for consenting to reproduce some of his photographs in this book; to Christopher Makos for allowing us to use his portraits of Warhol; and to my friend the great American photographer Arnold Newman for kind permission to use his Warhol portrait collage.

Jacob Baal-Teshuva

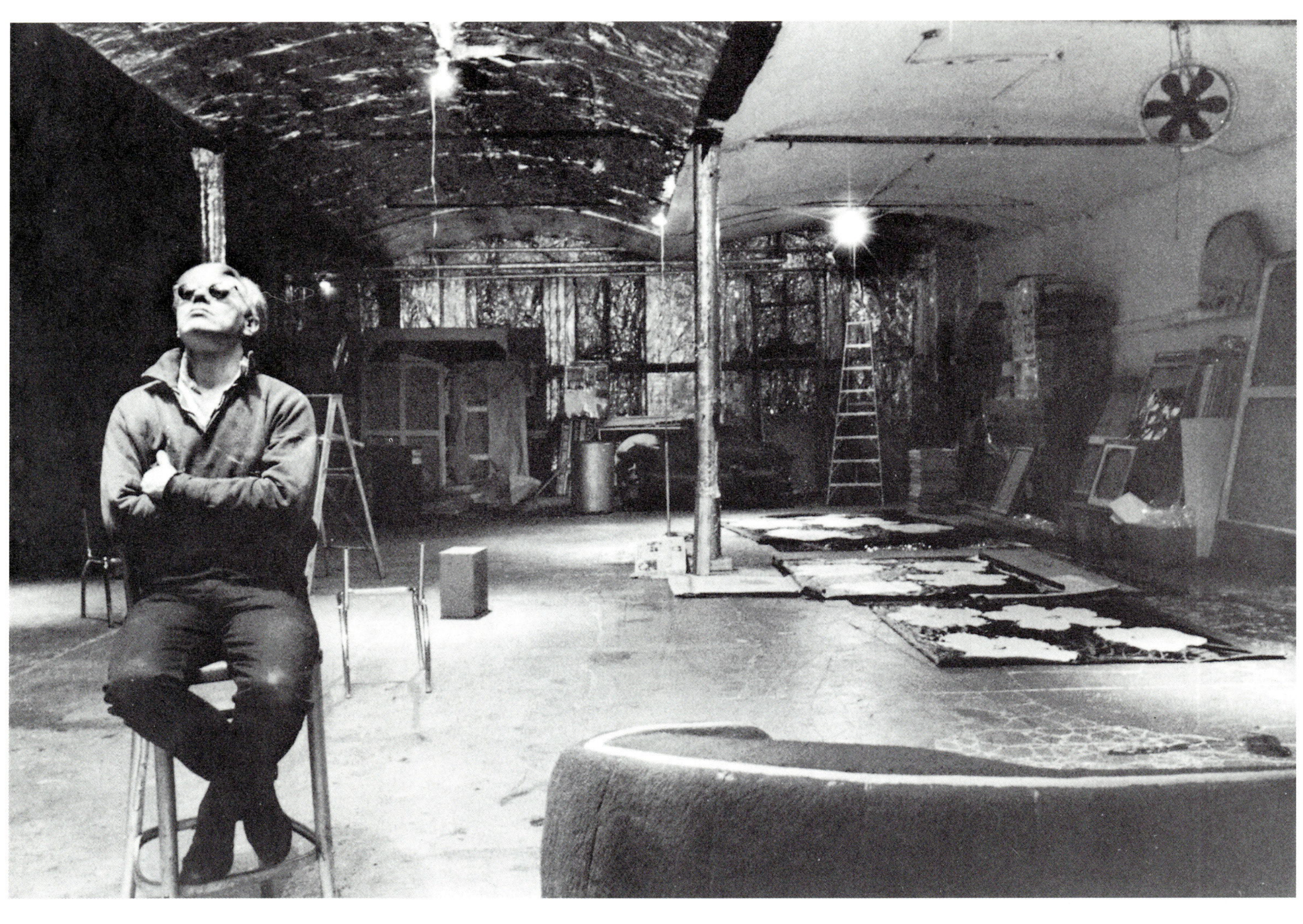

Andy Warhol, ca. 1964/65. Photo: Ugo Mulas

David Bourdon

Andy Warhol and the American Dream

Andy Warhol was an optimist who believed wholeheartedly in the American ideal that every hardworking citizen, given an equal opportunity, earned the inalienable right to become rich and famous. This, after all, was the American Dream. In its emphasis upon egalitarianism and material prosperity, the American Dream now seems a little naive: equality remains hard to come by in the nation's educational and economic sectors, while materialism appears to be at the root of the national debt. But more than fifty years ago, when Andy was a child of poor, hardworking Czech immigrants, it was easier to believe that anyone could rise to a higher station in life through diligent work and thrift.

Throughout the 1950s, Warhol was an extremely successful commercial artist, winning many awards and earning a great deal of money for his stylish illustrations for magazine articles and newspaper ads. He possessed an original and immediately recognizable style, as well as a shrewd instinct for determining which ideas and subjects would "sell" to his audience. But he was dissatisfied with his accomplishment, preferring to gain recognition as a "serious" artist. He also feared that magazine illustrators like himself were about to be replaced by photographers. The foremost question in his mind became how to make the transition from illustrator to painter.

At some point in 1960, Warhol's art underwent a dramatic change, based on his intuition that banal, commonplace subjects would permit him to enter the realm of "high" art. He determinedly transformed himself into a deadpan painter of comic strips and display ads, which he derived from newspapers and magazines. He meticulously simulated the appearance of comic strips, advertising art, and packaging design in large, hand-painted pictures that he presented with a minimum of artistic transformation. The newspapers and magazines that had formerly been the setting for his whimsical commercial art now became the subject of his serious painting.

Of all the Pop artists, Warhol was the most infatuated with tabloids. He doted on them because of their lively combination of scandals, celebrity photographs, and gossip columns. Newspaper headlines epitomized for him the pervasiveness and instant fame that the mass media could generate. From "ready-made" newspaper headlines and comic strips, it was an easy transition for Warhol to start appropriating brand-name products such as Campbell's Soup and Coca-Cola. These paintings gave an ironic, somewhat menacing new dimension to the American Dream by dramatizing the inherent materialism of American culture, with its entrenched consumerism and fascination with advertising, packaging, and promotion.

Many critics hated the pictures. Warhol's detractors, knowing that he had been a highly successful commercial artist, refused to take his new work seriously, viewing him as a flagrant self-promoter and cynical opportunist who degraded the seriousness of art through relentless commercialism. There was no shortage of observers who declared that the artist's brand-name subjects were too "low," "vulgar," and "commercial" to be considered seriously as fine art. The issue of transformation was especially troublesome. If Warhol was a true artist, people wanted to know, why couldn't he invent an image of his own? How, they wondered, could anyone call himself an artist who merely copied labels?

Many viewers were put off by the serial nature of Warhol's enterprise, believing – inaccurately – that he repeated the same composition over and over. They often failed to notice that he was doing something new with the idea of repetition, reiterating familiar images in rows to create seemingly abstract grids. His grid compositions enabled him to "abstract" his ready-made pictorial subjects and make them comply with the formal requirements of a "flat" painting style.

Warhol's insistence upon repetition as a unifying principle of composition attained one of its several apotheoses in his work with his extraordinary gallery installation of trompe l'oeil grocery-carton "sculptures" in 1964. Once again, he appropriated preexisting commercial products and advertising design, but now extended his principle of repetition into three dimensions. His grocery-carton sculptures were built to the exact dimensions of their cardboard prototypes – Brillo soap pads, Mott's apple juice, Kellogg's cornflakes, Del Monte peaches, Campbell's tomato juice, and Heinz ketchup. The sculptures were virtually indistinguishable from their original models. Warhol crammed the gallery with hundreds of his brand-name facsimiles, which he spread out in rows or piled high, making the place resemble a grocery distributor's warehouse.

At first glance, Warhol's box sculptures appeared to follow in the tradition of Marcel Duchamp, whose ready-mades established the aesthetic concept by which anyone could take an ordinary "found object" and present it as a work of art merely by denying its intended function and putting it into a new context. The essential difference, of course, is that Warhol's boxes are not found objects at all, but handmade objects, meticulously recreated in another medium.

Warhol appropriated still other brand-name subjects in the form of show-business celebrities. Stardom, like equal opportunity and material prosperity, was another key component of the American Dream. By latching onto the fame of stars such as Marilyn Monroe, Elizabeth Taylor, and Elvis Presley, he eventually parlayed his own name and face into commercial commodities. Within a few days of Monroe's death in August, 1962, Warhol purchased a 1950s publicity portrait of her, had it converted without any alteration into a silkscreen, then used the screen to imprint the photographic image on canvas. It was a seemingly mechanical process destined to distinguish him from all the other Pop artists. He had discovered toward the middle of 1962 that he could get just about any black-and-white newspaper or magazine illustration converted into a photographic silkscreen. (Silkscreening is a photomechanical stencil process, utilizing a fabric screen that has been chemically treated so that certain areas are impervious to pigment, while other areas let the pigment pass through. The process translates the picture into a series of halftone dots.) Within a brief period of time, he was screening photographic blowups not only of Marilyn Monroe, but also of Elizabeth Taylor, Marlon Brando, and Elvis Presley. Warhol's adaptation of the silkscreen process, complete with deliberately off-register printing, became one of his most important formal innovations, yielding the impersonal appearance of mechanical reproduction and suggesting that the image had been straightforwardly transposed without any mediation of the artist's psyche. The silkscreen process also enabled him to repeat the same portrait hundreds of times.

Two of the most famous faces that Warhol recycled during the course of 1963 belonged to the Mona Lisa and Jacqueline Kennedy. Realizing that Leonardo's masterpiece was about to make a month-long visit to New York's Metropolitan Museum of Art in Februry, Warhol created homages to the enigmatic Italian Renaissance lady, promoting her celebrity status by regimenting her portrait in row after row on his canvases. Warhol derived his powerful portraits of Jacqueline Kennedy from news photographs taken before and after President John F. Kennedy's assassination in Dallas in November. The "before" paintings show the First Lady, smiling as she sits beside her husband in the backseat of the car. The "after" photographs in the series show the grieving widow in mourning attire during the funeral ceremonies in Washington.

The fame and notoriety that played so crucial a role in Warhol's art soon spilled into his own studio, a large fourth-floor loft on East 47th Street, a few blocks from Grand Central Station. His friends called it the Factory because of the prodigious amount of painting and filmmaking that took place there. One of those friends was an off-Broadway theatrical lighting designer, then known as Billy Linich (later to become Billy Name). Warhol invited Billy to design the studio. Eventually, Billy served not only as the Factory's resident designer, but also its superintendent and concierge. He created the striking silvery decor, covering virtually all of the walls and ceiling with aluminium foil or silver paint. He continued his obsessive silver spray-painting until he had covered almost everything – desks, chairs, copying machine, toilet, dismembered mannikin and pay phone – with metallic pigment.

Almost instantaneously, the Factory became the epicenter of New York pop culture. The place functioned as a combination clubhouse, community center, lounge, and cruising area for some of New York's more outlandish types – preening fashion models, ranting amphetamine heads, sulky poets, underground moviemakers, and imperious magazine editors, as well as wide-eyed college students and occasional movie personalities and rock stars. Most of the drop-ins just wandered around and coolly sneaked sidelong stares at each other. Everyone, of course, vied for Warhol's attention. But he modestly claimed that his visitors were far more interested in seeing each other than they were in seeing him. If anyone was "hanging around," as he put it, it was *he* hanging around his visitors, not the other way around. Soon, professional photographers from all over the Western world were also hanging around the Factory, the new frontier of artistic far-outness.

The most truthful photographic documents, however, were the candid pictures that Billy Name snapped so casually that hardly anyone noticed that he had taken to carrying a 35mm camera around his neck. By day and night, he recorded vivid images of the Factory crowd in contrasty black-and-white, capturing Warhol and his entourage as they postured, worked, danced, and whiled away their time. Billy developed his negatives in an improvised darkroom at the rear of the Factory; it was actually a bathroom that he had converted into ascetic private quarters, where he slept on the floor. Most of Billy's photographs were lost for more than a decade, but then they resurfaced a few years ago, once again offering evidence of the frenetic, high-spirited energy that made the Factory *the* place to be for nearly four years.

Warhol's own, growing celebrity became a narcotic addiction for him. He expended tremendous energy in remaining a topical name in the news. He was obsessed with social dynamics – the ups and downs of who was "in" and "out." Always alert to new trends and social patterns, he constantly read personality-oriented magazines, movie-star biographies, and newspaper gossip columns to see who else was being talked about. The more fame he enjoyed, the more he needed it. He almost didn't seem to believe in his own existence until he saw it verified in print. His art increasingly became an intentional provocation, calculated to create controversy and elicit press coverage. His unflagging desire to generate shock waves often led him to impure sensationalism.

He certainly succeeded with a seemingly abstract series of 1978 paintings, known as Oxidations. The canvases were first coated with copper paint. Then, while the copper paint was still damp, Warhol and his assistants urinated on the canvases. In time, the uric acid and copper sulphate combined to produce a green patina. The artist, however, probably had far less interest in the chemical process, than in the alchemical implications of converting bodily waste into something aesthetic and precious. To add another overtone of perversity, the freely dribbled and "poured" pigment bears deliberate resemblances to Abstract Expressionism, particularly the looping lines and puddles in the famous "drip" paintings of Jackson Pollock.

Using more conventional pigments, Warhol could give a flattering patina to almost any face. His facility and flair at stylizing the human face made him one of the leading portraitists of his era. He could compose portraits in strikingly orchestrated colors of almost any face that came his way – sports stars, cats and dogs, even human skulls. But he preferred to paint the very rich because they not only paid their bills (most of the time) but also provided him with a pretext for going to more parties. After successfully wheedling them to commission their portraits, he aimed his Polaroid camera at them and took dozens of snapshots, later selecting some of the prints to be processes into silkscreens. He always preferred to base his portraits upon his own photographs, generally selecting the most complete and informative shot, usually a full-face or three-quarter-face view. He frequently lamented that, while it was easy to make ordinary people look good, he had difficulty making beautiful people look as attractive as they really were.

Departing from one of portraiture's most traditional ideals, Warhol made little attempt to portray people in character. His silkscreened faces are essentially stylized, cosmetic, skin-deep treatments of surfaces rather than personality studies. He typically made his portraits larger-than-lifesize, the face nearly filling each of the forty-inch square canvases. He emphasized the features he considered most important – the eyes (large, lustrous, brightly colored eyelids) and lips (full and sensuous). Noses were almost always diminished in importance.

Many of the portraits of the 1970s and '80s are slathered with sensuous, gestural brush strokes, suggesting a genuine affinity with "painterly" painting. He placed most of the showy, if erratic, brushwork on the canvas before the professional printers took over to screen the image, admitting that he "half-painted" the portraits to give them more style. It was more fun – and also faster – to be "sloppy," than to be neat.

Warhol rarely paid other people to pose for him. One of the few times he hired models was for a 1975 series of paintings and silkscreen prints, archly titled *Ladies and Gentlemen.* The subjects were black female impersonators. (Although he displayed a durable fascination with female impersonators in real life, this marked one of the few occasions when he chose to paint people of color.) To obtain authentic models, he sent a couple of his assistants out on midnight talent searches through some of the raunchier sections of Greenwich Village to collect amusingly dressed drag queens. Many of them seemed to fashion themselves after famous pop singers, such as Lena Horne and Diana Ross, and some of them apparently earned illicit livings as "ladies of the night." The female impersonators didn't care if they were contributing anything to fine art: for a fee, they gladly dropped by the Factory to pose, all decked out in their extravagant wigs, wide-brimmed hats, or simple bandannas. In a perverse way, these portraits demonstrate Warhol's lingering egalitarianism, his willingness to treat street people with as much dignity and style as his monied clients.

As the 1970s ended, Warhol looked at his most famous Pop images in retrospect and reshuffled some of them to come up with a couple of new series of paintings, the "Reversals" and the "Retrospectives," both initiated in 1979. These new series brought his Pop Art full circle by enabling him to reuse his "trademarked" motifs in new contexts. His Reversals recapitulate his portraits of famous faces – from Marilyn Monroe to the Mona Lisa – but with a reversal in tonal values. Spectators almost feel they are looking at photographic negatives because highlighted faces have receded in darkness while former shadows now rush forward in brilliant hues. The results are often quite melodramatic: the reversed Marilyns, for instance, cast a lurid, otherworldly glow, as if illuminated by infernal footlights.

While he typically repeated a single image in rows for the Reversals, Warhol scattered several different subjects across the surfaces of his Retrospectives. These paintings present a sort of souvenir assortment of Warholian themes, from soup cans and corn flakes cartons to Marilyn Monroe, with electric chairs oddly juxtaposed with bucolic flowers and cows. He casually arrayed the images, sometimes overlapping them or screening them in reverse. In making a pastiche of his former subjects, he clearly called into question earlier interpretations of their significance. In ransacking his own past to produce the Reversals and Retrospectives, Warhol also revealed himself to be one of the shrewdest of the new wave of post-Modernists, displaying – once again – a cool, ironic attitute toward all aesthetic camps, as well as a total indifference to traditional hierarchies of "high" and "low" art.

Like a true post-Modernist, Warhol valued advertising images as much as those from art history. He claimed to buy magazines primarily for their advertisements and to watch television mainly for the commercials. He became less apologetic about his years as a commercial artist and he increasingly accepted corporate commissions that were explicitly tied in with advertising. Obviously feeling no qualms about collaborating with corporate advertising departments, he accepted commissions to produce paintings for Absolut vodka, Perrier water, and Mercedez-Benz automobiles. Even the Campbell's Soup Company hired Warhol in 1985 to produce a new series of paintings, promoting the company's dry soup mixes. On his own, he turned out a series of paintings and silkscreen prints, glorifiying print ads for famous products, including Paramount Pictures, Life Savers, Chanel No.5, and Volkswagen automobiles. Some critics maintained that his career had gone full circle, beginning with and returning to advertising illustration after a fling with fine art. But Warhol cut the grass from under their feet, claiming that he had *always* been a commercial artist and had *never* made the transformation from commercial to "real" artist. But, when he said that, just how serious was he?

His art continued to demonstrate that he was an elusive character, not easy to categorize. Just when it appeared he was hopelessly cynical, he produced an ingratiating series of brightly colored paintings based on children's toys. And just as his audience might have given him up as heartless, his respect for the victims of a natural disaster prompted a series of ominously stylized views of Vesuvius. No one could second-guess Warhol.

In 1986, only about a year before his premature death, Warhol set out to do an ambitious series of works based on Leonardo da Vinci's *Last Supper.* He was impressed, but not at all intimidated, by Leonardo, possibly because he had "recycled" the *Mona Lisa* many years earlier. In some of his silkscreened versions of the *Last Supper,* he repeated Leonardo's composition in grids as many as sixty times. In hand-painted versions, he juxtaposed the religious figures with advertising images of motorcycles, Dove soap bars, and Wise potato chips, insinuating that Leonardo's masterpiece had become a commonplace, brand-name product.

Throughout his long career, Warhol injected "serious" painting with a prodigal amount of topical and seemingly ephemeral subjects, ranging from display ads and comic strips to news photographs and publicity stills. In the process, he became a pictorial chronicler of the American way of life, depicting many of the faces, products, and events that exemplified his era. Although he never claimed any intellectual significance for his artworks, he knew they were aesthetically innovative and exemplary reflections on the American Dream.

First published in *Andy Warhol* (Tel Aviv: Tel Aviv Museum of Art, 1992), pp. 176-180.

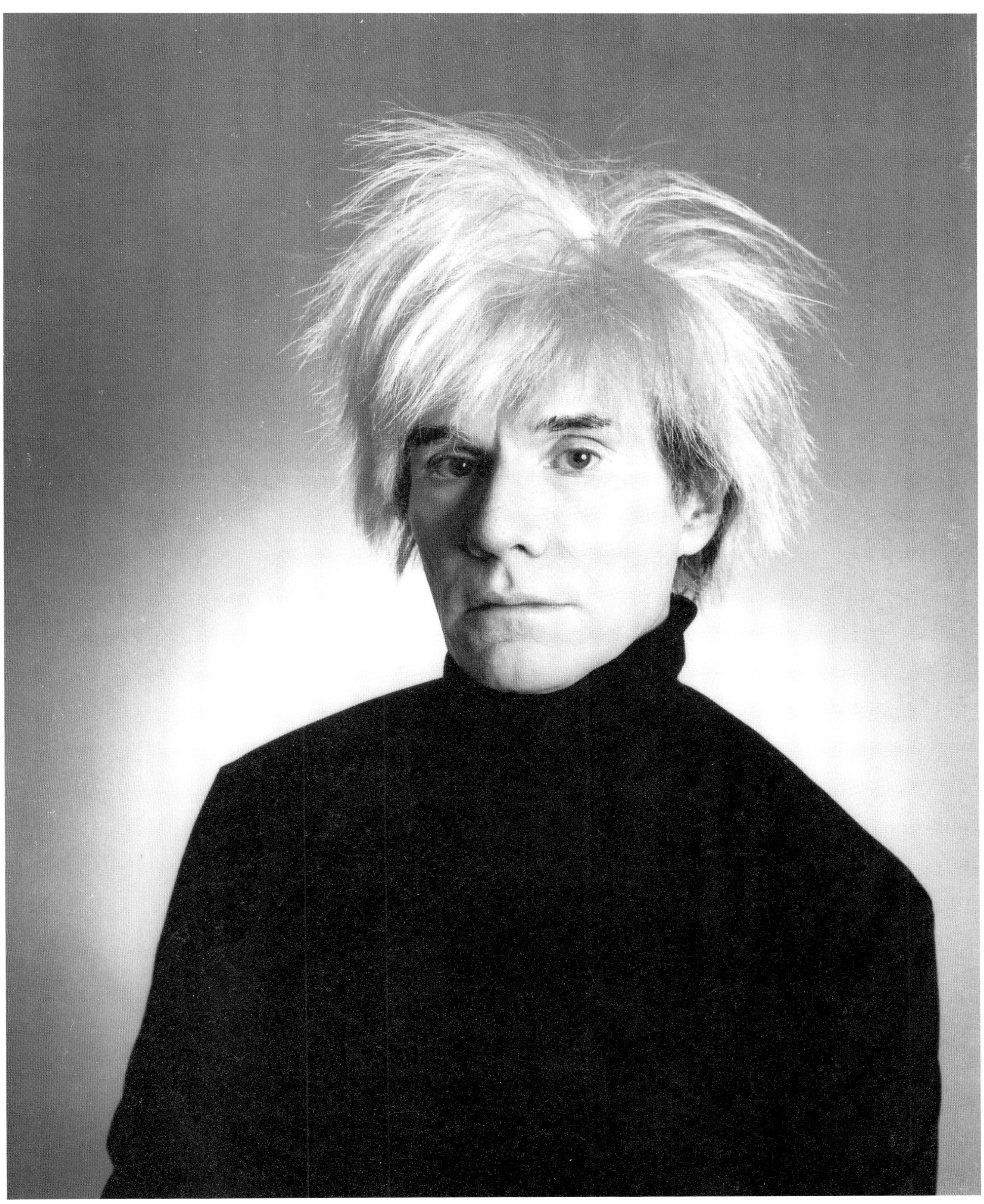

Andy Warhol, 1986. Photo: Christopher Makos

Jacob Baal-Teshuva

Pre-Pop

At the end of June 1949, shortly after graduating from the Carnegie Institute of Technology in Pittsburgh, where he had studied painting and drawing, a thin, pale, twenty-one-year-old Andrew Warhola arrived in New York in pursuit of his American Dream – to become rich and famous. For six months, he shared an apartment with Philip Pearlstein, his classmate, who later became a famous American Realist painter. Each morning, with a black leather portfolio containing his drawings, he would make his rounds of the advertising agencies and women's magazines, dressed in baggy pants, a leather jacket, and sneakers.

While still at college in Pittsburgh, he had been art editor of a student publication called *Cano*. One of his first stops in New York, therefore, was at the Condé Nast magazine *Glamour*, then based on the nineteenth floor of 420 Lexington Avenue. The building was known as the citadel of fashion, housing many photography and fashion agencies. It was ironic that Warhol, who loved and admired glamour, made his first call at *Glamour*, a magazine targeted at "the girl with a job." Tina S. Fredericks, who was its young art editor, describes her first encounter with Warhol: "I greeted a pale, blotchy boy, diffident almost to the point of disappearance, but somehow immediately and immensely appealing. He seemed all one color, pale chinos, pale wispy hair, pale eyes, a strange beige birthmark over the side of his face (almost like a Helen Frankenthaler wash). The big, black portfolio he carried was an emphatic accent.... The portfolio didn't have much in it, some nude figure studies, some flowers, and a charming abstraction of an orchestra playing, black and white circles. The musicians' heads were sketched in blotted lines and repeated all over the paper with multicolored accents slapped around to enliven the drawing even further. I was enchanted ... his ink lines were electrifying. Fragmented, broken, and intriguing, they grabbed at you with their spontaneous intensity. There was something wallpaperish about the way the drawing covered the space. Much later, of course, we could see these as the precursors to the multiple Coke bottles, the cow heads, the infinite, repetitive silkscreens of Marilyn and Mao.... He was fast, and that, in combination with intelligent, adaptable, and really good, made him an art director's dream come true .... Surprises were his trademark."[1]

Tina S. Fredericks gave him his first job: to draw six shoes. He came back the next day with beautiful drawings. The shoe drawings, which he continued to do, have come to represent his pre-Pop period. His next assignment was to illustrate a text for an article entitled "Success is a Job in New York." The result was a charming line drawing depicting the New York skyline with its skyscrapers, in which women are seen climbing the ladders of success.

Tina S. Fredericks was instrumental in launching Warhol's meteoric career. She bought his first drawing for herself for ten dollars, and introduced him to influential people. She describes Warhol as "quiet, inscrutable, talented, droll, magnetic, brilliant, possessed, manipulative, tolerant, strange, generous, elfish, shrewd, self-serving, kind, surprising, devout, astute, mysterious, plain, captivating."[2]

Warhol's images on paper were strong and powerful. He would place a water-resistant paper over the drawing and trace the original quickly in ink. The image then became bolder. These line drawings remind one of the work of the widely known American artist Ben Shahn.

Andy Warhol's commercial art began to be rich in opportunity. People reacted at that time to sophisticated advertising in the news media, radio, and television, and became consumers and purchasers of art.

His first exhibition in New York opened on June 16, 1952, at Gallery Hugo. It consisted of 15 drawings based on short stories by Truman Capote, who described Andy Warhol as "a sphinx without a riddle." Not one drawing was sold at the exhibition, but Warhol was not discouraged. It should be noted that these were the peak years of Abstract Expressionism in the United States.

Illustrating Christmas cards and record album covers, and designing window displays for a large department store, were the order of the day for Warhol. He also produced drawing portraits of Helena Rubenstein, and of the actresses Ginger Rogers and Joan Crawford, and other celebrities. These portraits were the forerunners of his portraits of the Pop period in the early 1960s. He was also commissioned to illustrate books, the first one in 1952 being *Amy Vanderbilt's Complete Book of Etiquette*. Other books he illustrated were *A Is an Alphabet*, *Love Is a Pink Cake*, *25 Cats Name Sam and One Blue Pussy*, *A La Recherche du Shoe Perdu*, *In the Bottom of My Garden*, *A Gold Book*, *Wild Raspberries*, and *Amy Vanderbilt's Complete Cookbook*.

He continued to draw shoes, and the signature "Warhol" on the drawings was done by his mother, who moved to New York to live with her son. When asked why he didn't sign the drawings himself, he replied that his mother's handwriting was very beautiful.

Warhol was introduced to Emile de Antonio, an influential artist's agent nicknamed "De," who was credited for bringing Jasper Johns and Robert Rauschenberg to the attention of Leo Castelli, the dean of American dealers in contemporary art. De and Warhol became good friends. He said to Warhol, "I don't know why you don't become a painter, Andy – you've got more ideas than anybody around."[3]

Warhol's commercial art of the 1950s was a prologue to the Pop Art with which he was to go down in art history. It was in the early 1960s that he broke with commercial art and began to use images taken from everyday life and objects at hand. His daily lunches in his studio consisted of Campbell's soup and Coca-Cola. The cans and bottles accumulated on his desk, and inspired him to paint them on canvas. De found the paintings remarkable. "It's our society. And it's who we are, it's absolutely beautiful and naked."[4] And it was De who introduced Warhol to Eleanor Ward, who put on an exhibition for him at her Stable Gallery in New York.

Notes

1 Tina S. Fredericks, "Remembering Andy: an Introduction," in Jesse Kornbluth, *Pre-Pop Warhol* (New York: Random House, 1988), p. 11.
2 Ibid., p. 9.
3 Ibid., p. 18.
4 Loc. cit.

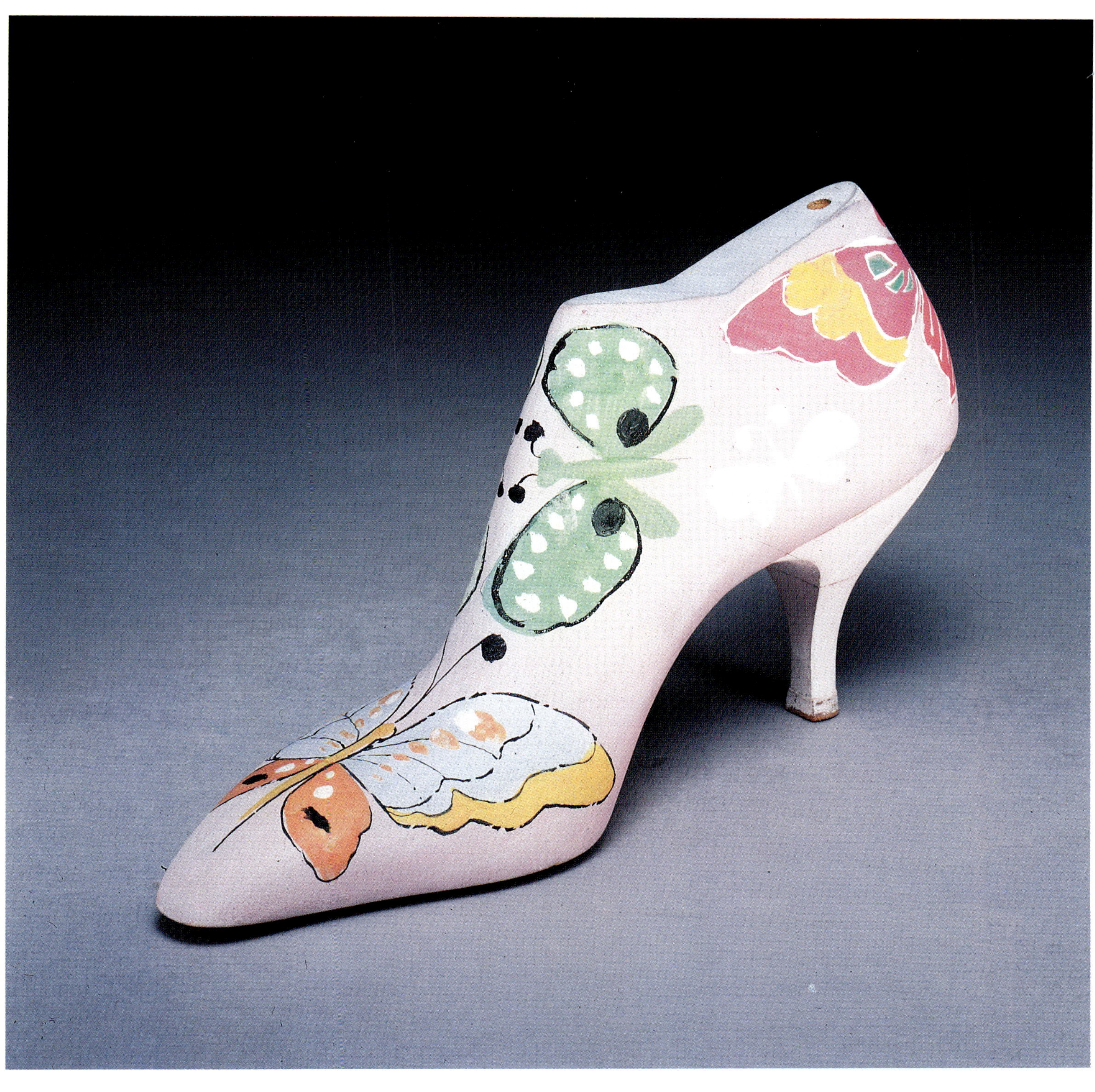

1 *Shoe*, ca. 1950

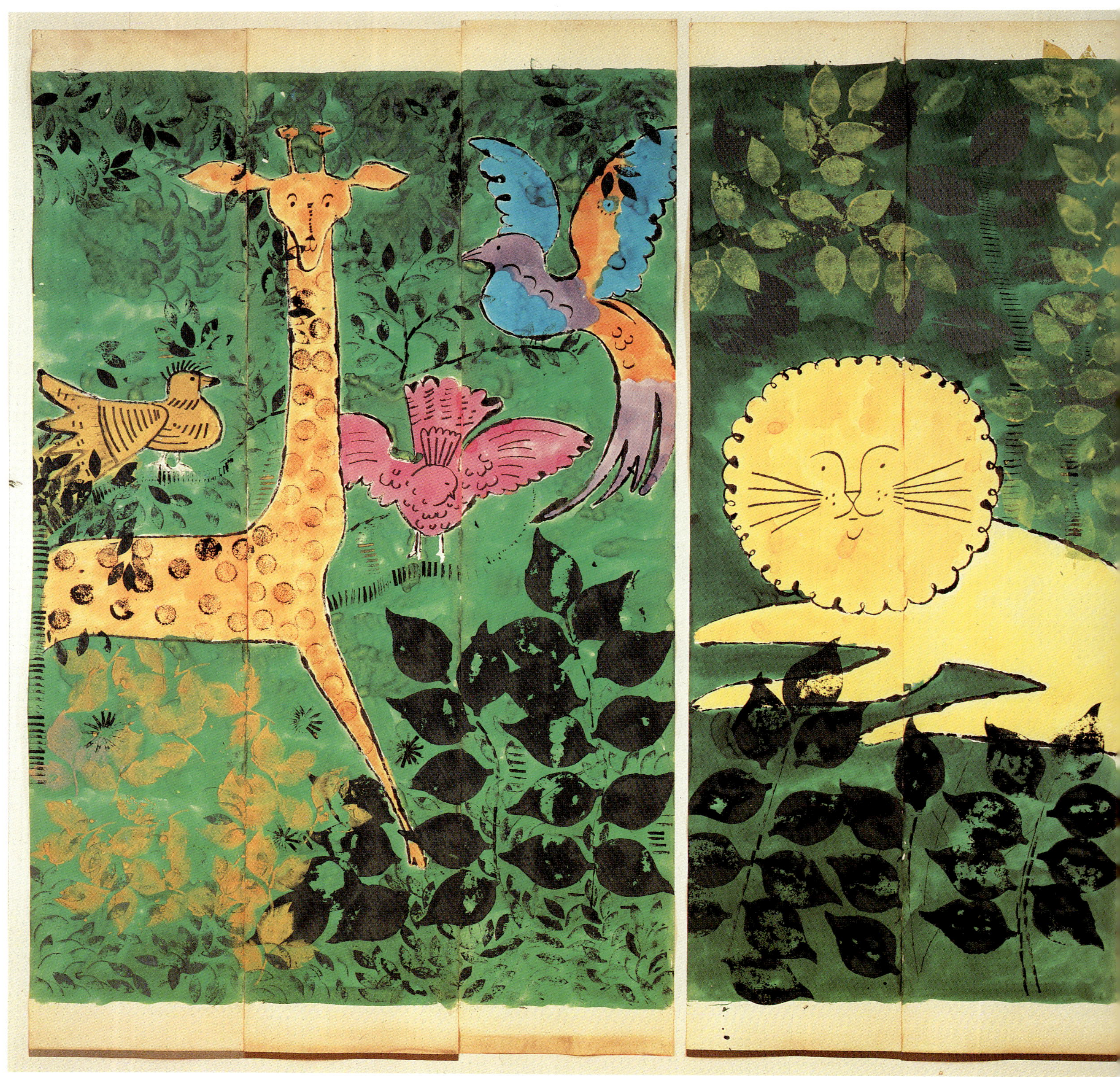

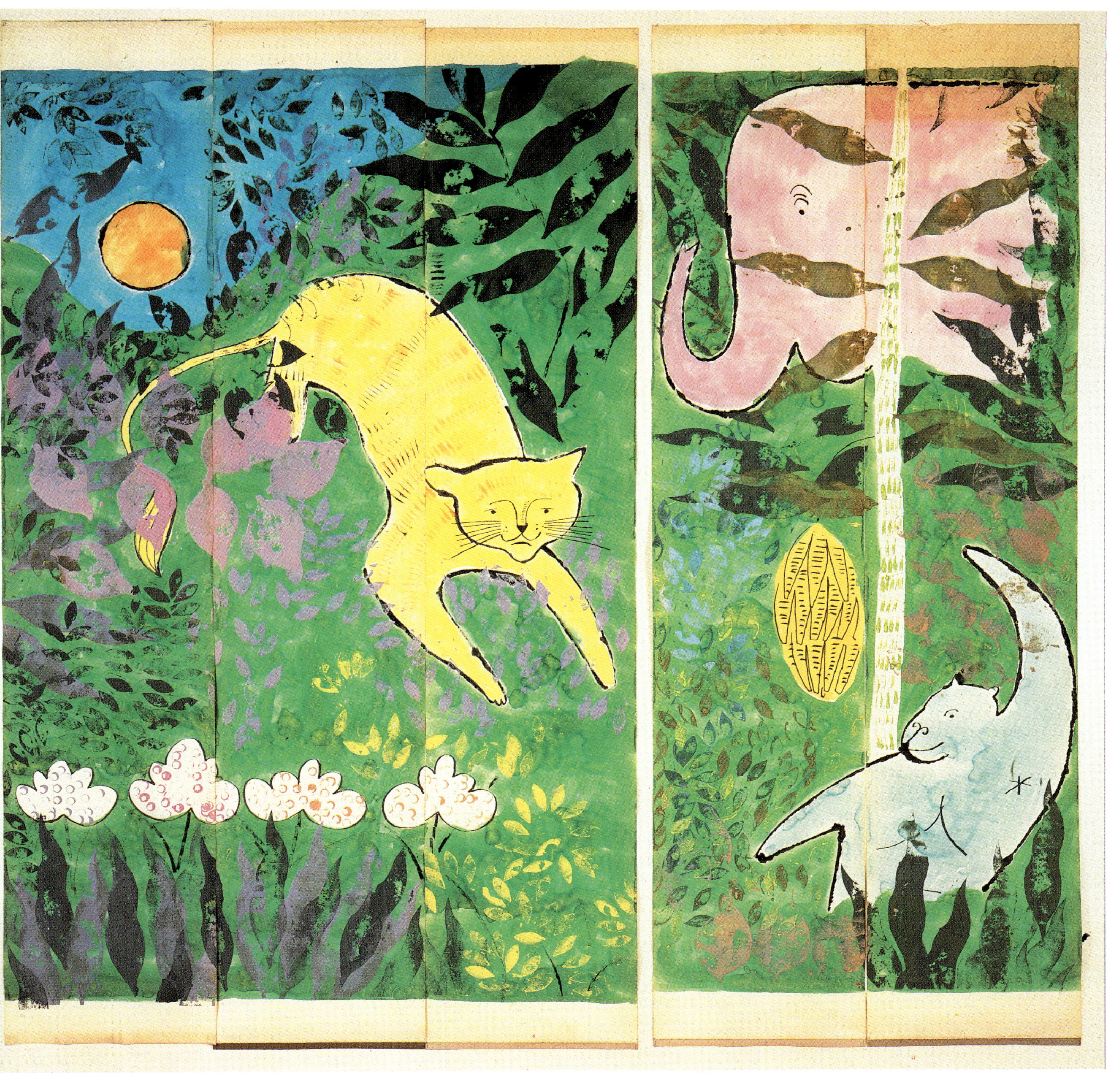

2 *Fashion Show Backdrop* (for *Glamour* magazine), 1955

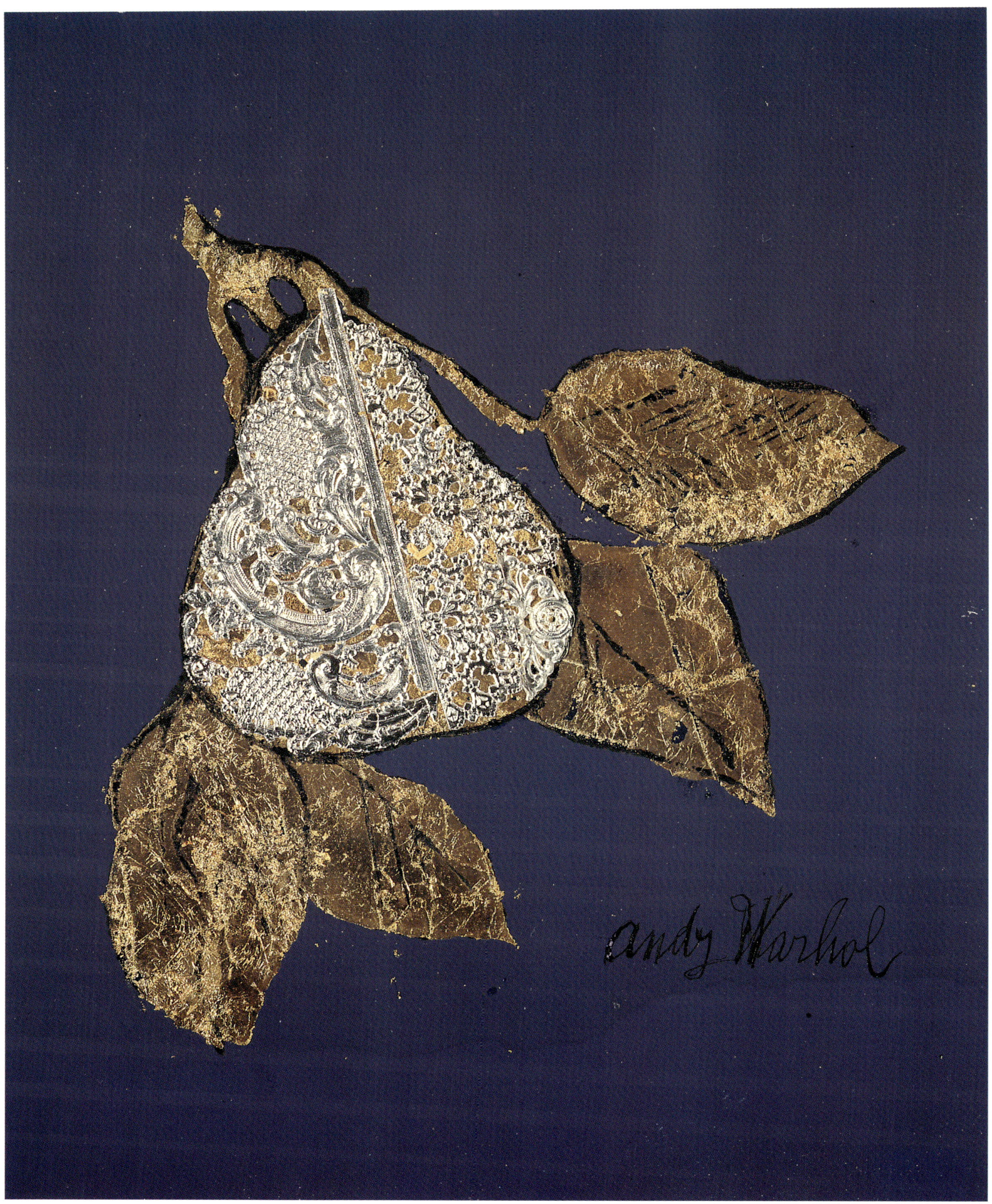

3 Untitled, ca. 1957

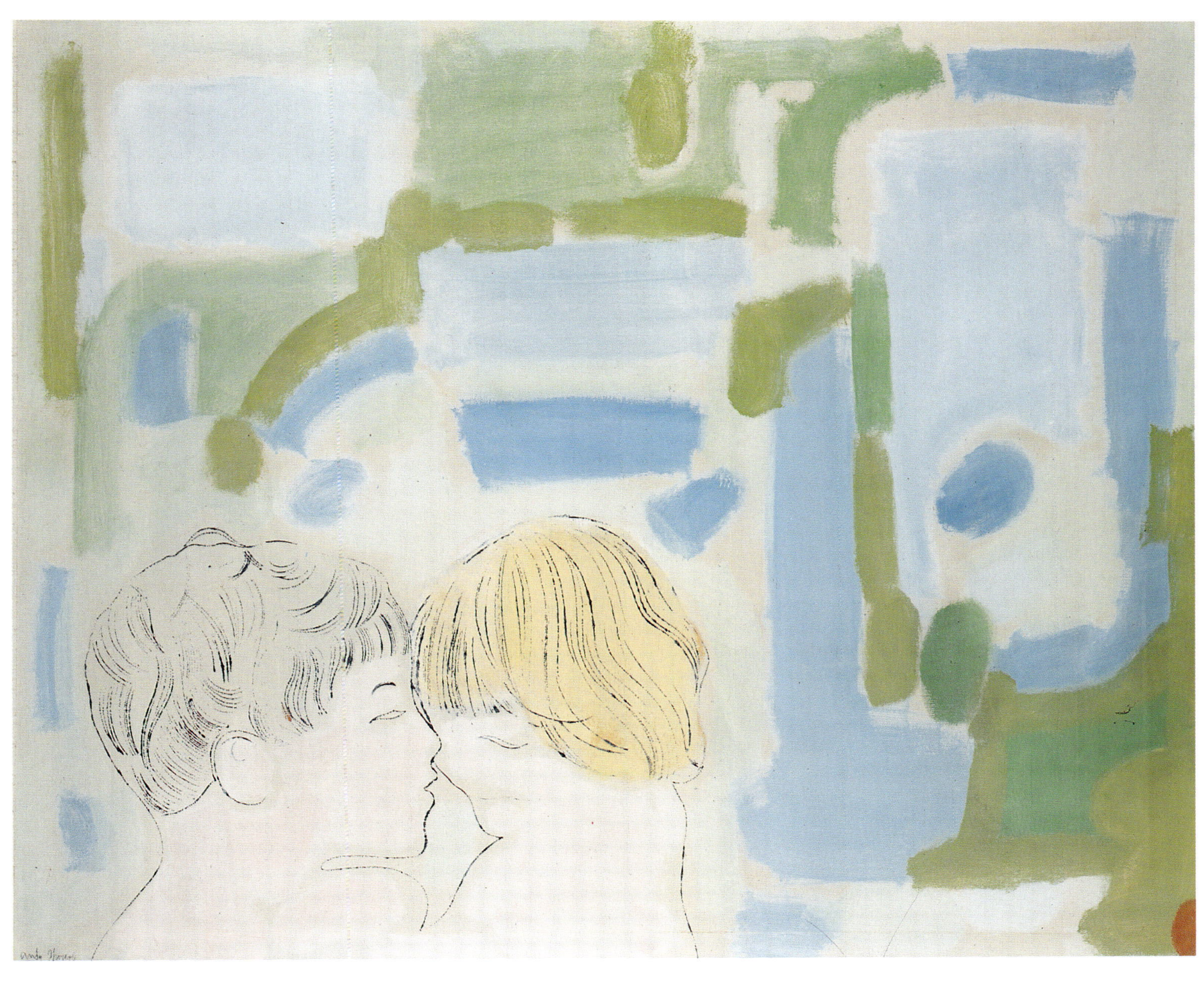

4 Untitled, ca. 1958

The interviewer should just tell me the words he wants me to say and I'll repeat them after him.

Let's say things intelligent.

I'm not more intelligent than I appear...

I still care about people but it would be so much easier not to care... it's too hard to care.... I don't want to get too involved in other people's lives.... I don't want to get too close.... I don't like to touch things... that's why my work is so distant from myself...

...and I don't really believe in love.

The reason I'm painting this way is because I want to be a machine. Whatever I do, and do machine-like, is because it is what I want to do. I think it would be terrific if everybody was alike.

I tried doing them by hand, but I find it easier to use a screen. This way, I don't have to work on my objects at all. One of my assistants or anyone else, for that matter, can reproduce the design as well as I could.

I like boring things...

"Do you think Pop Art is..."
"No."
"What?"
"No."
"Do you think Pop Art is..."
"No... No I don't."

I hate objects.

All is pretty.

I love Los Angeles. I love Hollywood. They're beautiful. Everybody's plastic – but I love plastic. I want to be plastic.

I never read, I just look at pictures.

I think we're a vacuum here at the Factory, it's great. I like being a vacuum; it leaves me alone to work. We are bothered though, we have cops coming up here all the time. They think we're doing awful things and we aren't.

I don't paint any more, I gave it up about a year ago and just do movies now. I could do two things at the same time but movies are more exciting.

People are so fantastic. You can't take a bad picture.

The Empire State Building is a star!

The lighting is bad, the camera work is bad, the projection is bad, but the people are beautiful.

I'd prefer to remain a mystery; I never like to give my background and, anyway, I make it all different all the time I'm asked. It's not just that it's part of my image not to tell everything, it's just that I forget what I said the day before and I have to make it all up over again. I don't think I have an image, anyway, favorable or unfavorable.

All my films are artificial, but then everything is sort of artificial. I don't know where the artificial stops and the real starts. The artificial fascinates me, the bright and shiny...

I don't worry about art or life. I mean, the war and the bomb worry me but usually there's not much you can do about them. I've represented it in some of my films and I'm going to try and do more. Money doesn't worry me, either, though I sometimes wonder where is it? Somebody's got it all!

These quotes by Andy Warhol were taken from *Andy Warhol* (Stockholm: Moderna Museet), 1968.

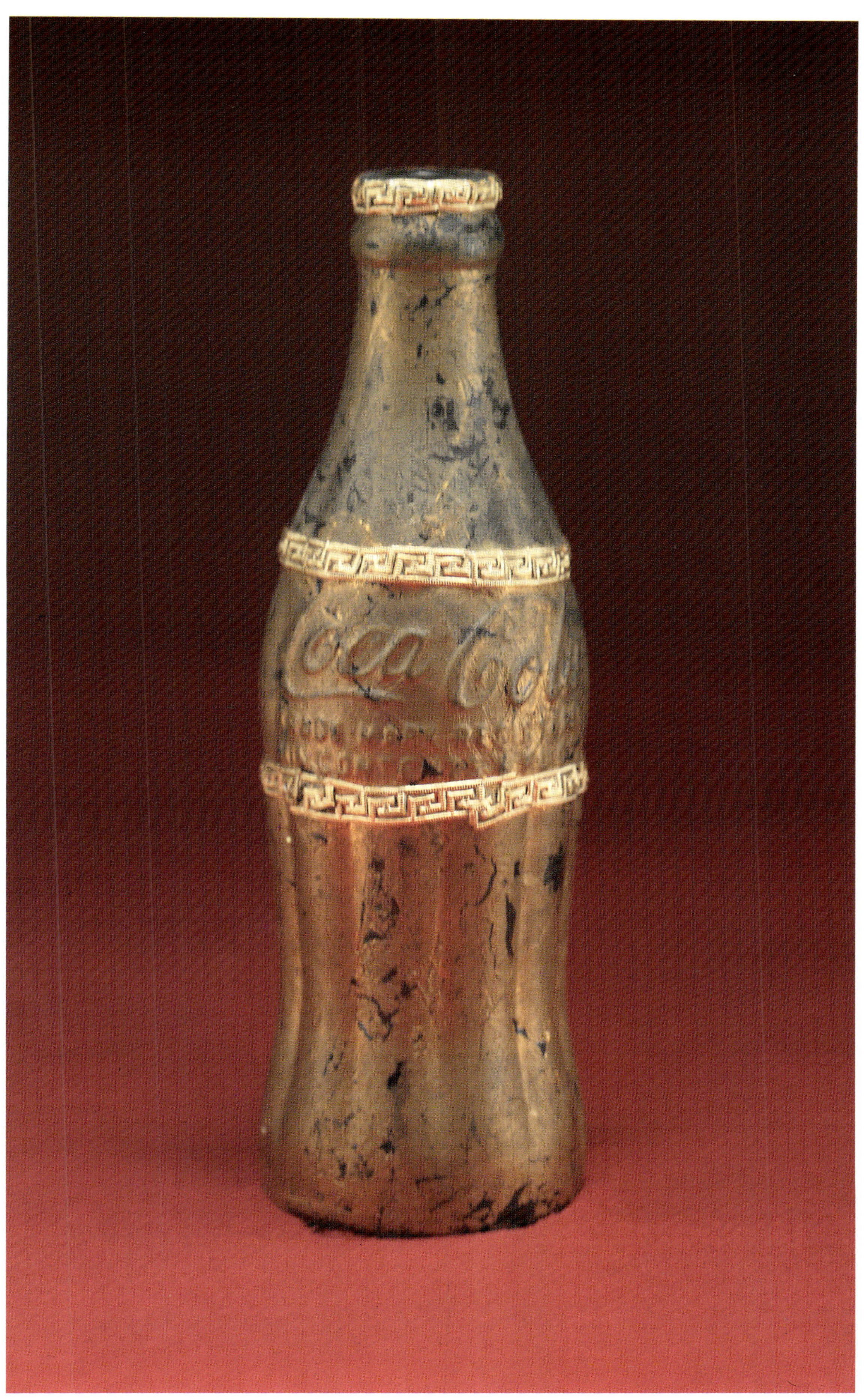

5 *Coca-Cola*, ca. 1962

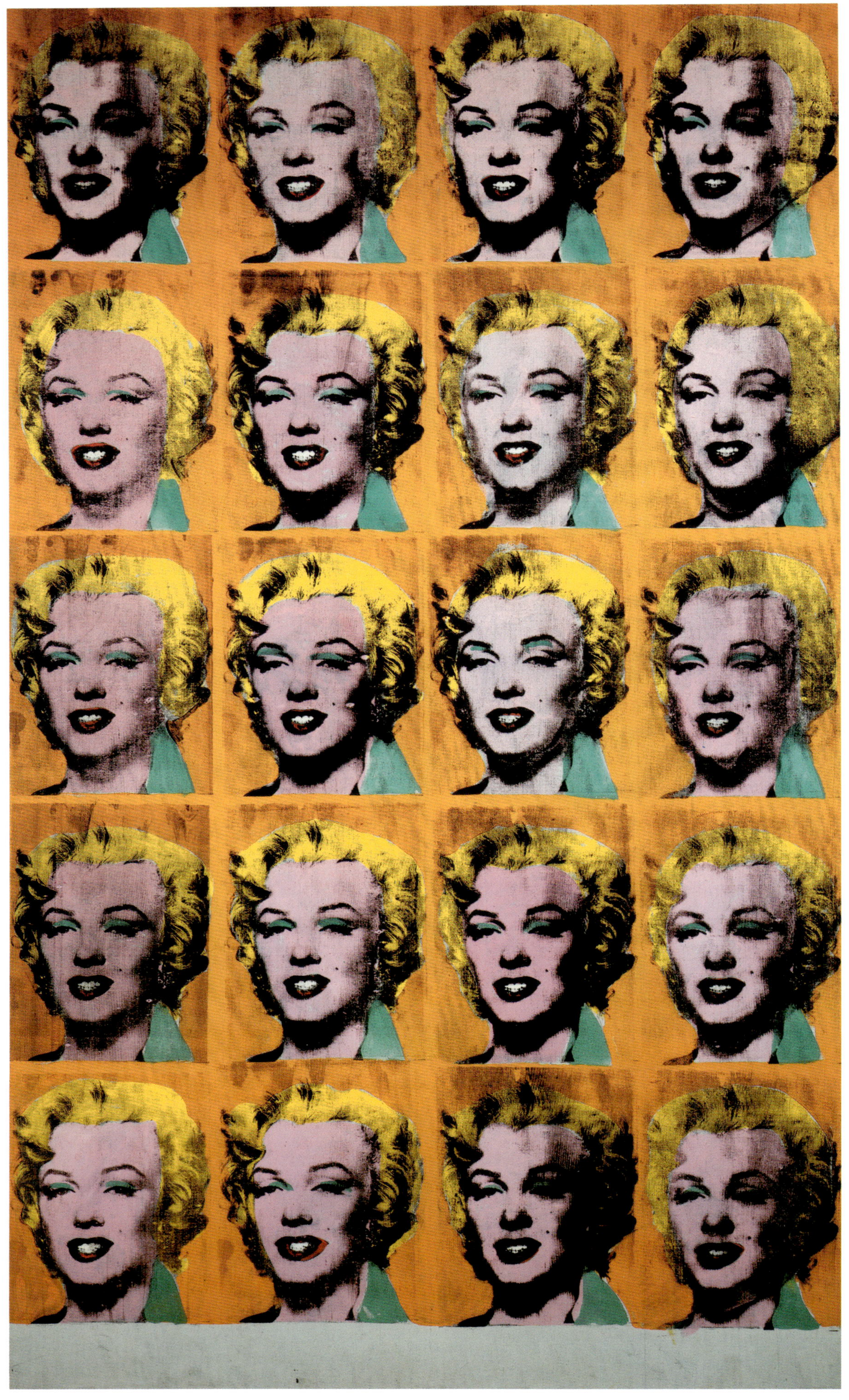

6 *Marilyn Monroe* (Twenty Times), 1962

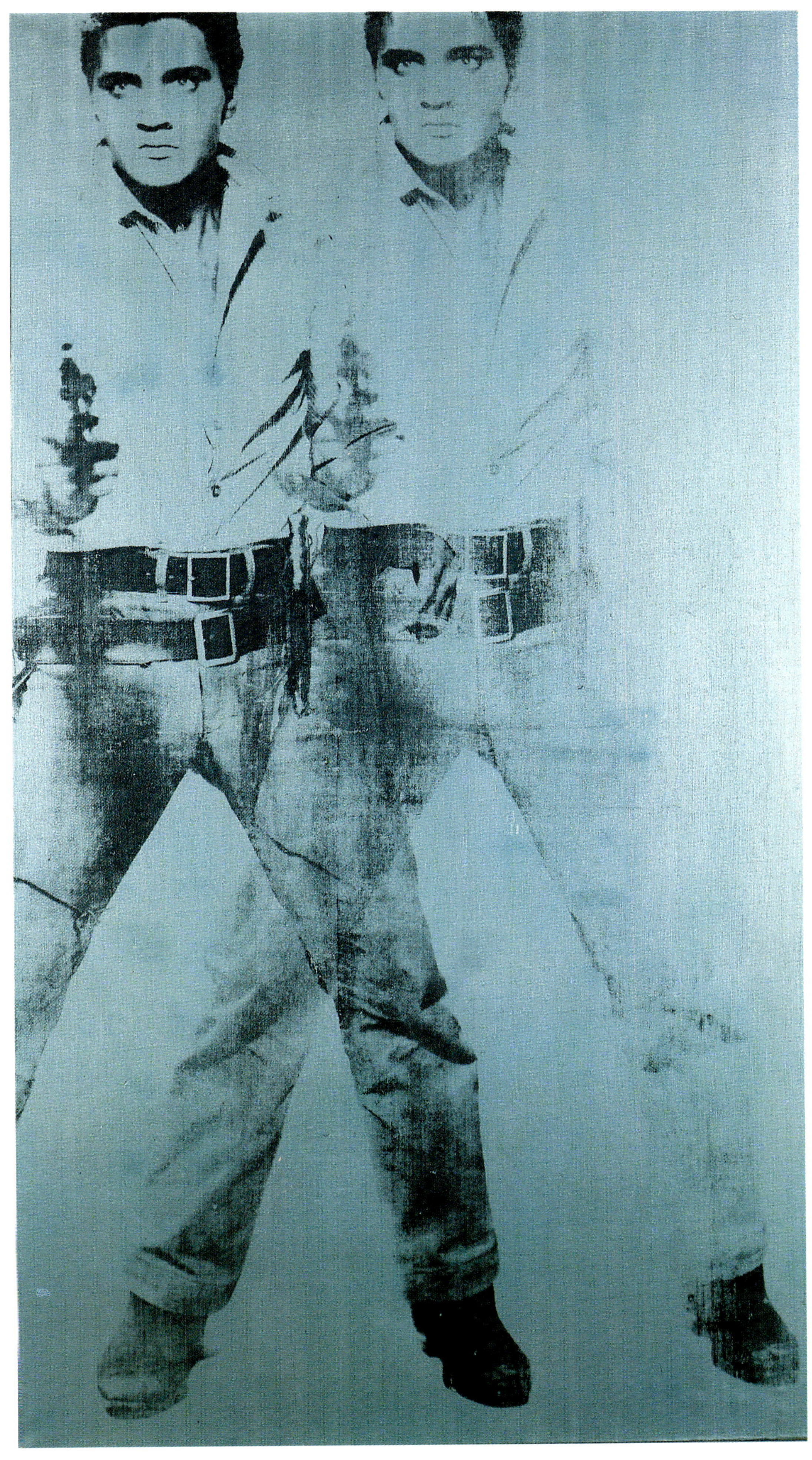

7 *Double Elvis*, 1963

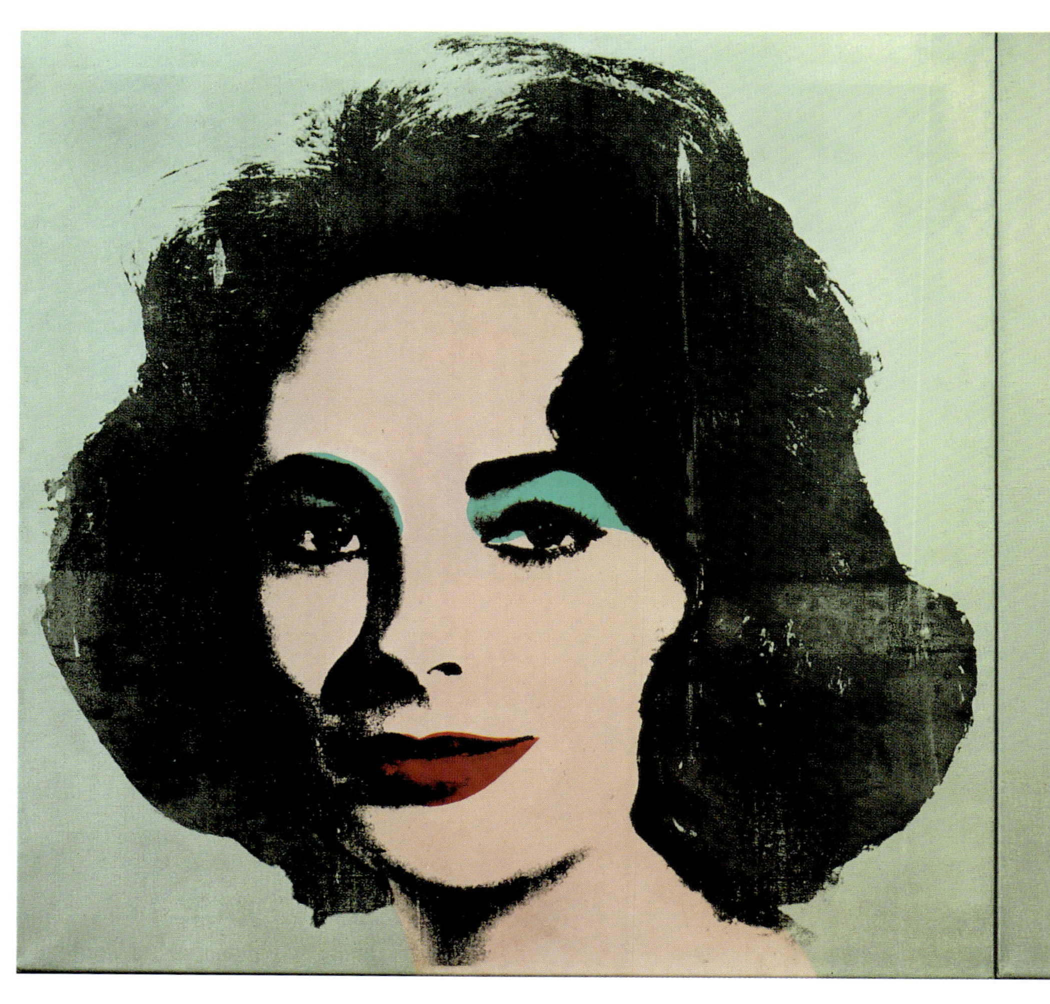

8 *Liz*, 1963

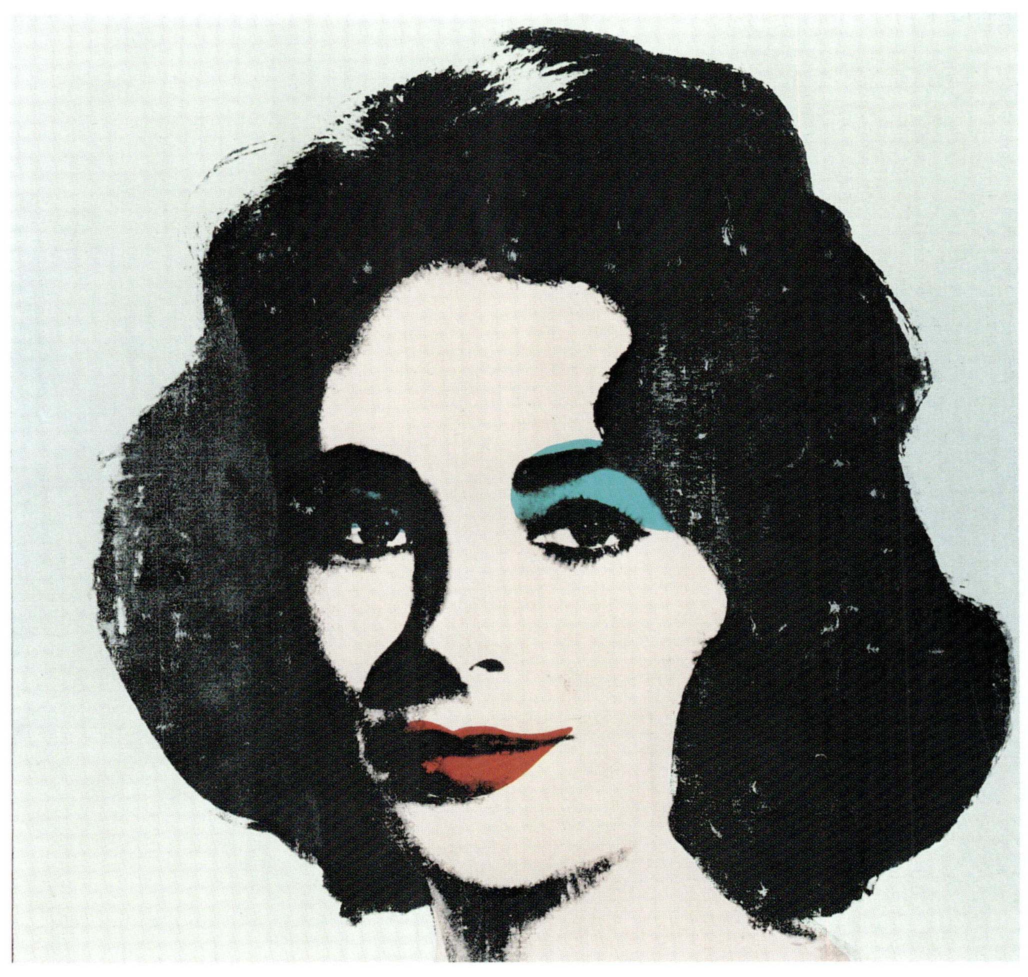

9 *Liz Taylor*, 1965

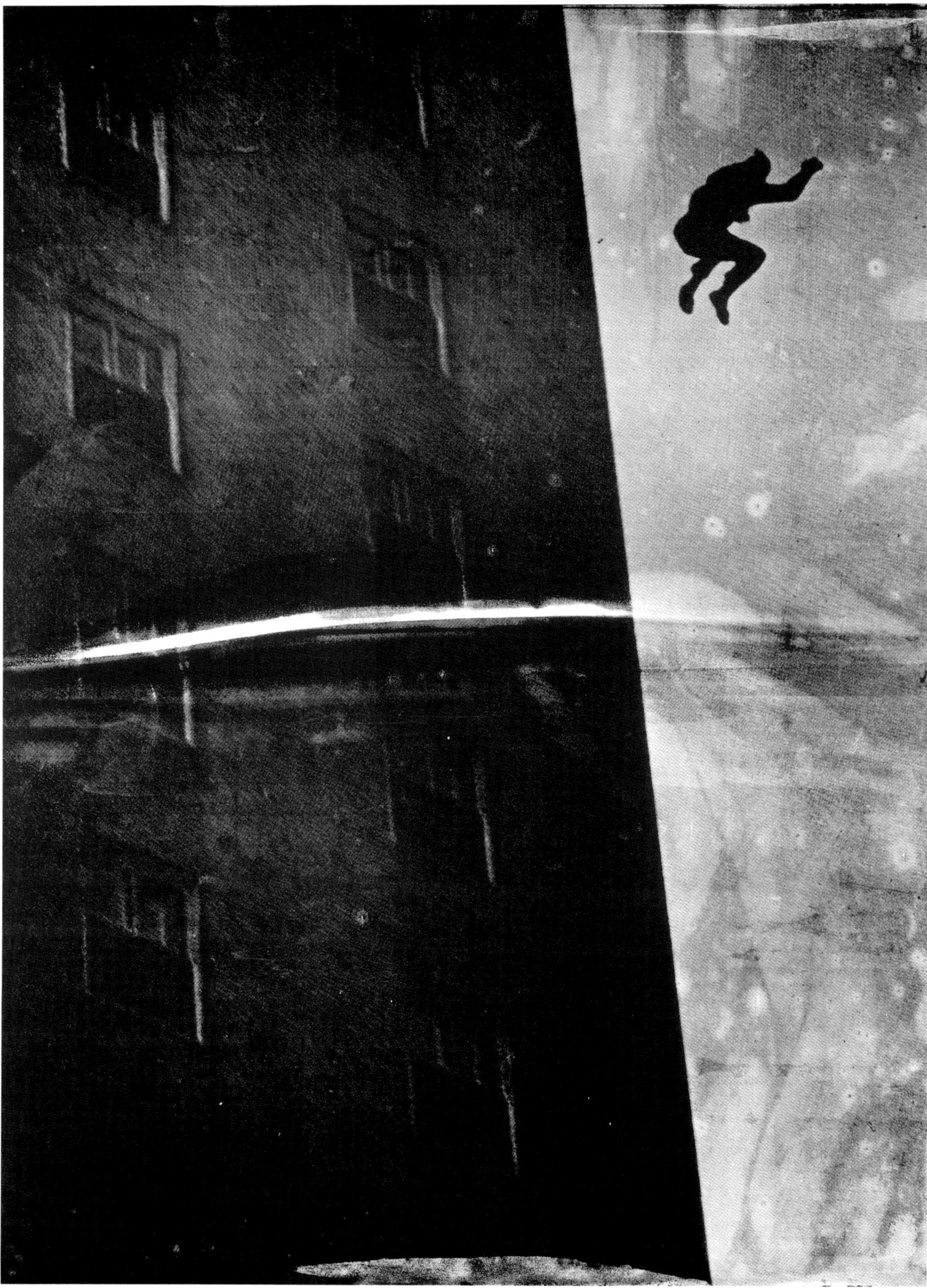

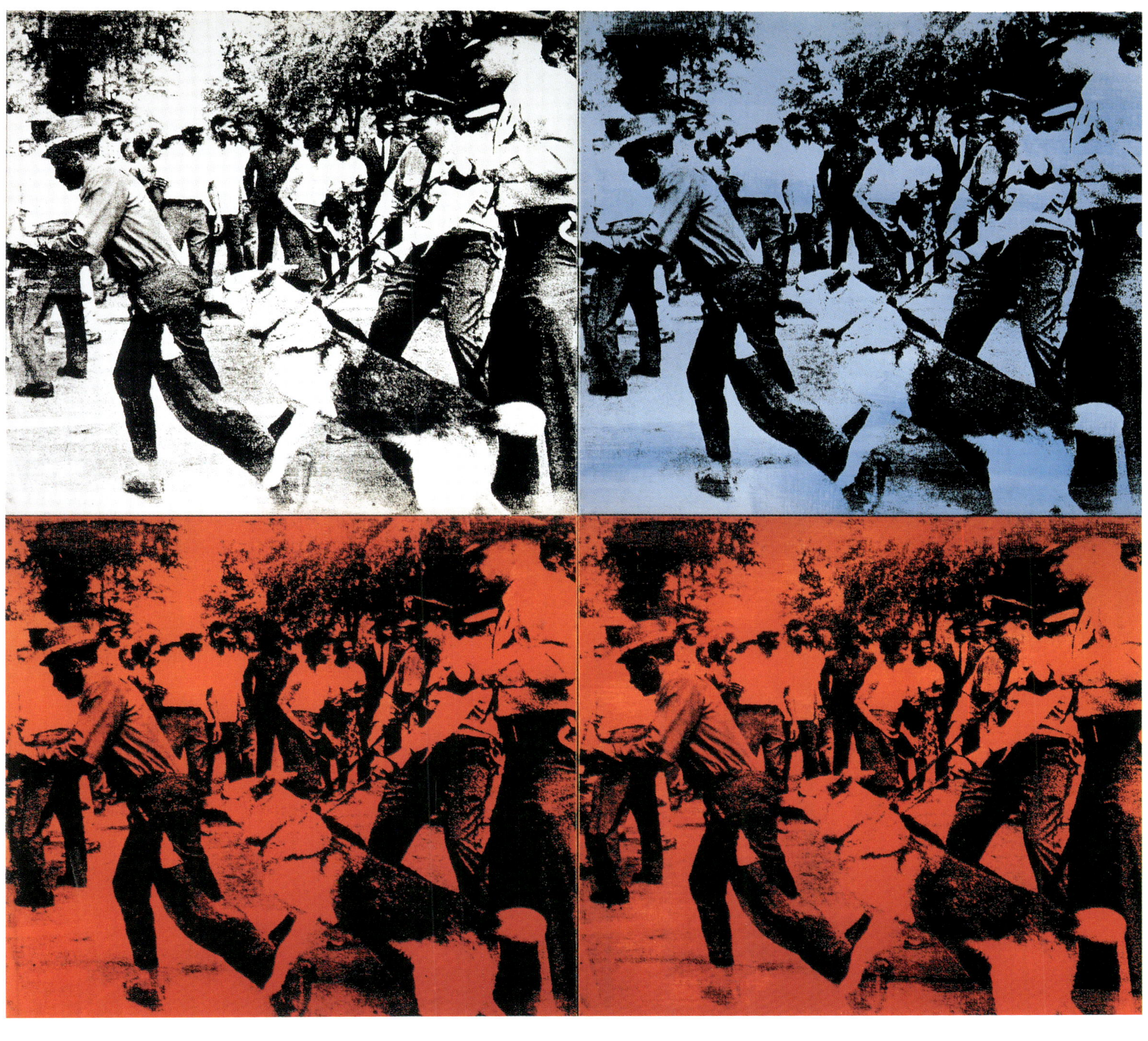

10 *Suicide*, 1964

11 *Race Riot*, 1964

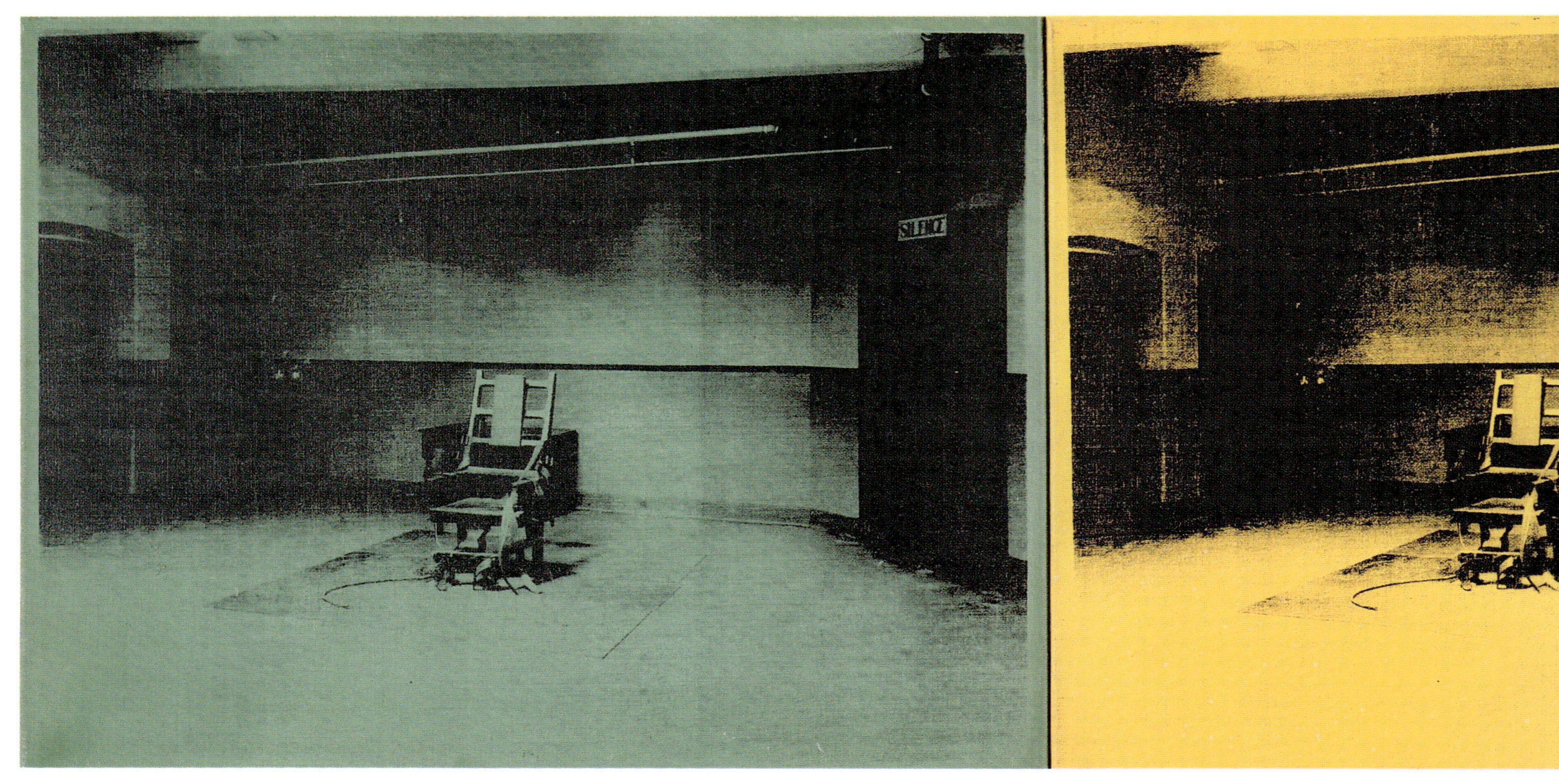

12 *Electric Chair*, 1964

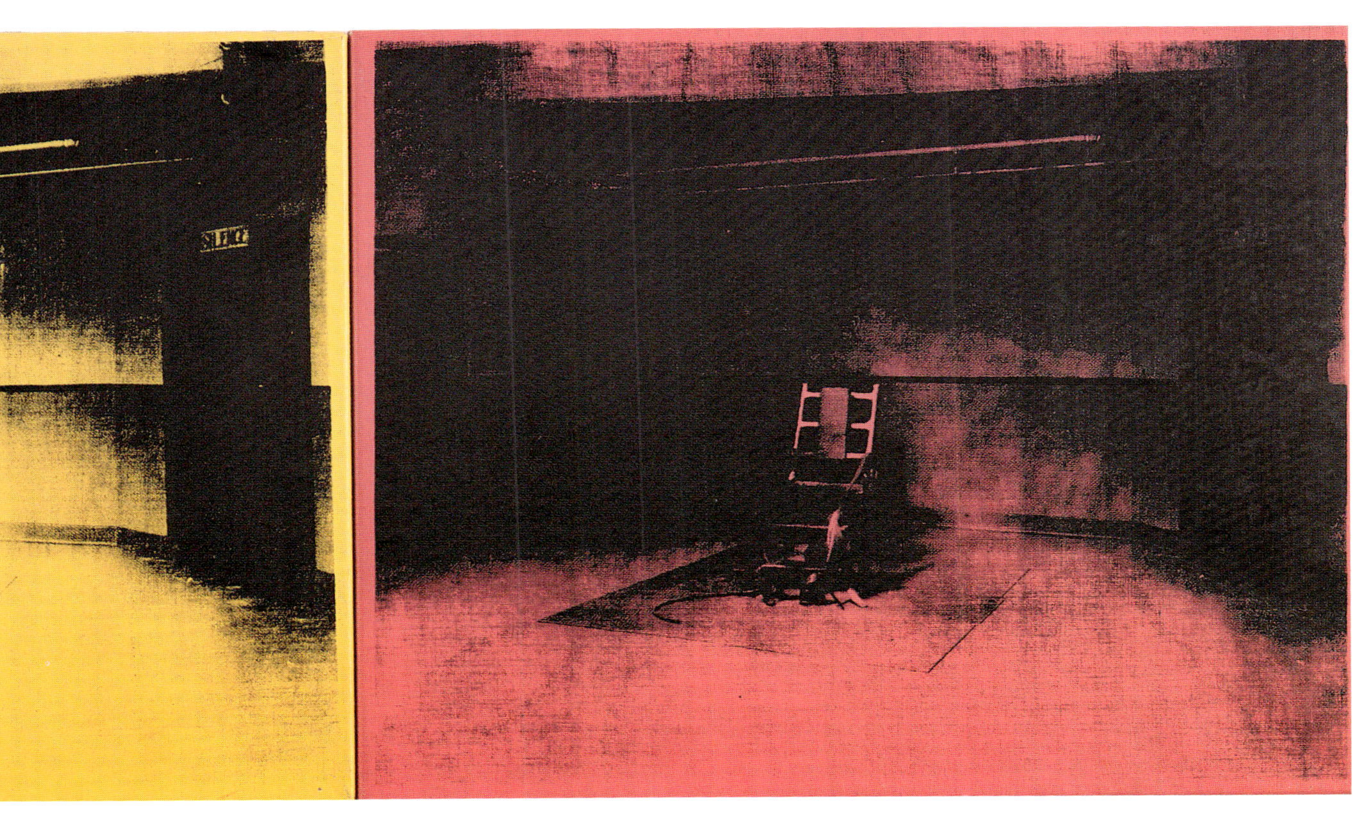

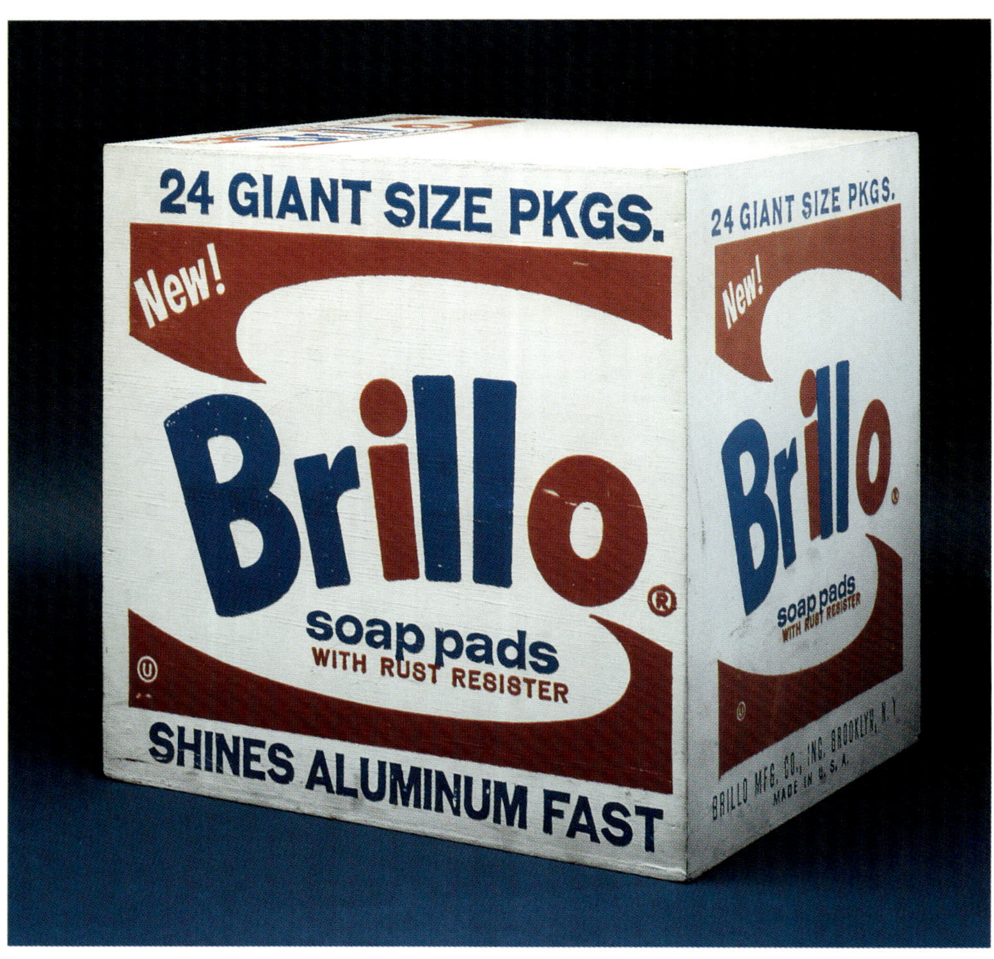

13 and 14 (not illustrated) *Brillo Box*, 1964

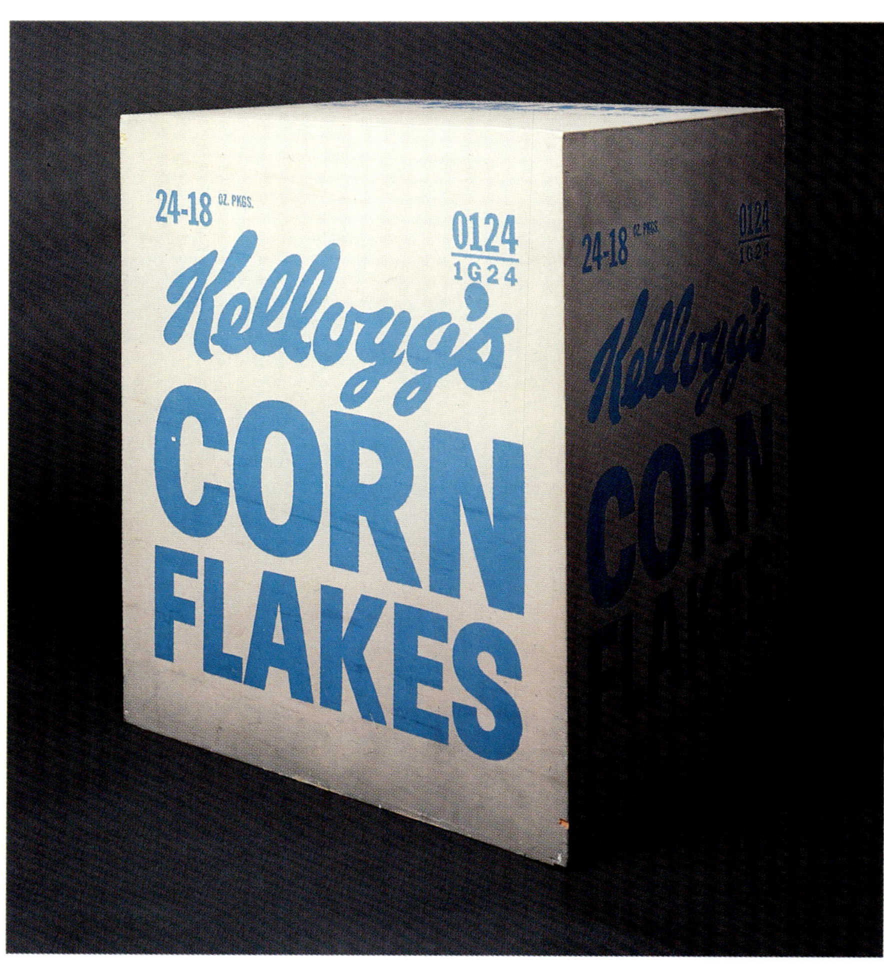

15 *Kellogg's Corn Flakes Box*, 1964

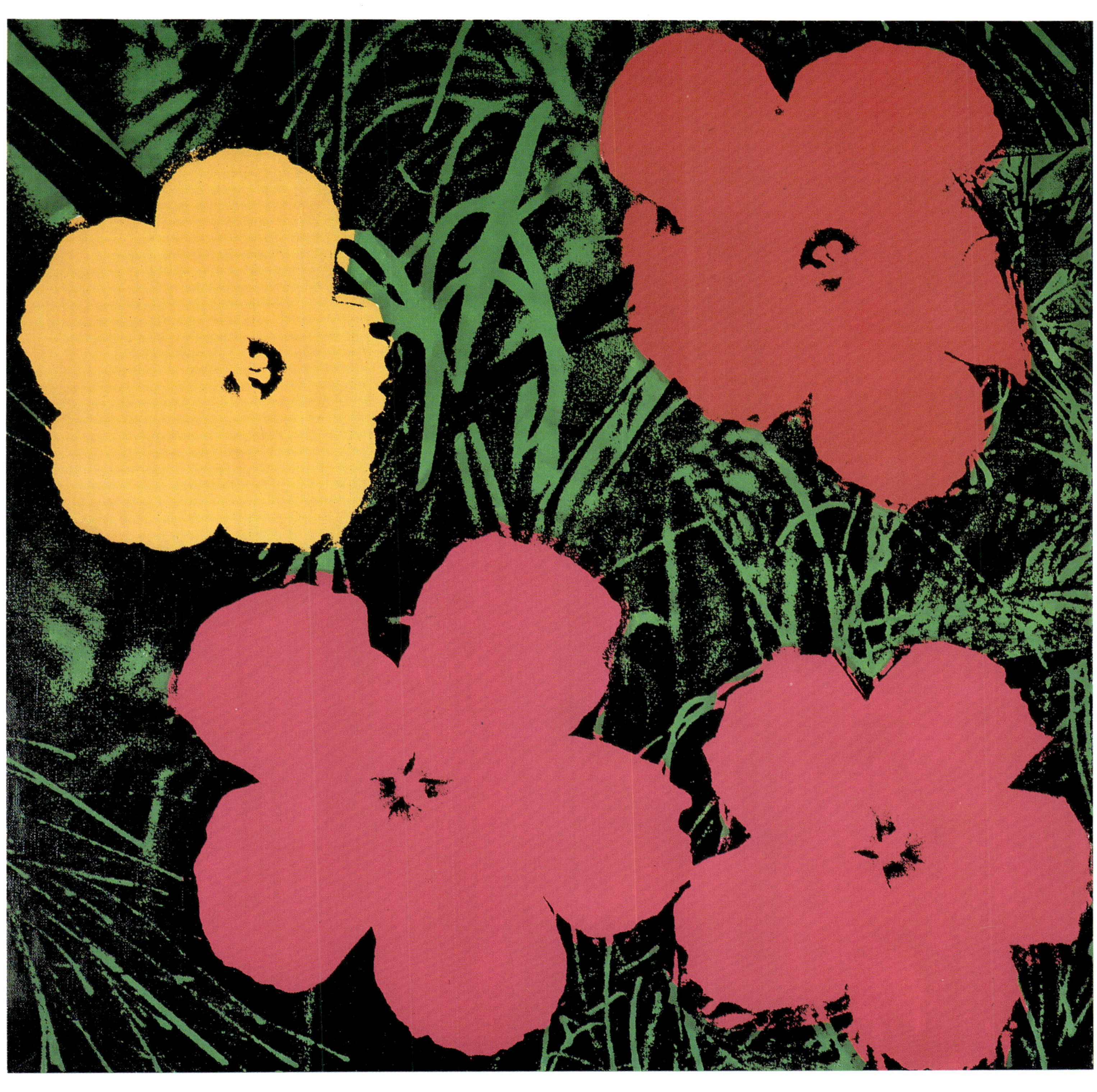

16 *Flowers*, 1964

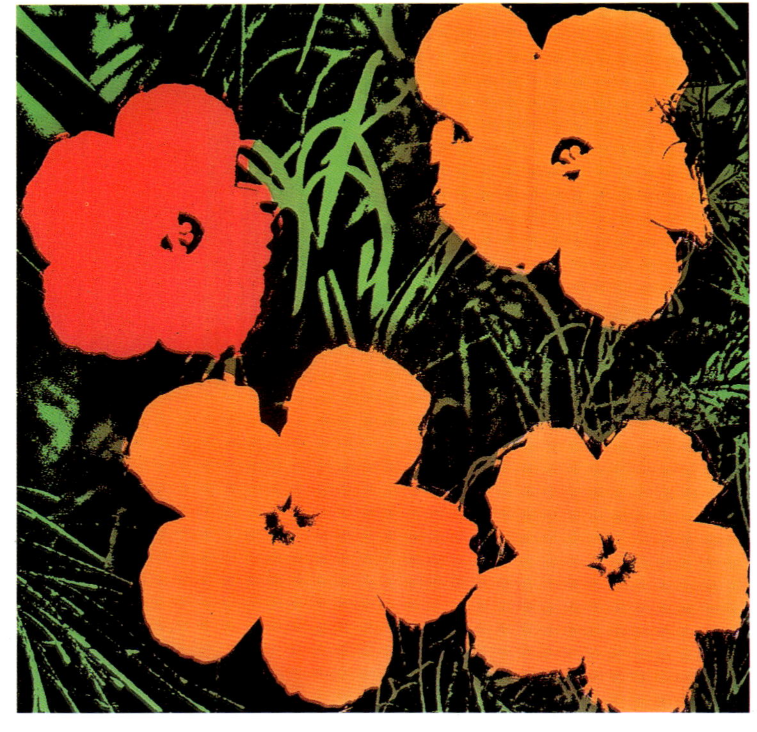

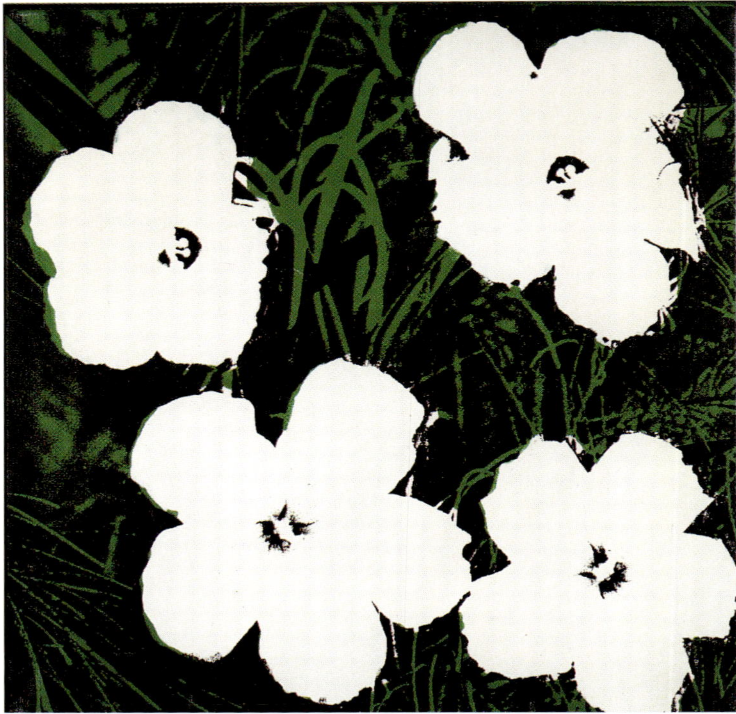

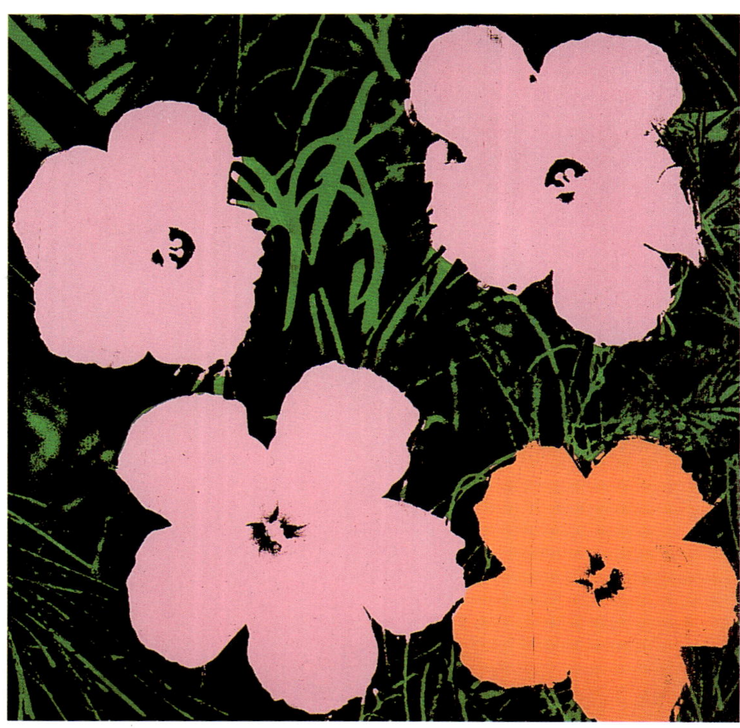

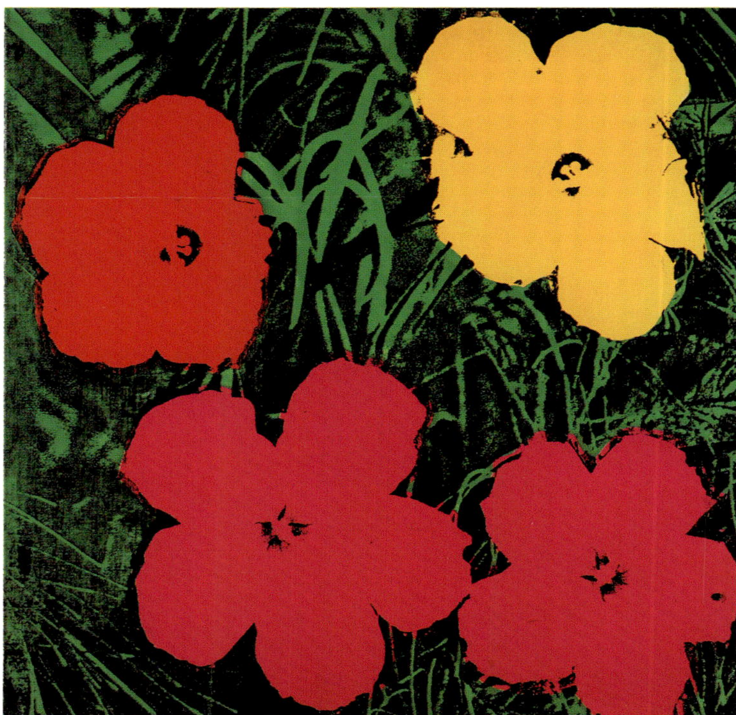

17 *Flowers*, 1964

18 *Flowers*, 1964

19 *Flowers*, 1964

20 *Flowers*, 1964

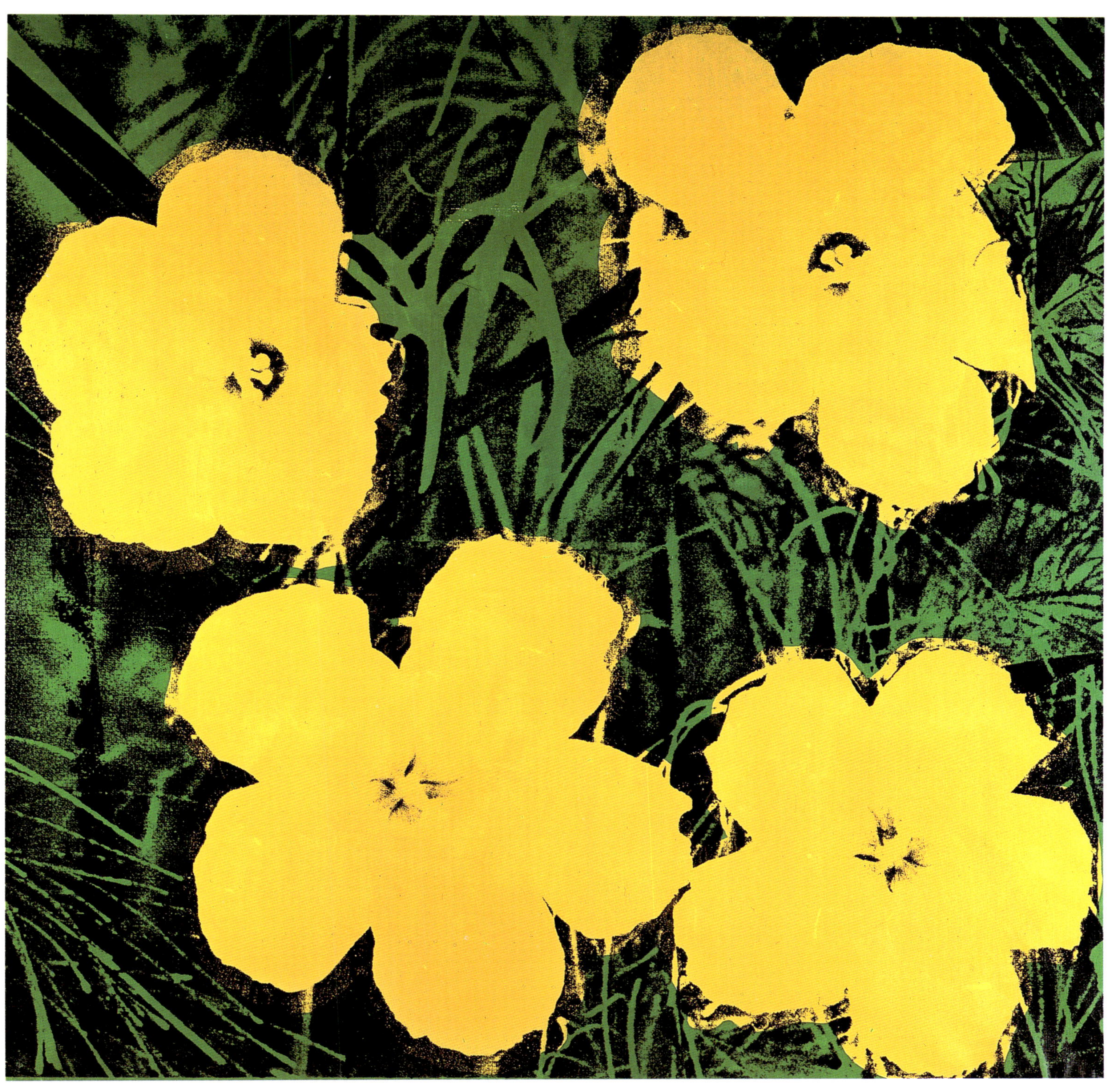

21 *Flowers*, 1964

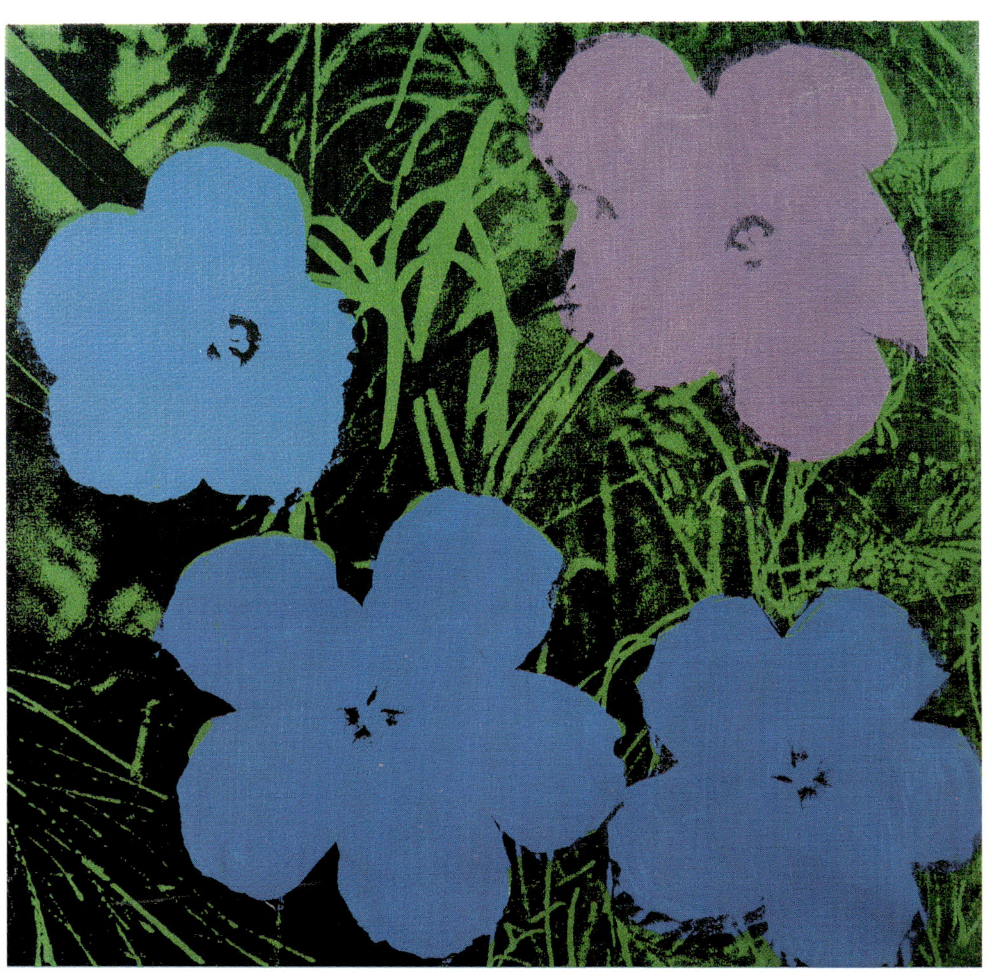

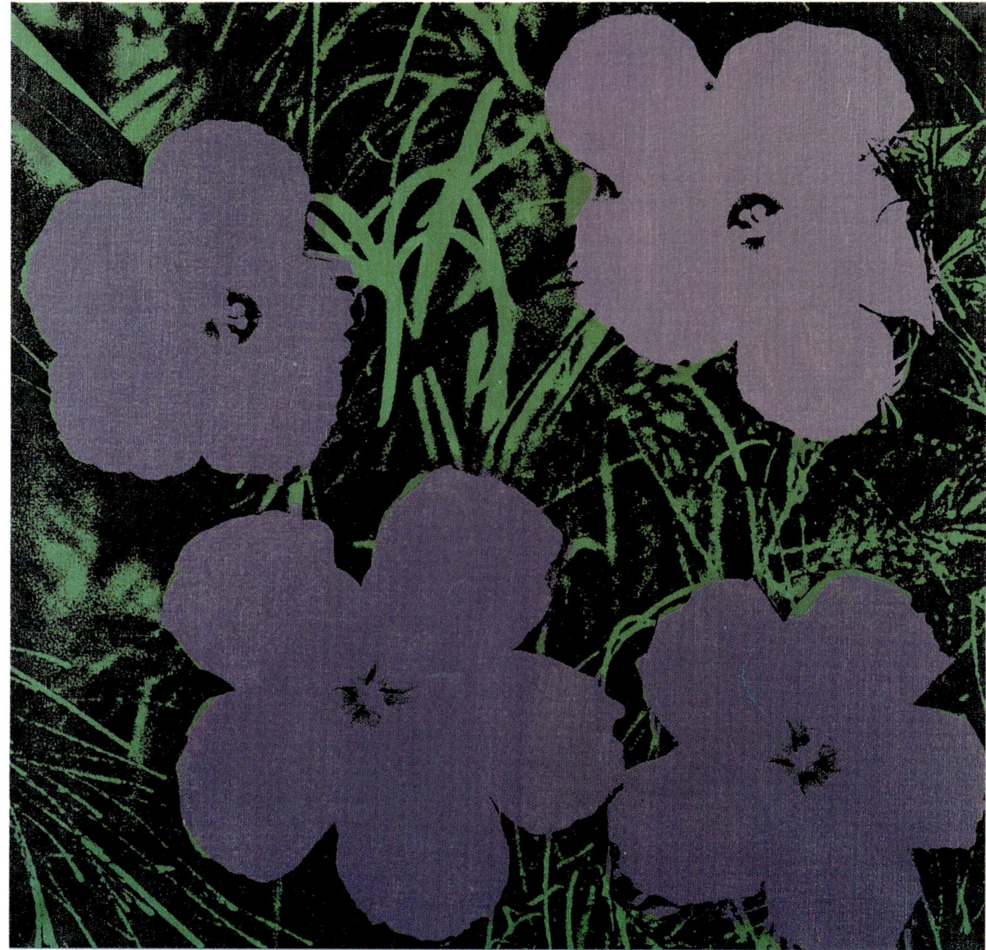

22 *Flowers*, 1964

23 *Flowers*, 1964

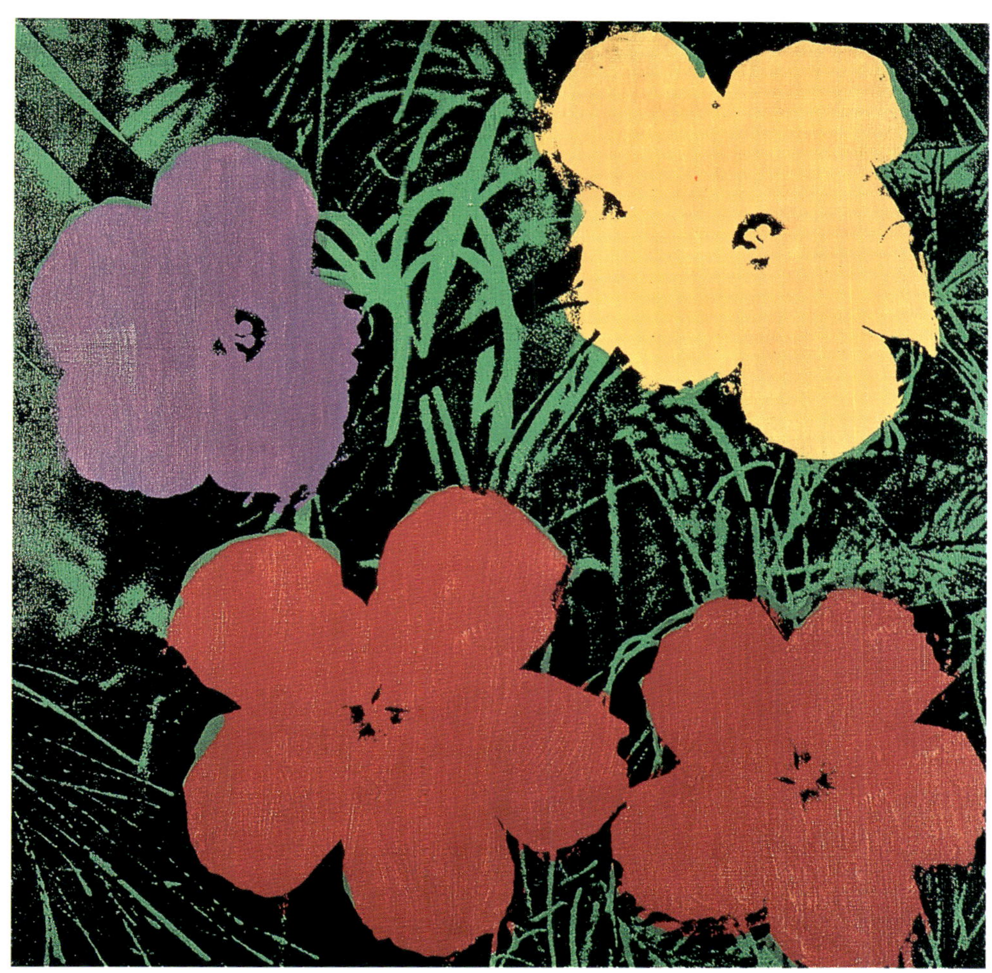

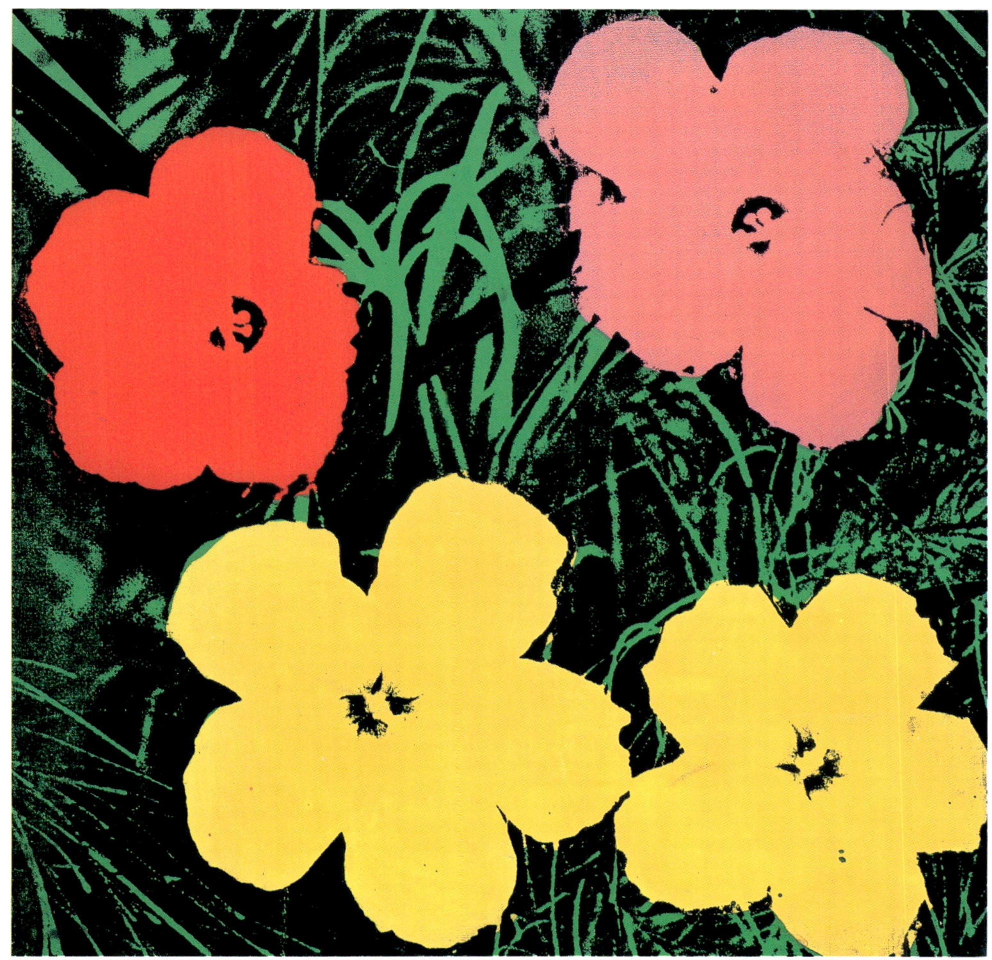

24 *Flowers*, 1964

25 *Flowers*, 1964

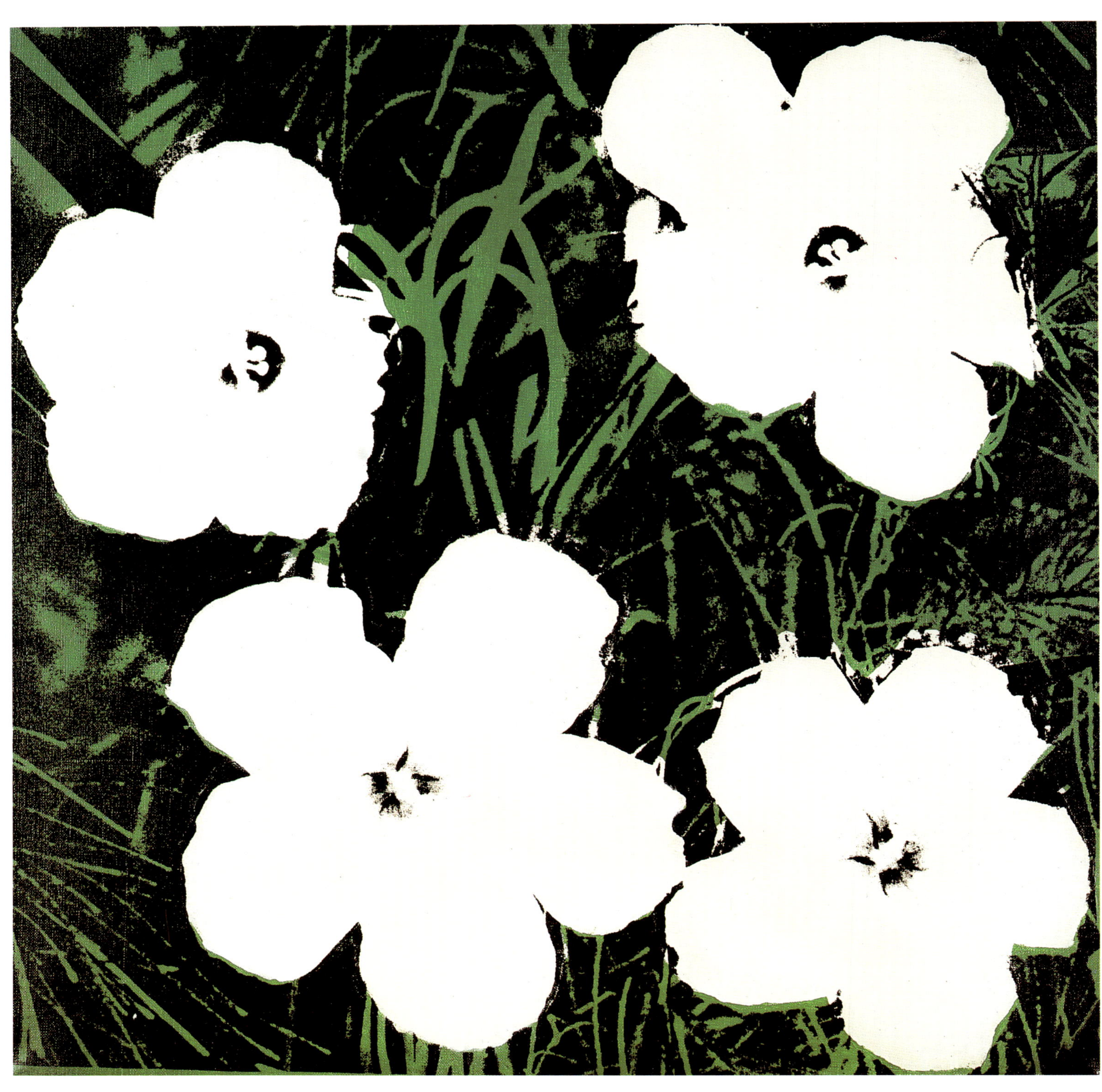

26 *Flowers*, 1964

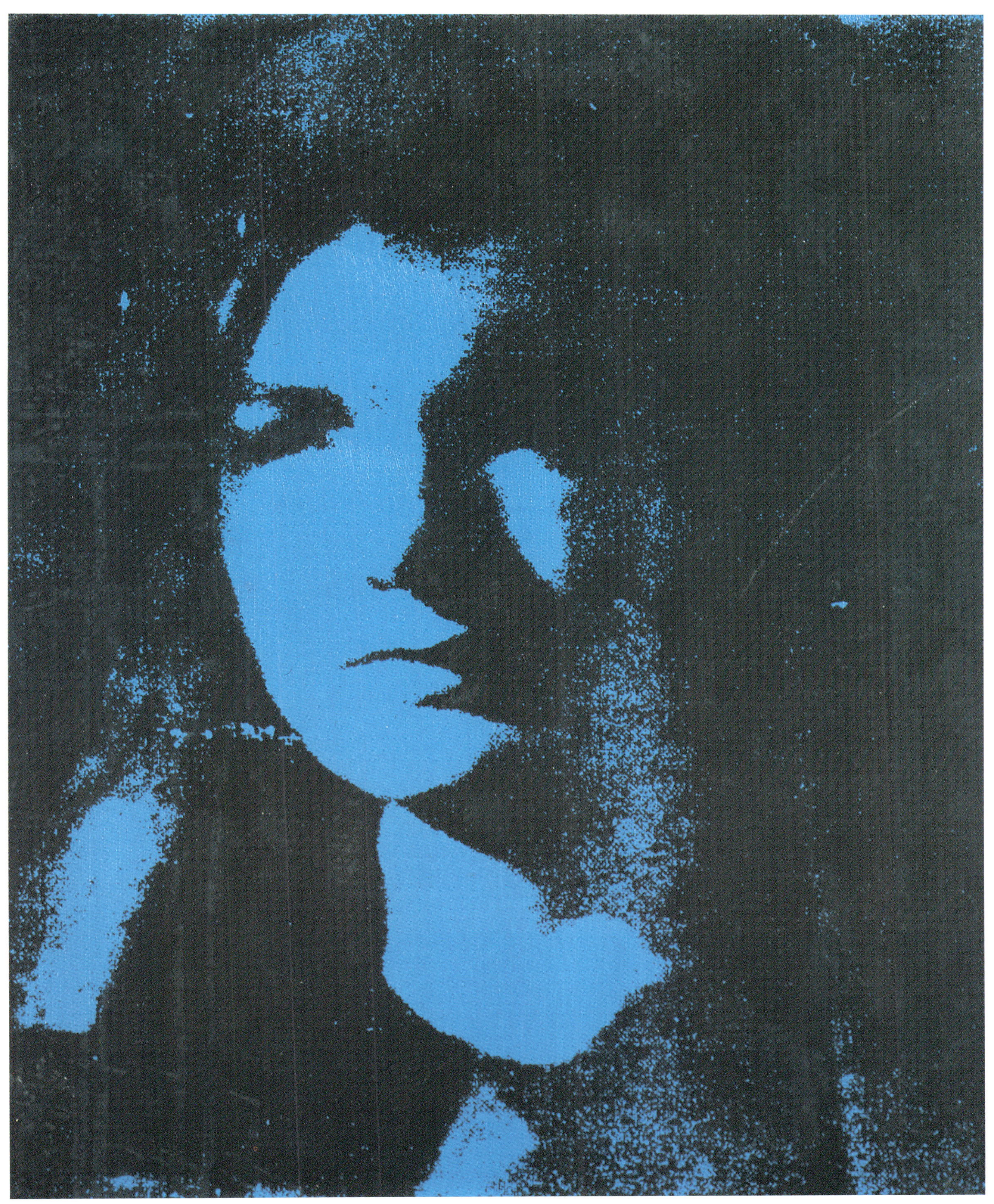

27 *Jackie*, 1964

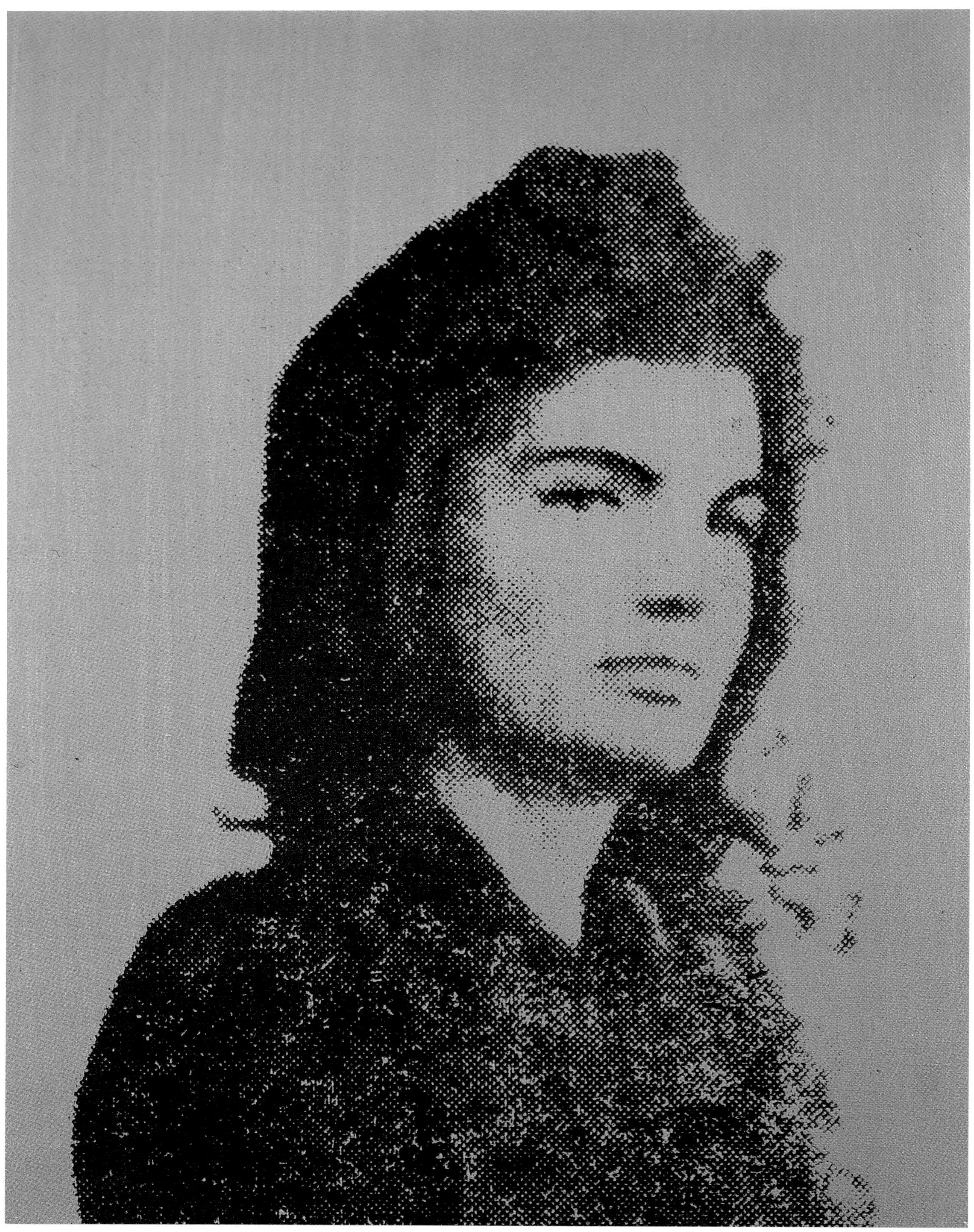

28 *Blue Jackie*, 1964

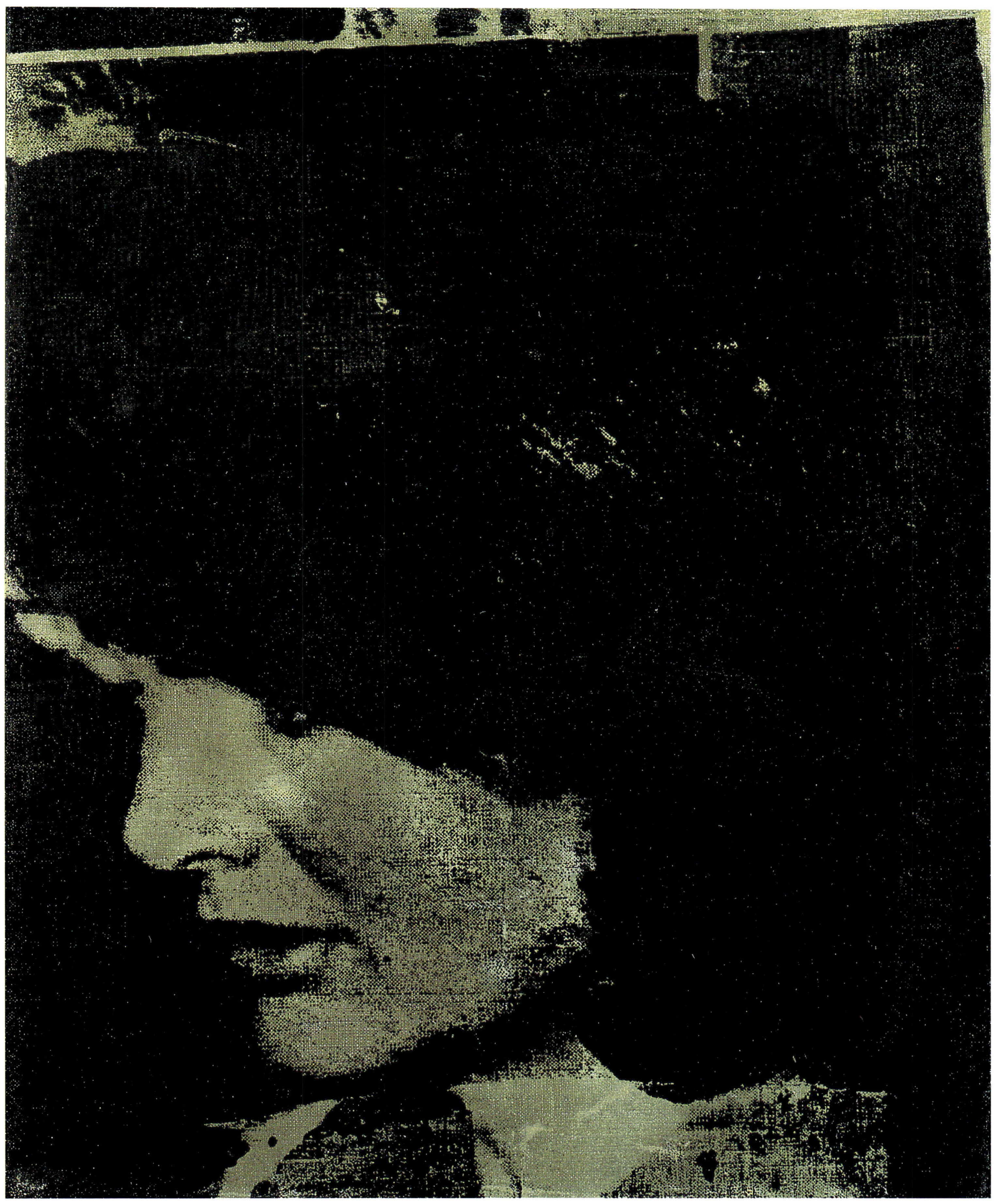

29 *Gold Jackie*, 1964

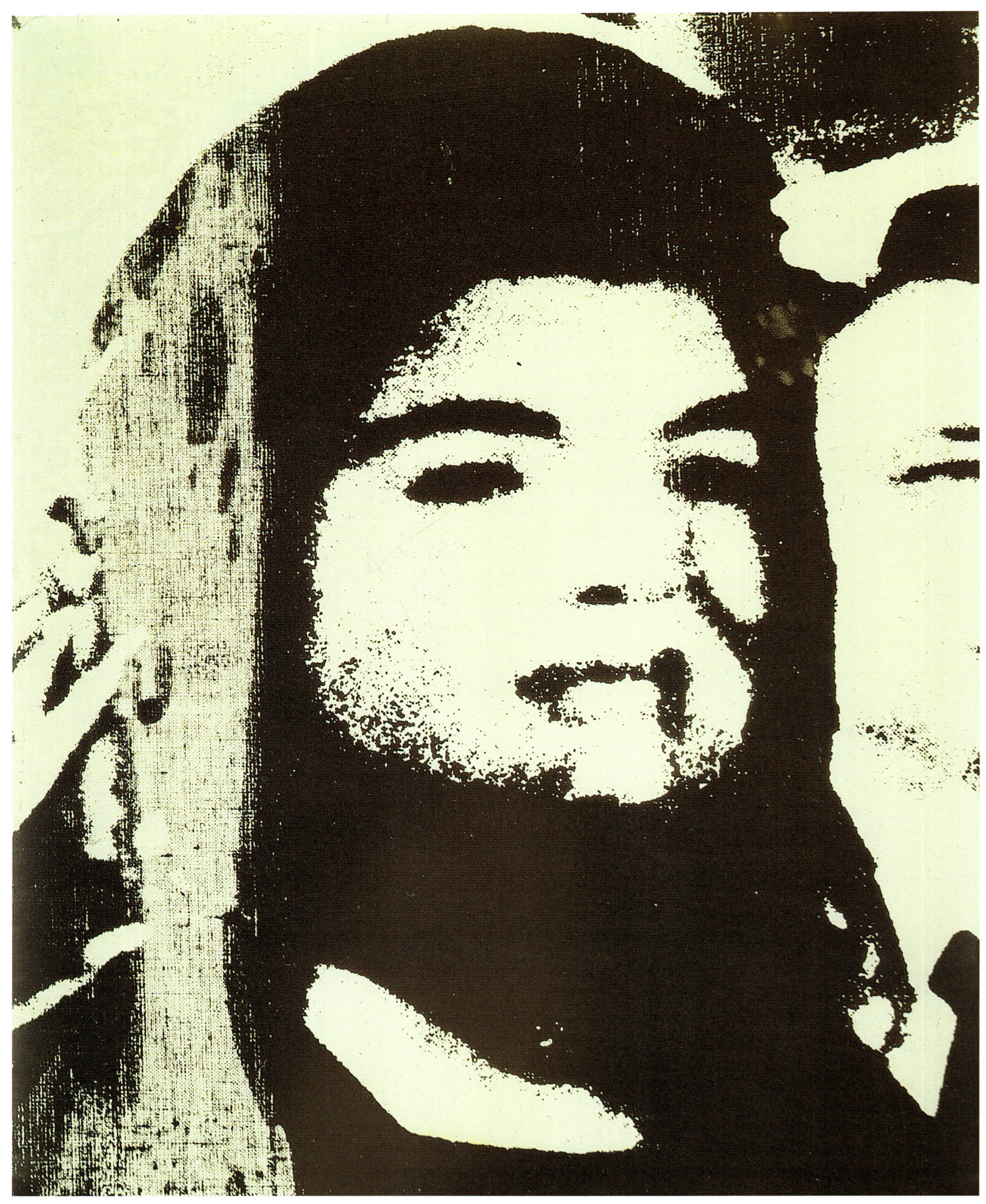

30 *Jackie*, 1964

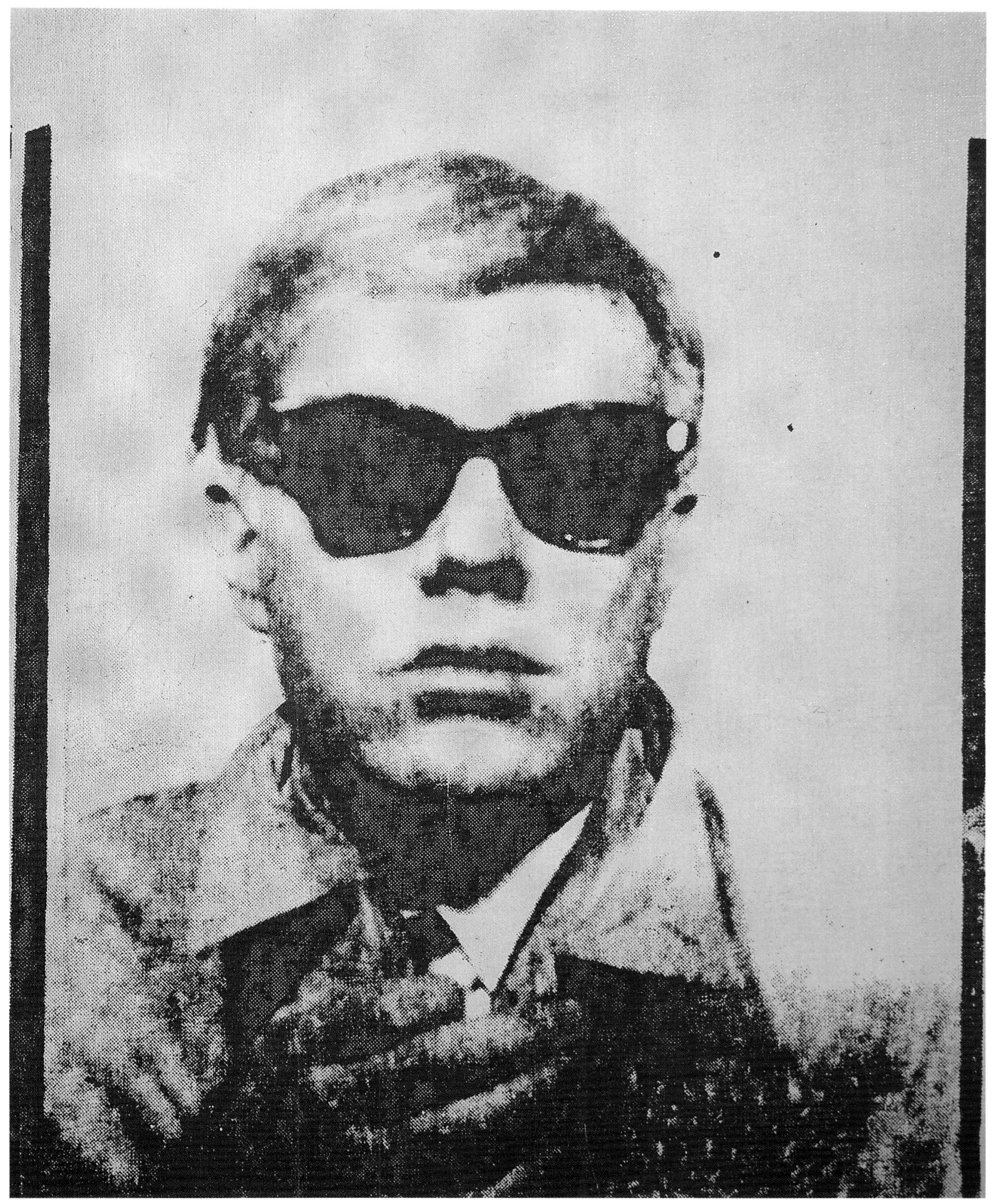

31 *Self-Portrait*, 1964

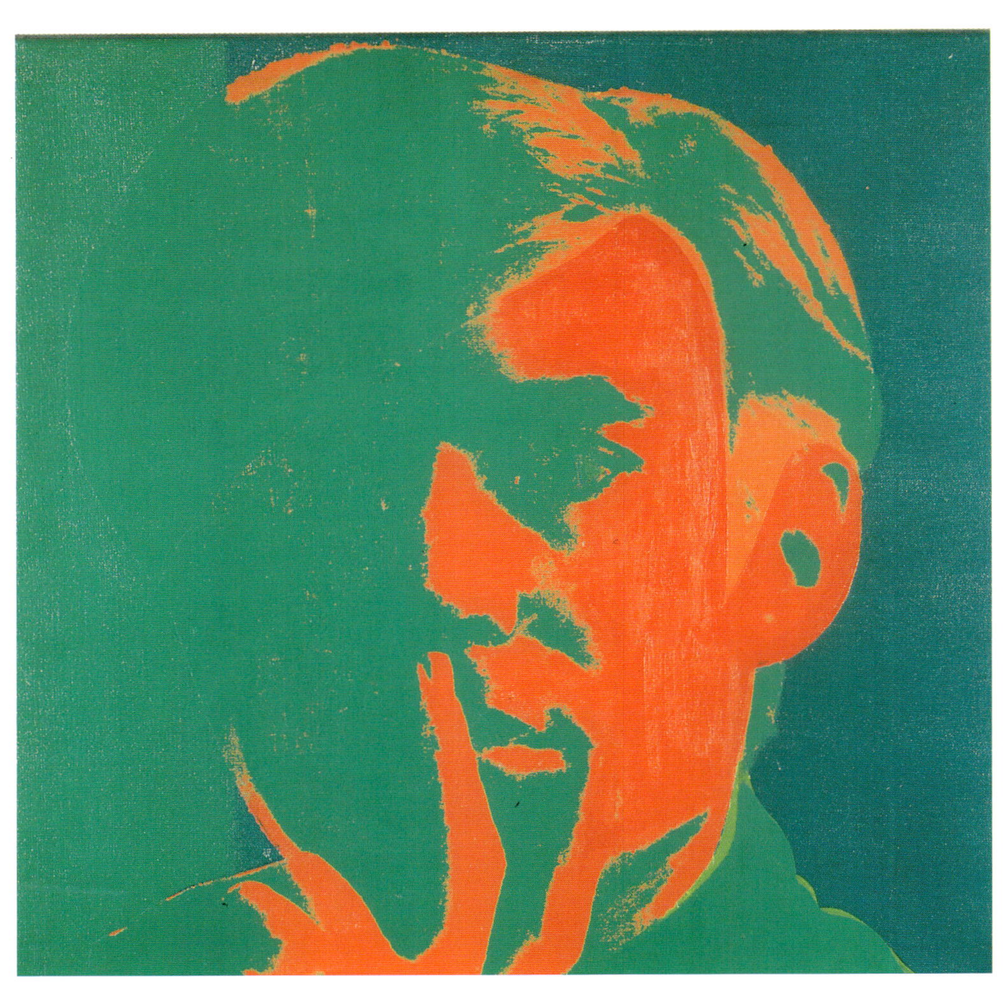

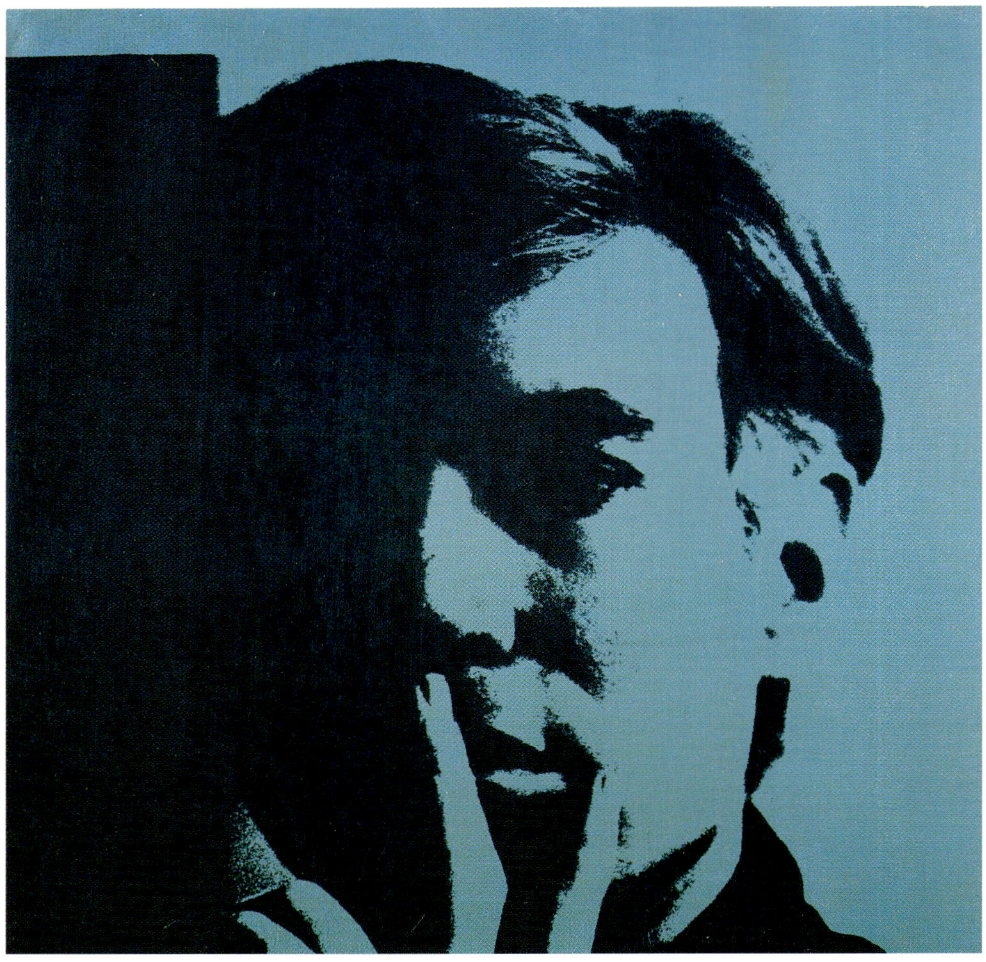

32 *Self-Portrait*, 1966/67

33 *Self-Portrait*, 1966

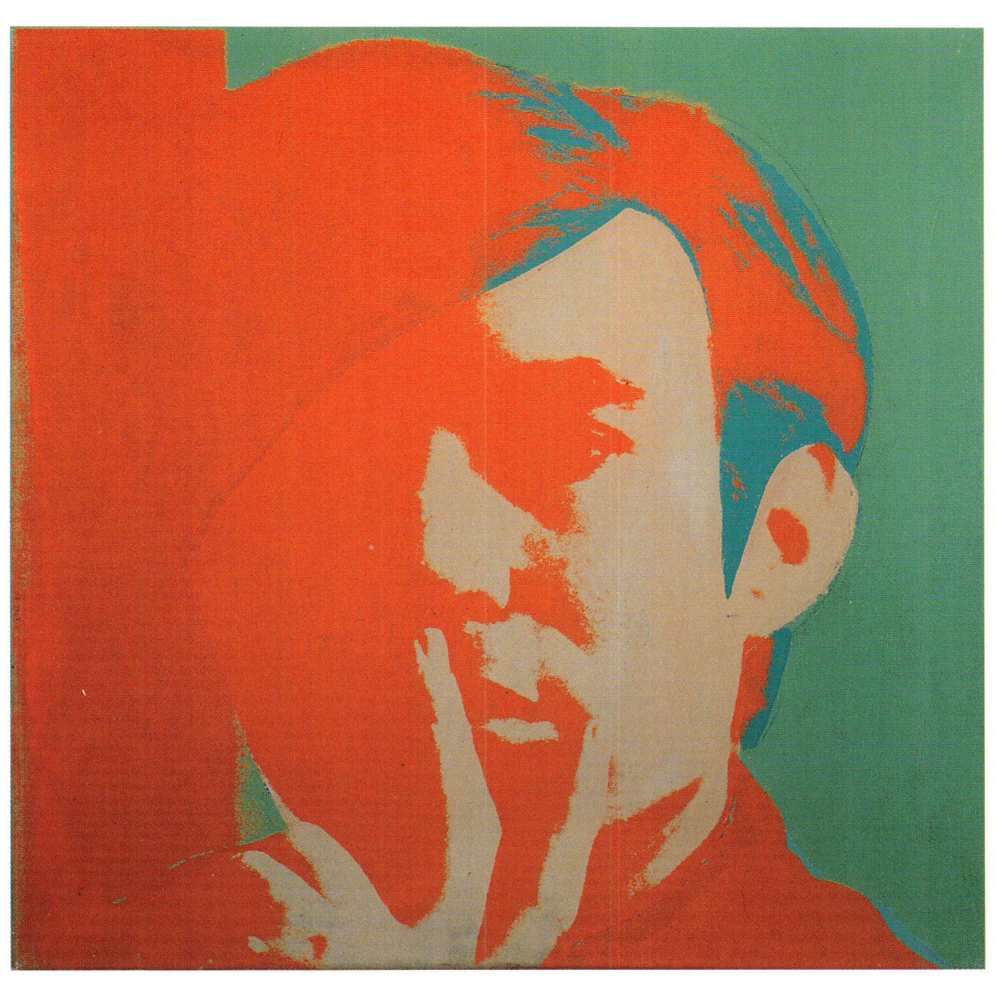

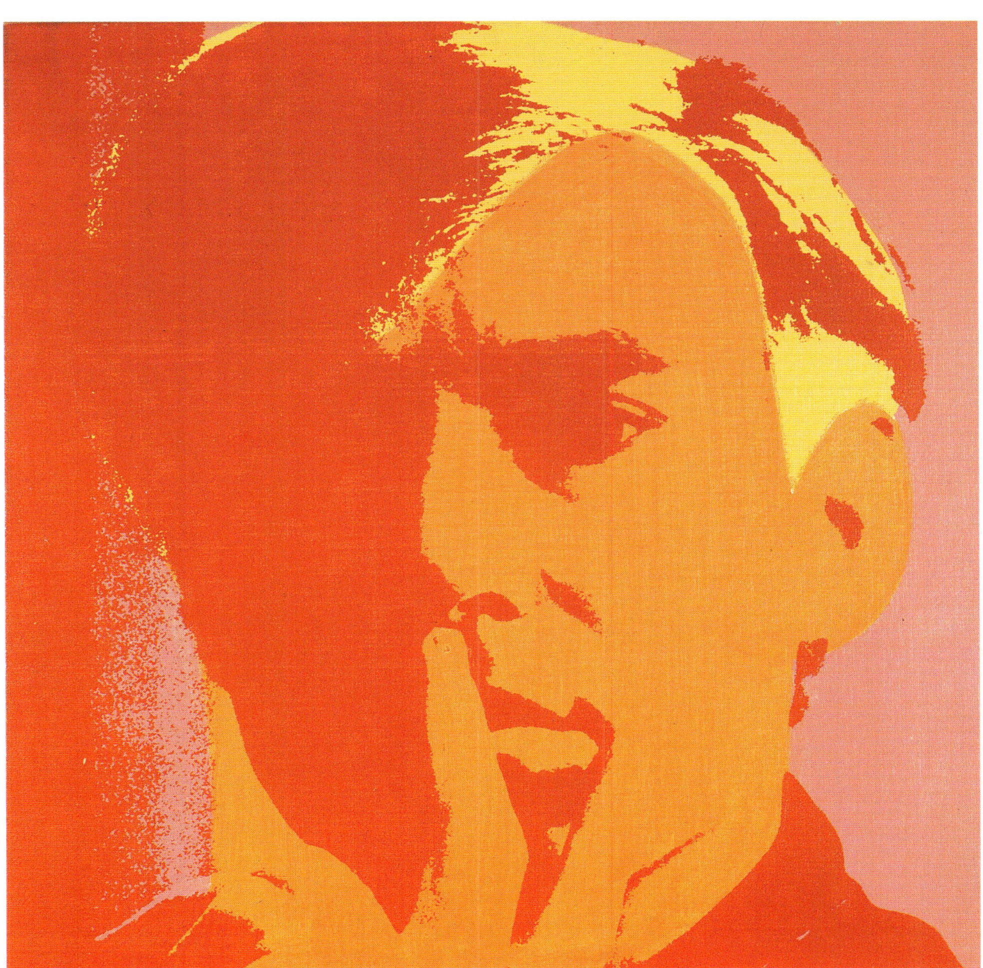

34 *Self-Portrait*, 1967

35 *Self-Portrait*, 1966

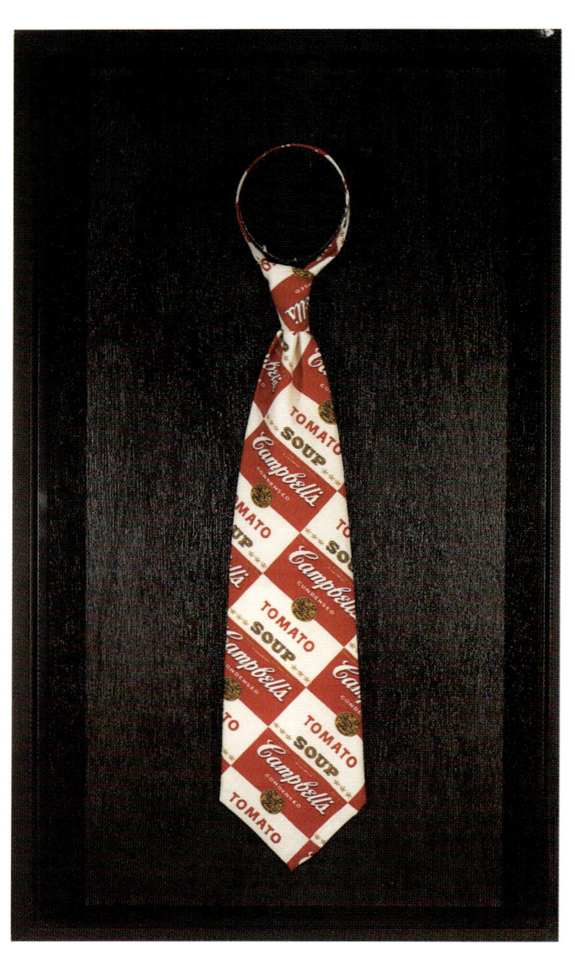

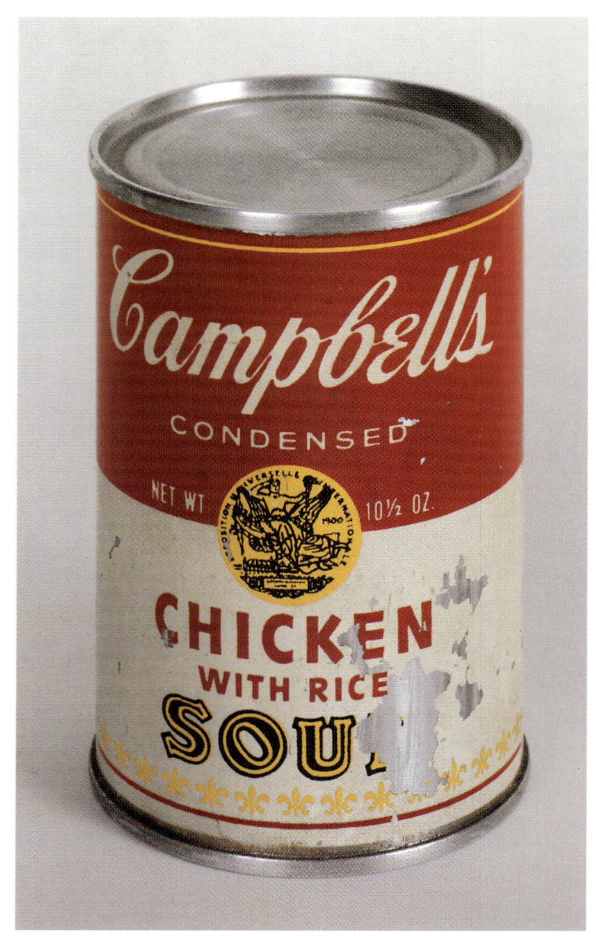

36 *Campbell's Soup*, 1975

37 *Campbell's Soup Can*, 1966

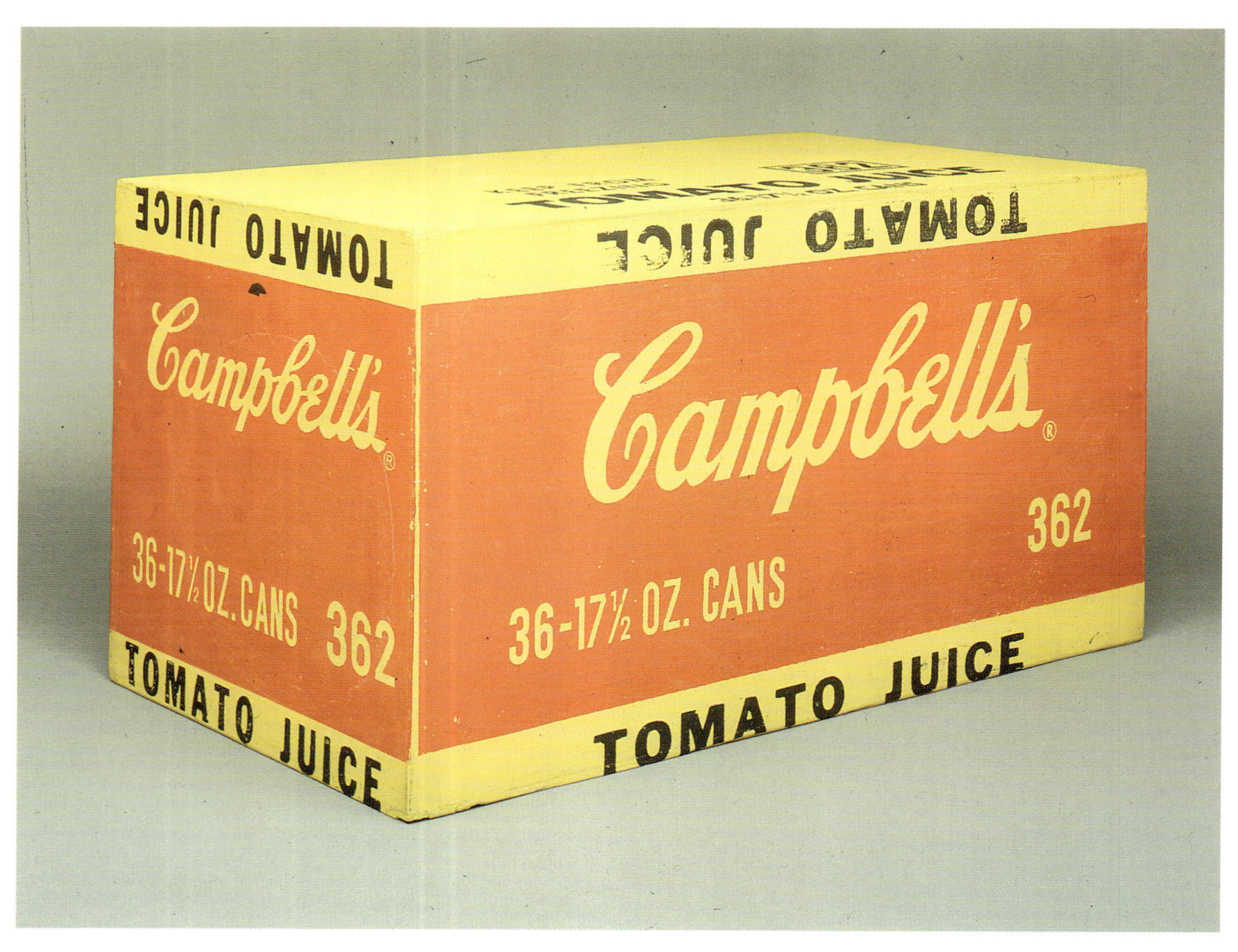

38 *Campbell's Tomato Juice Box*, 1964

39 *Campbell's Tomato Soup Can*, 1968

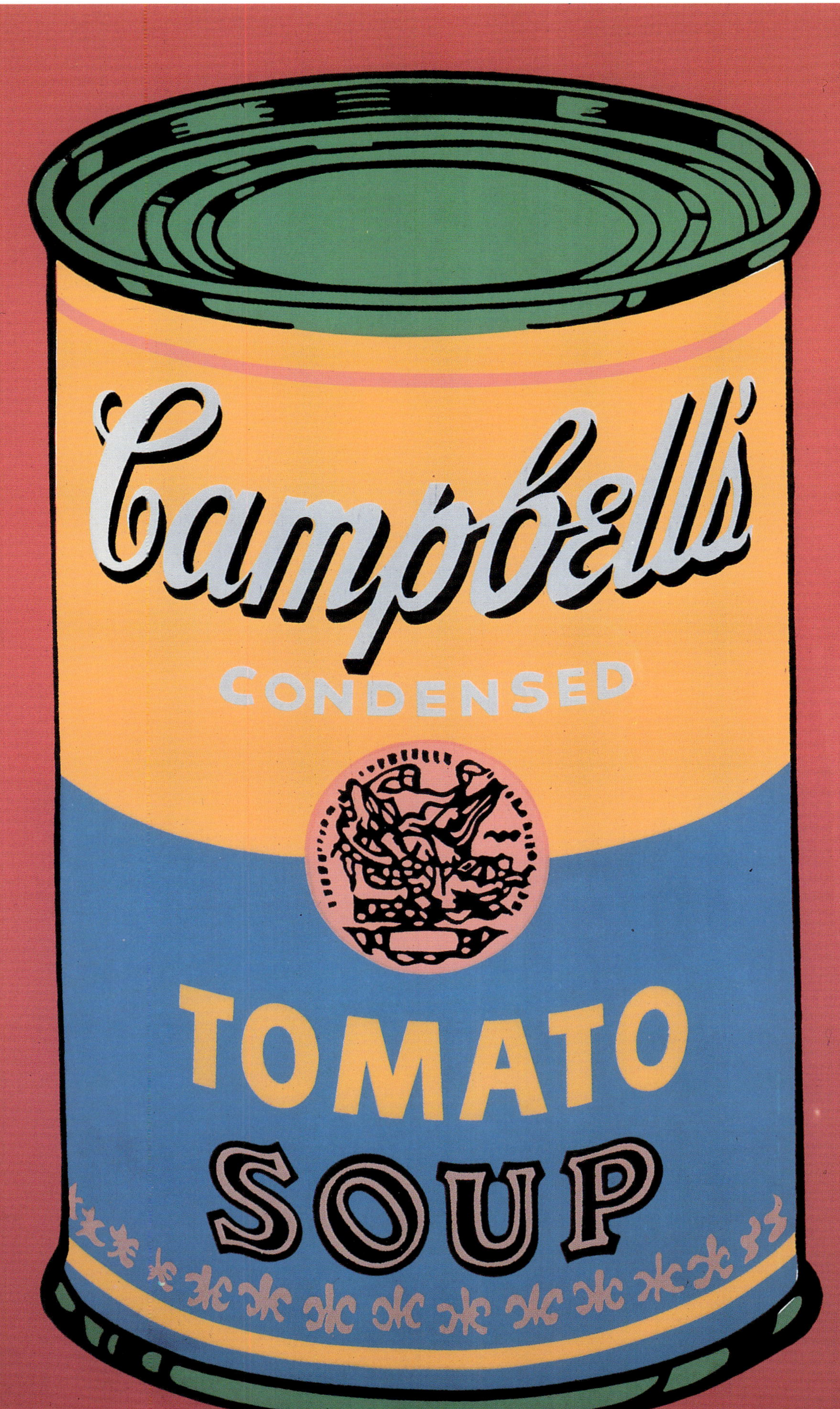
Campbell's
CONDENSED
TOMATO
SOUP

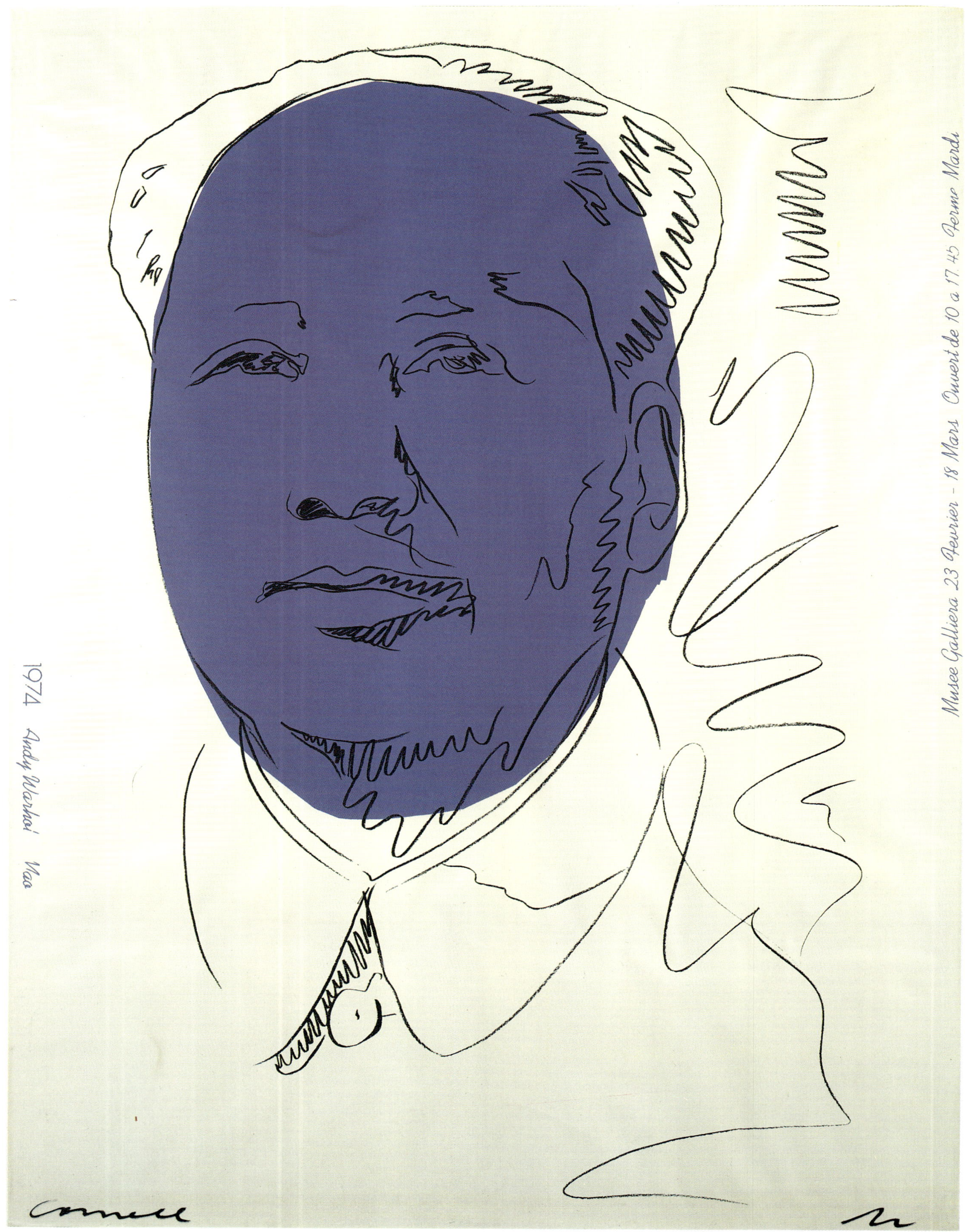

40 *Mao Tse-tung*, 1974

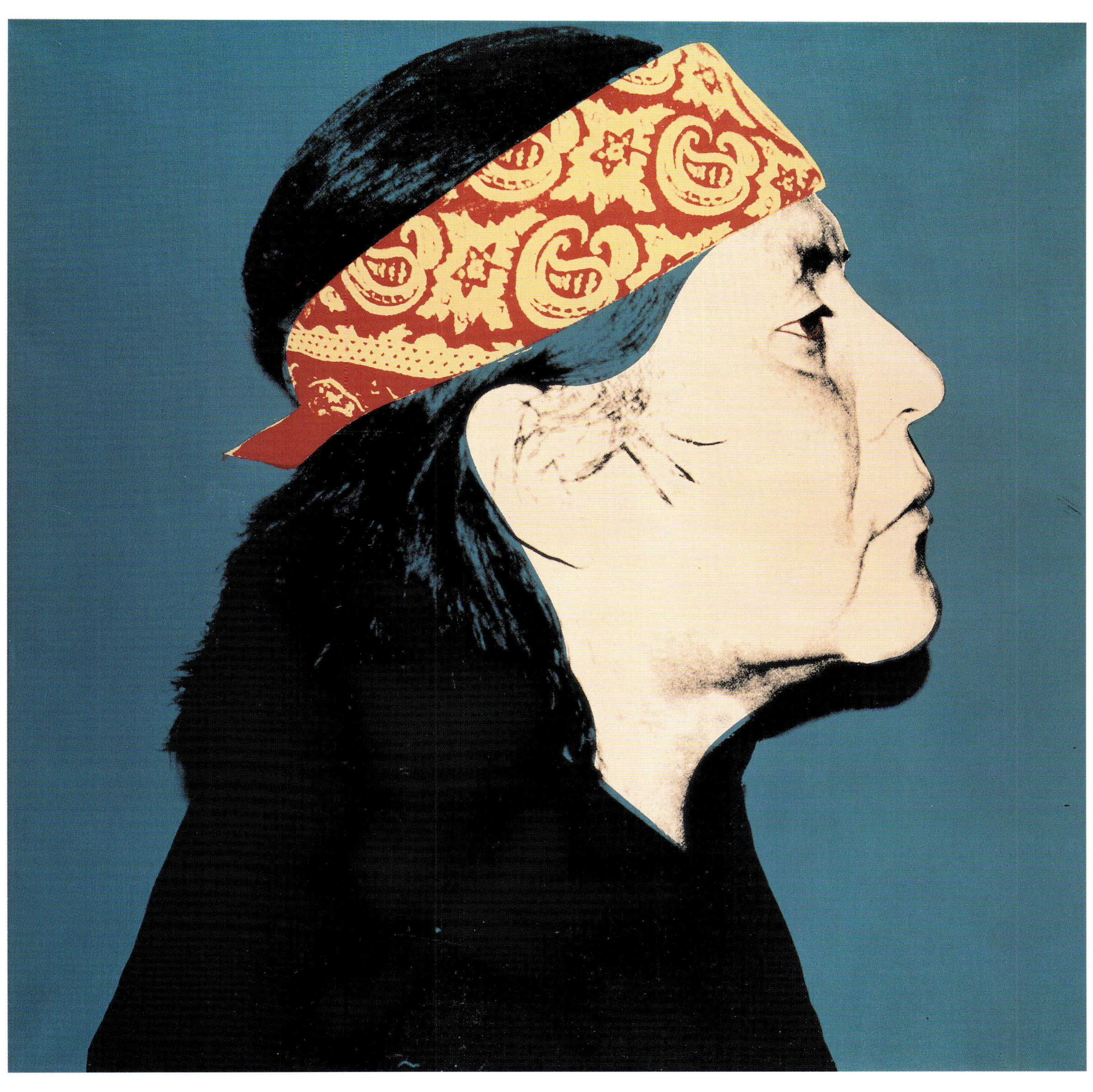

41 *Portrait of R. C. Gorman*, 1979

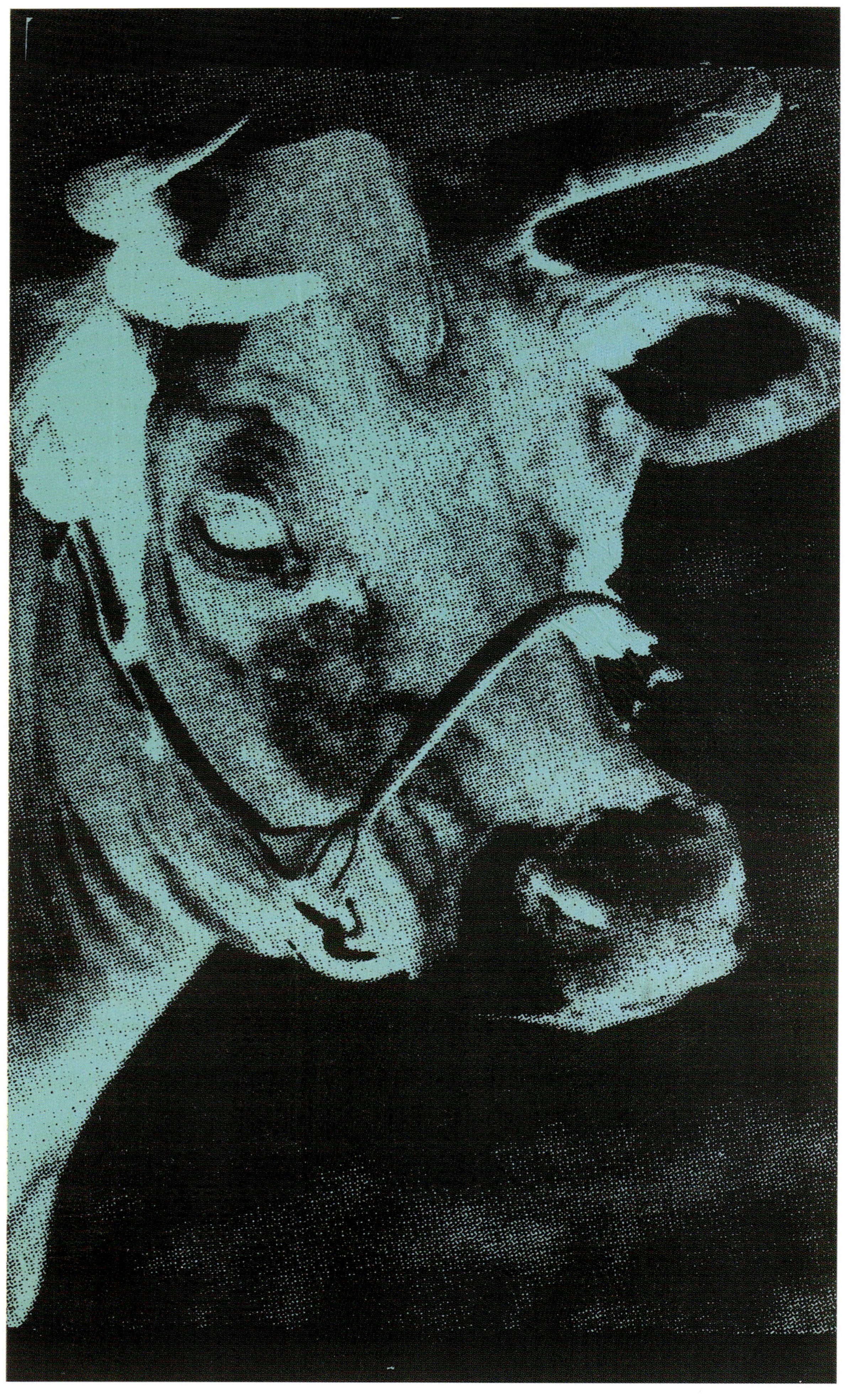

42 *One Green Cow*, 1979

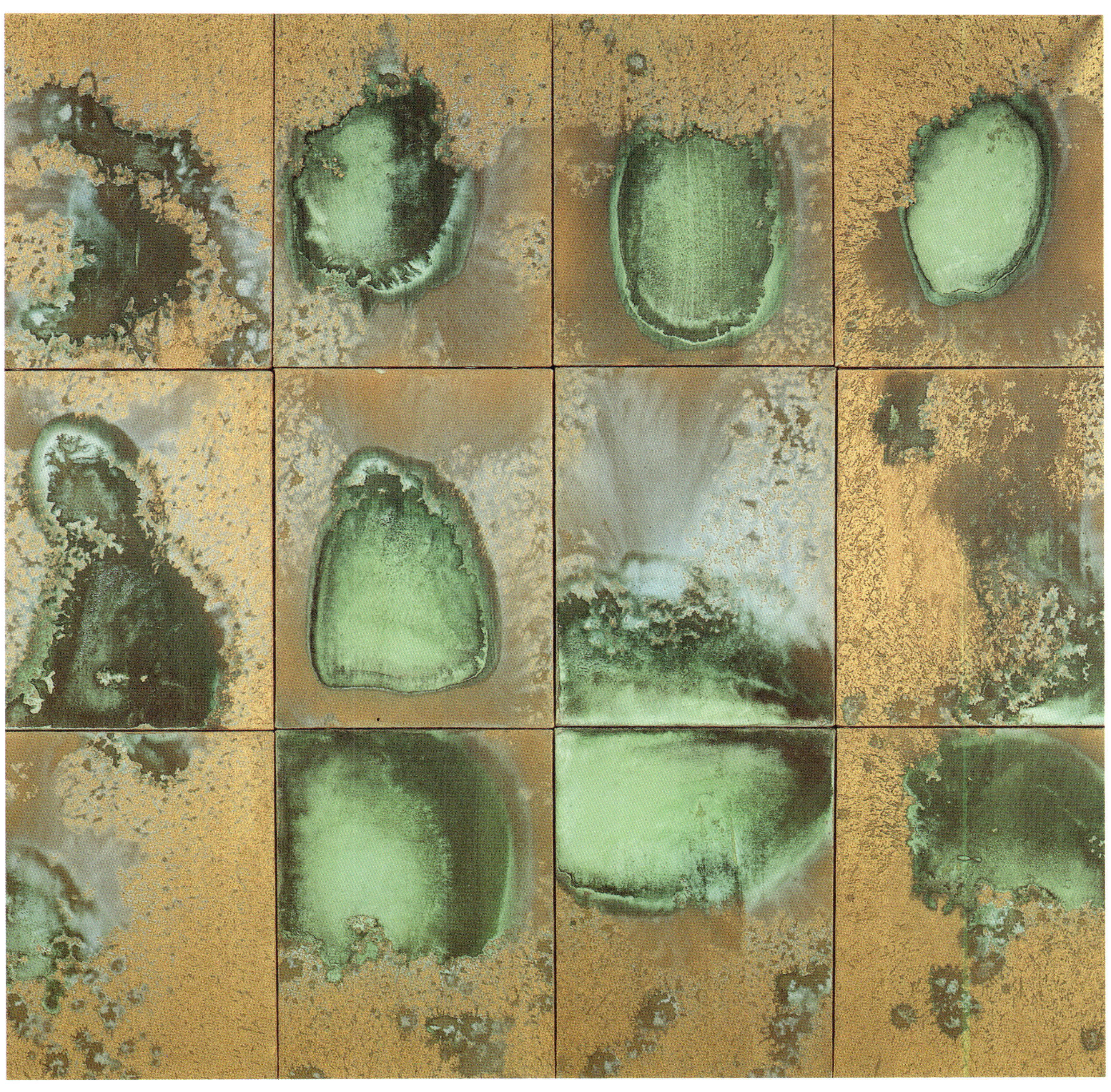

43 *Oxidation Painting*, 1978

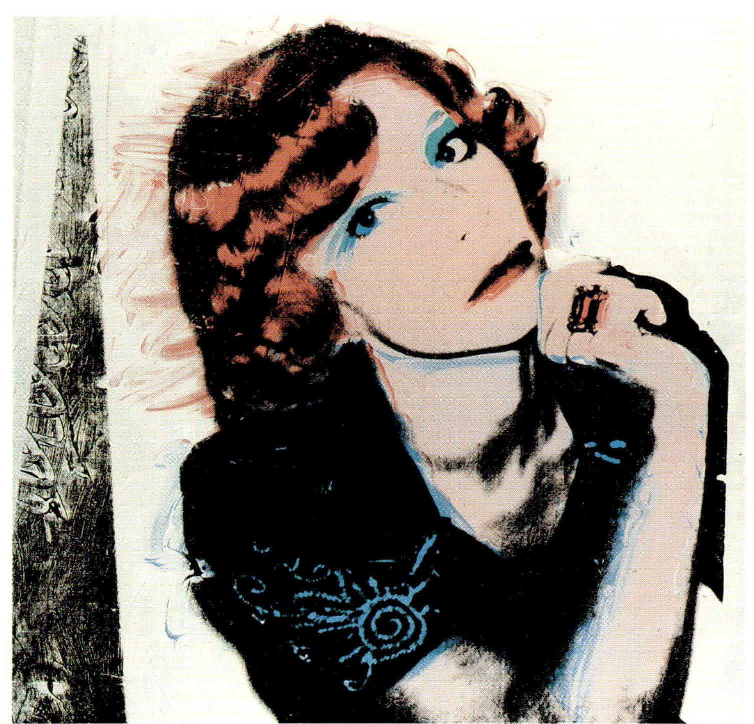

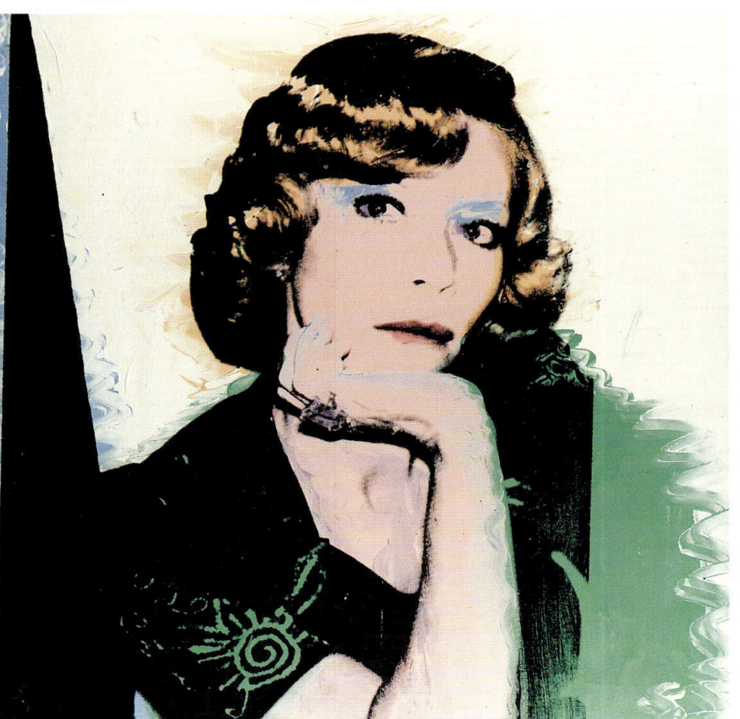

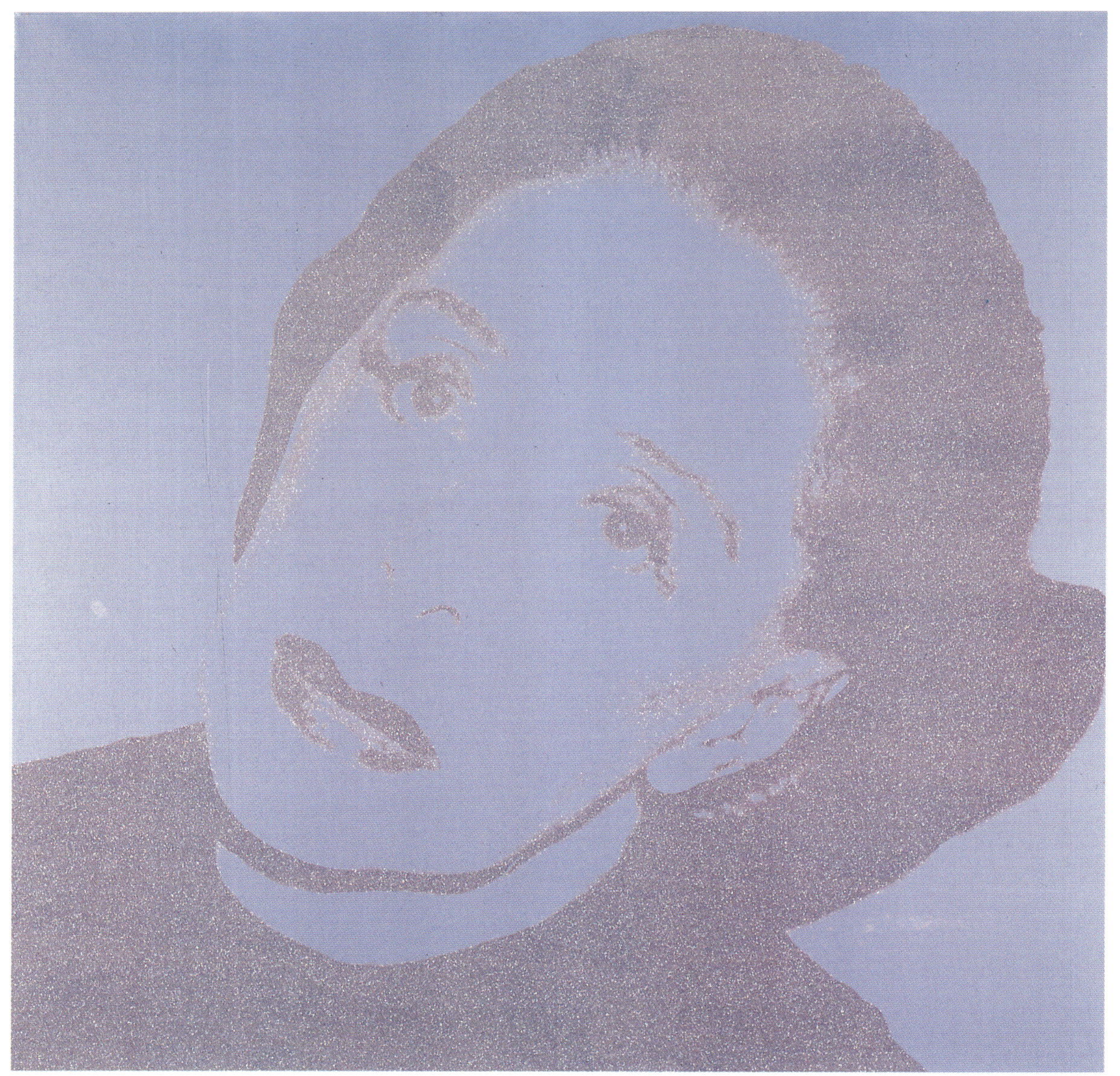

44 *Portrait of Madame Smith*, 1970s

45 *Portrait of Martha Graham*, 1980

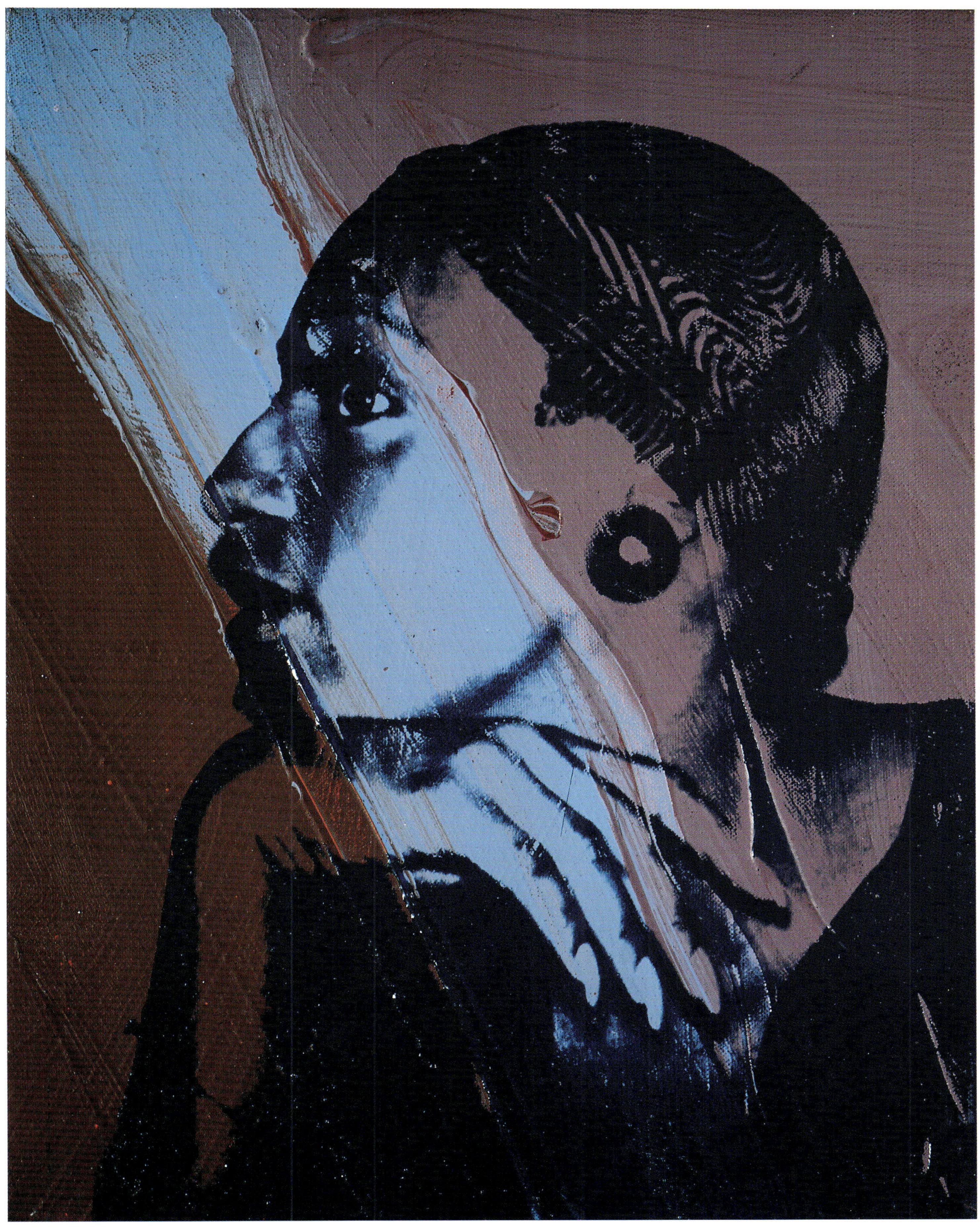

46 *Drag Queen*, 1977

47 *One White on White Mona Lisa*, 1979

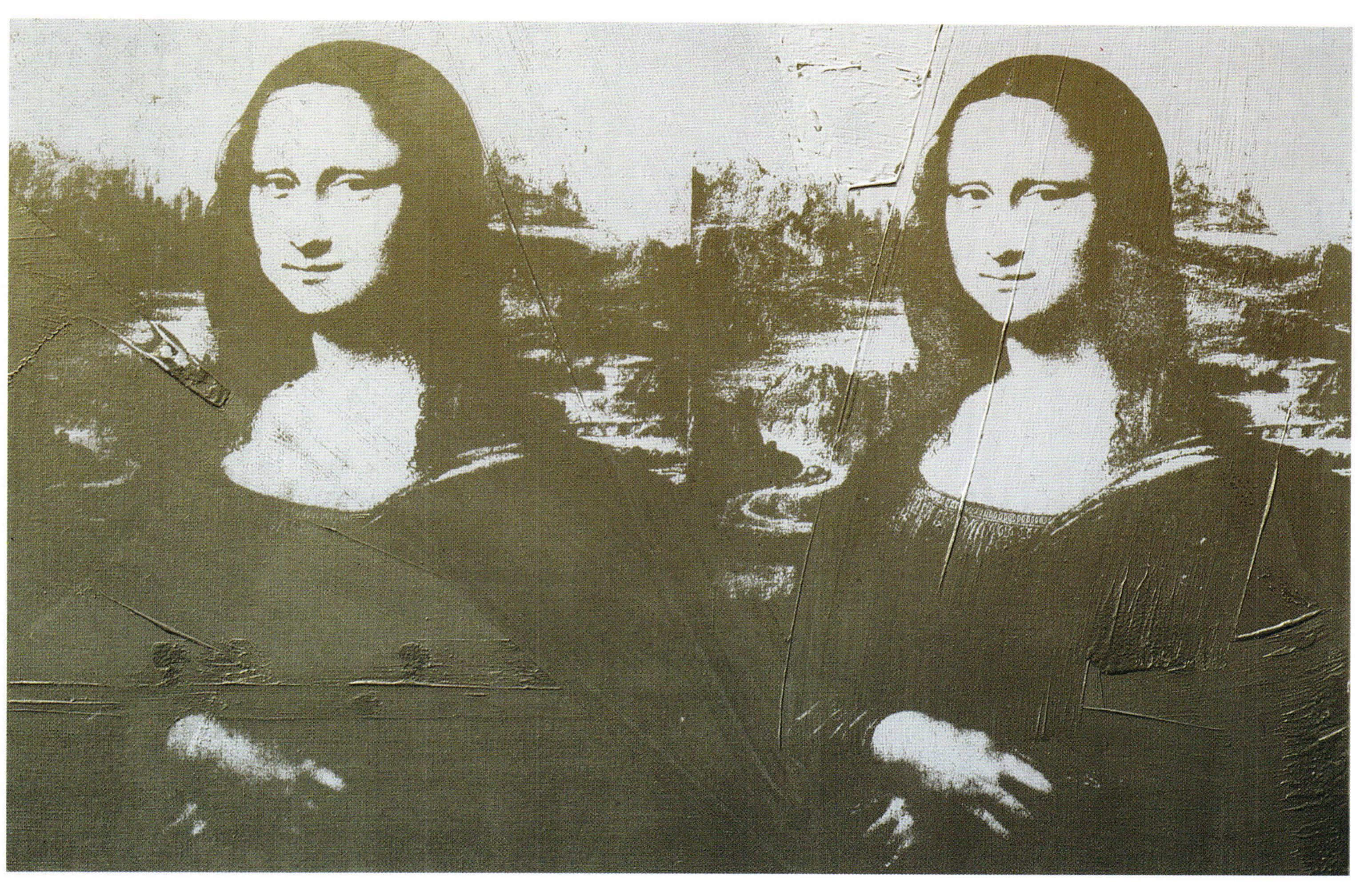

48 *Two Golden Mona Lisas*, 1980

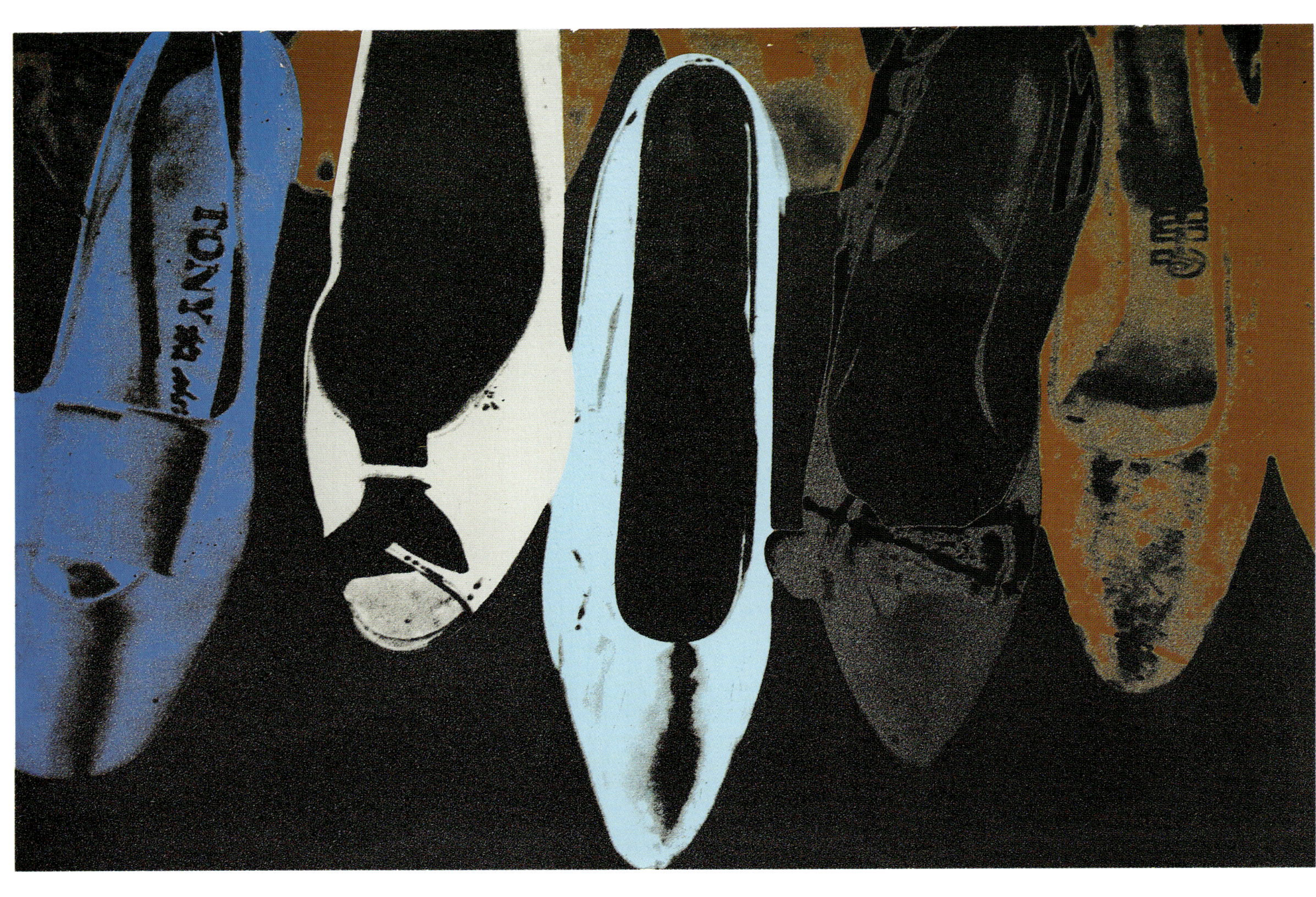

49 *Shoes* (Tony), 1980

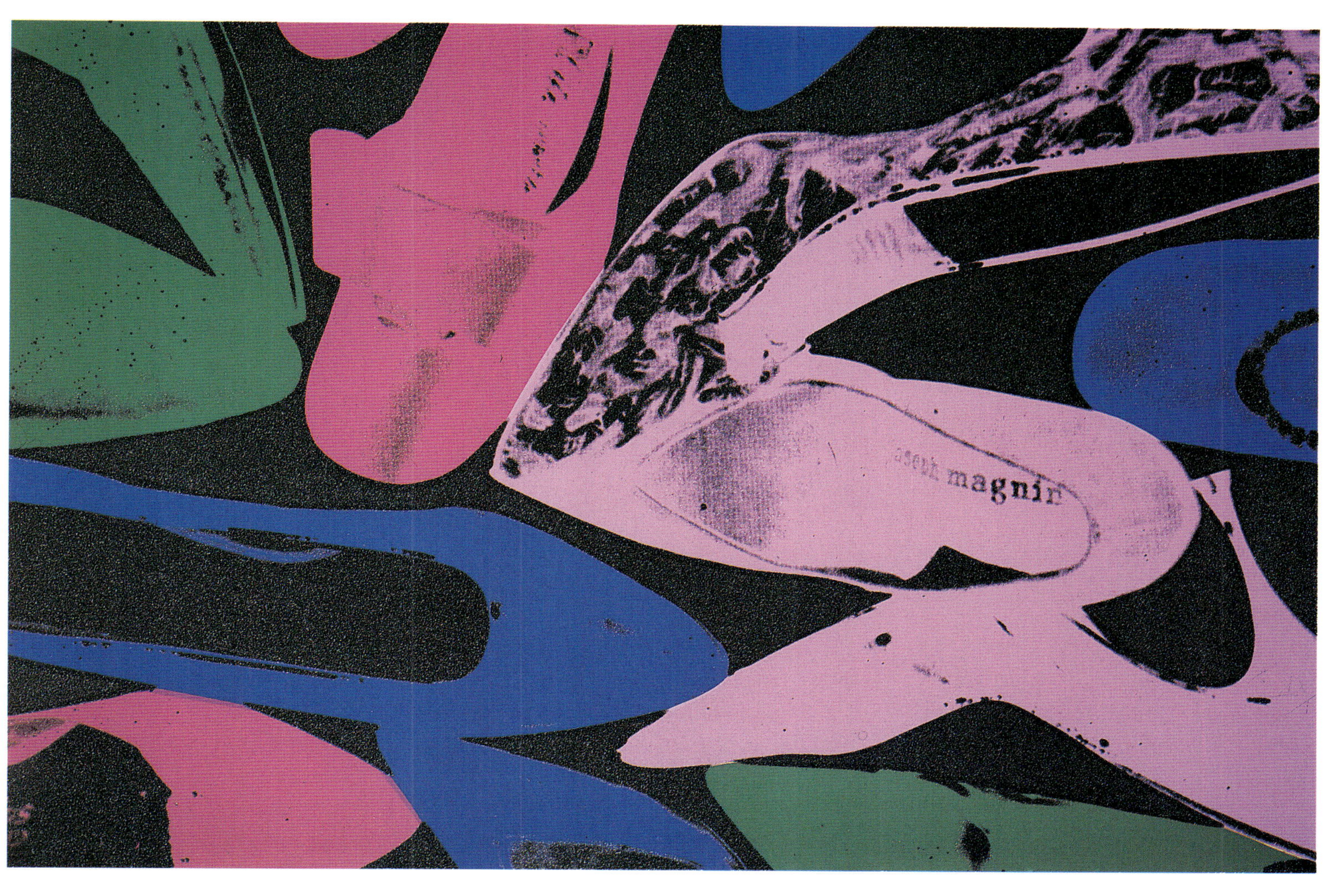

50 *Shoes* (Magnin), 1980

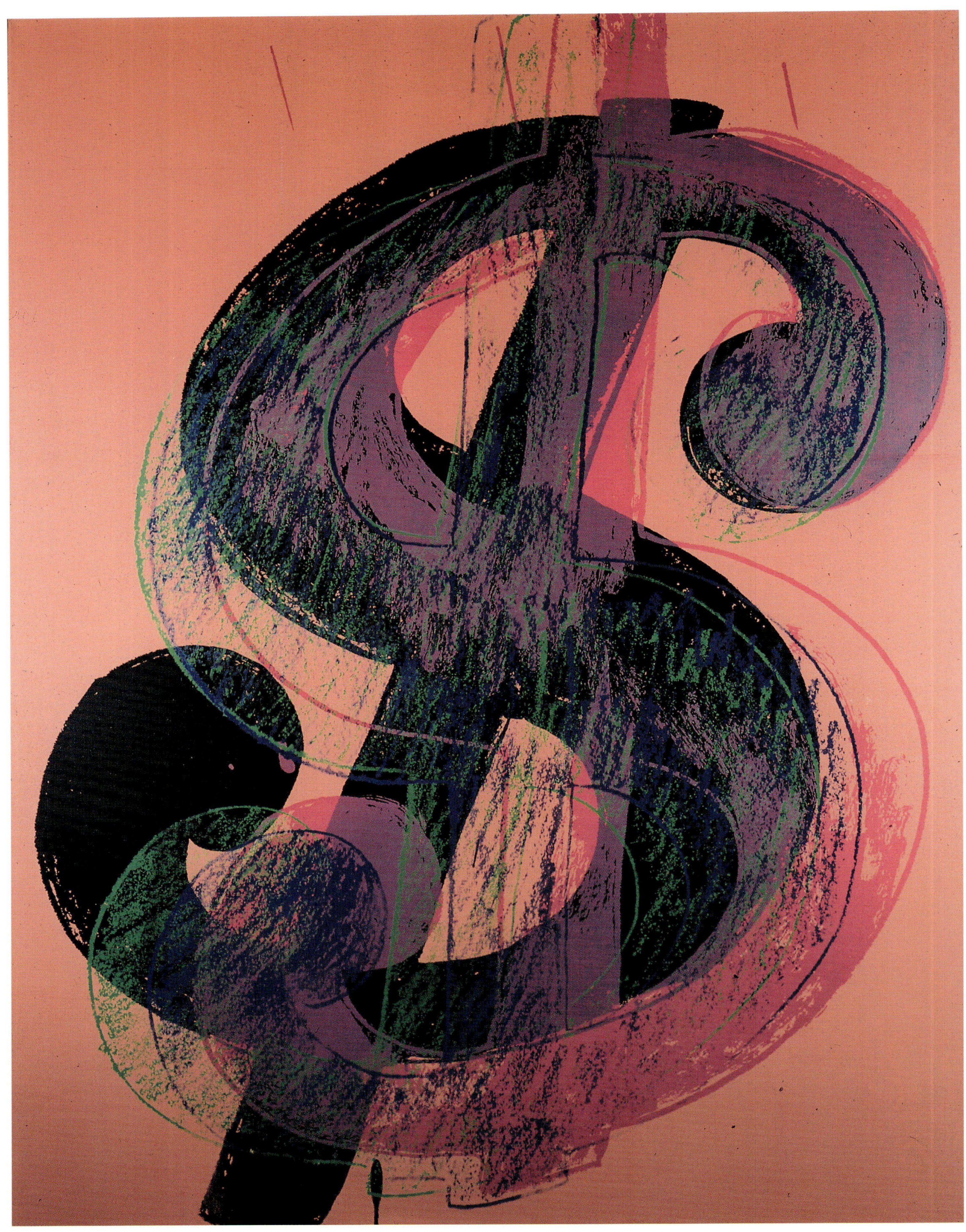

51 *$*, 1981

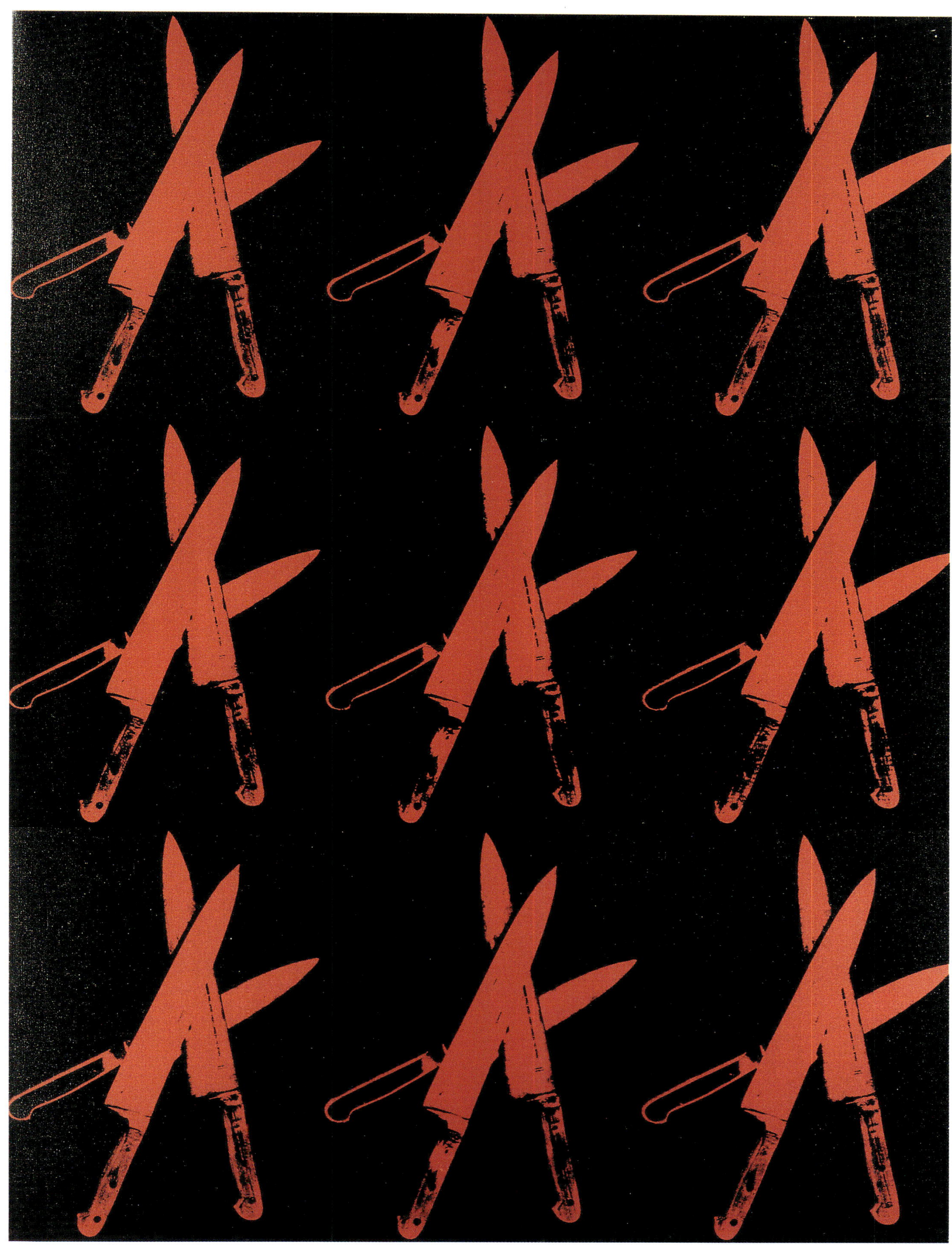

52 *Knives*, 1982

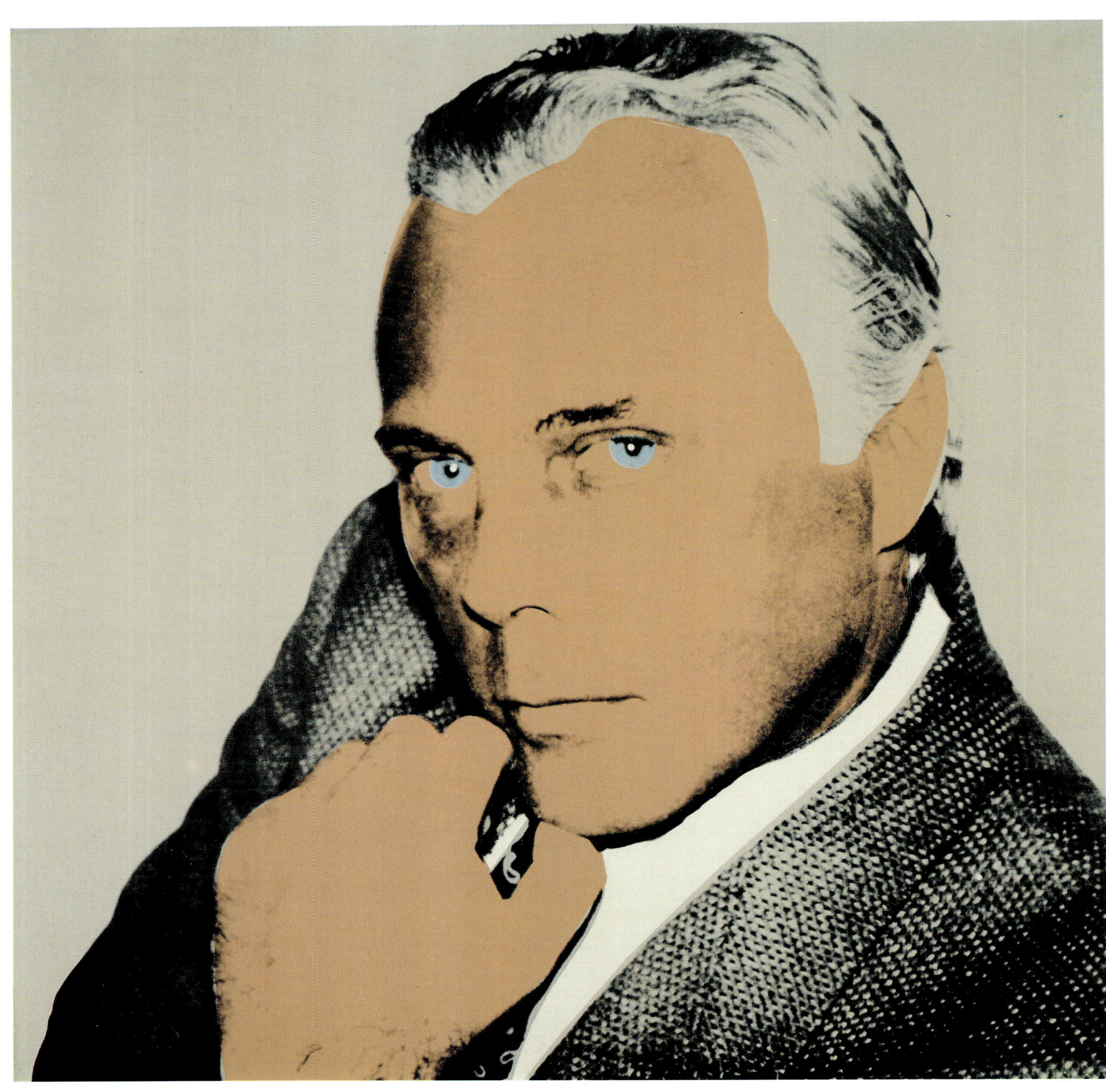

53 *Giorgio Armani*, 1983

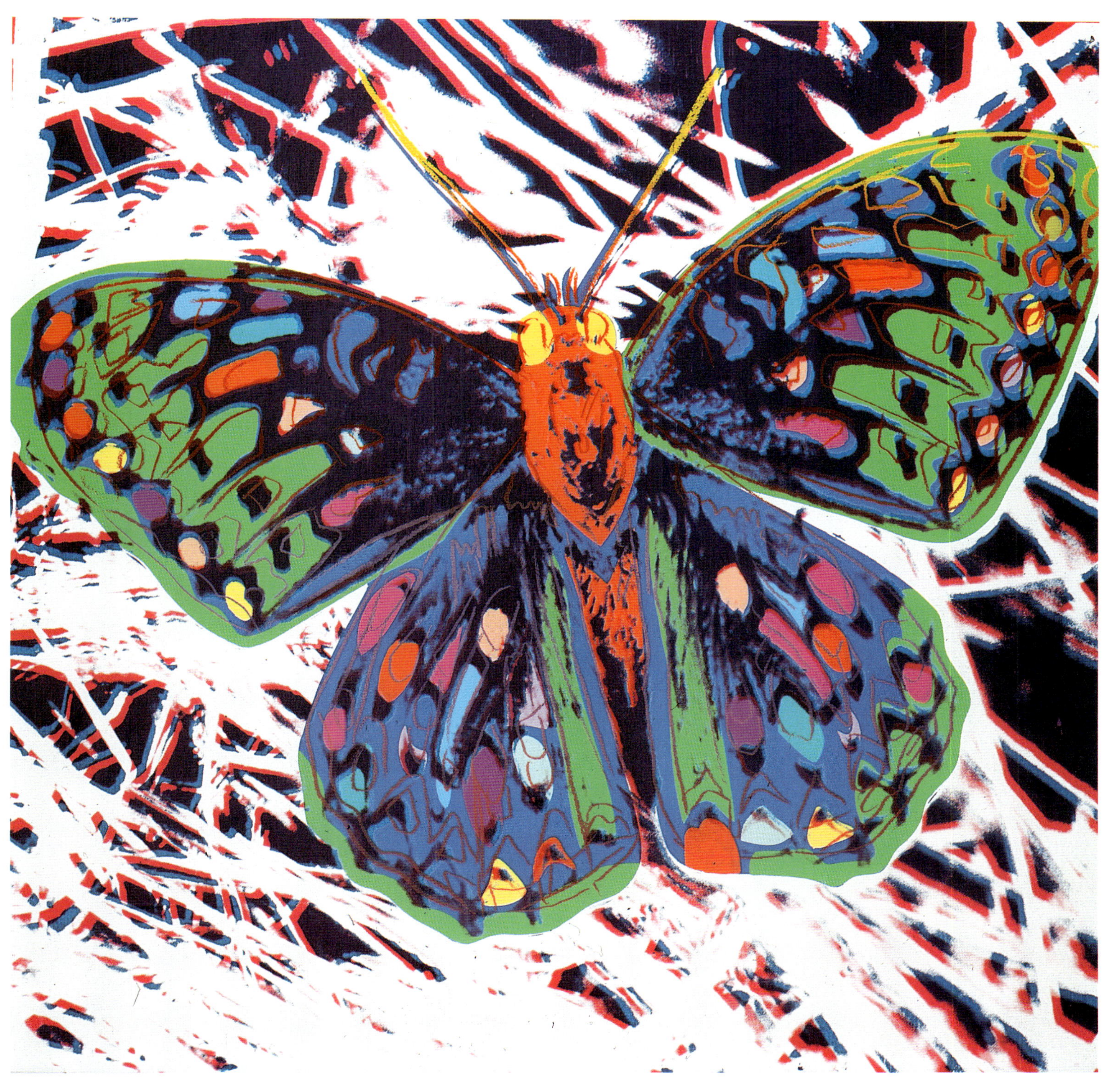

54 *San Francisco Silverspot*, 1983

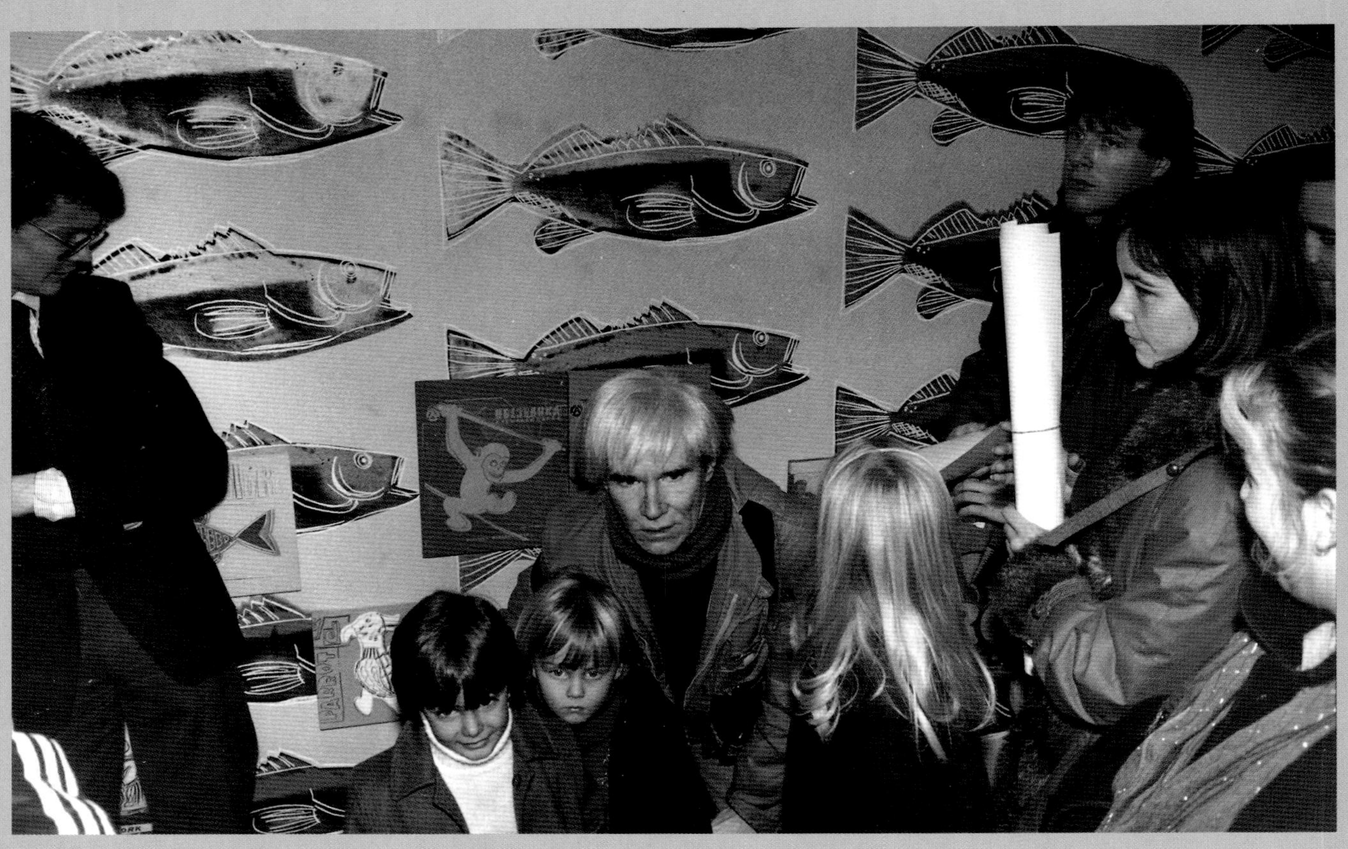

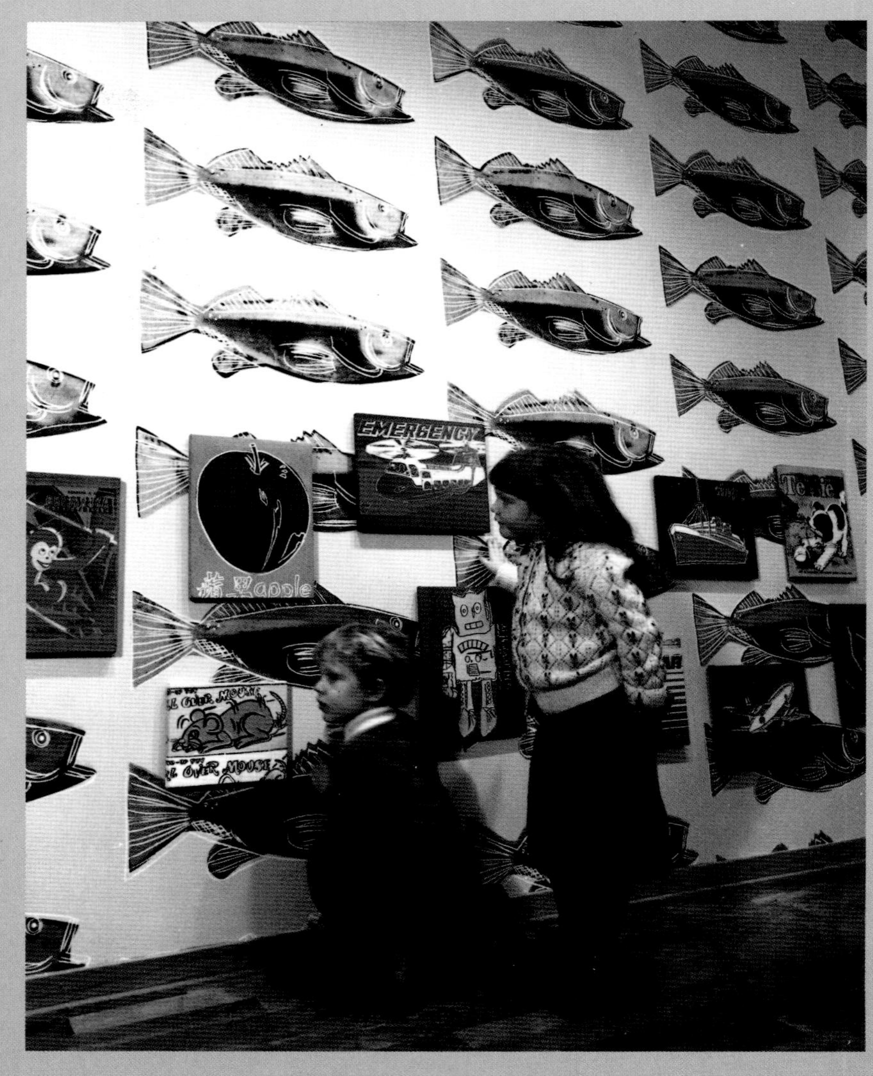
EMERGENCY

Jacob Baal-Teshuva

Paintings for Children

One aspect of Andy Warhol's work is unknown to the wider public, and even to many Warhol collectors and admirers, despite his popularity: his "Paintings for children," also known as the "Toy Paintings." Even the major Warhol retrospective organized by the Museum of Modern Art in New York in 1989, which traveled to several museums in Europe, for some reason failed to include any of these paintings.

Deep down, Andy Warhol was a child – a grown-up child. His passion for collecting toys and other items was legendary. Nearly every weekend, he went with his friend, Stuart Pivar, to New York flea markets and antique stores. He bought hundreds of toys, cookie jars in every form, color, and shape, watches and jewelry, and American and other folk art; he bought Art Deco and Art Nouveau furniture, as well as furniture of other periods, and a great deal of kitsch. His purchases filled rooms in his five-story town house. Many packages had not even been opened at the time of his death. His collection could be described as an eclectic compendium of popular culture. More than a year after Warhol's death in 1987, over six thousand people attended the Sotheby auction on April 23, 1988 in New York, which became a major media event. Many items went for several times the estimated value.

It was in 1983 that Warhol's Zurich dealer, Bruno Bischofberger, had asked him to produce a series of paintings for children. "When I took my kids to a museum I had to hold them up so they could see the pictures. That's when I got the idea of asking my friend Andy Warhol to paint pictures for children on the subject of toys and to hang them in my gallery at a low height, so that children could see them without any trouble."[1] Warhol was taken by the idea and began working on the project enthusiastically. He chose the simplest subjects: monkeys, parrots, fish, dogs, pandas, circus clowns, mice, and apples. All in all, between twenty and thirty of these subjects were painted on standard-size canvases measuring 28x36cm, with different color variations.

On December 3, 1983, the exhibition opened at the Bischofberger Gallery in Zurich, with Warhol present. Dozens of children crowded into the gallery, which was decorated with wallpaper featuring a fish pattern in various colors. The gallery actually looked like a huge aquarium or fish pond. Altogether, there were 128 paintings, hung low so that the children could view them easily. The exhibition was a great success, and drew the attention of the conservative Swiss press, as well as the international media.

Andy Warhol, a bachelor all his life, was very fond of children, as his close friend and personal photographer, Christopher Makos, recalled: "Andy needed to have contact with at least four or five kids a day. He loved smart ones as much as beautiful ones, but if they were dumb, he'd say, 'Oh God, not another one.' He got a lot from young people, and at work he surrounded himself with them .... He felt more comfortable with children than he did with art collectors and serious fans."[2] Warhol is not the only artist to have painted for children. One of his many predecessors in the field was Pablo Picasso, who, between 1949 and 1951, while living with Françoise Gilot, painted dolls, roosters, and other toys in brilliant colors for the amusement and pleasure of his children, Claude and Paloma. Warhol's "Paintings for Children," or "Toy Paintings," reflect not only his love for children, but also his own toy collection, which inspired the works.

Notes

1 Personal communication.
2 Christopher Makos, *Warhol: A Personal Photographic Memoir* (New York: New American Library, 1988), p.34.

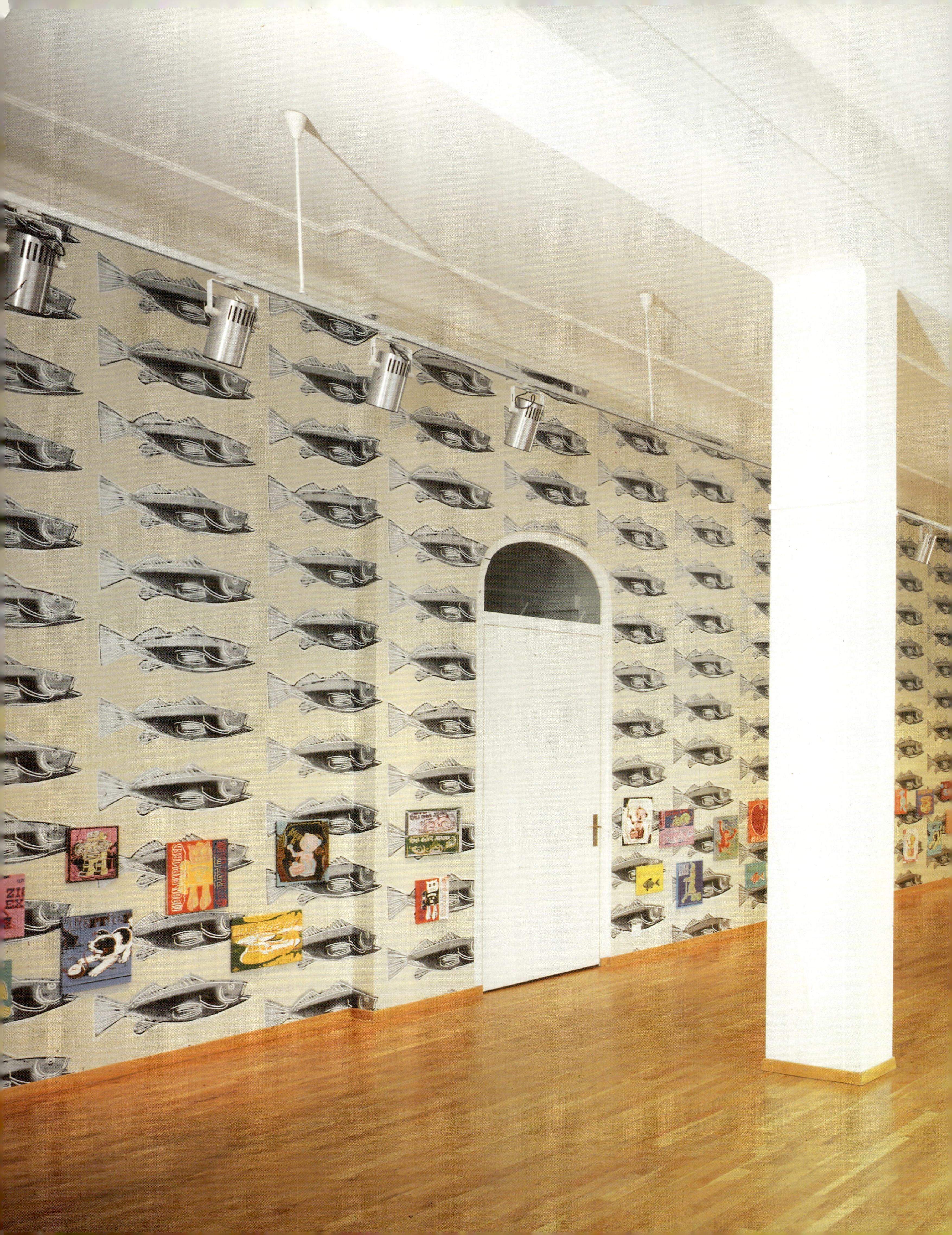

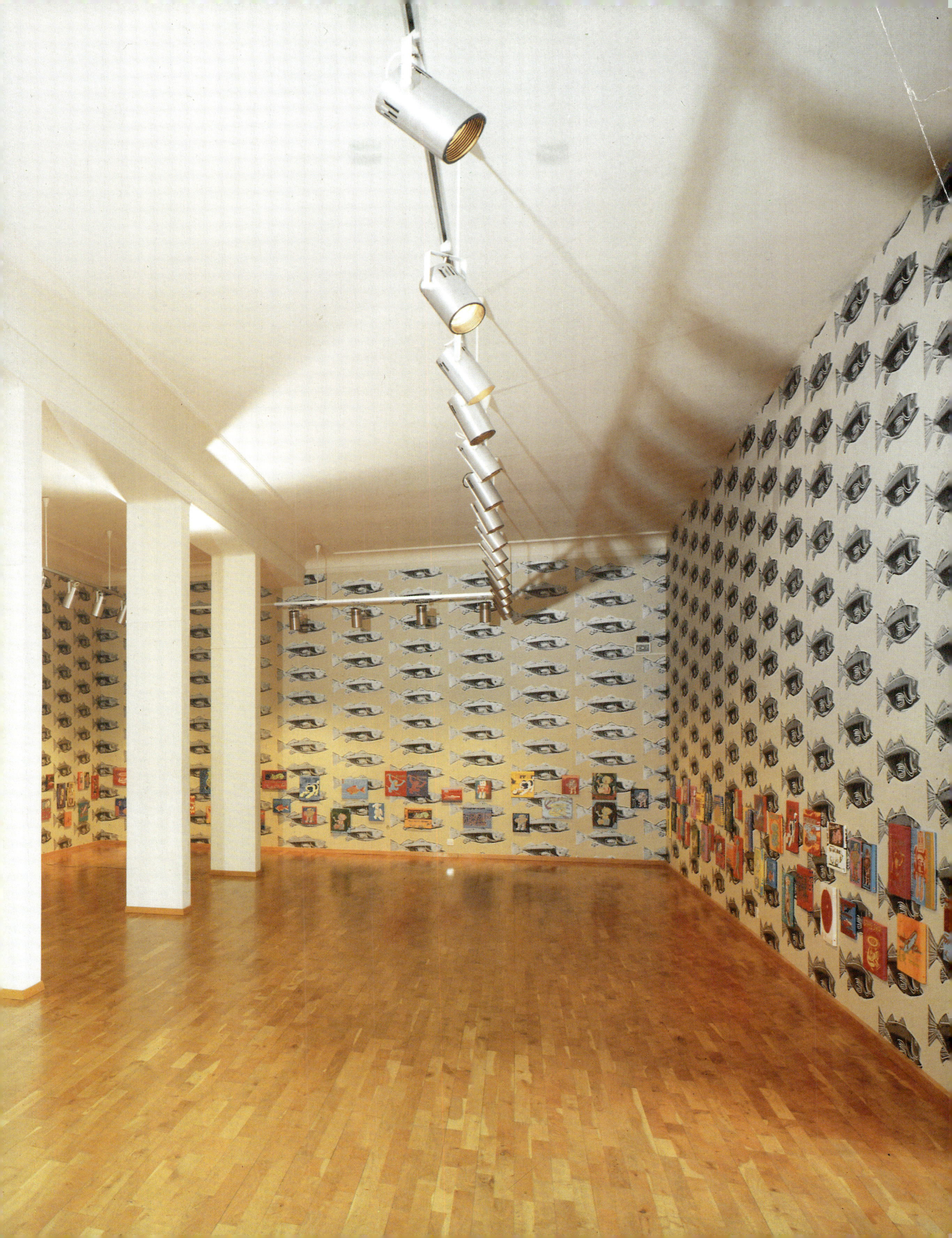

55 *Toy Panda*, 1983

56 *Airplane*, 1983

57 *Fish Small* (No. 1), 1983

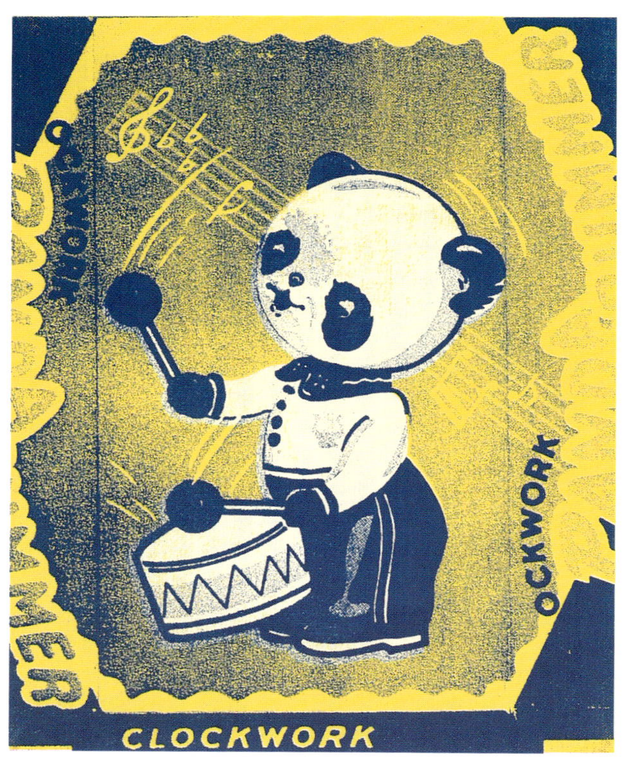

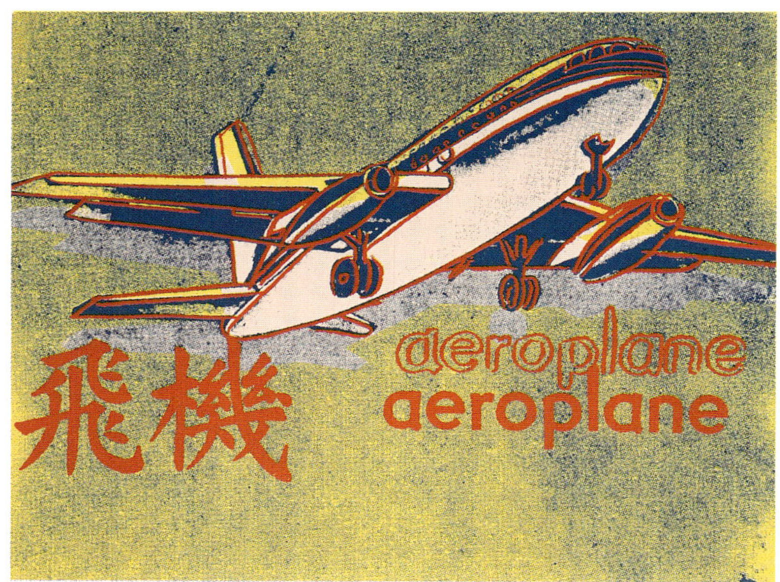

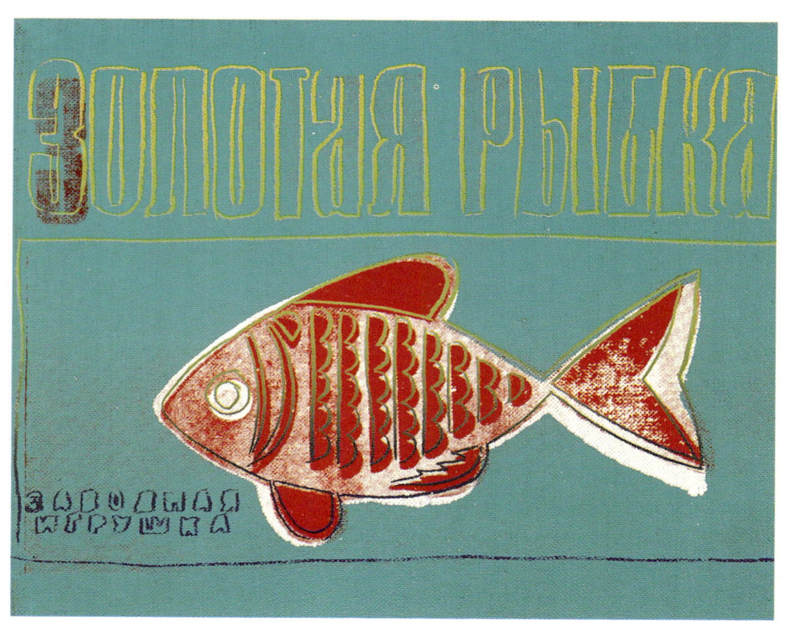

58 *Parrot*, 1983

59 *Police Car*, 1983

60 *Roli Zoli*, 1983

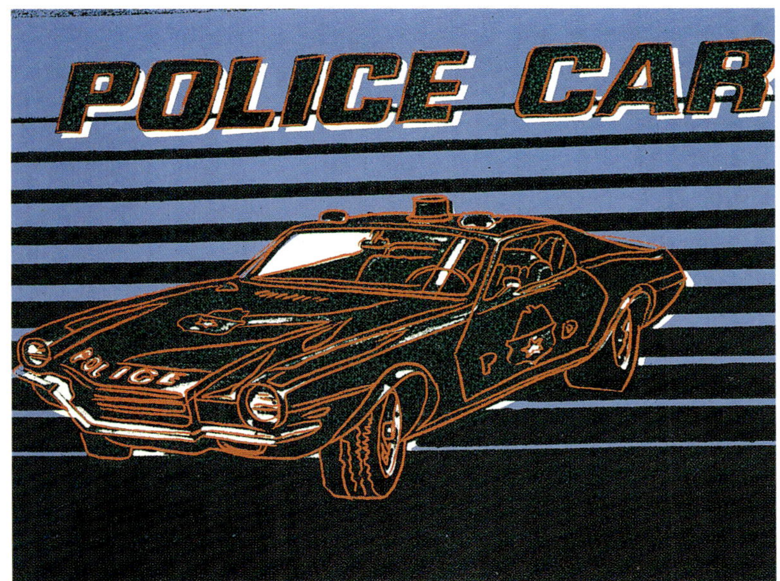

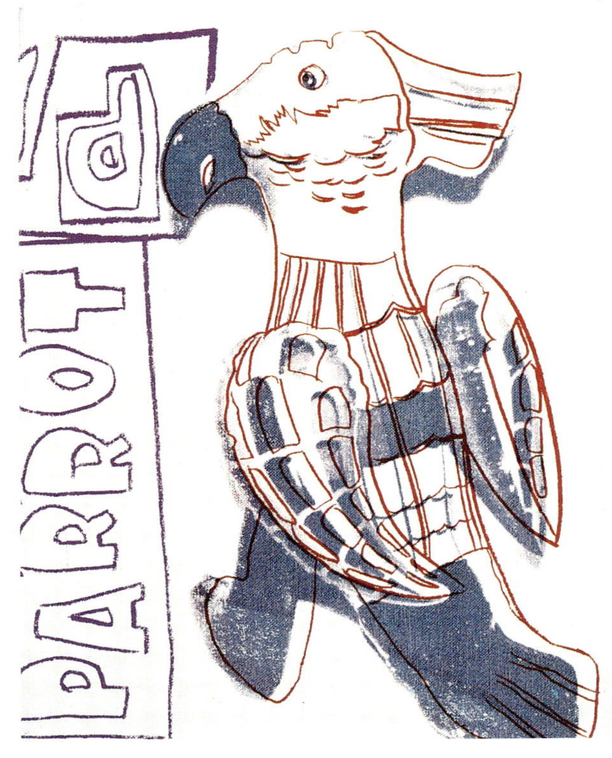

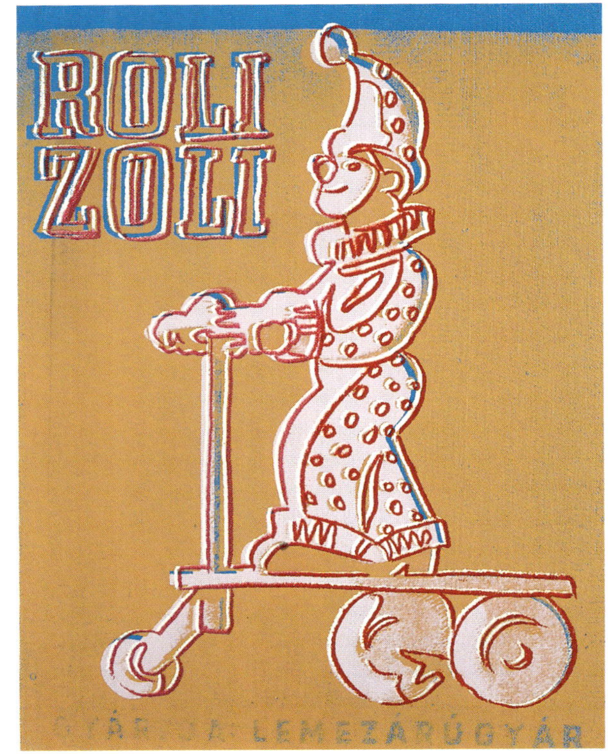

61 *Locomotive*, 1983

62 *Apple*, 1983

63 *Space Ship*, 1983

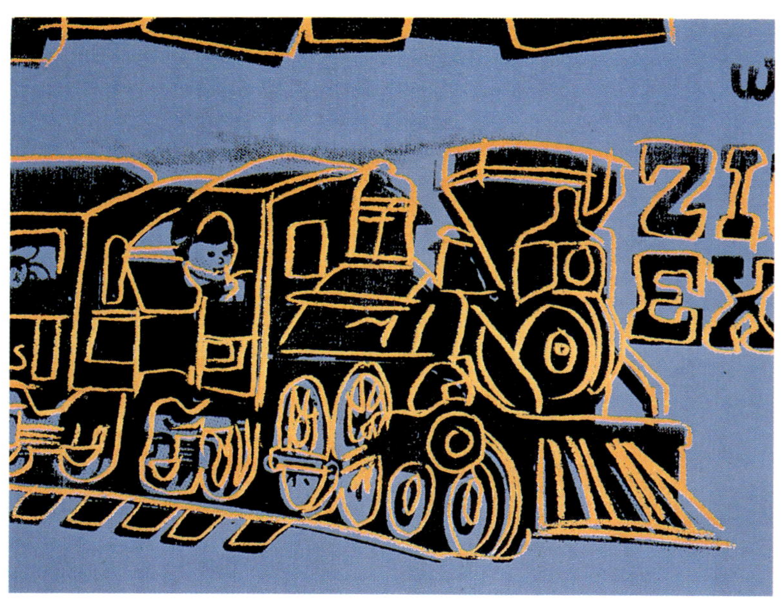

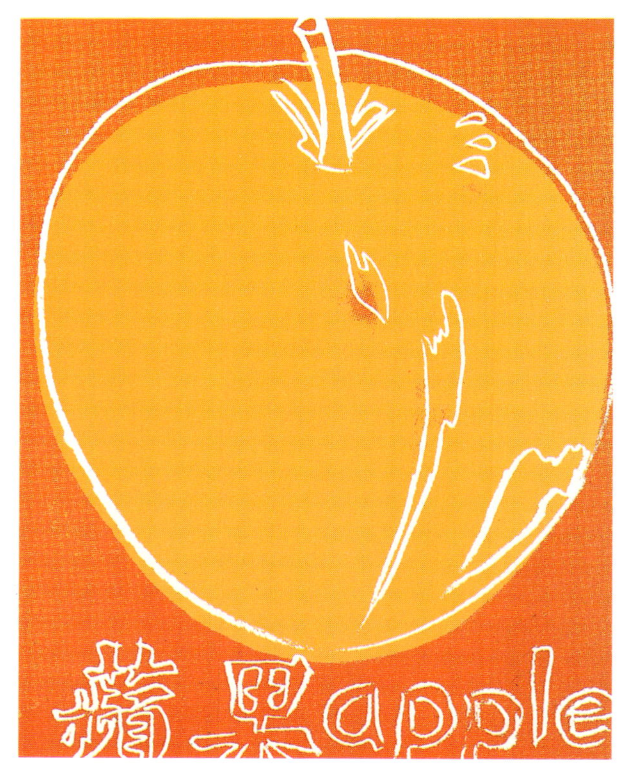

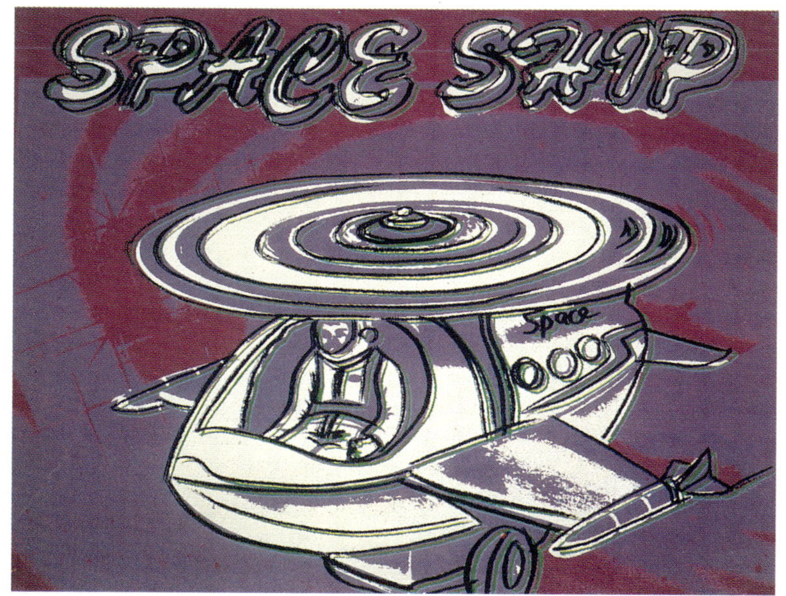

64 *Ship*, 1983

65 *Emergency Helicopter*, 1983

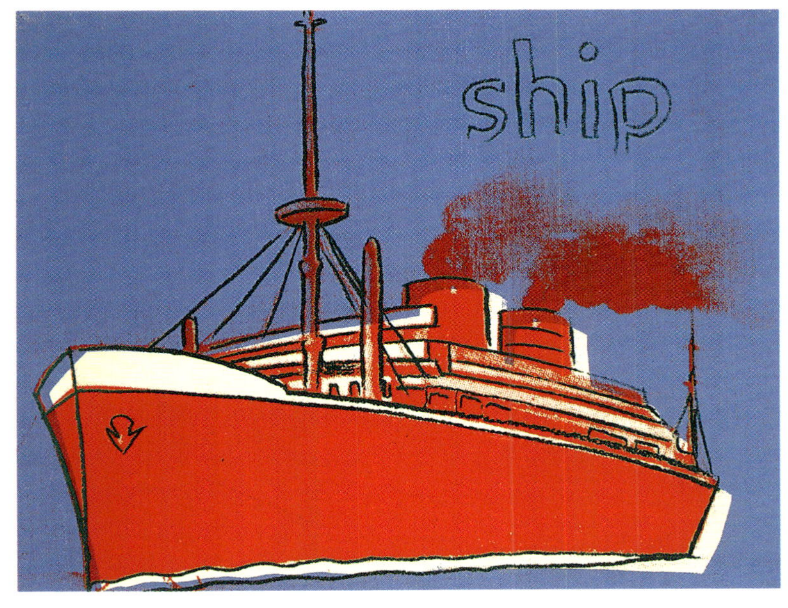

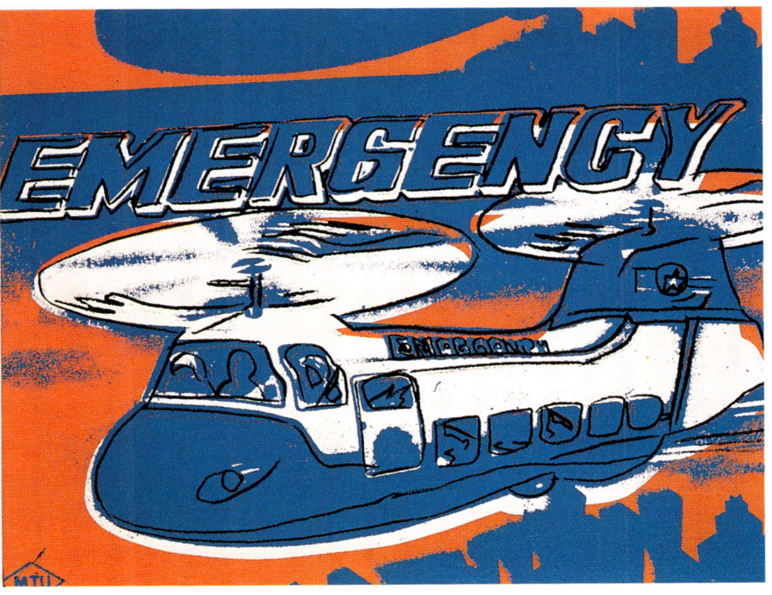

66 *Moon Explorer* (No. 8), 1983

67 *Apple*, 1983

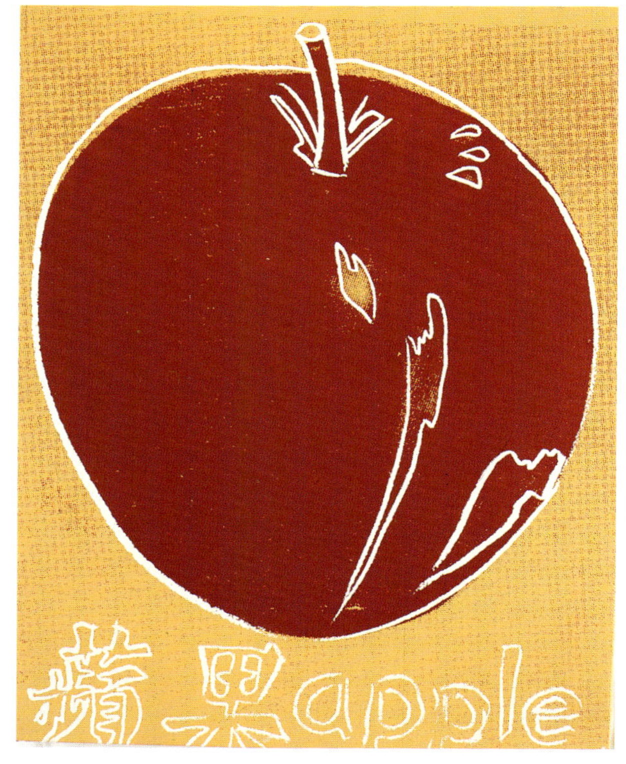

74 *Ship*, 1983

75 *Space Ship*, 1983

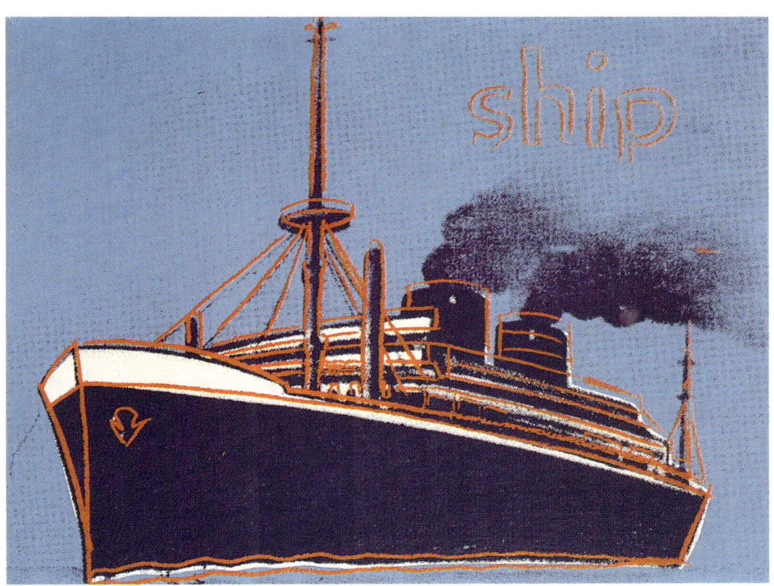

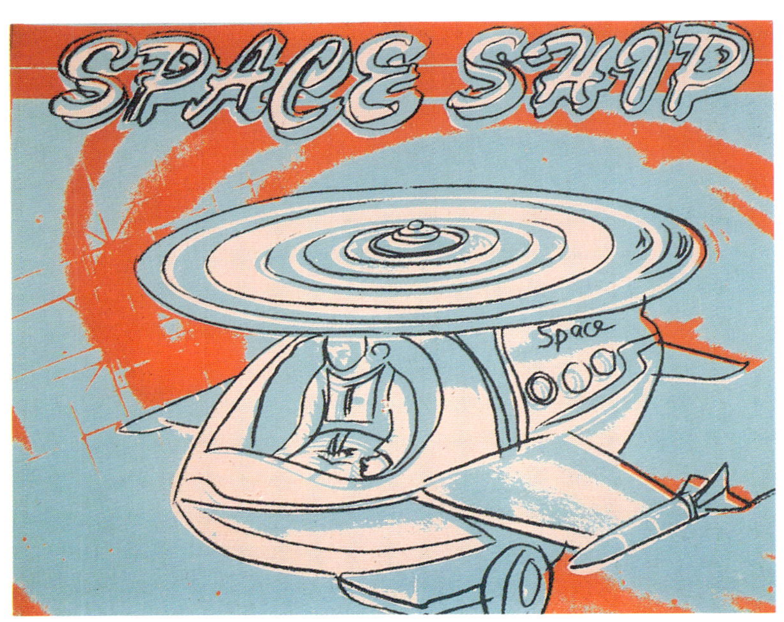

76 *Ship*, 1983

77 *Police Car*, 1983

78 *Space Ship*, 1983

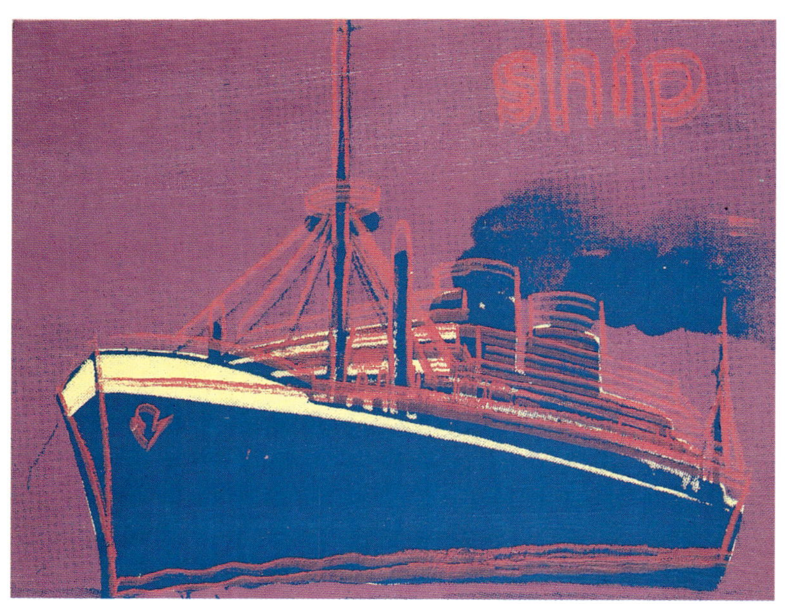

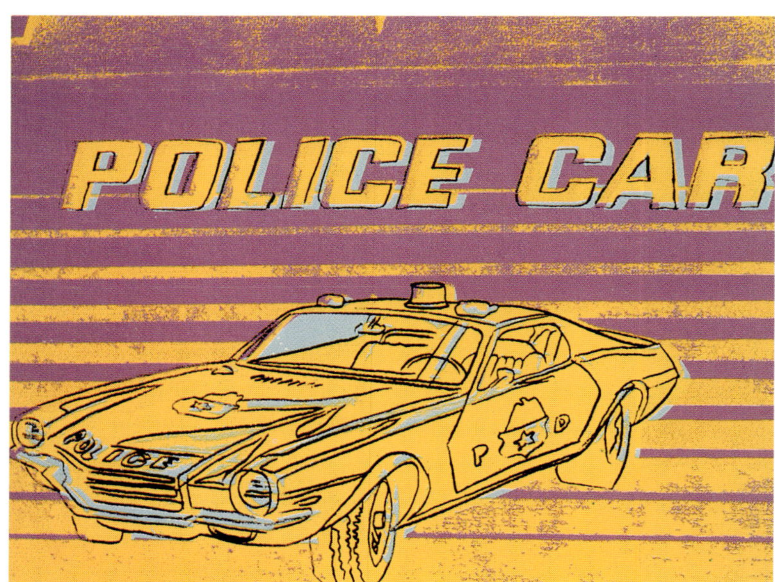

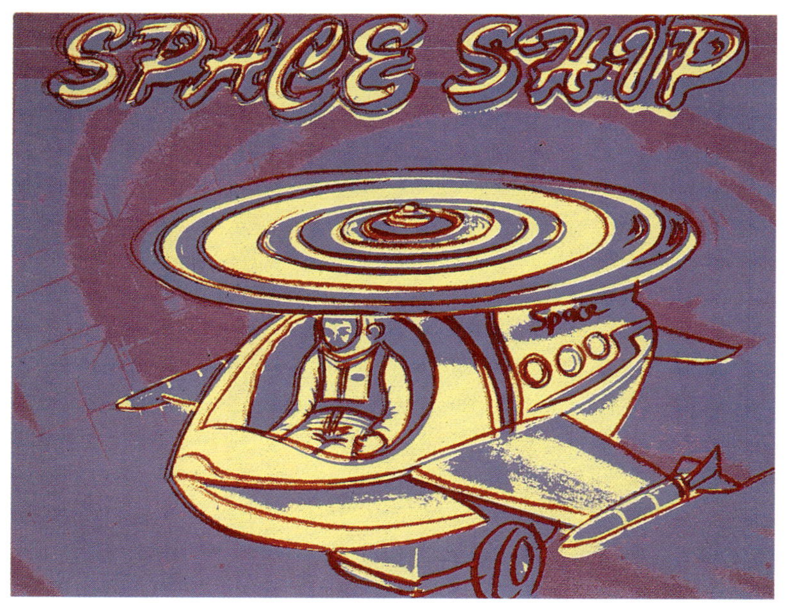

79 *Emergency Helicopter*, 1983

80 *Panda Bear* (No. 100), 1983

81 *Police Car*, 1983

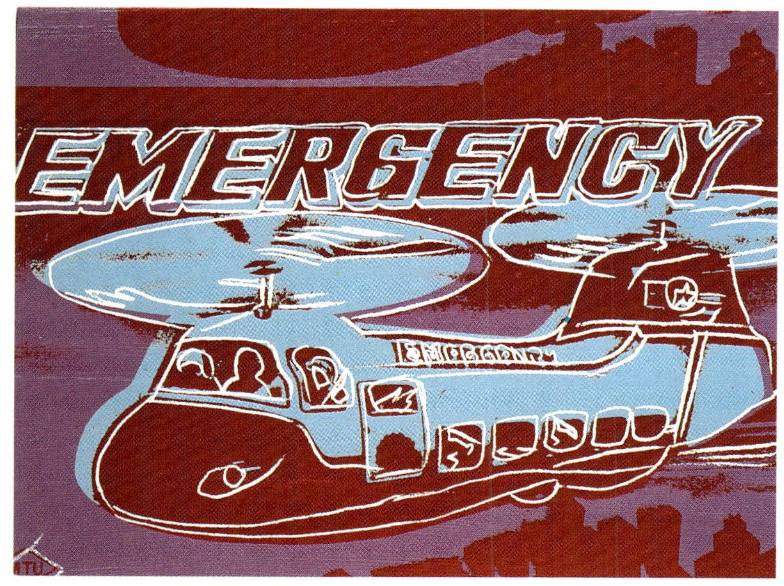

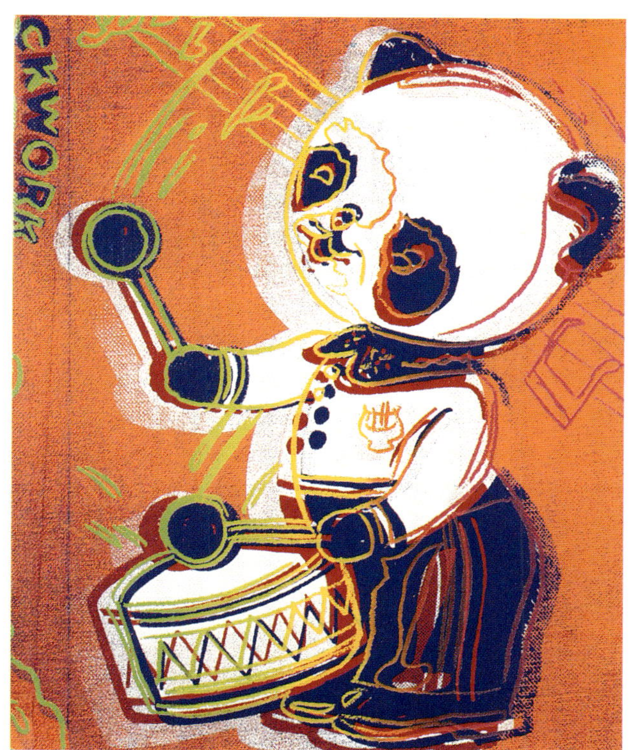

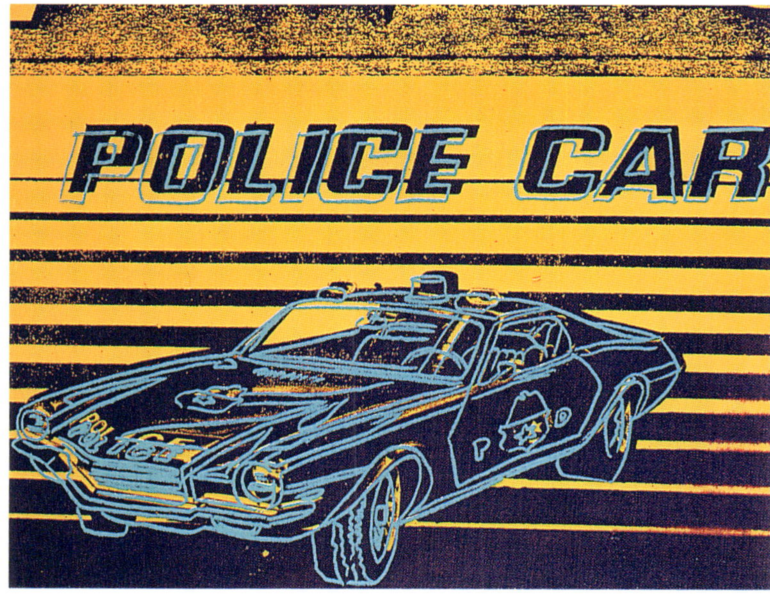

82 *Airplane*, 1983

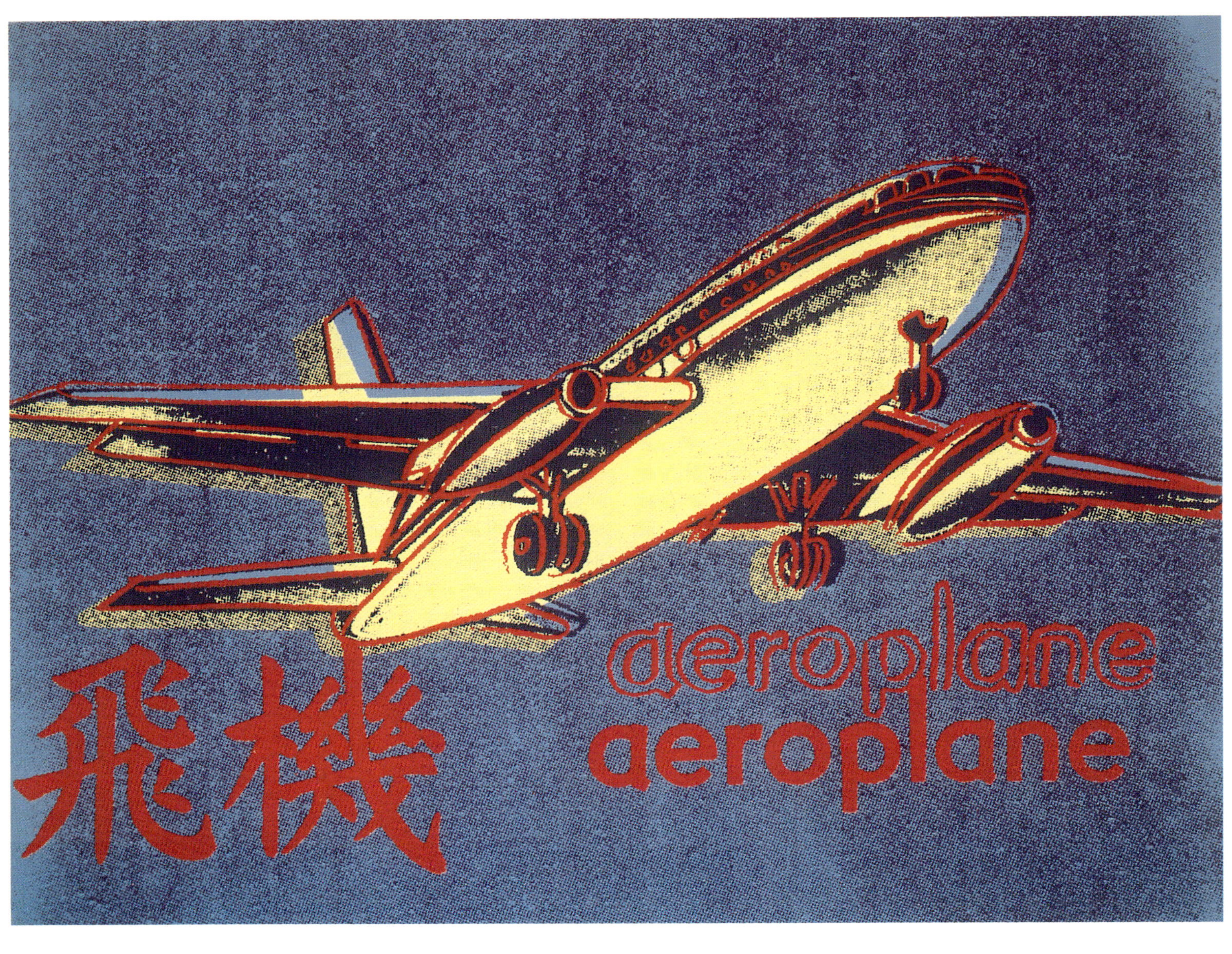

83 *Police Car*, 1983

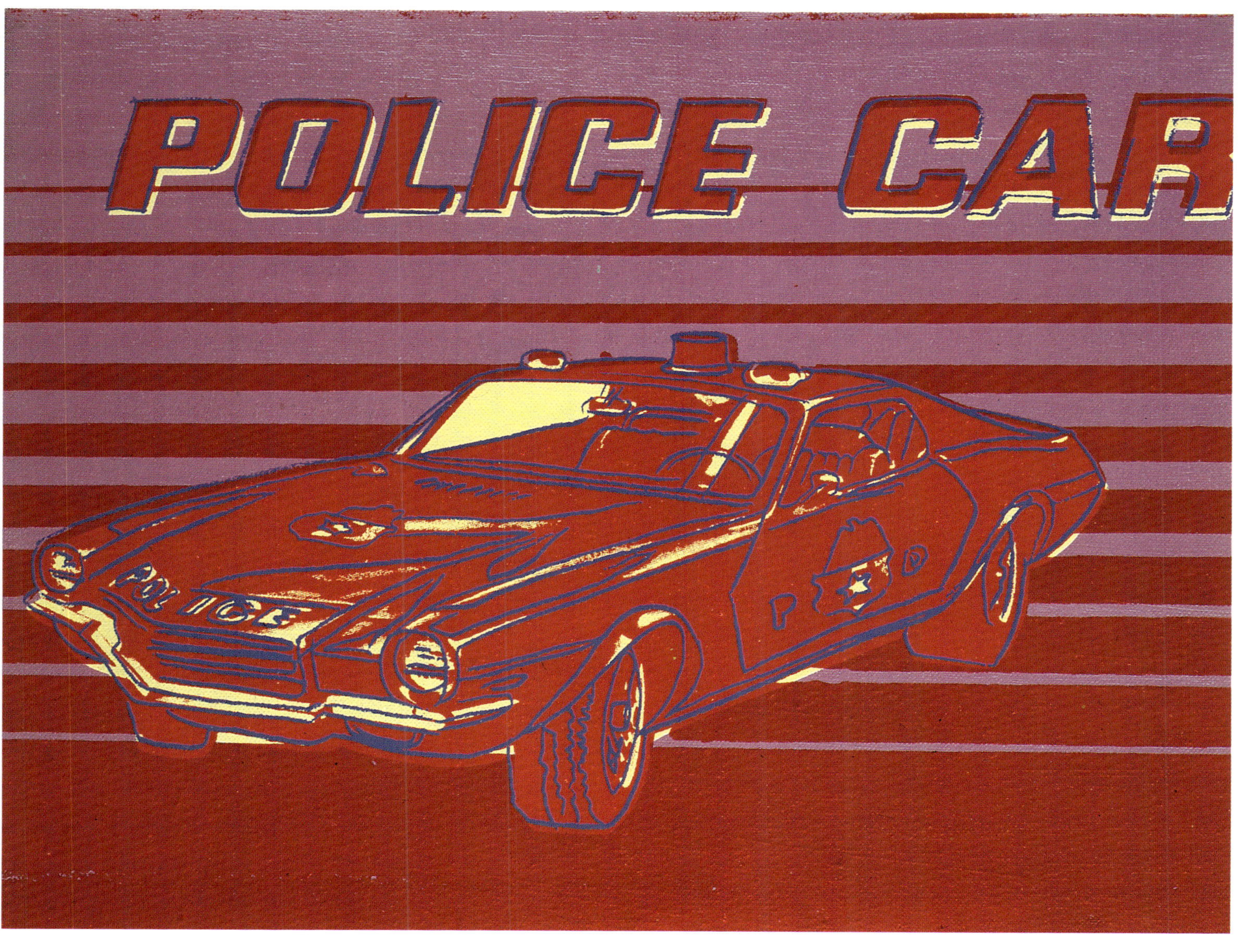

84 *Locomotive*, 1983

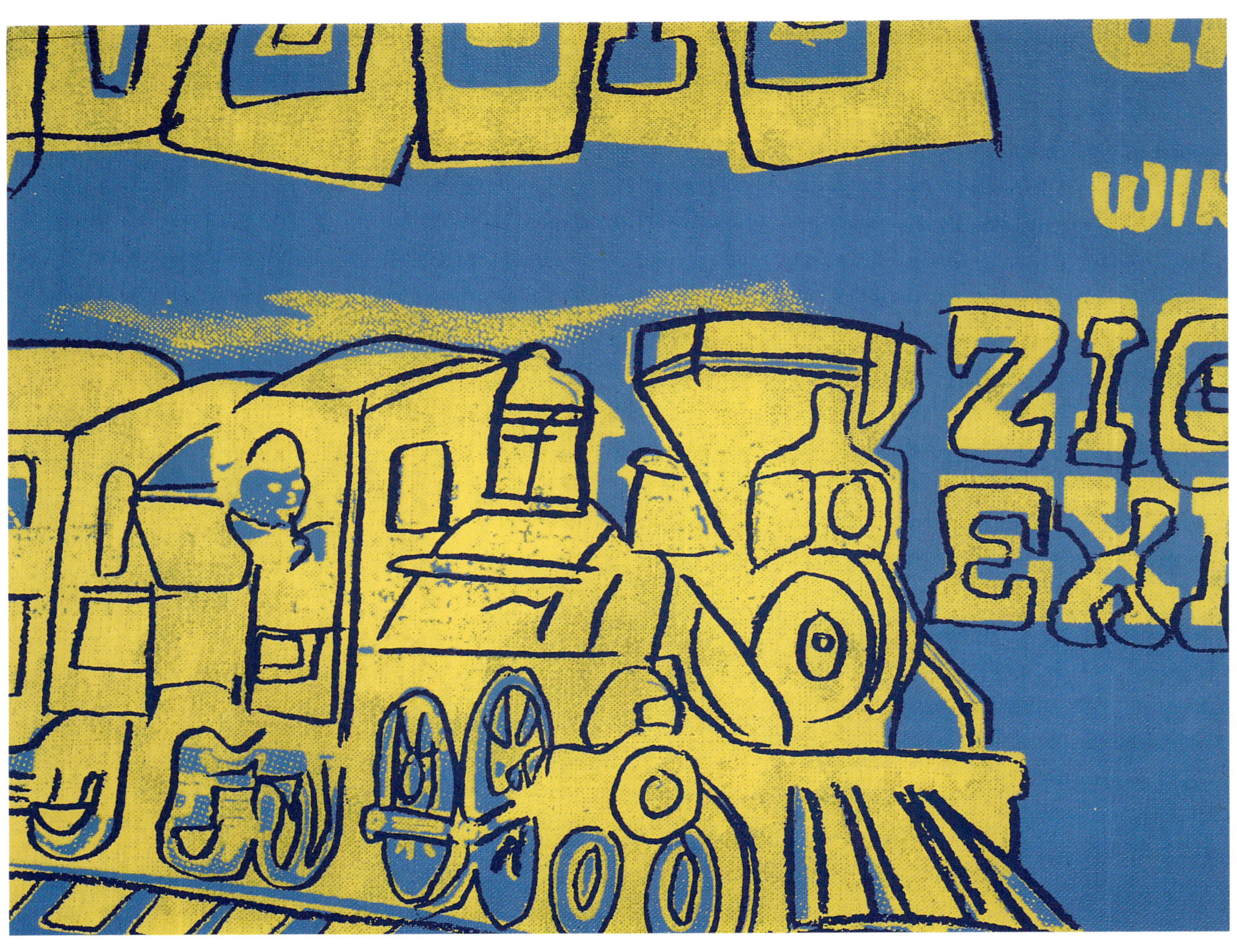

85 *Apple*, 1983

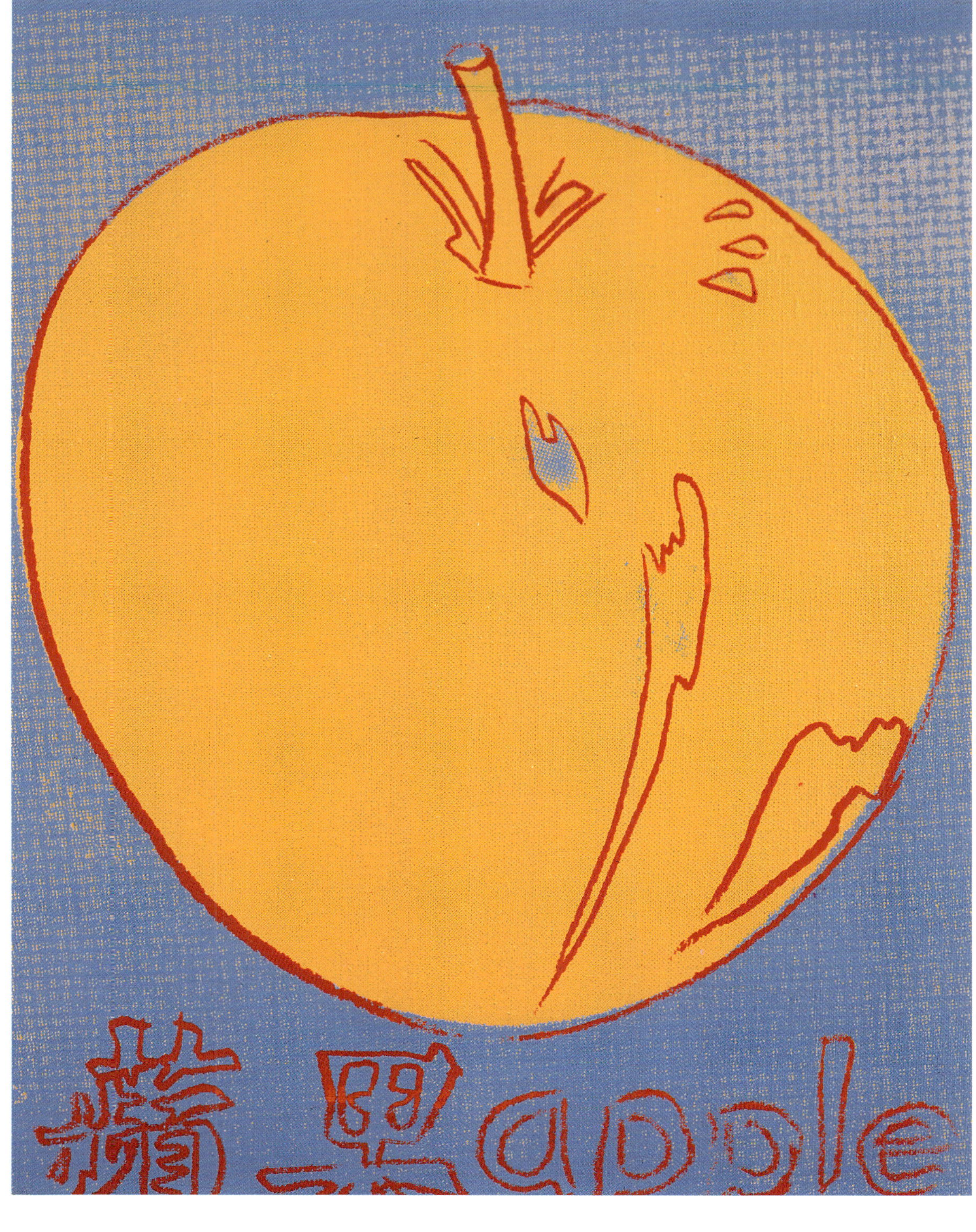

I always admired De Chirico. He inspired so many painters. The retrospective at the MOMA was great and showed what a great painter he was. I met him in Venice so many times and I thought I loved his work so much. I love his art and then the idea he repeated the same paintings over and over again. I like that idea a lot, so I thought it would be great to do it.... I believe he did it not only because people and dealers asked him to do it, but because he liked it and viewed repetition as a way of expressing himself. This is probably what we have in common....

I think that once you see the emotions from a certain angle you can never think of them as real again.

...I've made a career out of being the right thing in the wrong space. And the wrong thing in the right space. That's one thing I really do know about.

But when you see a gruesome picture over and over again, it doesn't really have any effect.

Publicity is like eating peanuts. Once you start you can't stop.

When you think about it, department stores are kind of like museums.

Someone said that Brecht wanted everybody to think alike. I want everbody to think alike.

Someone said my life has dominated me, I liked that idea.

Money doesn't worry me, though I sometimes wonder where is it? Somebody's got it all.

You should always have a product that has nothing to do with who you are, or what people think about you. An actress should count up her plays, a model should count up her photographs... a writer should count up his words, and an artist should count up his pictures so that you never start thinking that your product is you, or your fame, or your aura.

If everybody's not a beauty, then nobody is.

I never fall apart because I never fall together.

The thing is to think of nothing.... Look, nothing is exciting, nothing is sexy, nothing is not embarrassing. The only time I ever want to be something is outside a party so I can get in.

I don't feel I'm representing the main sex symbols of our time in some of my pictures, such as Marilyn Monroe or Elizabeth Taylor. I just see Monroe as just another person. As for whether it's symbolical to paint Monroe in such violent colors: it's beauty, and she's beautiful and if something's beautiful it's pretty colors, that's all. Or something. The Monroe picture was part of a death series I was doing, of people who had died by different ways. There was no profound reason for doing a death series, no victims of their time; there was no reason for doing it all, just a surface reason.

I think of myself as an American artist; I like it here, I think it's so great. It's fantastic. I'd like to work in Europe but I wouldn't do the same things, I'd do different things. I feel I represent the U.S. in my art but I'm not a social critic. I just paint those objects in my paintings because those are the things I know best. I'm not trying to criticize the U.S. in any way, not trying to show up any ugliness at all. I'm just a pure artist, I guess. But I can't say if I take myself seriously as an artist. I just hadn't thought about it.

I suppose I have a really loose interpretation of "work," because I think that just being alive is so much work at something you don't always want to do. Being born is like being kidnapped. And then sold into slavery. People are working every minute. The machinery is always going. Even when you sleep.

These quotes by Andy Warhol were taken from *Andy Warhol: A Retrospective,* McShine, Kynaston, ed. (New York: Museum of Modern Art) 1989. The quote on De Chirico was taken from *Warhol verso De Chirico* (New York: Marisa del Re Gallery) 1985.

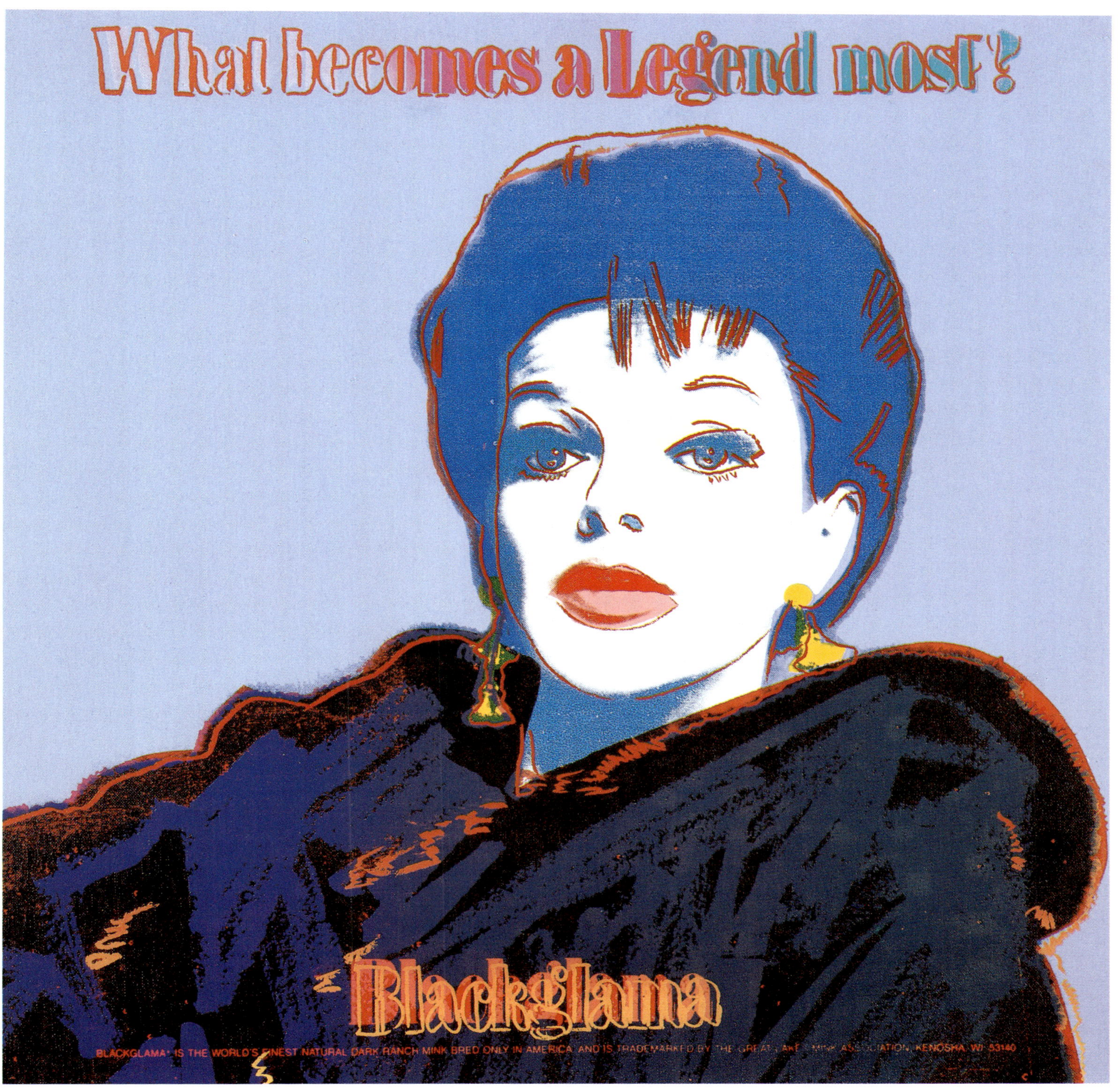

86 *Blackglama*, 1985

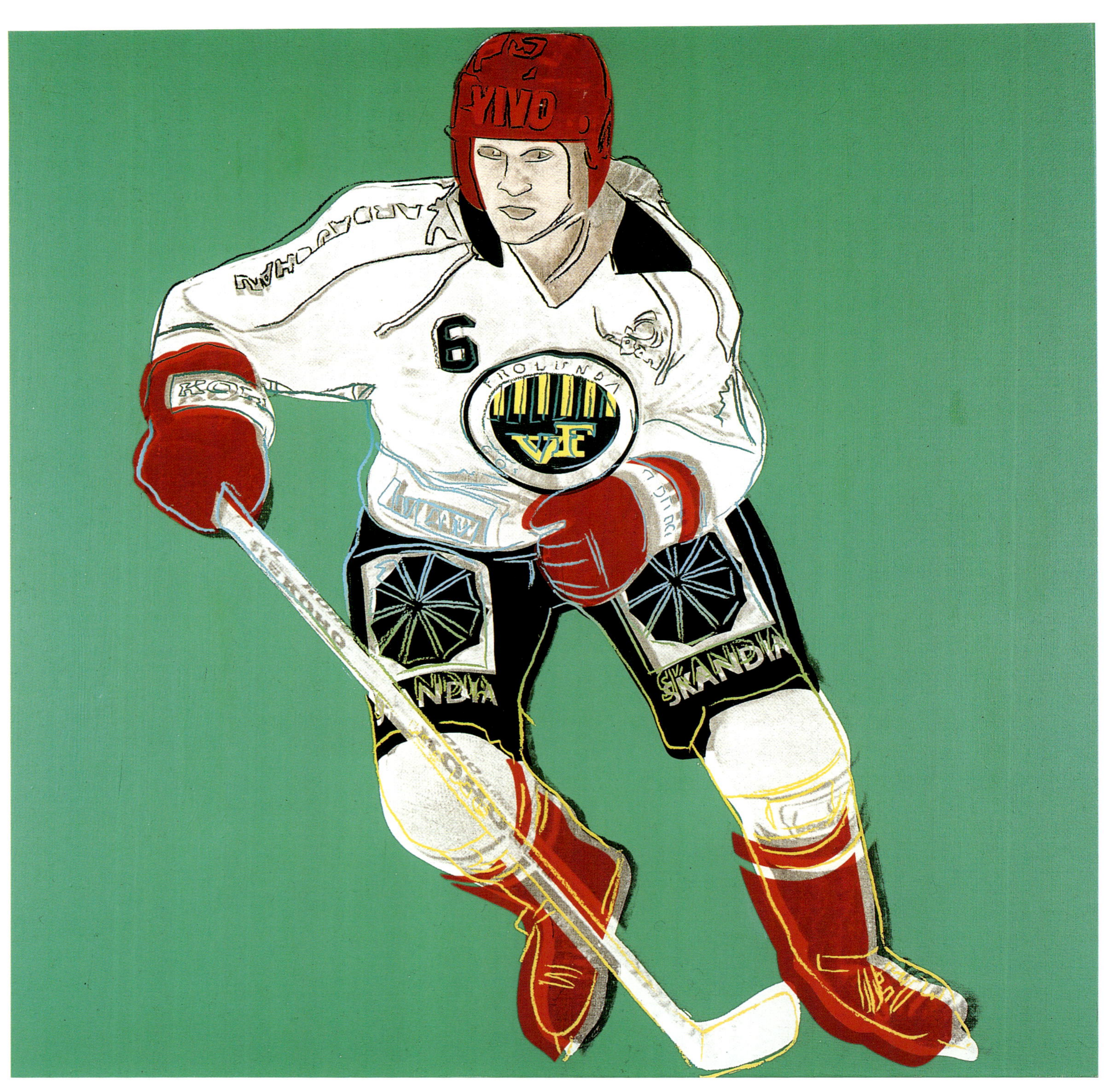

87 *Ice Hockey Player*, 1984

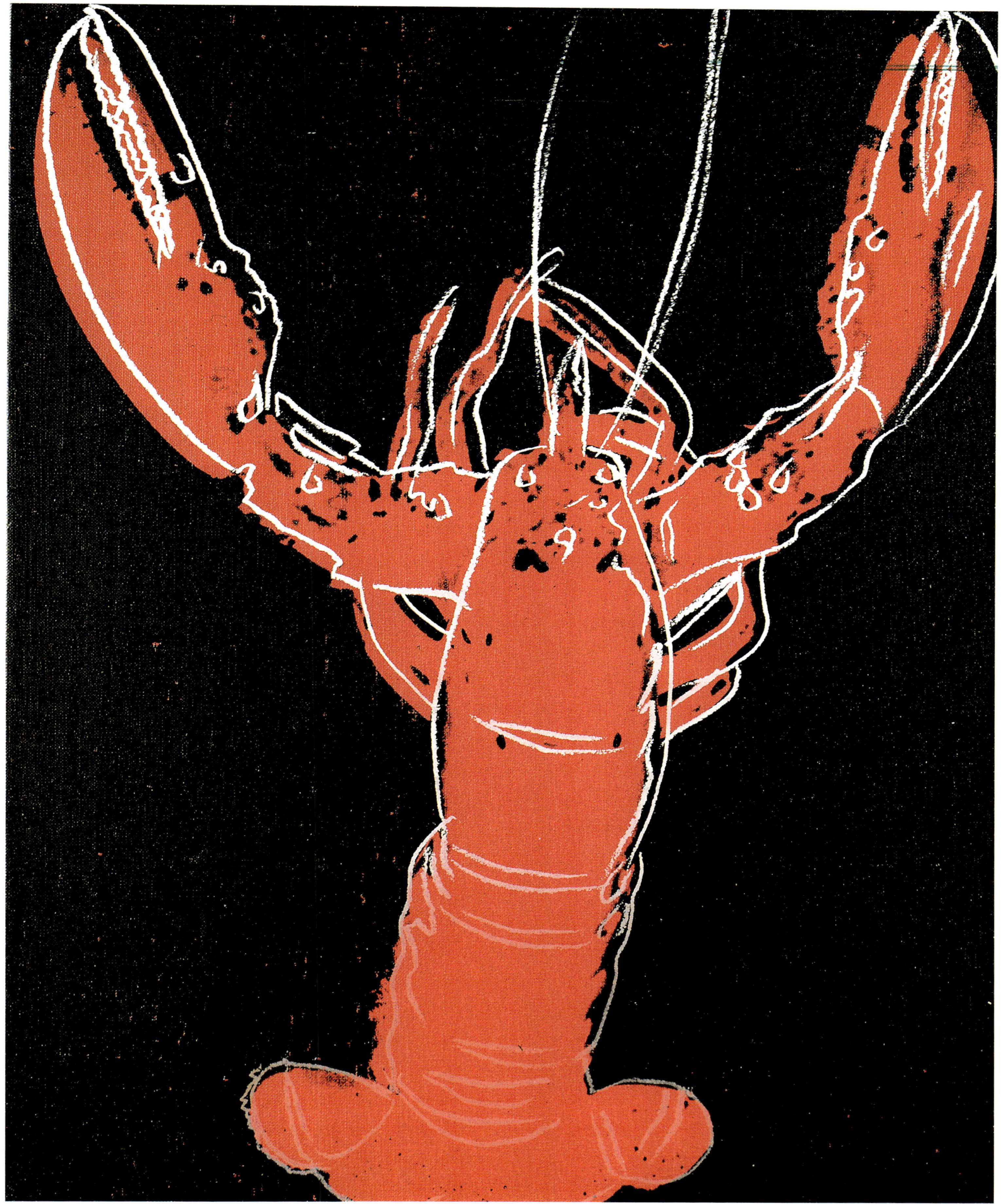

88 *Untitled* (Lobster), 1984

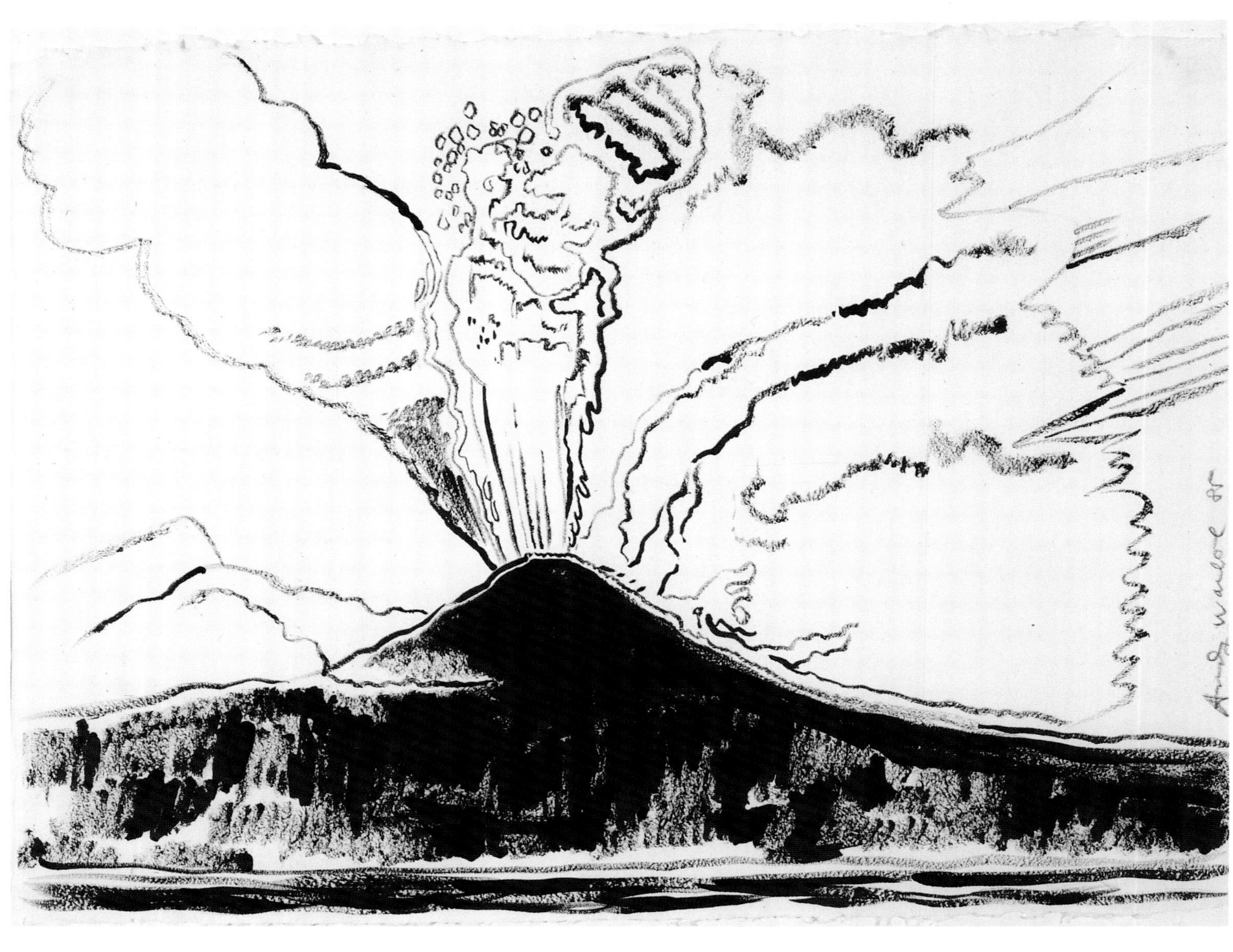

89 *Vesuvius*, 1985

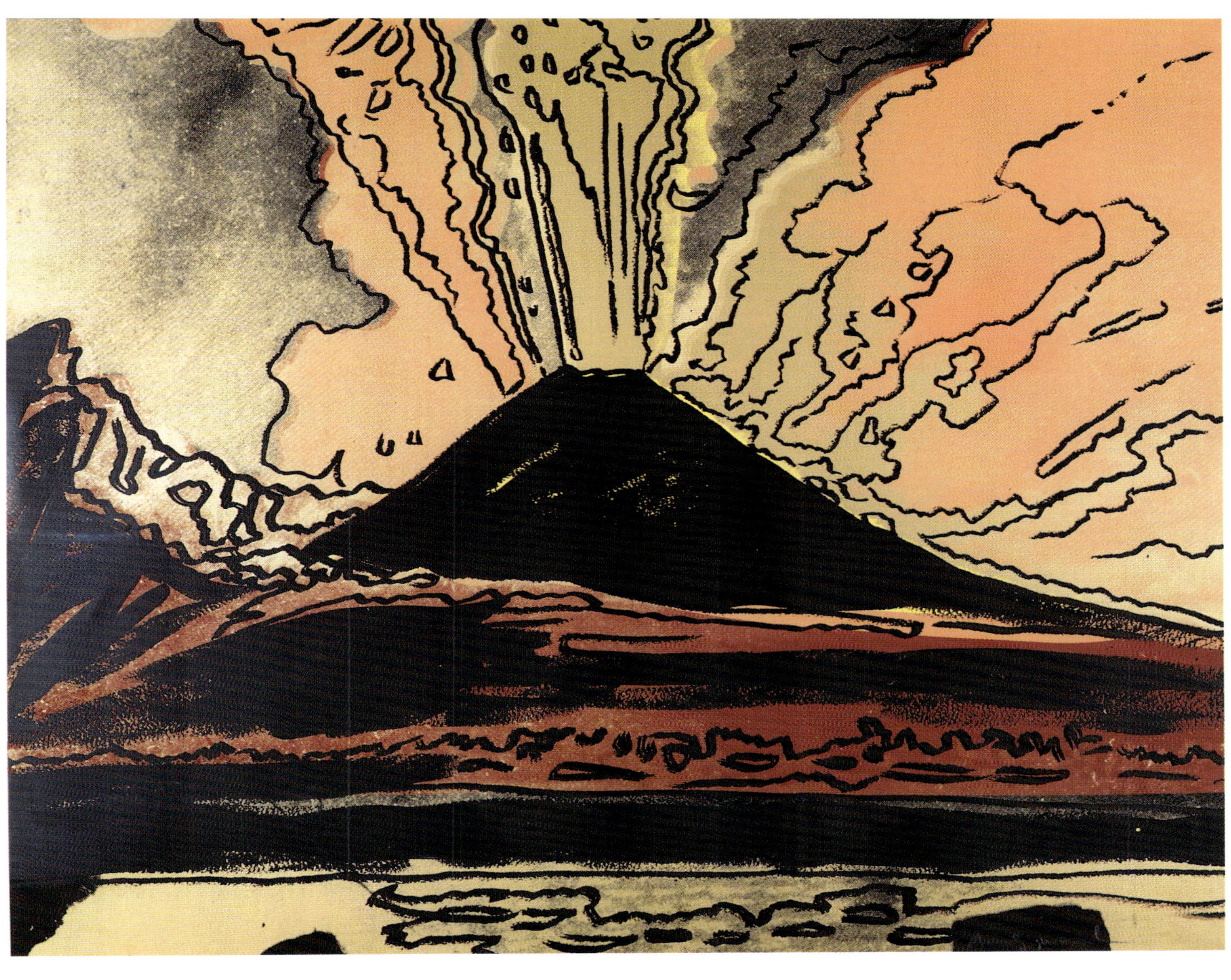

90 *Vesuvius*, 1985

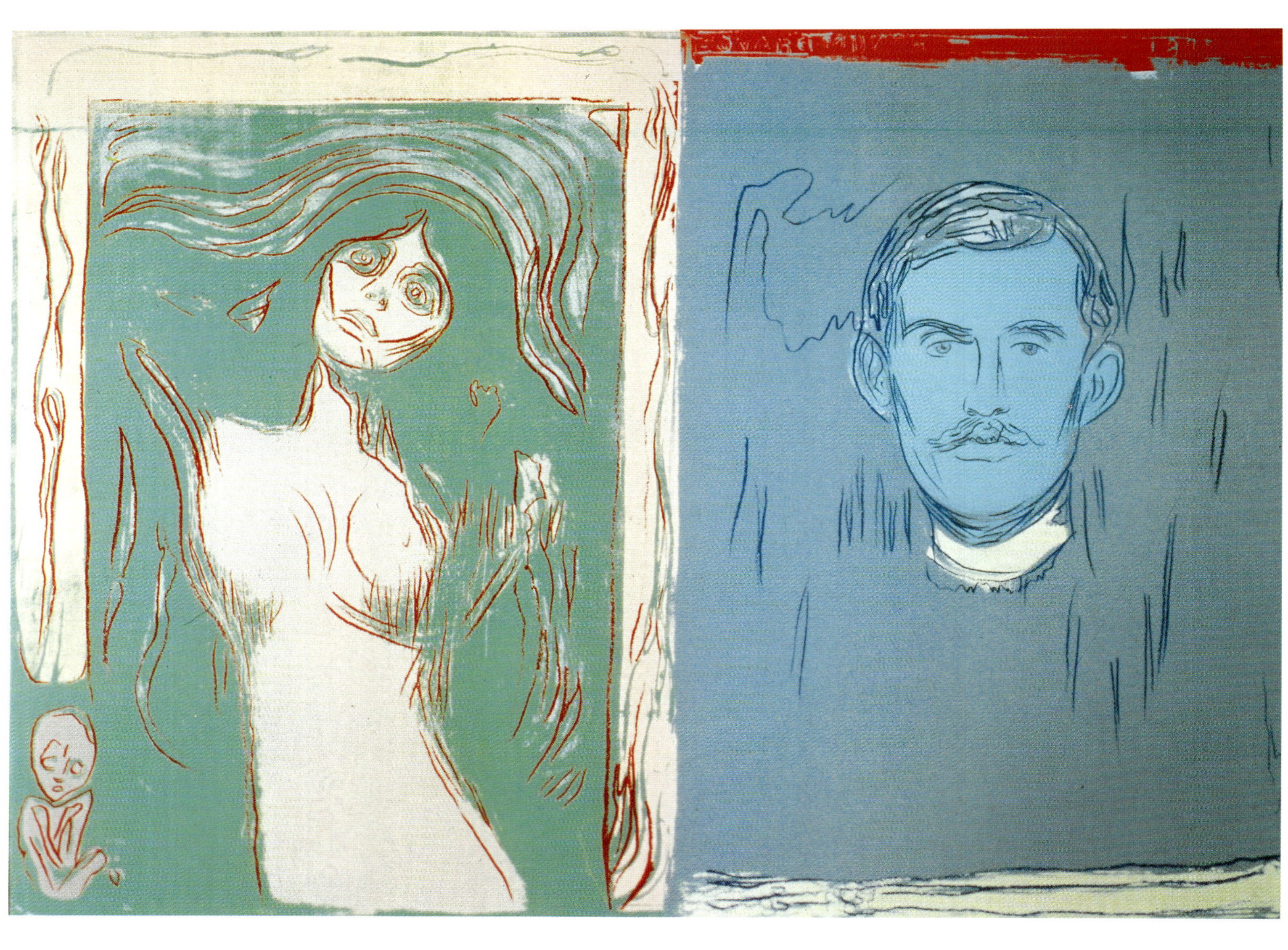

91 *Self-Portrait with Skeleton's Arm and Madonna* (after Edvard Munch), 1984

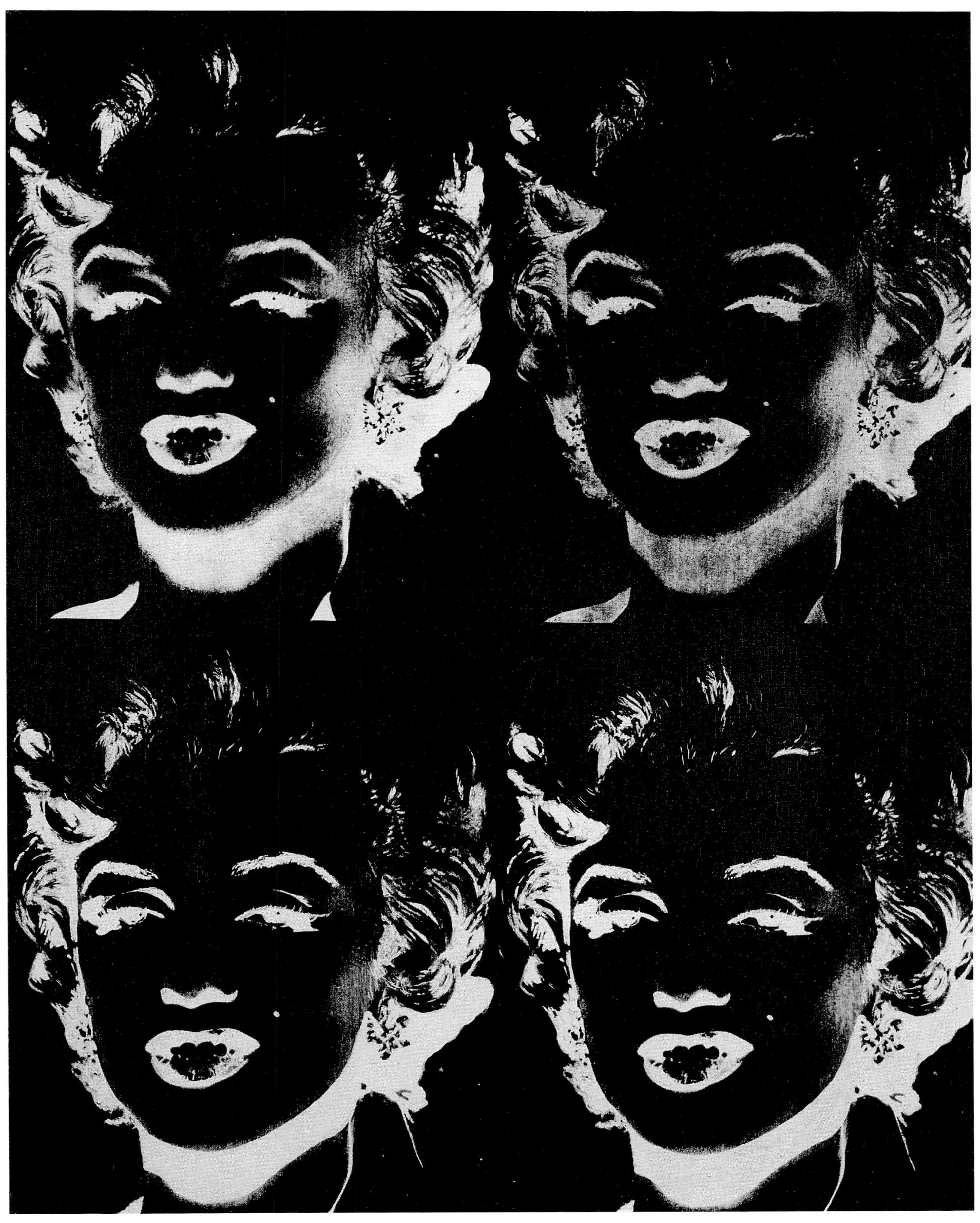

92 *Four Marilyns* (Reversal). *Black on Light Green*, 1979-86

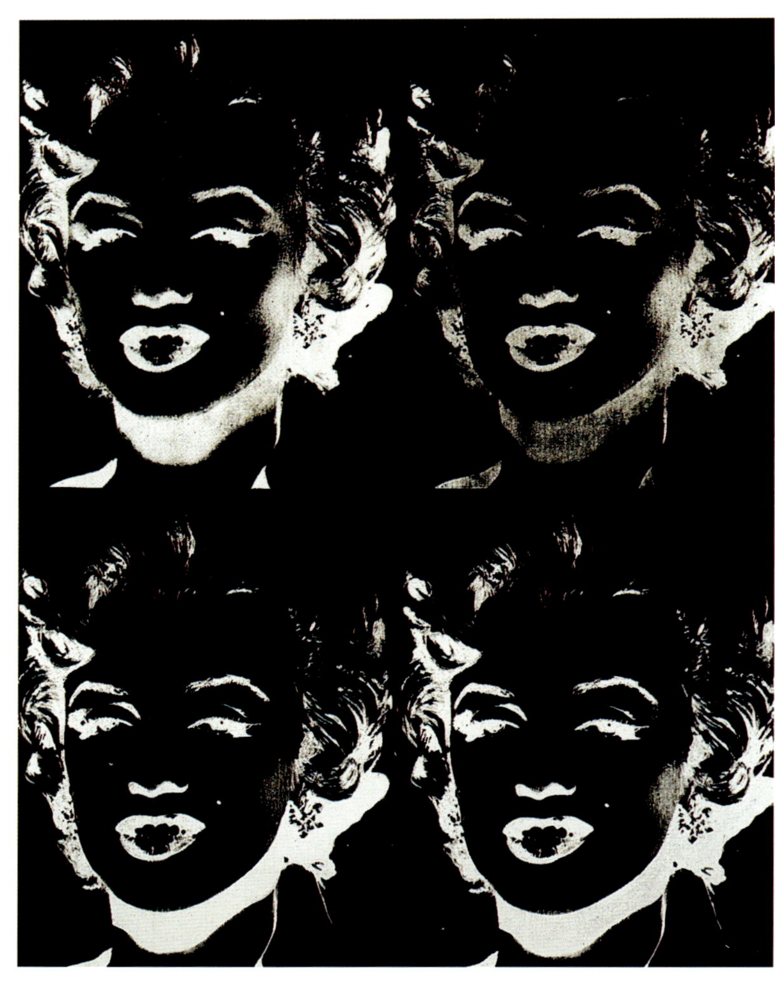

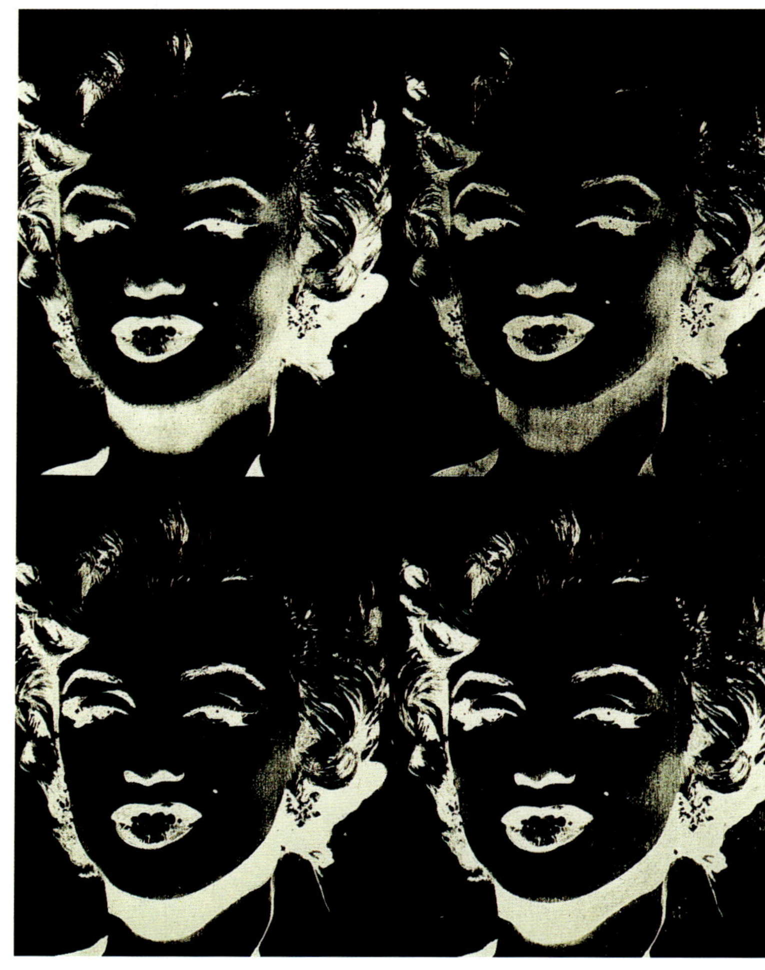

93 *Four Marilyns* (Reversal). *Black on White*, 1979-86

94 *Four Marilyns* (Reversal). *Black on White*, 1979-86

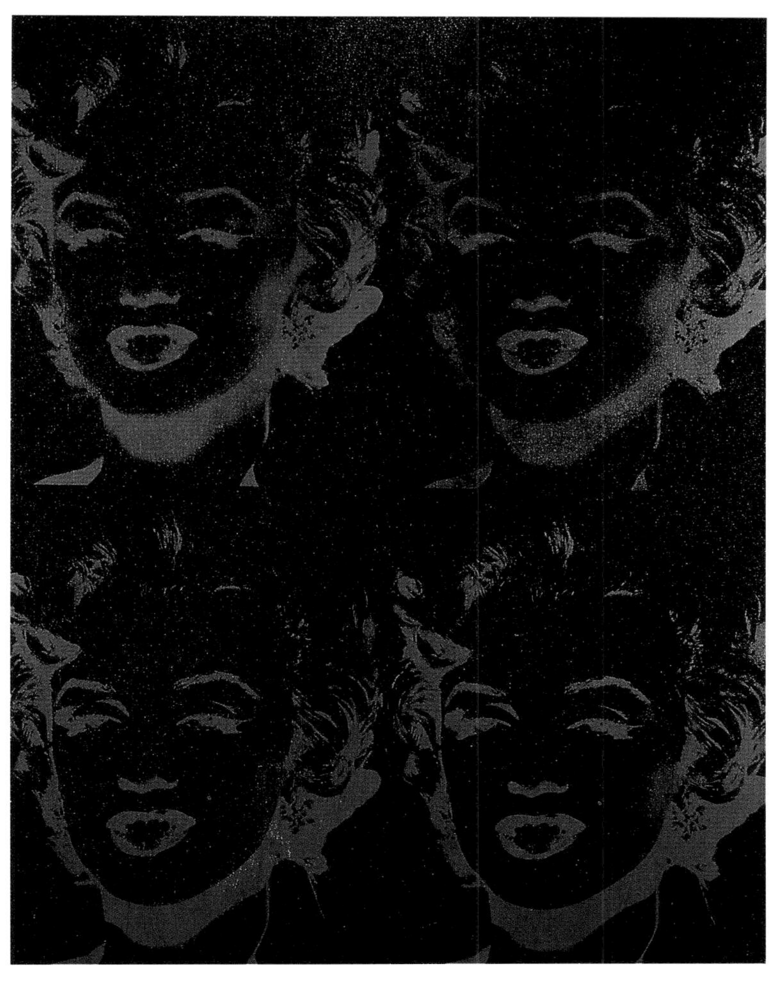

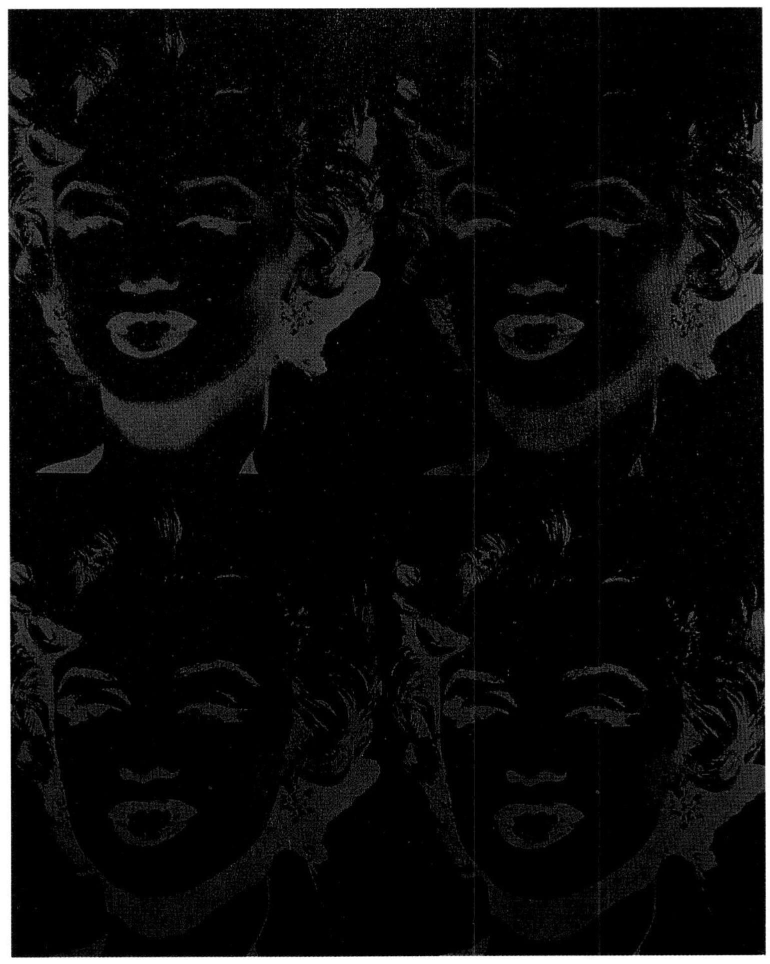

95 *Four Marilyns* (Reversal). *Black on Black*, 1979-86

96 *Four Marilyns* (Reversal). *Black on Black*, 1979-86

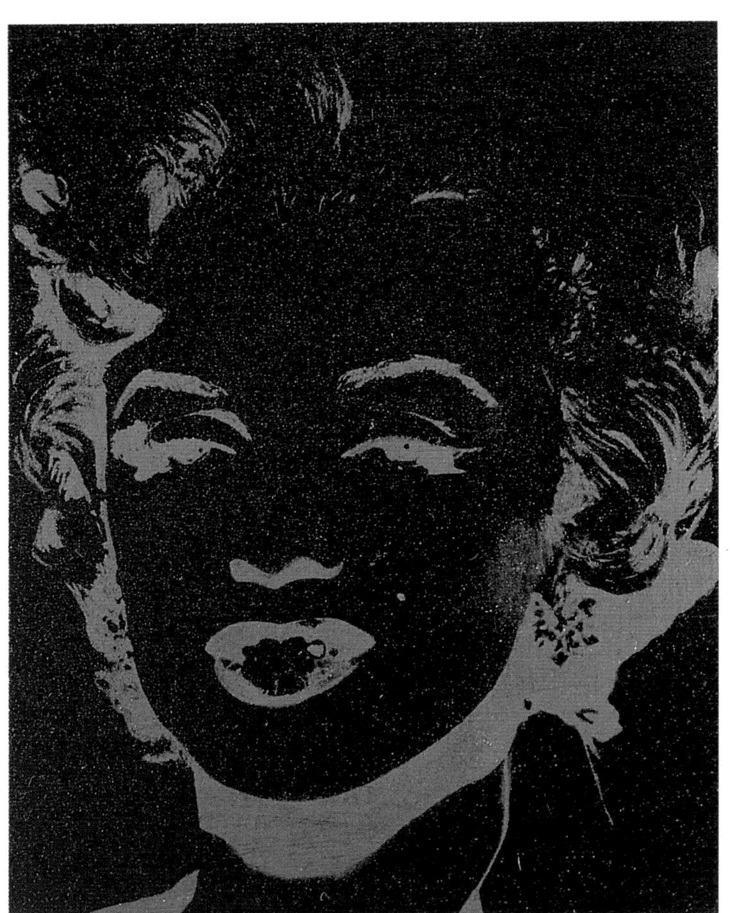

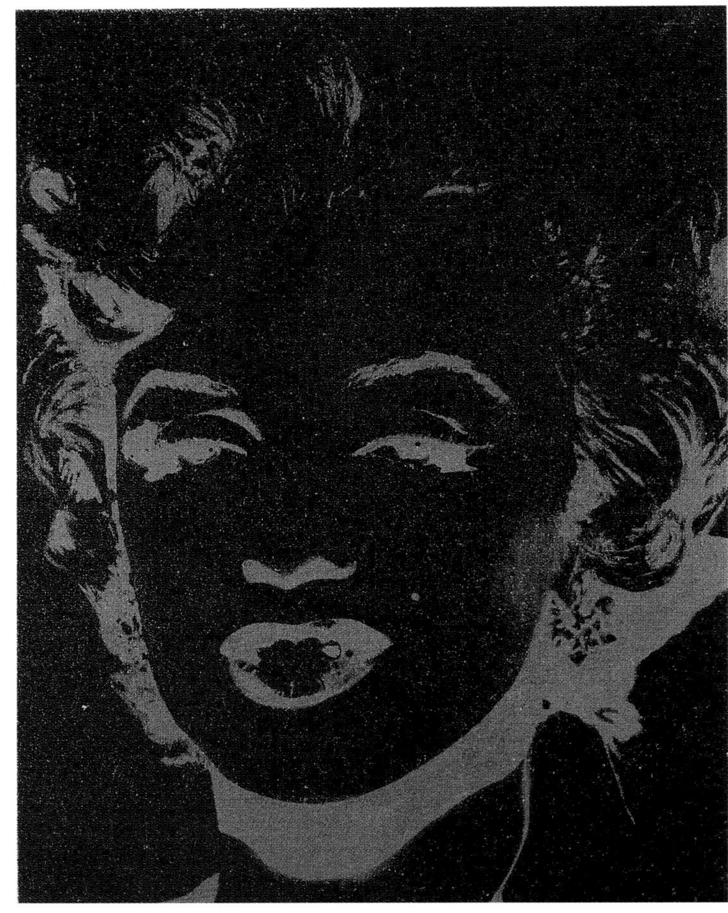

97 *Marilyn* (Reversal). *Black on Black*, 1979-86

98 *Marilyn* (Reversal). *Black on Gray* (Black), 1979-86

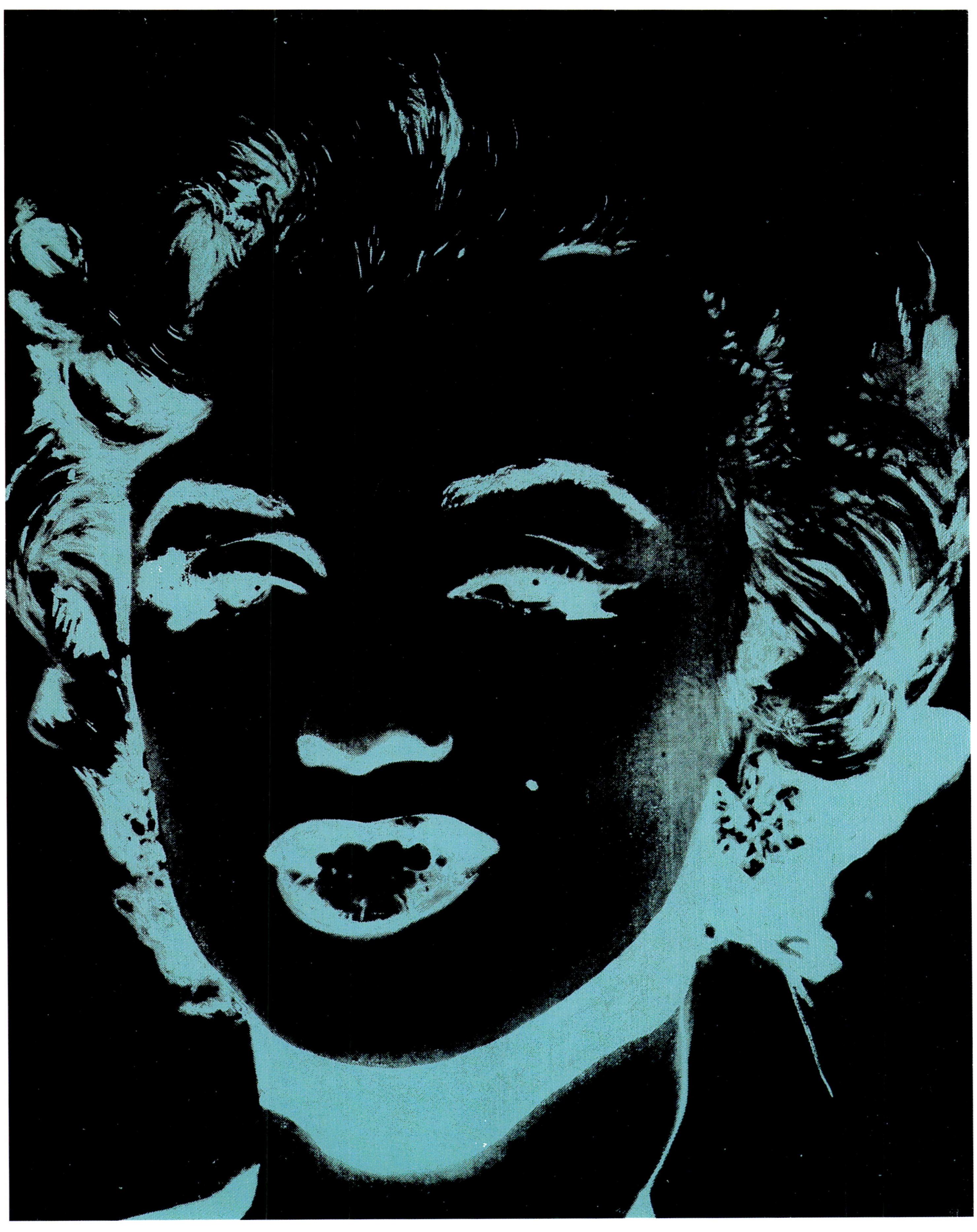

99 *Marilyn* (Reversal). *Black on Blue-Green*, 1979-86

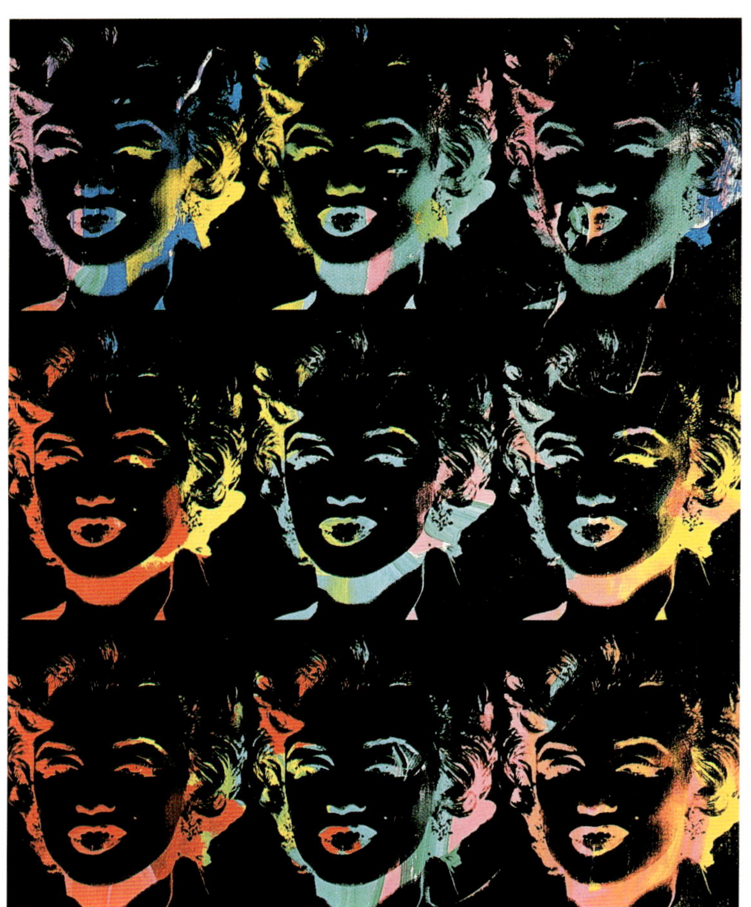

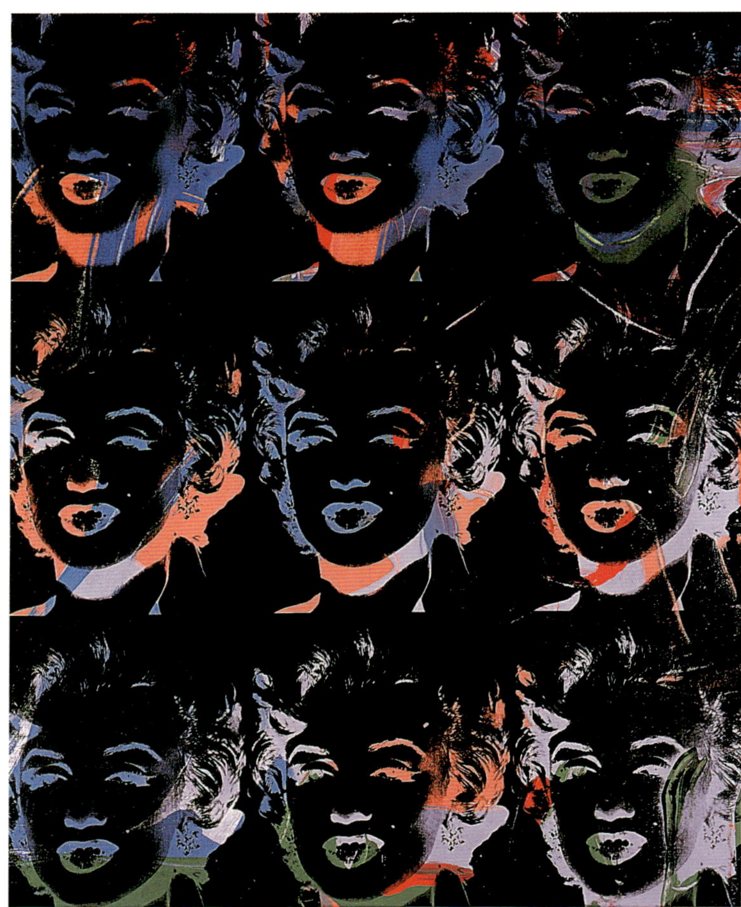

100 *Nine Multicolored Marilyns*, 1979-86

101 *Nine Multicolored Marilyns*, 1979-86

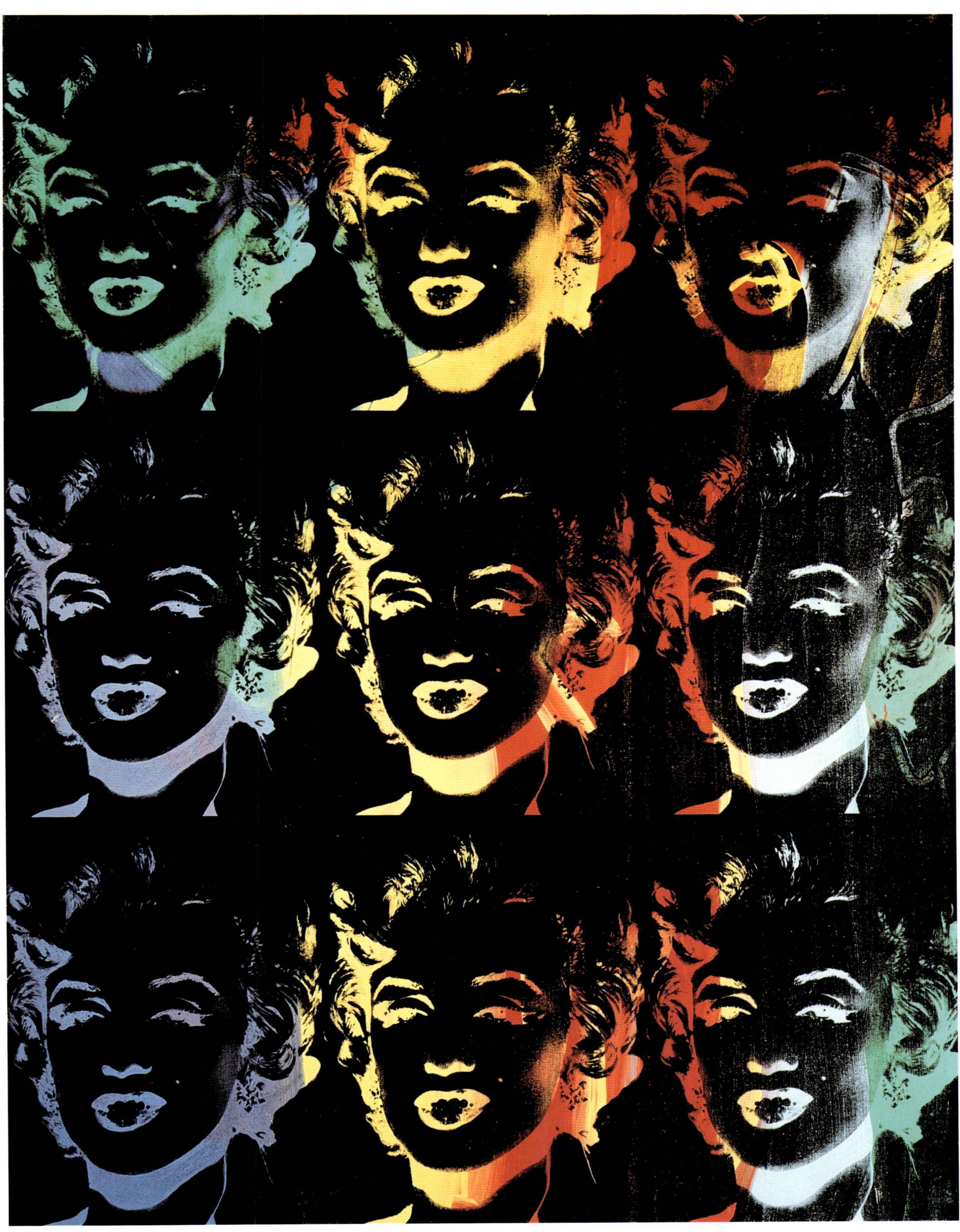

102 *Marilyn – Nine Multicolored Marilyns* (Reversal), 1986

103 *Last Supper. Black on Black*, 1986

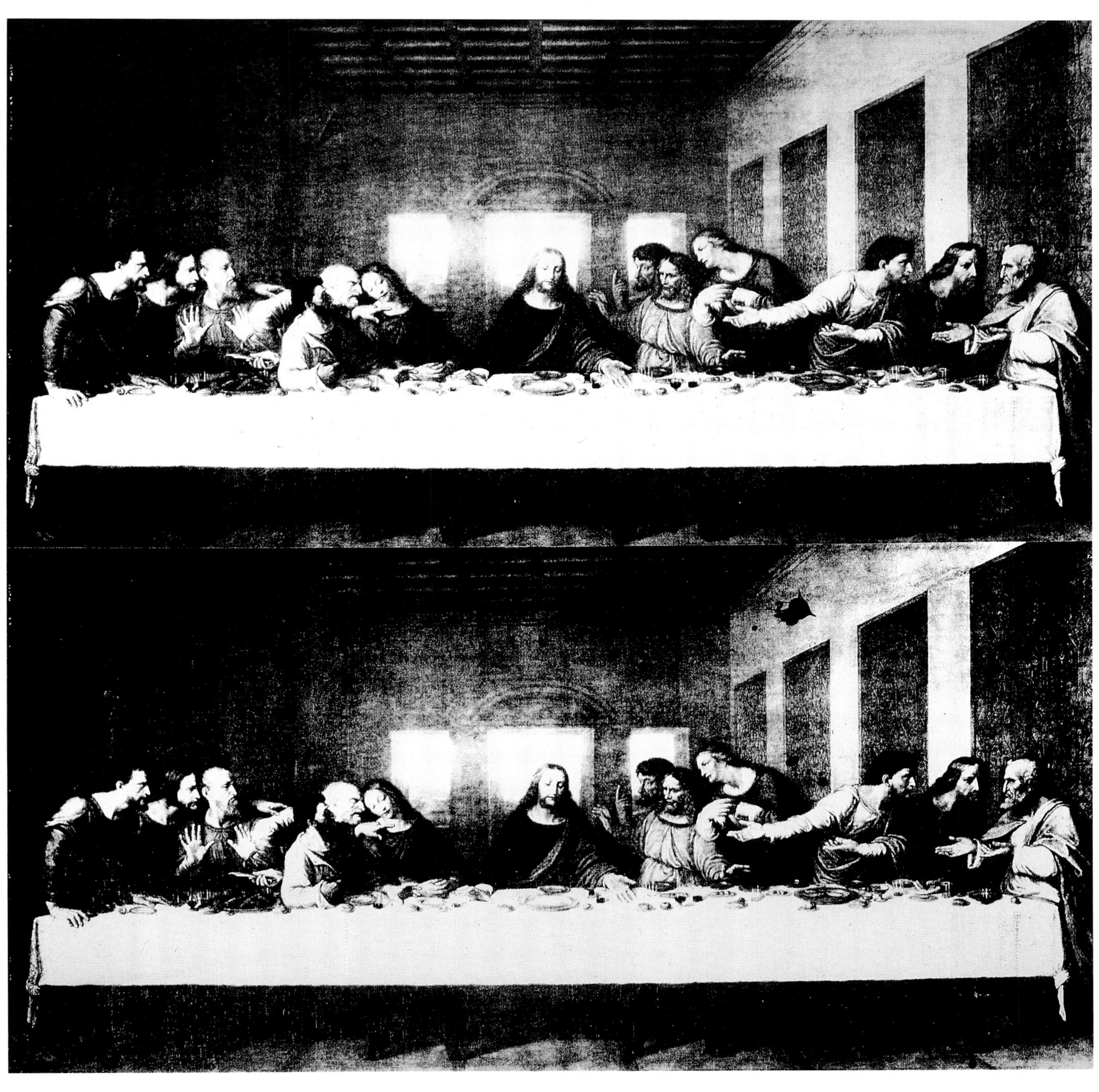

104 *Last Supper. Black/White*, 1986

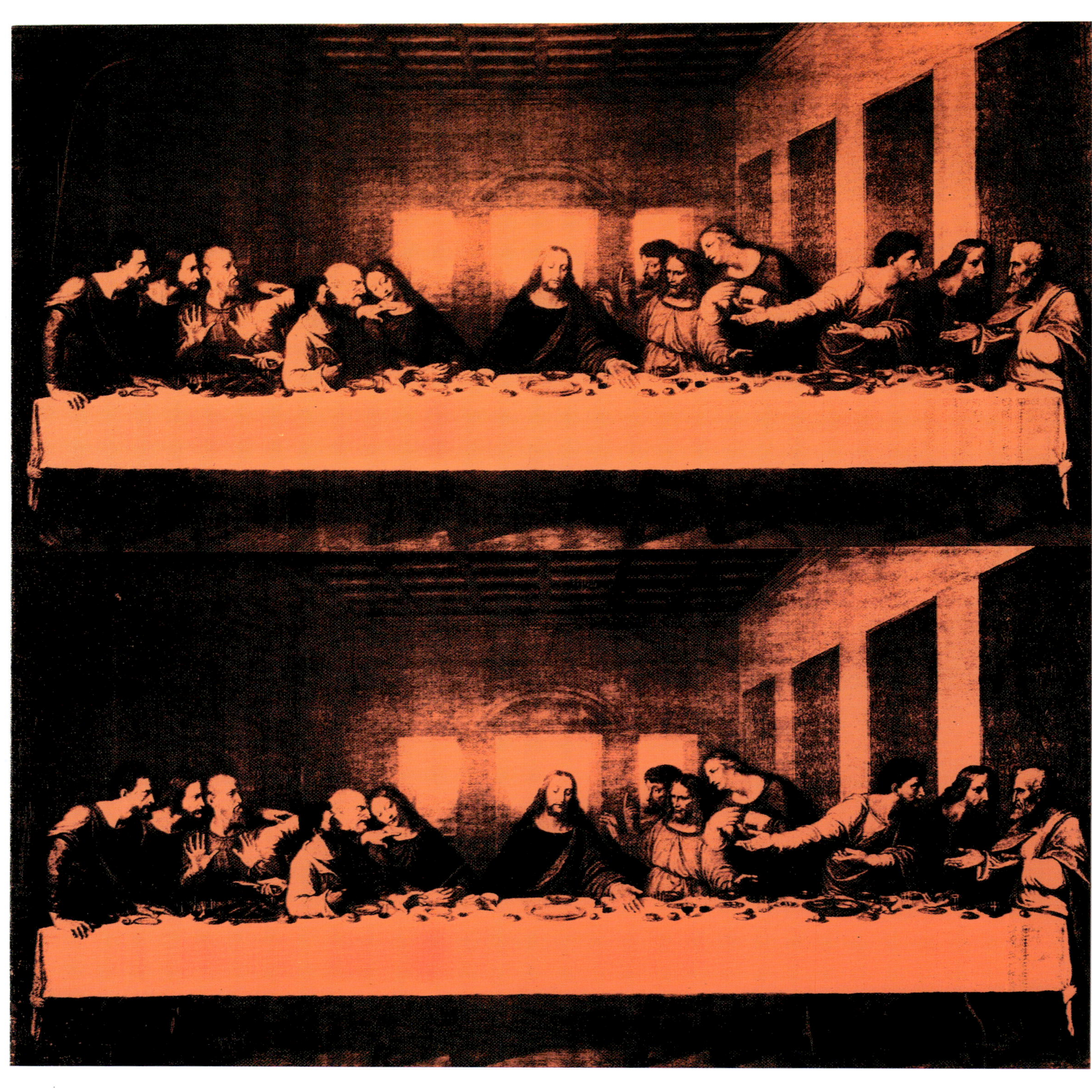

105 *Last Supper. Black/Orange*, 1986

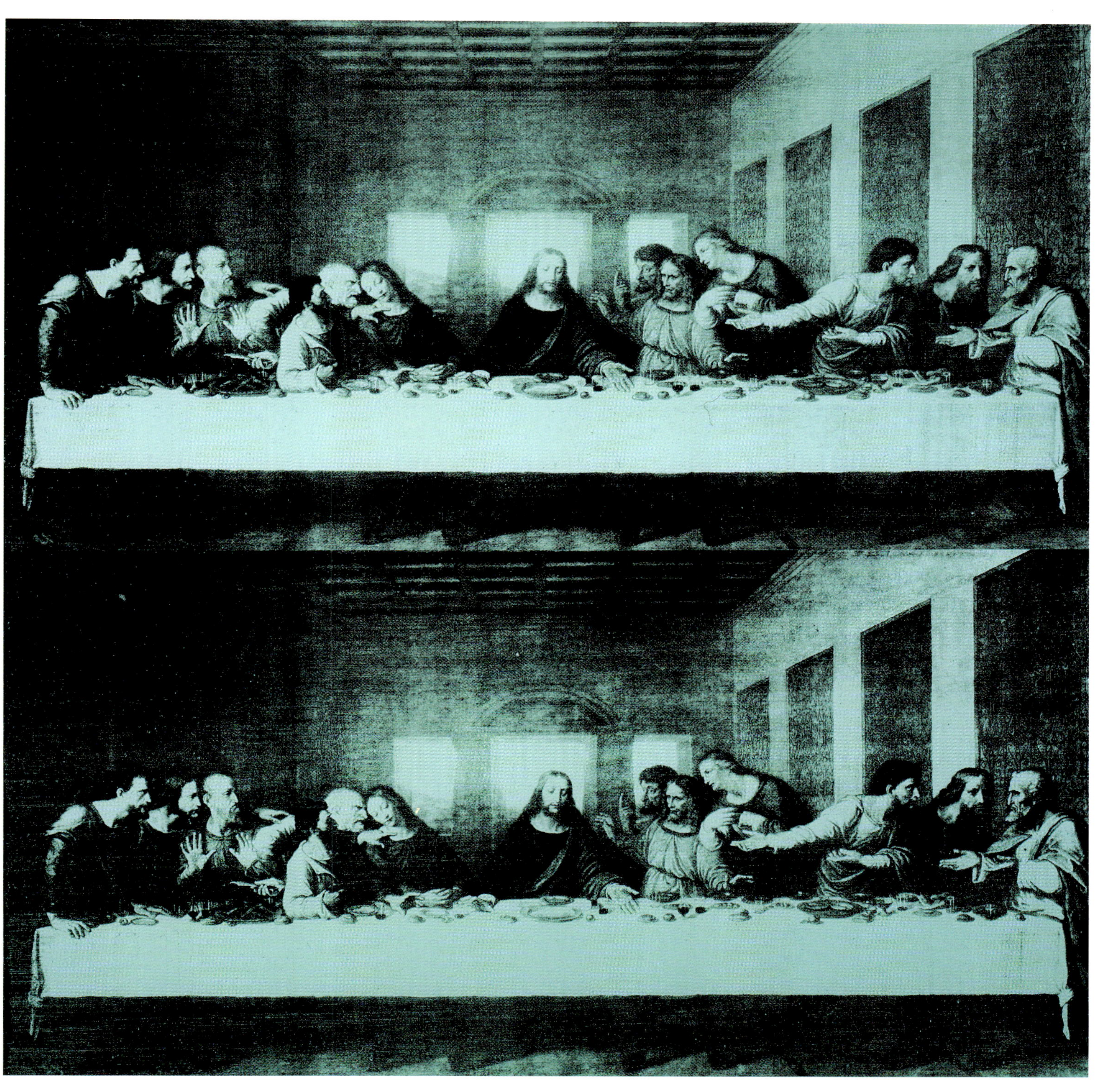

106 *Last Supper. Black/Green*, 1986

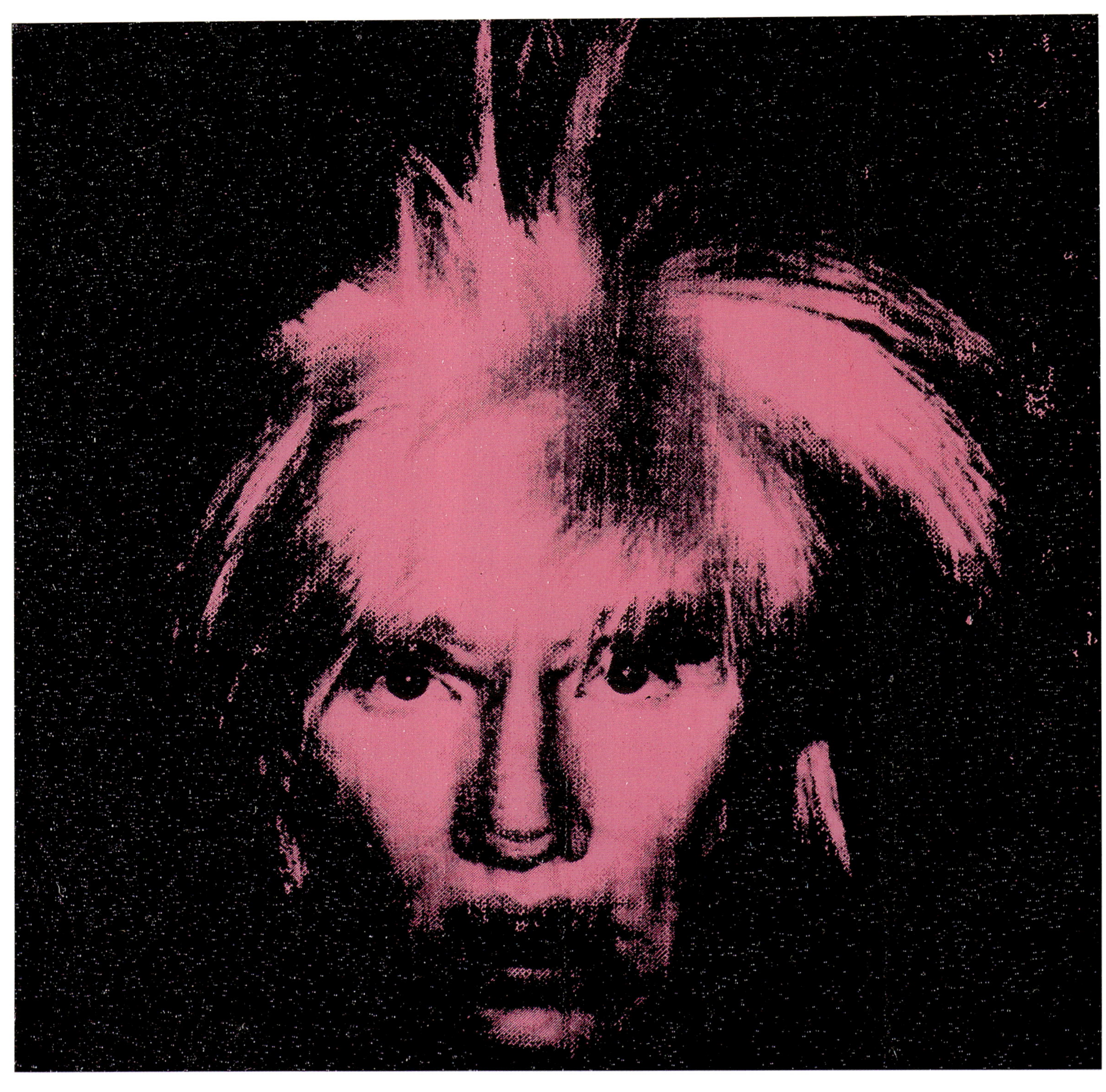

107 *Self-Portrait*, 1986

List of Works

1
Shoe, ca. 1950
Tempera on wood
5 x 8¾″
Collection José Mugrabi
Acquired from the artist
Literature: McShine 1989, fig. 2, p. 64

2
Fashion Show Backdrop
(for *Glamour* magazine), 1955
Tempera and ink on ten canvas window shades
106¼ x 215″
Collection José Mugrabi
Provenance: Acquired from the artist; Collection Kate Rand Lloyd
Exhibited: "'Success Is a Job in New York...': The Early Art and Business of Andy Warhol," 1989-1990: Grey Art Gallery and Study Center, New York; Carnegie Museum of Art, Pittsburgh; Institute of Contemporary Art, University of Pennsylvania, Philadelphia; Fondation Cartier, Jouy-en-Josas, France
Literature: Kornbluth 1988, pl. no. 34, pp. 94-97

3
Untitled, ca. 1957
Gold leaf, collage, pen and black ink on paper
10 x 8″
Signed
Collection José Mugrabi and Isle of Man Co.
Provenance: Gotham Book Mart Gallery, New York

4
Untitled, ca. 1958
Oil and ink on canvas
40 x 48″
Signed
Collection José Mugrabi
Acquired from the artist

5
Coca-Cola, ca. 1962
Gold leaf and collage on Coca-Cola bottle
Height 7¾″
Collection José Mugrabi and Isle of Man Co.
Provenance: Acquired from the artist; Henry Geldzahler, New York

6
Marilyn Monroe (Twenty Times), 1962
Synthetic polymer handpainted and silkscreened on canvas
76¾ x 44¾″
Signed and dated on the reverse
Collection José Mugrabi
Provenance: Stable Gallery, New York; Galerie Sonnabend, Paris; René de Montaigue, Paris; Leo Castelli Gallery, New York; Mr. and Mrs. François de Menil
Exhibited: "Andy Warhol," 1970: Pasadena Art Museum, CA; Museum of Contemporary Art, Chicago; Stedelijk Van Abbe Museum, Eindhoven; Musée d'Art Moderne de la Ville de Paris; Tate Gallery, London; Whitney Museum of American Art, New York; "Paris – New York," 1977: Musée National d'Art Moderne, Centre Georges Pompidou, Paris
Literature: Ratcliff 1983; Crone 1970, cat. no. 64 (size incorrect); Coplans 1970, repr. p. 72

7
Double Elvis, 1963
Synthetic polymer silkscreened on canvas
83 x 45¼″
Collection José Mugrabi and Isle of Man Co.
Provenance: Ferus Gallery, Los Angeles
Exhibited: Pasadena Art Museum, CA, 1973
Literature: To be included in the forthcoming catalogue raisonné of the artist's work by Thomas Ammann

8
Liz, 1963
Diptych
Silver paint and synthetic polymer silkscreened on canvas
40 x 80¼″
Signed and dated on the overlap of the right panel; signed again and dated 64 on the stretcher of the left panel
Unframed
Collection José Mugrabi and Isle of Man Co.
Provenance: Leo Castelli Gallery, New York

9
Liz Taylor, 1965
Silkscreen ink on aluminum paint on canvas
41 x 42½″
Authenticated by Frederick W. Hughes on the overlap
Collection José Mugrabi and Isle of Man Co.
Provenance: Acquired from the artist; private collection
Exhibited: "Faces and Figures," 1989: Thomas Ammann Fine Art, Zurich
Literature: To be included in the forthcoming catalogue raisonné of the artist's work by Thomas Ammann

10
Suicide, 1964
Silkscreen on paper
40 x 30″
Signed and dated 1964 on the reverse
Collection José Mugrabi
Provenance: Leo Castelli Gallery, New York; private collection (acquired in 1964)
Literature: Crone 1970, cat. nos. 603 and 607, p. 272; Morphet 1971, fig. 56, p. 82; Ratcliff 1983, cat. no. 35, p. 37; Hopps 1988, plate 2, p. 47; McShine 1989, cat. no. 266, p. 260

11
Race Riot, 1964
Four panels
Silkscreened ink and synthetic polymer on canvas
30¾ x 33¾″ (each), 61½ x 67⅝″ (total)
Signed and dated 64 on the overlap
Private collection, Monte Carlo
Provenance: Leo Castelli Gallery, New York; Sam Wagstaff, New York; The Estate of Robert Mapplethorpe, New York
Exhibited: "Andy Warhol," 1970/71 Pasadena Art Museum; Museum of Contemporary Art, Chicago; Stedelijk Van Abbe Museum, Eindhoven; Musée d'Art Moderne de la Ville de Paris; Tate Gallery, London; Whitney Museum of American Art, New York; "Pop Art: 1955-1970," 1985: Art Gallery of New South Wales; Queensland Art Gallery; National Gallery of Victoria; "Made in the U.S.A. – An Americanization of Modern Art – The 50s & 60s," 1987: University Art Museum, University of California, Berkeley; Nelson-Atkins Museum, Kansas City; Virginia Museum of Fine Arts, Richmond
Literature: Crone 1970, cat. nos. 416-19; Geldzahler 1985, p. 89; McShine 1989, plate 275

12
Electric Chair, 1964
3 plates mounted together
22 x 84″
Collection José Mugrabi
Exhibited: "Andy Warhol," 1970-71: Pasadena Art Museum, CA; Museum of Contemporary Art, Chicago; Stedelijk Van Abbe Museum, Eindhoven; Musée d'Art Moderne de la Ville de Paris; Tate Gallery, London; Whitney Museum of American Art, New York
Literature: To be included in the forthcoming catalogue raisonné by Thomas Ammann

13
Brillo Box, 1964
Oil and stencil on wood
17 x 17 x 14″
Signed and dated on the underside
Collection José Mugrabi and Isle of Man Co.
Provenance: private collection, Antwerp

14
Brillo Box, 1964 (not illustrated)
Oil and stencil on wood
17 x 17 x 14″
Collection José Mugrabi

15
Kellogg's Corn Flakes Box, 1964
Synthetic polymer silkscreened on wood
25 x 21 x 17″
This work is from an unnumbered edition which was executed in the same size as the commercially used boxes
Collection José Mugrabi
Provenance: Estate of Alan R. Solomon, New York
Literature: Crone 1970, cat. no. 636, repr. p. 283; McShine 1989, pl. 189, p. 200

16
Flowers, 1964
Oil and acrylic on canvas
23⅝ x 23⅝″
Signed and dated on the overlap
Label: OK Harris Works of Art, New York
Collection José Mugrabi
Exhibited: Institute of Contemporary Art, University of Pennsylvania, Philadelphia, in conjunction with the exhibition "'Success Is a Job in New York...': The Early Art and Business of Andy Warhol," 1989-1990

17
Flowers, 1964
Red, orange
Acrylic silkscreened on canvas
24 x 24″
Signed and dated on the overlap
LC (111) written on the stretcher
Unframed
Collection José Mugrabi
Provenance: Leo Castelli Gallery, New York
Exhibited: Institute of Contemporary Art, University of Pennsylvania, Philadelphia, in conjunction with the exhibition "'Success Is a Job in New York...': The Early Art and Business of Andy Warhol," 1989-1990

18
Flowers, 1964
White
Synthetic polymer silkscreened on canvas
23⅝ x 23⅝″
Signed and dated
Collection José Mugrabi

19
Flowers, 1964
Pink, orange
Silkscreen ink and synthetic polymer on canvas
23⅝ x 23⅝″
Signed and dated
Collection José Mugrabi

20
Flowers, 1964
Pink, orange, red
Silkscreen ink on synthetic paint on canvas
24 x 24″
Signed and dated on the overlap
Unframed
Collection José Mugrabi and Isle of Man Co.
Provenance: Leo Castelli, LC #232, New York; Jane Holzer, New York

21
Flowers, 1964
Synthetic polymer silkscreened on canvas
82 x 82″
Collection José Mugrabi and Isle of Man Co.
Provenance: Leo Castelli Gallery, New York; William Zierler, New York; Leon Kraushar, Long Island; Karl Ströher, Munich (acquired from Kraushar in 1968)
Exhibited: Neue Nationalgalerie, Berlin, 1969; Kunsthalle, Bern, 1969; Hessisches Landesmuseum, Darmstadt, 1970; Städtische Kunsthalle, Düsseldorf, 1976; Kestner GmbH, Hannover, 1981
Literature: Crone 1970, cat. no. 575, p. 309; Schmidt 1982, cat. no. 612, repr. p. 238. To be included in the forthcoming catalogue raisonné by Thomas Ammann

22
Flowers, 1964
Purple, blue
Acrylic silkscreened on canvas
24 x 24″
Signed and dated on the overlap
LC (228) written on the stretcher
Collection José Mugrabi
Provenance: Leo Castelli Gallery, New York
Exhibited: Institute of Contemporary Art, University of Pennsylvania, Philadelphia, in conjunction with the exhibition "'Success Is a Job in New York...': The Early Art and Business of Andy Warhol," 1989-1990

23
Flowers, 1964
Purple
Silkscreen ink on synthetic paint on canvas
24 x 24″
Stamp signed and certified with date on the overlap
Unframed
Collection José Mugrabi and Isle of Man Co.
Provenance: Leo Castelli, LC #227, New York; Jane Holzer, New York

24
Flowers, 1964
Red, orange, purple
Silkscreen ink on synthetic paint on canvas
24 x 24″
Framed
Collection José Mugrabi and Isle of Man Co.
Provenance: Leo Castelli, LC #236, New York; Carter Burden Collection, #11.63, New York; Jane Holzer, New York

25
Flowers, 1964
Orange, red, pink
Silkscreen ink on synthetic paint on canvas
24 x 24″
Framed
Collection José Mugrabi and Isle of Man Co.
Provenance: Leo Castelli, LC #235, New York; Carter Burden Collection, #11.64, New York; Jane Holzer, New York

26
Flowers, 1964
White
Silkscreen ink on synthetic paint on canvas
24 x 24″
Signed and dated on the overlap
Unframed
Collection José Mugrabi and Isle of Man Co.
Provenance: Leo Castelli, LC #150, New York; Jane Holzer, New York

27
Jackie, 1964
Synthetic polymer silkscreened on canvas
20 x 16″
Collection José Mugrabi
Provenance: Ferus Gallery, Los Angeles

28
Blue Jackie, 1964
Synthetic polymer silkscreened on canvas
20 x 16″
Signed and dated on the overlap
Unframed
Collection José Mugrabi
Provenance: Leo Castelli Gallery, New York; CORE, New York

29
Gold Jackie, 1964
Synthetic polymer silkscreened on canvas
20 x 16″
Stamped with artist's signature and authenticated by Vincent Fremont on the overlap
Collection José Mugrabi
Provenance: Acquired from the artist; Estate of Edward K. Walsh

30
Jackie, 1964
Synthetic polymer silkscreened on canvas
20 x 16″
Signed on the overlap
Collection José Mugrabi
Provenance: Eva Lee Gallery, Great Neck, N.Y.

31
Self-Portrait, 1964
Synthetic polymer silkscreened on canvas
20 x 16″
Unframed
Collection José Mugrabi and Isle of Man Co.
Provenance: The Paul Warhola Family, acquired directly from the artist

32
Self-Portrait, 1966/67
Synthetic polymer silkscreened on canvas
22½ x 22½
Collection José Mugrabi

33
Self-Portrait, 1966
Oil and acrylic on canvas
22 x 22″
Signed and dated on the overlap
Collection José Mugrabi

34
Self-Portrait, 1967
Green, orange
Silkscreen on canvas
22 x 22″
Collection José Mugrabi
Provenance: Collection Kraushar, New York
Galerie Heiner Friedrich, Munich;
Six Friedrich, Munich
Exhibited: Collection Karl Ströher, Galerie-Verein, Neue Pinakothek – Haus der Kunst, Munich, 1968
Literature: Crone 1970, cat. no. 187

35
Self-Portrait, 1966
Oil and acrylic on canvas
23⅝ x 23⅝
Stamp signed on the reverse
Authenticated by Frederick W. Hughes
Collection José Mugrabi

36
Campbell's Soup, 1975
Printed tie
Executed on the occasion of an Andy Warhol exhibition in New York
Collection José Mugrabi

37
Campbell's Soup Can, 1966
Mixed media
Diameter 2¾″
Height 4″
Collection José Mugrabi
Provenance: Six Friedrich, Munich

38
Campbell's Tomato Juice Box, 1964
Oil and stencil on wood
10 x 19 x 9½″
Collection José Mugrabi
Provenance: The Paul Warhola Family, acquired directly from the artist
Literature: To be included in the forthcoming catalogue raisonné of the artist's work by Thomas Ammann

39
Campbell's Tomato Soup Can, 1968
Acrylic silkscreened on painted paper
15 x 10″
Signed on the reverse
Collection José Mugrabi

40
Mao Tse-tung, 1974
Serigraph
40 x 30″
Collection José Mugrabi

41
Portrait of R. C. Gorman, 1979
Acrylic and silkscreen on canvas
40 x 40″
Signed on the reverse
Collection José Mugrabi and Isle of Man Co.
Provenance: Private collection, Beverly Hills, CA

42
One Green Cow, 1979
Acrylic and silkscreen on canvas
46½ x 27$\frac{3}{16}$
Signed, dated and titled on the overlap
Collection José Mugrabi
Provenance: Acquired from the artist, Galerie Bruno Bischofberger, Zurich
Literature: To be included in the forthcoming catalogue raisonné of the artist's work by Thomas Ammann

43
Oxidation Painting, 1978
Copper metallic pigment mixed with mixed media on canvas
48 x 49½″
Signed and dated on the reverse of each panel
Collection José Mugrabi
Provenance: Estate of the artist; Gagosian Gallery, New York

44
Portrait of Madame Smith, 1970s
Synthetic polymer silkscreened on canvas
40 x 40″ (each)
Collection José Mugrabi
Acquired from the artist

45
Portrait of Martha Graham, 1980
Synthetic polymer with diamond dust silkscreened on canvas
40 x 40″
Signed, dated and inscribed M. G. on the overlap
Collection José Mugrabi
Acquired from the artist

46
Drag Queen, 1977
Synthetic polymer silkscreened on canvas
14 x 11″
Signed and dated on the overlap
Unframed
Collection José Mugrabi and Isle of Man Co.
Acquired from the artist

47
One White on White Mona Lisa, 1979
Acrylic and silkscreen on canvas
24¾ x 19⅞″
Signed, dated and titled on the overlap
Collection José Mugrabi
Provenance: Acquired from the artist; Galerie Bruno Bischofberger, Zurich
Literature: To be included in the forthcoming catalogue raisonné of the artist's work by Thomas Ammann

48
Two Golden Mona Lisas, 1980
Acrylic and silkscreen on canvas
26⅝ x 40″
Collection José Mugrabi
Provenance: Acquired from the artist; Galerie Bruno Bischofberger, Zurich
Literature: To be included in the forthcoming catalogue raisonné of the artist's work by Thomas Ammann

49
Shoes (Tony), 1980
Serigraph on paper mounted on panel, with diamond dust
49 3/16 x 58 1/16″
Collection José Mugrabi

50
Shoes (Magnin), 1980
Serigraph on paper mounted on panel, with diamond dust
25⅜ x 58″
Collection José Mugrabi

51
$, 1981
Synthetic polymer silkscreened on canvas
90 x 70″
Signed and dated on the overlap
Collection José Mugrabi

52
Knives, 1982
Silkscreen ink and synthetic polymer on canvas
70 x 48 13/16
Signed
Collection José Mugrabi

53
Giorgio Armani, 1983
Acrylic on canvas
39¾ x 39¾
Collection José Mugrabi

54
San Francisco Silverspot, 1983
Synthetic polymer paint silkscreened on canvas
60 x 60″
Signed and dated on the overlap
Collection José Mugrabi
Provenance: Ronald Feldman Gallery, New York

55
Toy Panda (from the series "Paintings for Children"), 1983
Acrylic on canvas
11 x 14 3/16
Collection José Mugrabi
Provenance: Acquired from the artist; Rupert-Jasen Smith; Hans Mayer

56
Airplane (from the series "Paintings for Children"), 1983
Acrylic and silkscreen on canvas
11 x 14 3/16″
Collection José Mugrabi and Isle of Man Co.

57
Fish Small (No. 1, from the series "Paintings for Children"), 1983
Acrylic and silkscreen on canvas
7⅞ x 9⅞″
Signed and dated on the overlap
Collection José Mugrabi
Provenance: Acquired from the artist; Galerie Bruno Bischofberger, Zurich
Literature: To be included in the forthcoming catalogue raisonné of the artist's work by Thomas Ammann

58
Parrot (from the series "Paintings for Children"), 1983
Acrylic and silkscreen on canvas
14 3/16 x 11″
Collection José Mugrabi and Isle of Man Co.

59
Police Car (from the series "Paintings for Children"), 1983
Acrylic and silkscreen on canvas
11 x 14 3/16″
Collection José Mugrabi and Isle of Man Co.

60
Roli Zoli (from the series "Paintings for Children"), 1983
Acrylic and silkscreen on canvas
11 x 14 3/16″
Collection José Mugrabi and Isle of Man Co.

61
Locomotive (from the series "Paintings for Children"), 1983
Acrylic and silkscreen on canvas
11 x 14 3/16″
Collection José Mugrabi and Isle of Man Co.

62
Apple (from the series "Paintings for Children"), 1983
Acrylic and silkscreen on canvas
11 x 14 3/16″
Collection José Mugrabi and Isle of Man Co.

63
Space Ship (from the series "Paintings for Children"), 1983
Acrylic and silkscreen on canvas
11 x 14 3/16″
Collection José Mugrabi and Isle of Man Co.

64
Ship (from the series "Paintings for Children"), 1983
Acrylic and silkscreen on canvas
11 x 14 3/16″
Collection José Mugrabi and Isle of Man Co.

65
Emergency Helicopter (from the series "Paintings for Children"), 1983
Acrylic and silkscreen on canvas
11 x 14 3/16″
Collection José Mugrabi and Isle of Man Co.

66
Moon Explorer (No. 8, from the series "Paintings for Children"), 1983
Acrylic and silkscreen on canvas
9⅞ x 7⅞″
Signed and dated on the overlap
Collection José Murgrabi
Provenance: Acquired from the artist; Galerie Bruno Bischofberger, Zurich
Literature: To be included in the forthcoming catalogue raisonné of the artist's work by Thomas Ammann

67
Apple (from the series "Paintings for Children"), 1983
Acrylic and silkscreen on canvas
11 x 14 3/16″
Collection José Mugrabi and Isle of Man Co.

68
Fish Small (No. 99, from the series "Paintings for Children"), 1983
Acrylic and silkscreen on canvas
8 x 10″
Signed and dated on the overlap
Collection José Mugrabi
Provenance: Acquired from the artist; Galerie Bruno Bischofberger, Zurich
Literature: To be included in the forthcoming catalogue raisonné of the artist's work by Thomas Ammann

69
Ship (from the series "Paintings for Children"), 1983
Acrylic and silkscreeen on canvas
11 x 14 3/16″
Collection José Mugrabi and Isle of Man Co.

70
Parrot (No. 3, from the series "Paintings for Children"), 1983
Acrylic and silkscreen on canvas
9⅞ x 7⅞″
Signed and dated on the overlap
Collection José Mugrabi
Provenance: Acquired from the artist; Galerie Bruno Bischofberger, Zurich
Literature: To be included in the forthcoming catalogue raisonné of the artist's work by Thomas Ammann

71
Roli Zoli (from the series "Paintings for Children"), 1983
Acrylic and silkscreen on canvas
11 x 14 3/16"
Collection José Mugrabi and Isle of Man Co.

72
Apple (from the series "Paintings for Children"), 1983
Acrylic and silkscreen on canvas
11 x 14 3/16"
Collection José Mugrabi and Isle of Man Co.

73
Airplane (from the series "Paintings for Children"), 1983
Acrylic and silkscreen on canvas
11 x 14 3/16"
Collection José Mugrabi and Isle of Man Co.

74
Ship (from the series "Paintings for Children"), 1983
Acrylic and silkscreen on canvas
11 x 14 3/16"
Collection José Mugrabi and Isle of Man Co.

75
Space Ship (from the series "Paintings for Children"), 1983
Acrylic and silkscreen on canvas
11 x 14 3/16"
Collection José Mugrabi and Isle of Man Co.

76
Ship (from the series "Paintings for Children"), 1983
Acrylic and silkscreen on canvas
11 x 14 3/16"
Collection José Mugrabi and Isle of Man Co.

77
Police Car (from the series "Paintings for Children"), 1983
Acrylic and silkscreen on canvas
11 x 14 3/16"
Collection José Mugrabi and Isle of Man Co.

78
Space Ship (from the series "Paintings for Children"), 1983
Acrylic and silkscreen on canvas
11 x 14 3/16"
Collection José Mugrabi and Isle of Man Co.

79
Emergency Helicopter (from the series "Paintings for Children"), 1983
Acrylic and silkscreen on canvas
11 x 14 3/16"
Collection José Mugrabi and Isle of Man Co.

80
Panda Bear (No. 100, from the series "Paintings for Children"), 1983
Acrylic and silkscreen on canvas
9 7/8 x 7 7/8"
Signed and dated on the overlap
Collection José Mugrabi
Provenance: Acquired from the artist;
Galerie Bruno Bischofberger, Zurich
Literature: To be included in the forthcoming catalogue raisonné of the artist's work by Thomas Ammann

81
Police Car (from the series "Paintings for Children"), 1983
Acrylic and silkscreen on canvas
11 x 14 3/16"
Collection José Mugrabi and Isle of Man Co.

82
Airplane (from the series "Paintings for Children"), 1983
Acrylic and silkscreen on canvas
11 x 14 3/16"
Collection José Mugrabi and Isle of Man Co.

83
Police Car (from the series "Paintings for Children"), 1983
Acrylic and silkscreen on canvas
11 x 14 3/16"
Collection José Mugrabi and Isle of Man Co.

84
Locomotive (from the series "Paintings for Children"), 1983
Acrylic and silkscreen on canvas
11 x 14 3/16"
Collection José Mugrabi and Isle of Man Co.

85
Apple (from the series "Paintings for Children"), 1983
Acrylic and silkscreen on canvas
11 x 14 3/16"
Collection José Mugrabi and Isle of Man Co.

86
Blackglama, 1985
Synthetic polymer paint silkscreened on canvas
22x22"
Signed and dated 85 on the overlap
Collection José Mugrabi
Provenance: Martin Lawrence Galleries, Los Angeles

87
Ice Hockey Player, 1984
Synthetic polymer silkscreened on canvas
40x40"
Stamped with artist's signature and inscribed with authentication by Frederick W. Hughes on the overlap.
Depicts a member of the World Champion Swedish ice hockey team
Collection José Mugrabi commissioned from the artist;
Literature: To be included in the forthcoming catalogue raisonné of the artist's work by Thomas Ammann

88
Untitled (Lobster), 1984
Synthetic polymer silkscreened on canvas
20x 16"
Signed and dated on the reverse
Collection José Mugrabi and Isle of Man Co.
Acquired from the artist

89
Vesuvius, 1985
Ink and charcoal on Arches paper
23x31"
Collection José Mugrabi
Provenance: Lucio Amelio, Naples
Literature: Bonuomo 1985

90
Vesuvius, 1985
Original serigraph, painted
31½x41½
Trial proof – unique
Collection José Mugrabi
Provenance: Lucio Amelio, Naples
Literature: Bonuomo 1985

91
Self-Portrait with Skeleton's Arm and Madonna (after Edvard Munch), 1984
Acrylic and silkscreen on canvas
51x71"
Signed and dated on the reverse
Collection José Mugrabi

92
Four Marilyns (Reversal). *Black on Light Green*, 1979-1986
Acrylic and silkscreen on canvas
36x28"
Collection José Mugrabi
Literature: To be included in the forthcoming catalogue raisonné of the artist's work by Thomas Ammann

93
Four Marilyns (Reversal). *Black on White*, 1979-1986
Acrylic and silkscreen on canvas
36x28"
Collection José Mugrabi
Literature: To be included in the forthcoming catalogue raisonné of the artist's work by Thomas Ammann

94
Four Marilyns (Reversal). *Black on White*, 1979-1986
Acrylic and silkscreen on canvas
36x28"
Collection José Mugrabi
Provenance: Galerie Bruno Bischofberger, Zurich
Literature: To be included in the forthcoming catalogue raisonné of the artist's work by Thomas Ammann

95
Four Marilyns (Reversal). *Black on Black*, 1979-1986
Acrylic and silkscreen on canvas
36x28"
Collection José Mugrabi
Literature: To be included in the forthcoming catalogue raisonné of the artist's work by Thomas Ammann

96
Four Marilyns (Reversal). *Black on Black*, 1979-1986
Acrylic and silkscreen on canvas
36x28"
Collection José Mugrabi
Literature: To be included in the forthcoming catalogue raisonné of the artist's work by Thomas Ammann

97
Marilyn (Reversal). *Black on Black*, 1979-1986
Acrylic and silkscreen on canvas
18x 14"
Collection José Mugrabi
Provenance: Galerie Bruno Bischofberger, Zurich
Literature: To be included in the forthcoming catalogue raisonné of the artist's work by Thomas Ammann

98
Marilyn (Reversal). *Black on Gray* (Black), 1979-1986
Acrylic and silkscreen on canvas
18 x 14"
Collection José Mugrabi
Literature: To be included in the forthcoming catalogue raisonné of the artist's work by Thomas Ammann

99
Marilyn (Reversal). *Black on Blue-Green*, 1979-1986
Acrylic and silkscreen on canvas
18 x 14"
Collection José Mugrabi
Literature: To be included in the forthcoming catalogue raisonné of the artist's work by Thomas Ammann

100
Nine Multicolored Marilyns, 1979-1986
Synthetic polymer silkscreened on canvas
54 3/16 x 42"
Signed and dated on the overlap
Collection José Mugrabi
Provenance: Galerie Bruno Bischofberger, Zurich

101
Nine Multicolored Marilyns, 1979-1986
Acrylic and silkscreen on canvas
50 7/16 x 40 1/4"
Signed and dated 1986 and authenticated by Frederick W. Hughes on the overlap
Collection José Mugrabi
Provenance: Acquired from the artist; Galerie Bruno Bischofberger, Zurich
Literature: To be included in the forthcoming catalogue raisonné of the artist's work by Thomas Ammann

102
Marilyn – Nine Multicolored Marilyns (Reversal), 1986
Synthetic polymer silkscreened on canvas
54 1/4 x 41 1/2"
Signed and dated on the overlap
Collection José Mugrabi
Provenance: Galerie Bruno Bischofberger, Zurich; The Waddington Galleries, London

103
Last Supper. Black on Black, 1986
Acrylic and silkscreen on canvas
39 3/8 x 39 3/8"
Collection José Mugrabi
Provenance: Acquired from the artist; Galerie Bruno Bischofberger, Zurich
Exhibited: "American Masters of the 60's," 1990: Tony Shafrazi Gallery, New York
Literature: To be included in the forthcoming catalogue raisonné of the artist's work by Thomas Ammann

104
Last Supper. Black/White, 1986
Acrylic on canvas
39 3/8 x 39 3/8"
Collection José Mugrabi
Provenance: Acquired from the artist; Hans Mayer
Exhibited: "American Masters of the 60's," Tony Shafrazi Gallery, New York, 1990

105
Last Supper. Black/Orange, 1986
Acrylic on canvas
39 3/8 x 39 3/8"
Collection José Mugrabi
Provenance: Acquired from the artist; Hans Mayer
Exhibited: "American Masters of the 60's," Tony Shafrazi Gallery, New York, 1990

106
Last Supper. Black/Green, 1986
Acrylic on canvas
39 3/8 x 39 3/8"
Collection José Mugrabi
Provenance: Acquired from the artist; Hans Mayer
Exhibited: "American Masters of the 60's," Tony Shafrazi Gallery, New York, 1990

107
Self-Portrait, 1986
Acrylic silkscreened on canvas
Signed and dated on the overlap
Collection José Mugrabi and Isle of Man Co.
Provenance: Sho Gallery, Tokyo

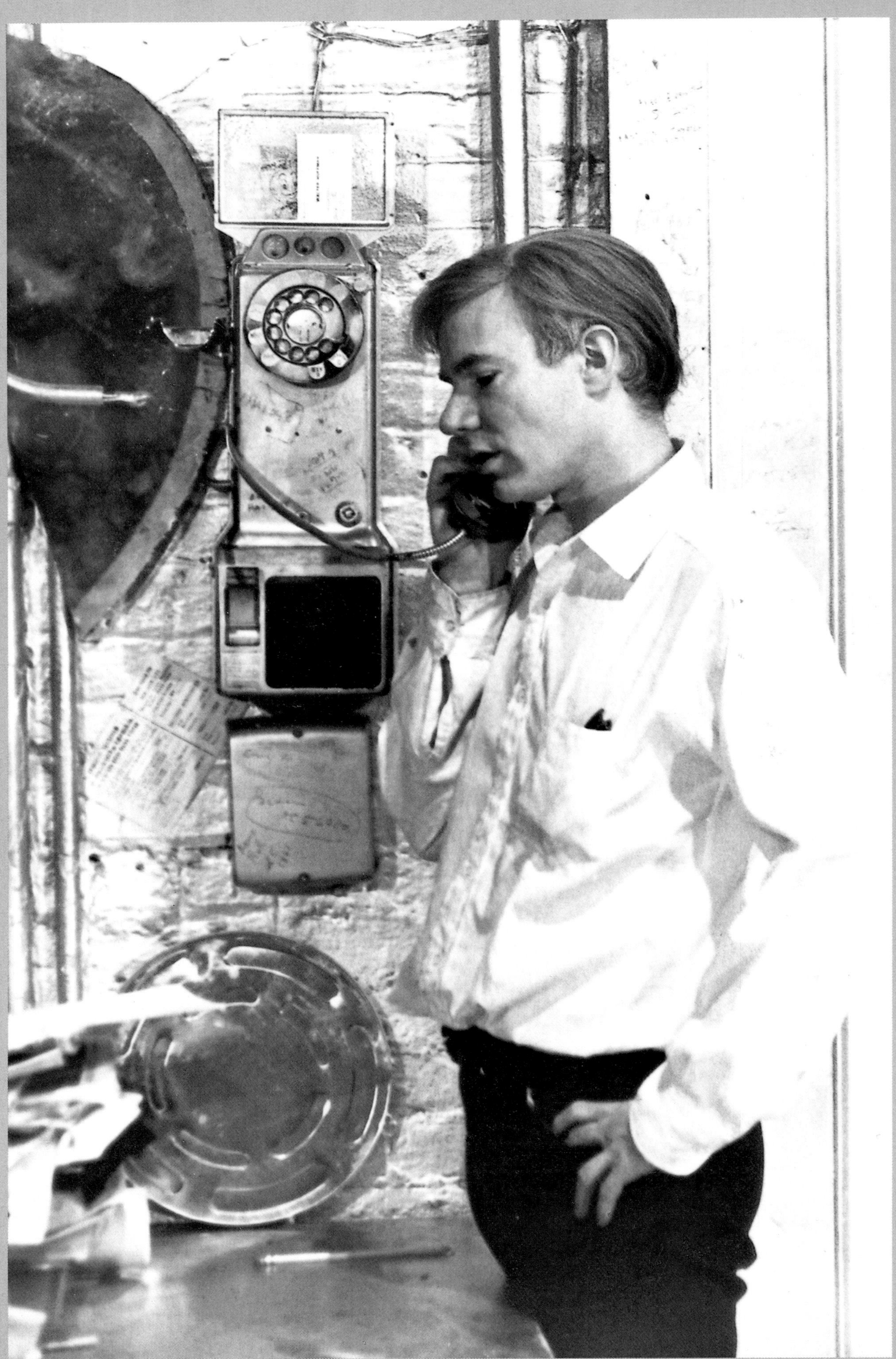

Andy Warhol, 1964. Photo: Billy Name

Illustrated Biography

The works by Andy Warhol shown here are not from the same collections as those included in the plate section. The respective owners are given in the captions.

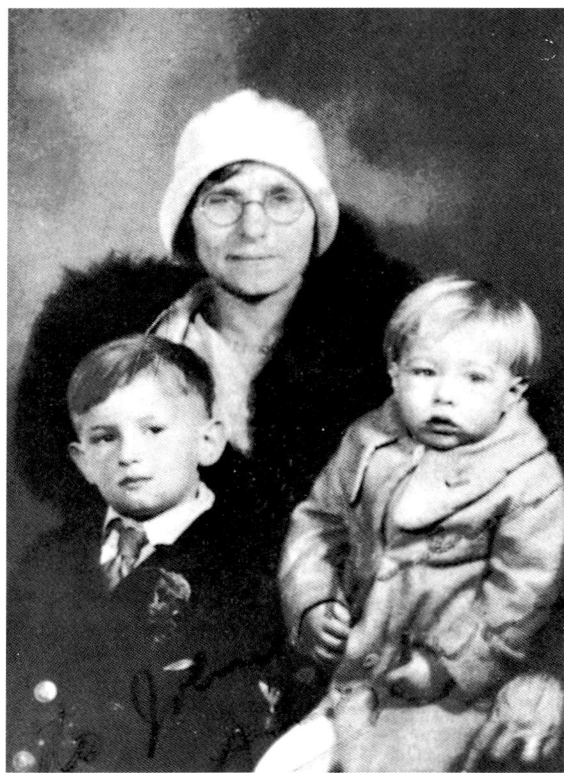

Warhol with his mother and his brother John, ca. 1931

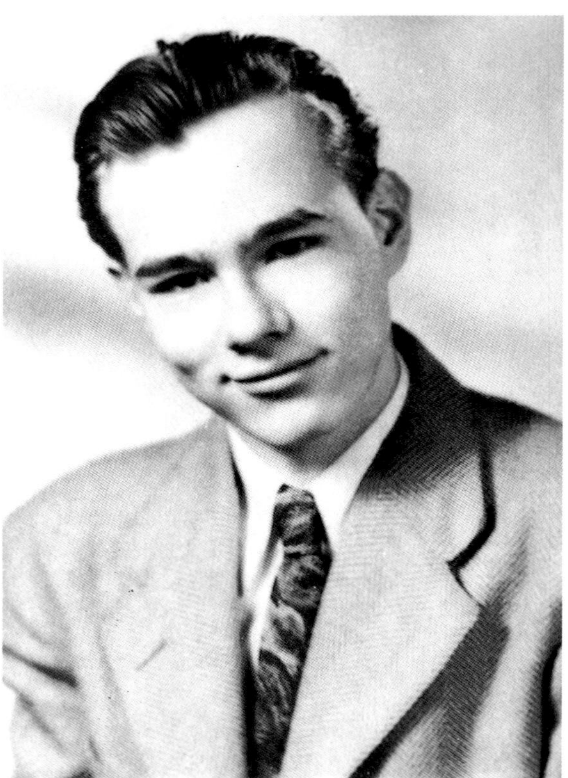

Warhol's school graduation photo, 1945

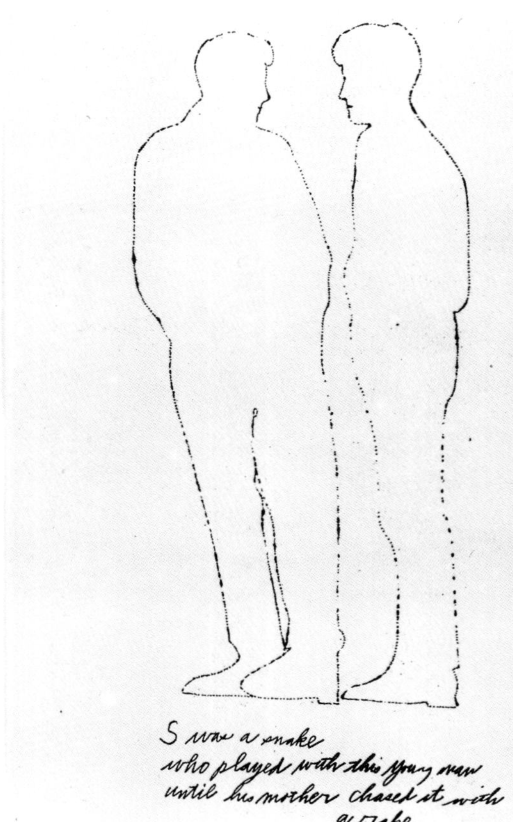

Illustration for Warhol's portfolio *A Is an Alphabet*, 1953. Offset lithography. Collection Richard F. Holmes

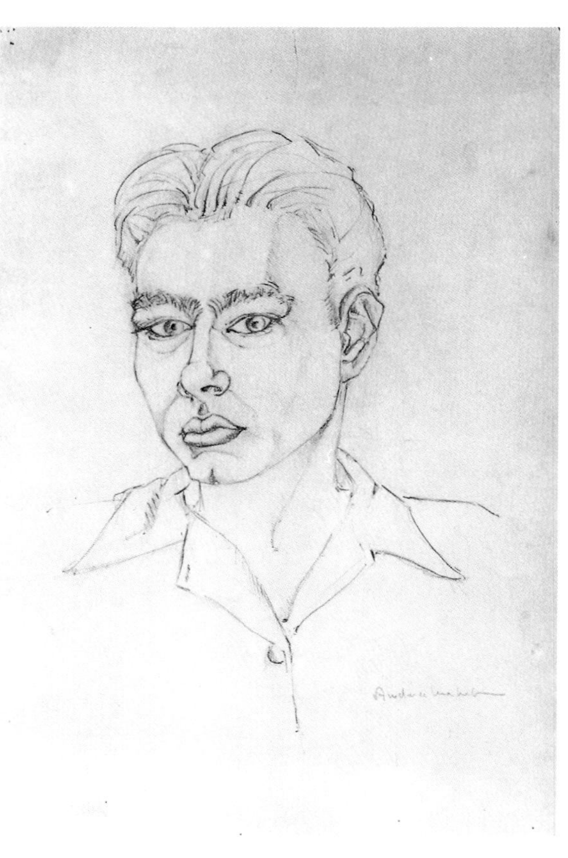

Self-portrait, 1942. Pencil on paper. 19 x 13 3/8". Private collection

1928
Andrew Warhola is born August 6 in Pittsburgh, Pennsylvania to Andrej and Julia Warhola. His parents are immigrants to the United States from Czechoslovakia. His father is a constsruction worker, and later a coal miner. His mother earned money from handicrafts, making flower sculptures out of fruit-tin cans and decorating Easter eggs. Andrew has two older brothers, Paul (born in 1922) and John (born in 1925).

1936-37
Suffers a nervous breakdown. While recuperating in bed, he cuts figures out of paper, paints, and fills coloring books. His brothers read to him, sometimes from the Dick Tracy comic strip, which he continues to read for the next few years. Drawings and paintings become his main interest, and he continues to collect autographed photographs of famous movie stars (a hobby of his since he was six).

1942
His father dies May 15.

At age fourteen, Warhol takes part in a study program at the Carnegie Institute of Technology in Pittsburgh (now Carnegie-Mellon University).

1945
Graduates from Schenley High School in Pittsburgh and enrolls at the Carnegie Institute of Technology to study drawing, pictorial and decorative art, and design. During his studies there, he meets Philip Pearlstein. Among his teachers are the artists Balcomb Greene and Robert Lepper. He experiments with the blotted-line technique, from which his reversing process develops.

1949-52
June 16. Graduates from the Carnegie Institute of Technology with a B. F. A. He shares an apartment with Philip Pearlstein. While looking for work as a graphic designer, he meets with Tina Fredericks, editor of *Glamour* magazine, who gives him his first assignment, to illustrate an article entitled "Success Is a Job in New York." He also works for *Vogue*, *Seventeen*, *The New Yorker, Harper's Bazaar*, as well as Tiffany & Co., Bergdorf Goodman, and Bonwit Teller, doing advertisements, window displays, book covers, record-album covers, and stationery.

He designs shoe advertisements for I. Miller, which appear in magazines and in the *New York Times*.

The credit line for his first illustration for *Glamour* reads "Andy Warhol," the first time he uses this name.

Lives with his mother in New York. Fritzie Miller is his agent for graphic work. He becomes one of the most sought-after illustrators of women's accessories in New York; for his design of newspaper advertisements, he receives the "Art Directors' Club Medal." Illustrates *Amy Vanderbilt's Complete Book of Etiquette*.

His first ***one-man show***: "Andy Warhol: Fifteen Drawings Based on the Writings of Truman Capote," Hugo Gallery, New York, 1952.

1953
Illustrates, with Ralph Thomas Ward, known as "Corkie," *A Is an Alphabet*, *There Was Snow on the Street and Rain in the Sky*, and *Love Is a Pink Cake*.

He is a member of the drama group "Theater 12," and designs several sets of stage scenery.

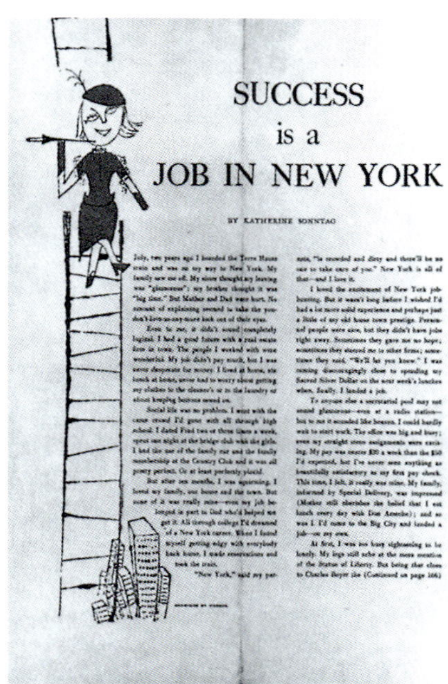
SUCCESS
is a
JOB IN NEW YORK

BY KATHERINE SONNTAG

Illustration for "Success Is a Job in New York" published in *Glamour* magazine, 1949

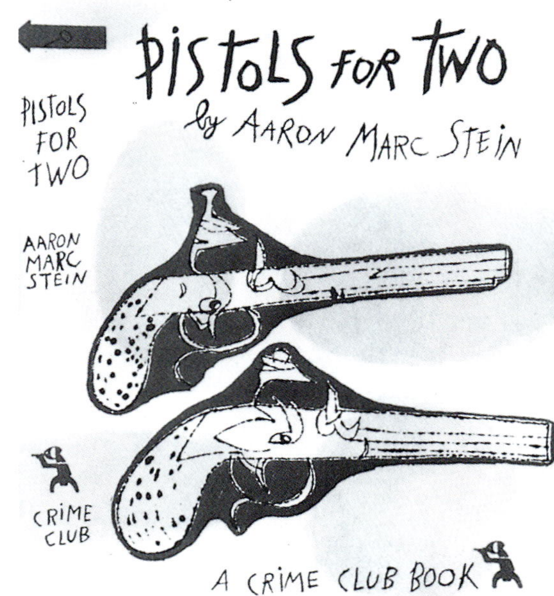

Pistols for two, design for a book cover, ca. 1951

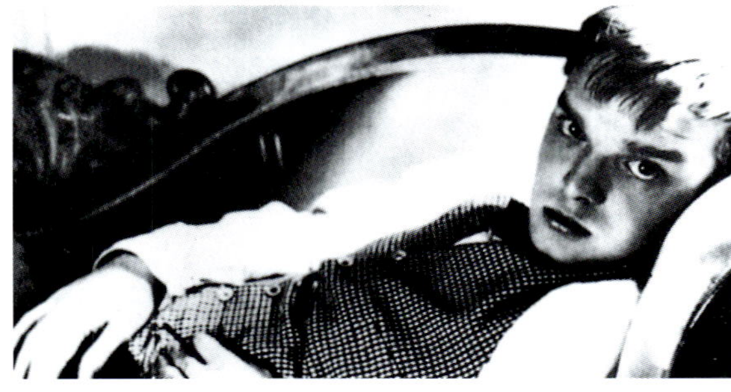
Photo of Truman Capote on the cover of his novel, *Other Voices, Other Rooms*, 1948.
Photo: Howard Halma

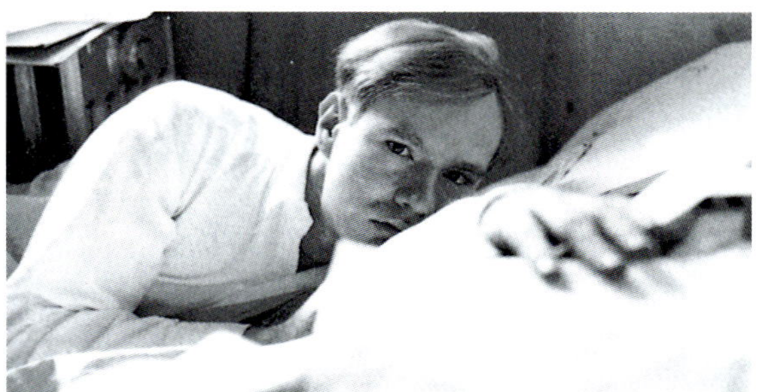
Warhol imitating Truman Capote, ca. 1949.
Photo: Duane Michals

Truman Capote, 1979. Acrylic and silkscreen on canvas. Two panels, each 40 x 40".
Dia Art Foundation, New York

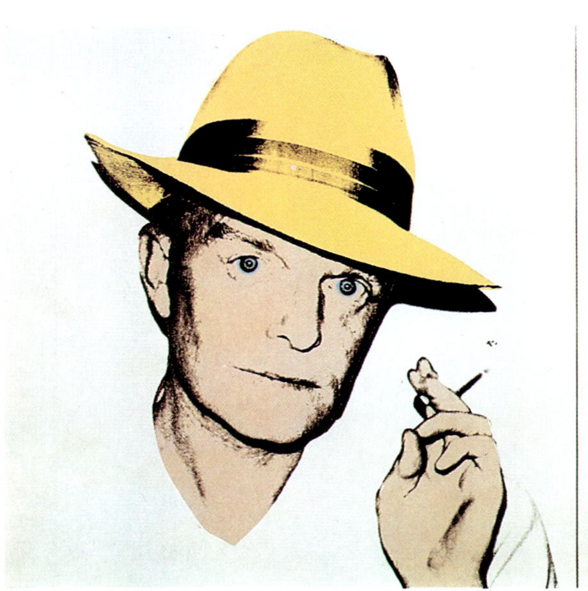
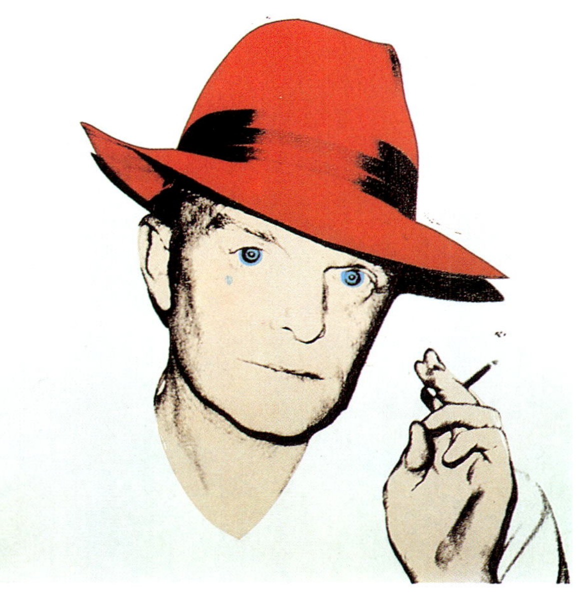

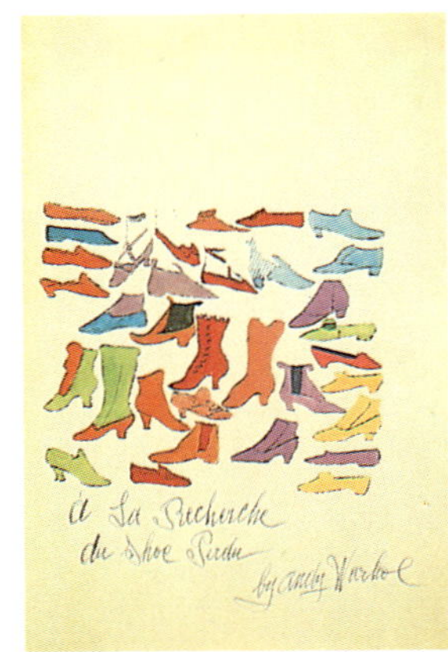

A La Recherche du Shoe Perdu, 1955. Offset lithography, watercolor and ink on paper. Cover (26 x 20"); 16 of 17 prints, each 9 3/4 x 13 3/4". Andy Warhol Estate

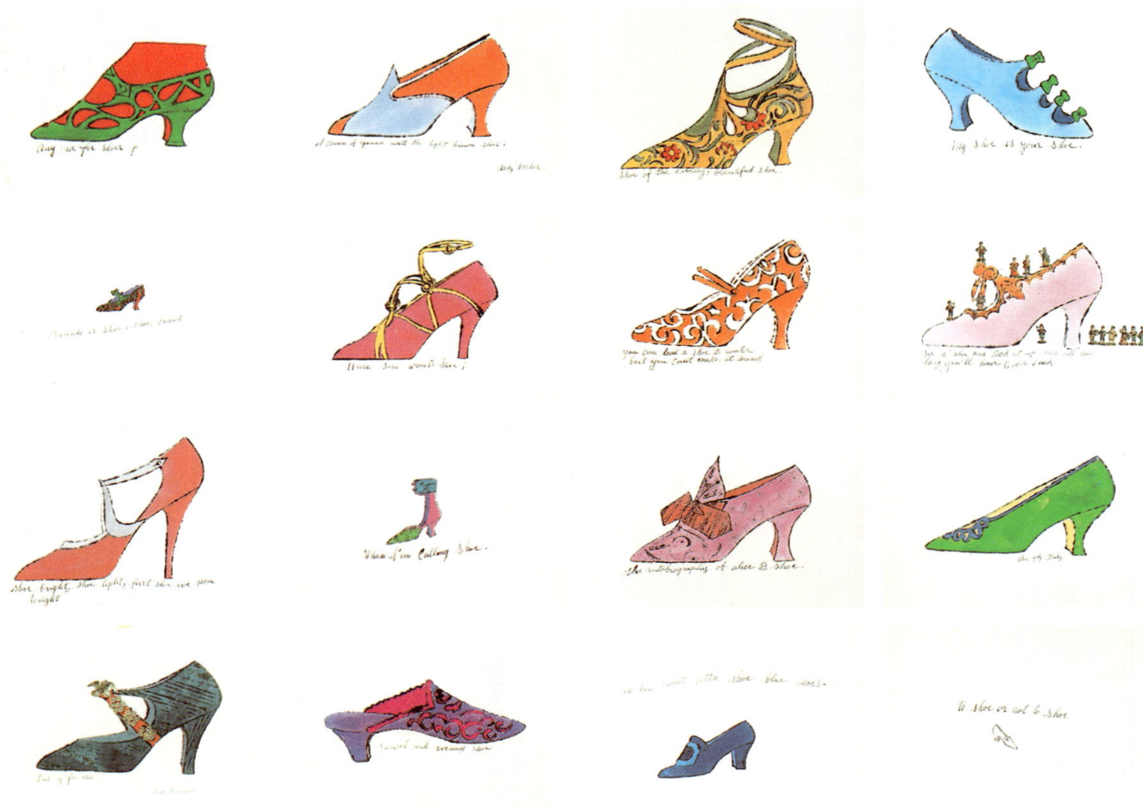

View of the exhibition "Andy Warhol: His Early Works, 1947-1959," Gotham Book Mart Gallery, New York, 1971

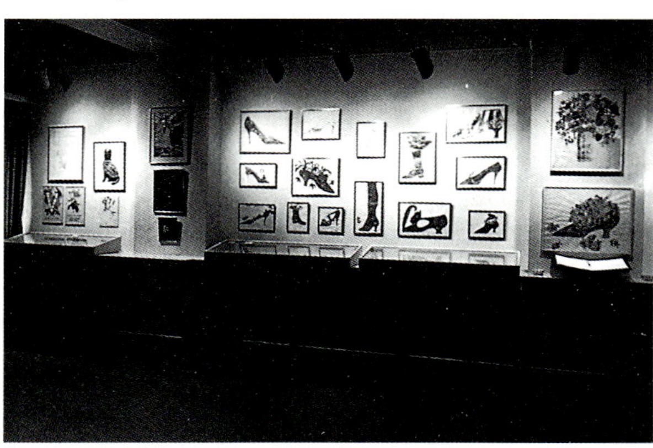

Babs, ca. 1956. India ink, collage, gold and silver leaf on paper, 12 x 16". Andy Warhol Estate

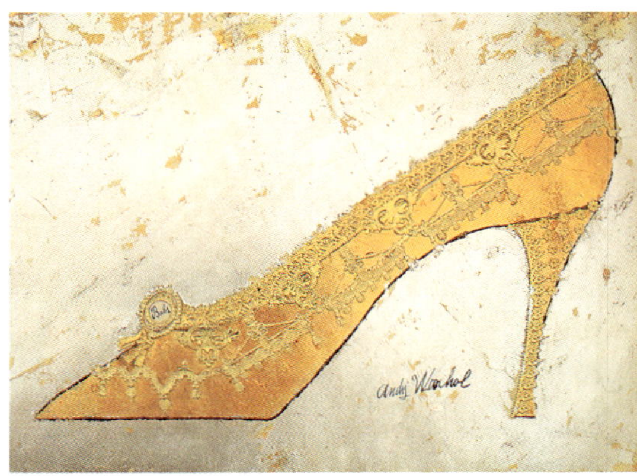

1954
"Certificate of Excellence" from the American Institute of Graphic Arts, an award he receives several times.

Illustrates and hand-colors *25 Cats Name Sam and One Blue Pussy*, with texts by Charles Lisanby.

October. "Warhol," a ***one-man show*** at a loft gallery in New York.

1955
Illustrates a book by Ralph Pomeroy: *A La Recherche du Shoe Perdu*. The texts are handwritten by Warhol's mother. Illustrates *In the Bottom of my Garden*.

1956
The Art Directors' Club honors Warhol for outstanding achievements, and he receives a second "Certificate of Excellence" from the American Institute of Graphic Arts for his commercial prints.

Makes a trip around the world, from June 16 to August 12, with Lisbany. He makes numerous sketchbooks during the journey.

Has first group exhibition, "Recent Drawings U.S.A.," Museum of Modern Art, New York, in which he exhibits shoe drawings. ***One-man shows***: "For a Boy," Bodley Gallery, New York, and "Andy Warhol: The Golden Slipper Show or Shoes Shoe in America," Bodley Gallery, New York.

1957
Receives the "Art Directors' Club Award for Distinctive Merit" and the "Art Directors' Club Medal," both for newspaper advertising art.

Illustrates and publishes *A Gold Book*, consisting of blotted-line drawings on gold paper, which was sent as a promotional item for Christmas.

Establishes the Andy Warhol Enterprises, Inc. for his commercial work.

Sells "personality" shoe collages at Serendipity.

Warhol has an operation to alter his nose.

Designs a book cover for *Madhouse on Washington Square*, published by J. B. Lippincott; it becomes a billboard in Times Square.

One-man show: "A Show of Golden Pictures by Andy Warhol," Bodley Gallery, New York.

1958

Warhol acquires a drawing by Jasper Johns entitled *Light Bulb*.

1959

Purchases a town house at 1342 Lexington Avenue in New York, near 89th Street, and moves there with his mother. Together with Suzie Frankfurt, publishes the humorous cookbook *Wild Raspberries*. The American Institute of Graphic Arts awards him a "Certificate of Excellence" for work carried out in 1958.

Warhol and his associate Nathan Gluck design wrapping paper using hand-carved stamps; Warhol meets the filmmaker Emile de Antonio.

One-man show: "Wild Raspberries," Bodley Gallery, New York.

1960

Makes first canvases of comic-strip characters such as Batman, Dick Tracy, Nancy, Saturday's Popeye, and Superman. He also makes his first paintings of commercial products, such as Coca-Cola bottles.

Filmmaker De Antonio introduces Warhol to painter Frank Stella.

Warhol meets Billy Linich, known later as Billy Name, who works with him and remains in his circle during the 1960s, also photographing Warhol and the Factory. A design by Warhol for a child's birthday party is reproduced in the book *Tiffany Table Settings*.

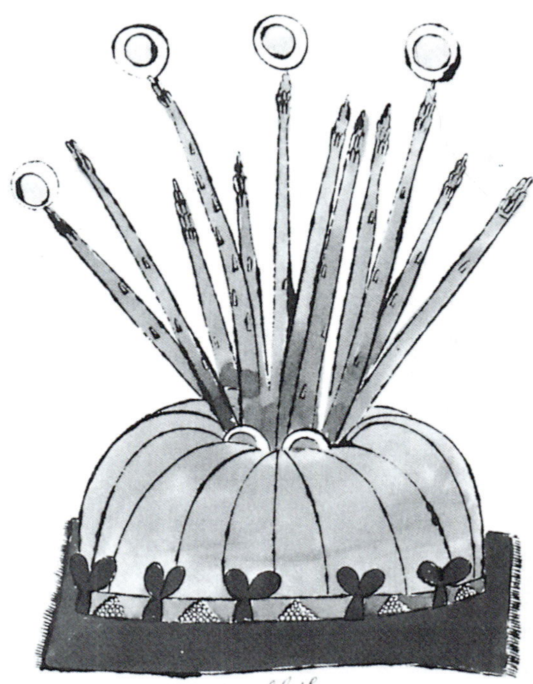

Page from *Wild Raspberries*, 1959. Texts handwritten by Warhol's mother

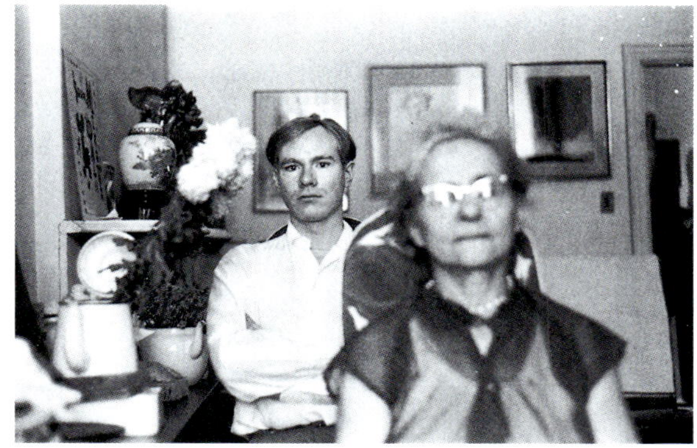

Andy Warhol and Julia Warhola, 1958. Photo: Duane Michals

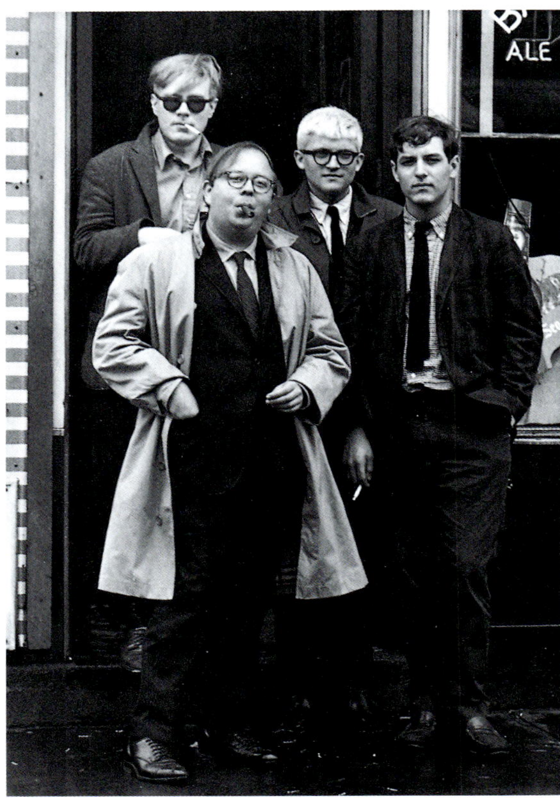

Right: Andy Warhol, Henry Geldzahler, David Hockney, and Geoffrey Goodman, 1963. Photo: Dennis Hopper

Superman, 1960. Acrylic and pastel on canvas, 67 x 52 3/8". Collection Gunter Sachs

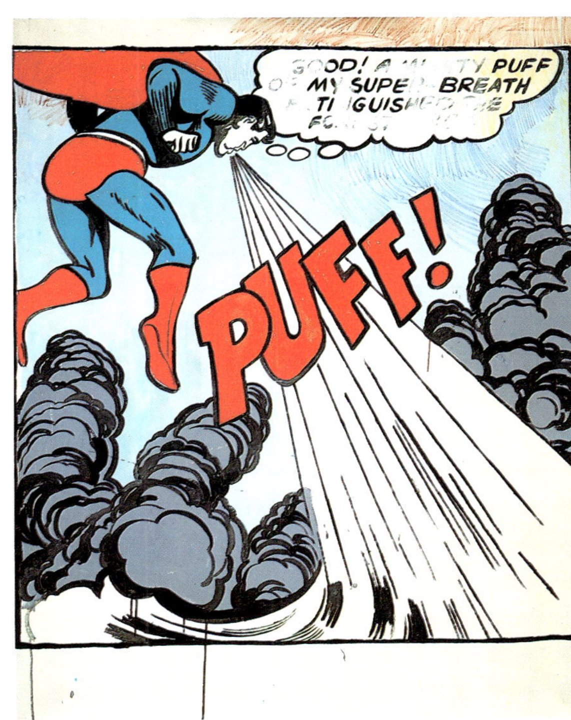

Henry Geldzahler, 1979. Acrylic and silkscreen on canvas, 40 x 40". Collection Henry Geldzahler

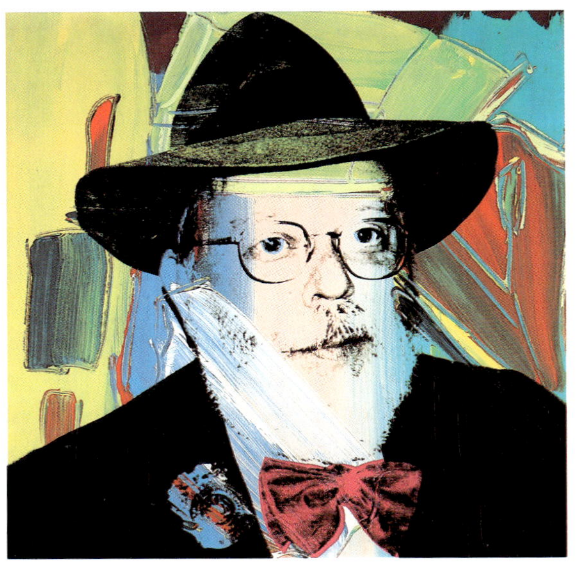

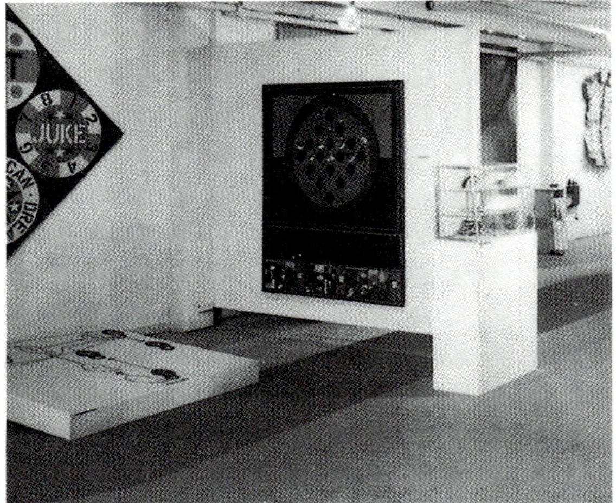

View of the exhibition "The New Realists," Sidney Janis Gallery, New York, 1962. *Dance Diagram* by Warhol (lower left)

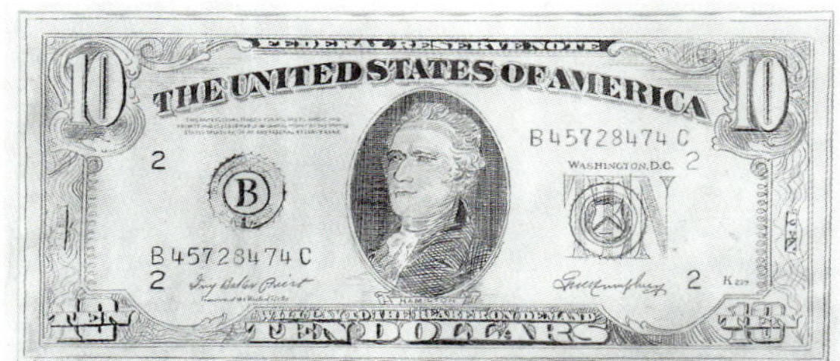

Ten-Dollar Bill, 1962. Pencil and watercolor on paper, 10 x 23″. Private collection, New York

Right: *Front and Back Dollar Bills*, 1962. Silkscreen on canvas, two panels, each 83 x 19″. Collection Jed Johnson

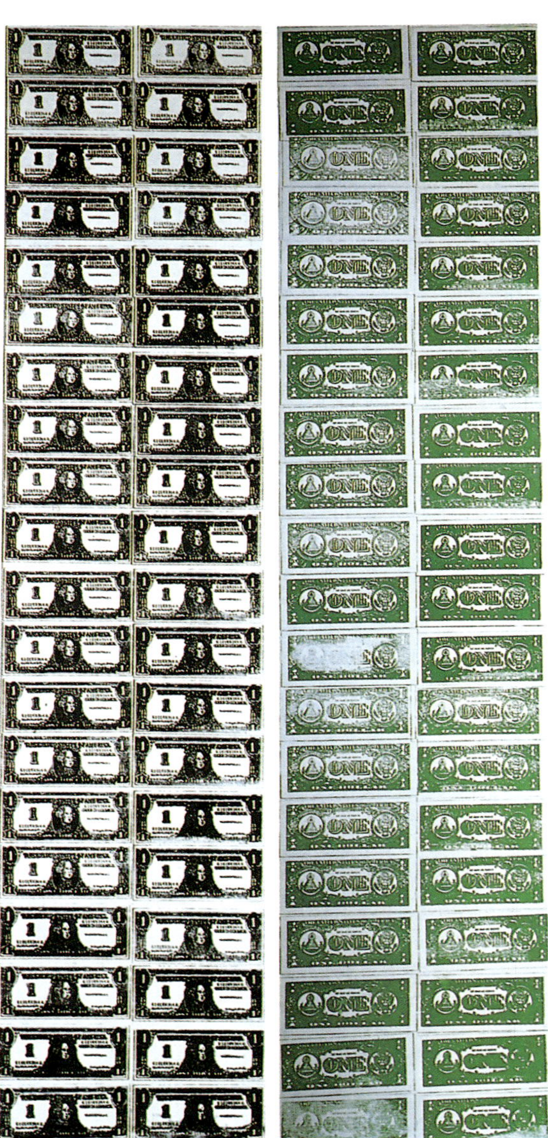

Do It Yourself (Landscape), 1962. Acrylic and Prestype lettering on canvas, 70 x 54″. Museum Ludwig, Cologne

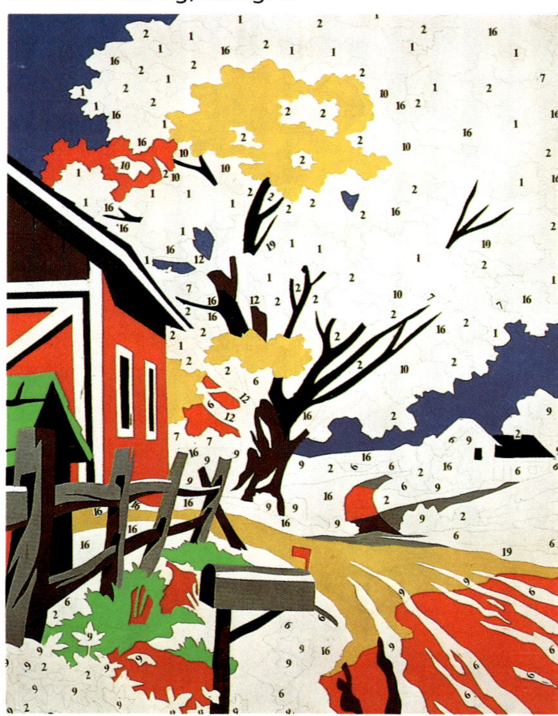

129 Die in Jet (Plane Crash), 1962. Acrylic and silkscreen on canvas, 100 x 72″. Museum Ludwig, Cologne

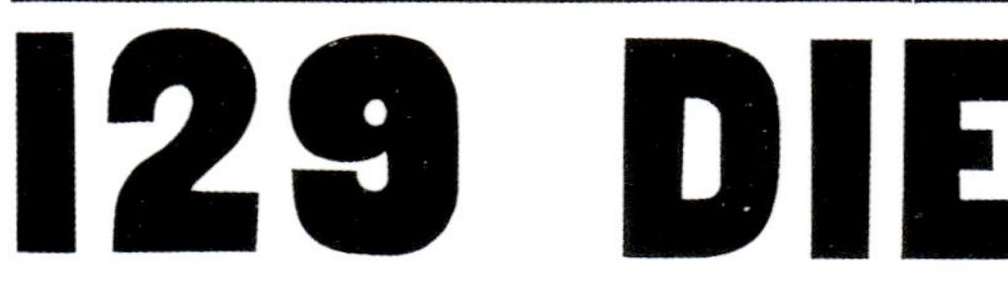

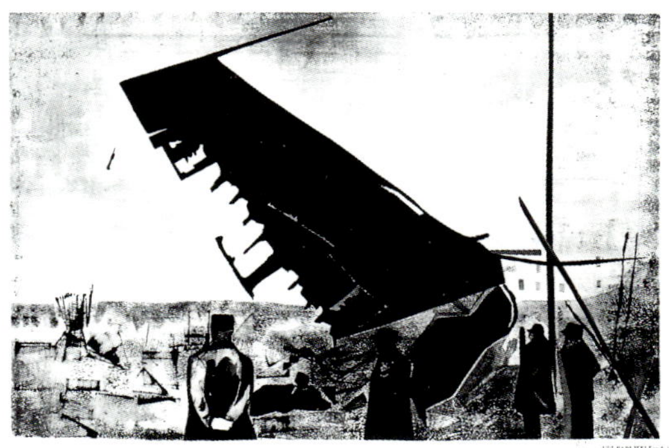

1961
He is commissioned to illustrate *Amy Vanderbilt's Complete Cookbook*, but in fact has his friend Ted Carey do the work, and pays him for it.

To his astonishment, Warhol sees Roy Lichtenstein's paintings of comic strips in the Leo Castelli Gallery. He invites Ivan Karp, who works at the gallery, to his studio to see his own comic strip paintings.

Meets Henry Geldzahler, who is on the curatorial staff of the Metropolitan Museum of Art in New York.

In April, he is invited to display *Advertisement, Before and After, Little King, Saturday's Popeye*, and *Superman*, as a background for mannequins in the store windows of Bonwit Teller on Fifth Avenue and 57th Street.

1962
Death of 129 people on June 4 in a jet accident, which becomes the subject of Warhol's first "Death and Disaster" series.

Further series: Campbell's Soup Cans, Disaster and Do It Yourself paintings, Elvis Presley and Marilyn portraits. First silkscreens on canvas: dollar bills and baseball pictures, as well as portraits of the actors Troy Donahue and Warren Beatty. He uses rubber stamps for *S & H Green Stamps* and *Red Air Mail Stamps*. He makes a Coca-Cola print from a balsawood block. He starts experiments with oxidation paintings, which he resumes in 1978. He places canvases on street sidewalks so as to include the footprints of passers-by.

De Antonio introduces Warhol to Eleanor Ward from the Stable Gallery in New York, who later exhibits his work. Geldzahler brings Robert Rauschenberg to Warhol's studio. Warhol buys six small paintings by Frank Stella, and another of his purchases around this time is *Box in a Valise*, by Marcel Duchamp, of whom he is a considerable admirer.

Exhibits "Dance Diagrams" at the exhibition "The New Realists," Sidney Janis Gallery, New York.

One-man-shows: "Campbell's Soup Cans," Ferus Gallery, Los Angeles; "Andy Warhol," Stable Gallery, New York, (Dance Diagrams, Marilyns, Coca-Cola, Disaster and Do It Yourself paintings, *Handle with Care-Glass-Thank You*, and *Red Elvis*).

1963

Warhol starts two series of canvases, "Electric Chairs," and "Race Riots" (based on a photograph of clashes between civil rights demonstrators and the police in Birmingham, Alabama, published in *Life* on May 17, 1963). He begins a series of Jacqueline Kennedy portraits after President John F. Kennedy is assassinated on November 22.

Purchases a 16-mm movie camera and shoots his first film, *Sleep*. He also films *Andy Warhol Films Jack Smith Filming "Normal Love,"* the films *Blow Job*, *Dance Movie*, *Eat*, *Haircut*, *Kiss*, *Salome and Delilah*, and *Tarzan and Jane Regained... Sort of*.

Creates a layout for *Harper's Bazaar*, for the first time using photographs taken in a photo booth.

Creates a costume concept for the Broadway musical *The Beast in Me* by James Thurber.

Warhol moves his studio to a firehouse on East 87th Street. Later in the year, he moves his studio again to 231 East 47th Street, which becomes known as the Factory. Billy Name moves in, and covers the Factory in aluminum foil and silver paint. For the

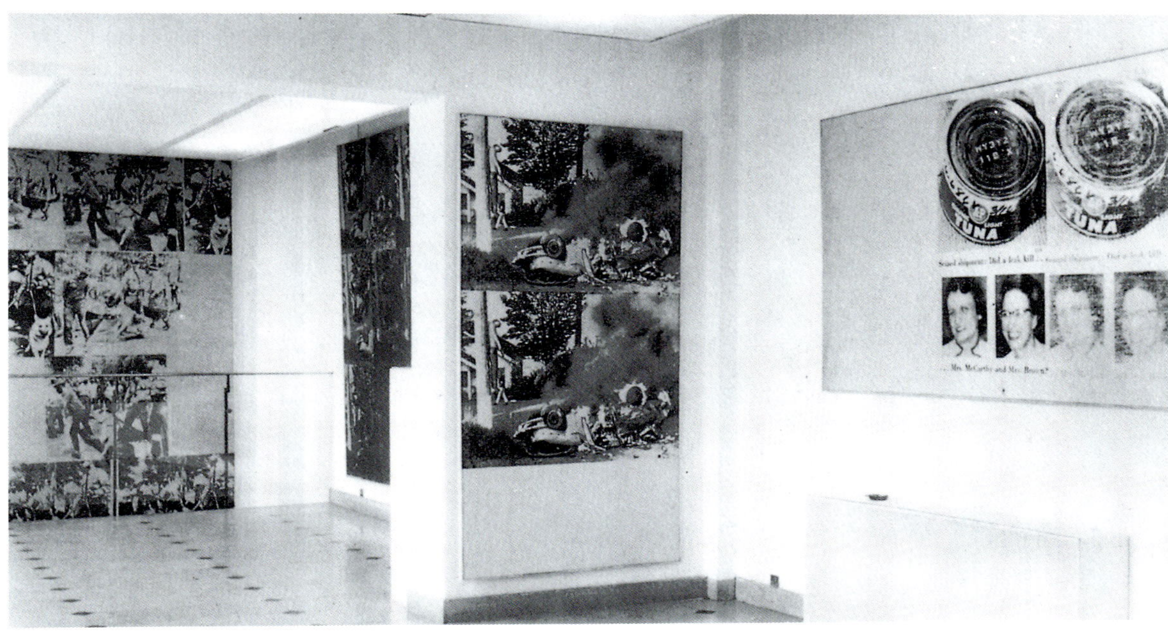

View of the exhibition "Warhol," Galerie Ileana Sonnabend, Paris, 1964

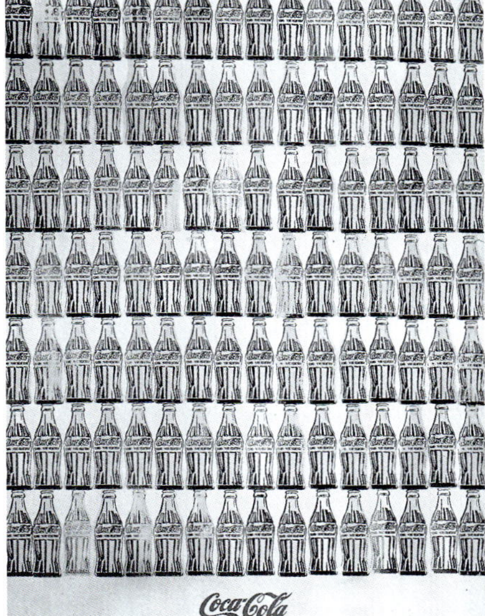

Green Coca-Cola Bottles, 1962. Oil on canvas, 82x57". Whitney Museum of American Art, New York. Acquired from funds of the Friends of the Whitney Museum of American Art

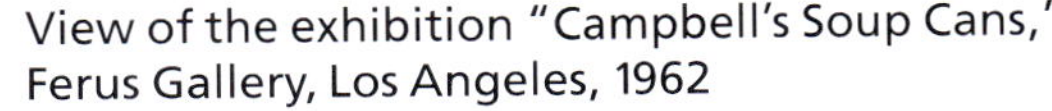

View of the exhibition "Campbell's Soup Cans," Ferus Gallery, Los Angeles, 1962

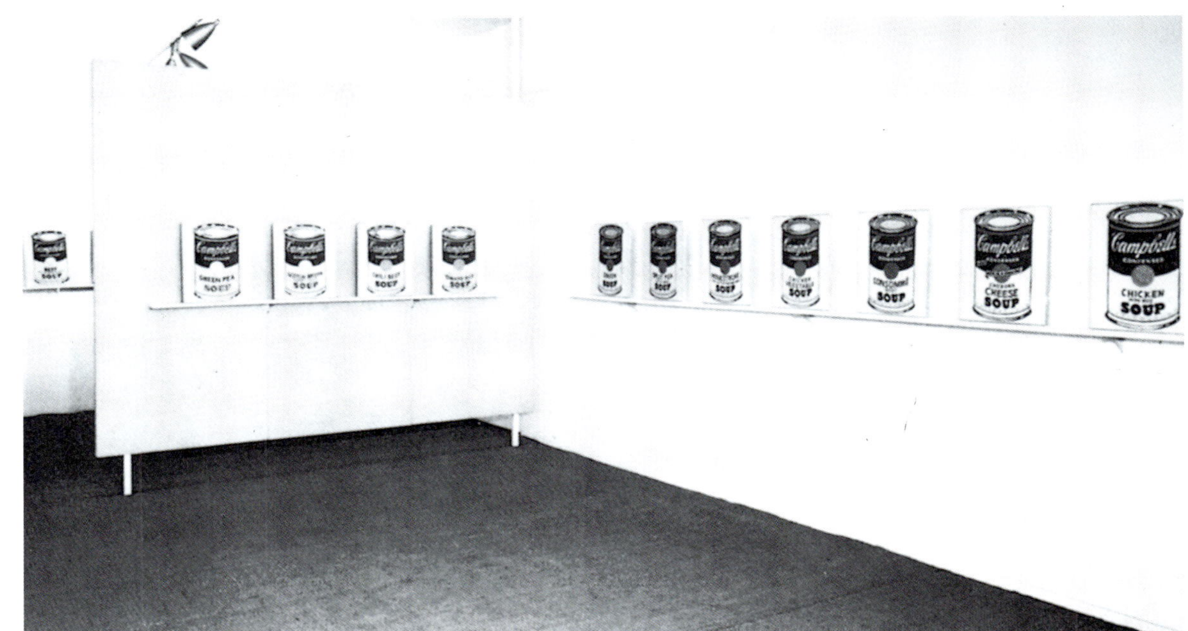

first time, Warhol uses a Polaroid camera to produce a cover for the magazine, *C.*

Gerard Malanga, a young poet, becomes Warhol's main assistant, (working with him until 1967 and from 1968 to 1970). Appearing in Warhol's films are "baby" Jane Holzer, Brigid Polk (Brigid Berlin), and Ondine (Robert Olivio), who all become frequenters of the Factory.

Warhol meets Jonas Mekas, director of the Filmmakers' Cooperative, who shows many Warhol films for the first time. Warhol replaces the gray wig, which he has worn since the early 1950s, with a silver-sprayed wig.

He travels by car to Los Angeles with Malanga, painter Wynn Chamberlain, and actor Taylor Mead, to attend the opening of his exhibition at the Ferus Gallery. While in California, he attends the opening of a Marcel Duchamp retrospective at the Pasadena Art Museum, and meets Marcel Duchamp whom he later films.

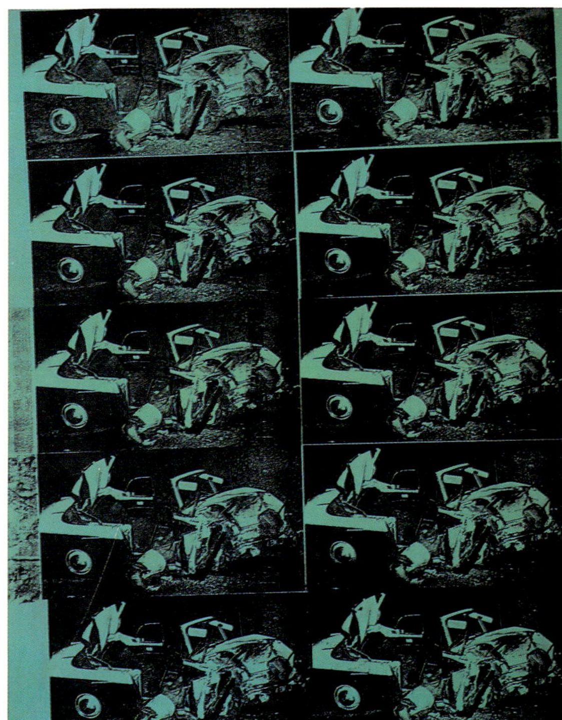

Green Disaster Ten Times, 1963. Acrylic and silkscreen on canvas, 105 1/4 x 79 1/8". Museum für Moderne Kunst, Frankfurt

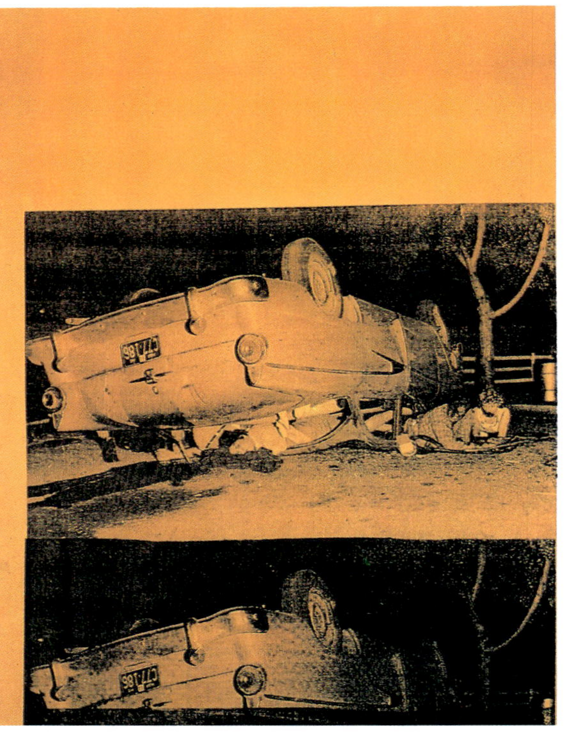

Five Death on Orange, 1963. Acrylic and silkscreen on canvas, 44 1/8 x 33". Private collection

Lower right: *Self-Portraits*, ca. 1964. Photobooth pictures, strip of four images, each 7 3/4 x 1 5/8". Collection Robert Mapplethorpe

Left and right: Warhol filming in New York in the 1960s. Photo: Billy Name

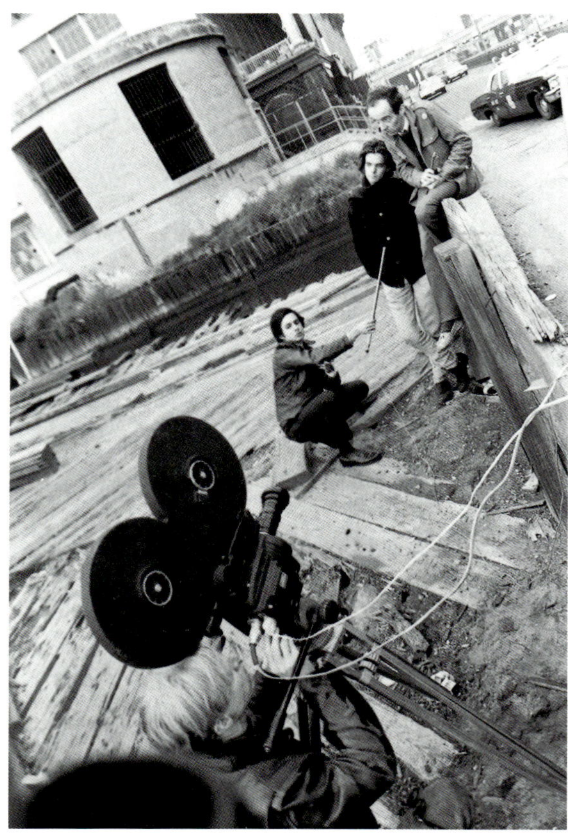

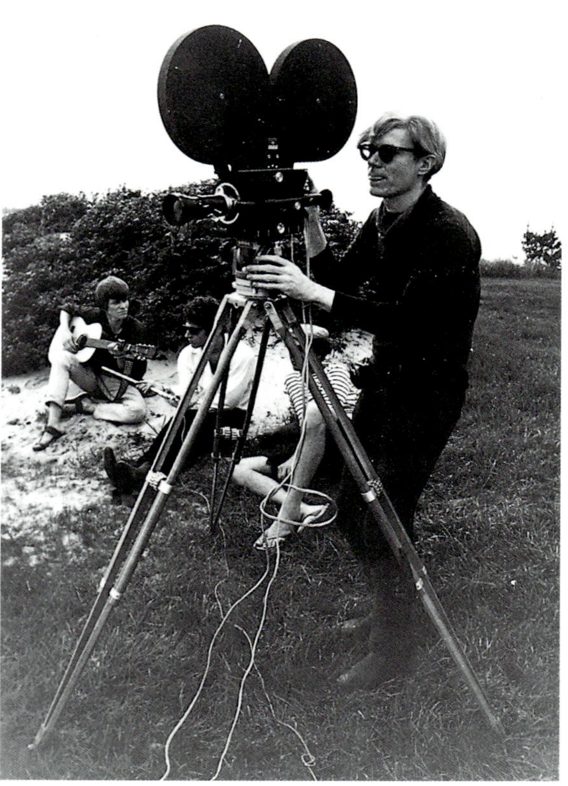

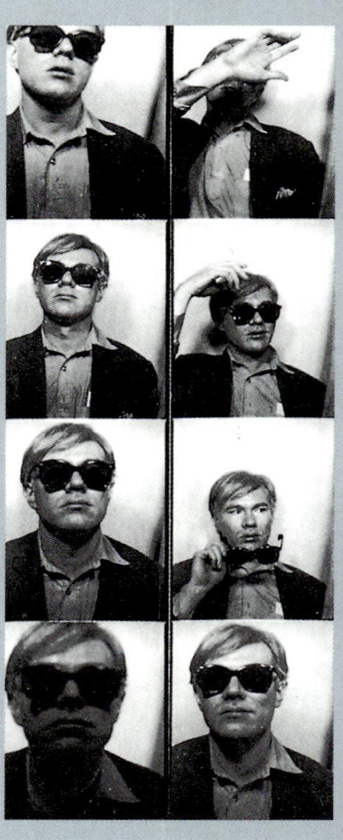

One-man show: "Andy Warhol," Ferus Gallery, Los Angeles (portraits of Liz Taylor and Elvis Presley).

1964
He is commissioned to create a work for the New York State Pavilion, designed by architect Philip Johnson, at the New York World's Fair. He produces *Thirteen Most Wanted Men*, which is hung on the facade of the building. Fair officials feel the work is too political and controversial, and ask Warhol's permission to paint over it. He agrees.
Warhol receives the "Independent Film Award" from the magazine *Film Culture*. The photographer of the image that Warhol used for his flower paintings sues Warhol. The dispute is later settled out of court.
A woman with a gun enters the Factory and shoots at a group of four "Marilyns."

One-man shows: "Warhol," Galerie Ileana Sonnabend, Paris (Disaster paintings); "Warhol," Stable Gallery, New York (Boxes); and "Andy Warhol," Leo Castelli Gallery, New York (Flowers).

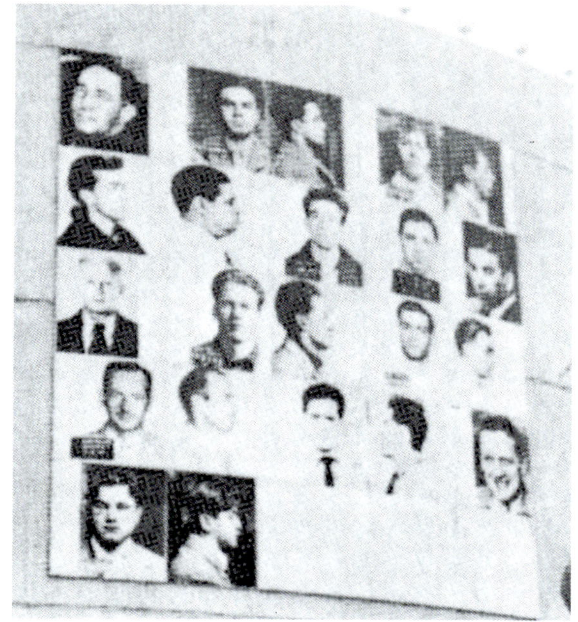
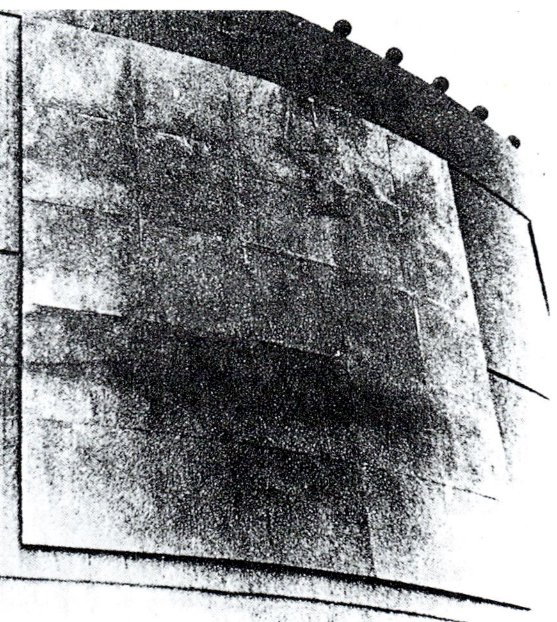

Thirteen Most Wanted Men, 1964. Installation at the New York State Pavilion, World Fair, New York. Silkscreen on fiberboard, 25 panels, 48x48" (each), 240x240" (total). Left: original condition; right: covered with aluminum paint. The Museum of Modern Art, New York

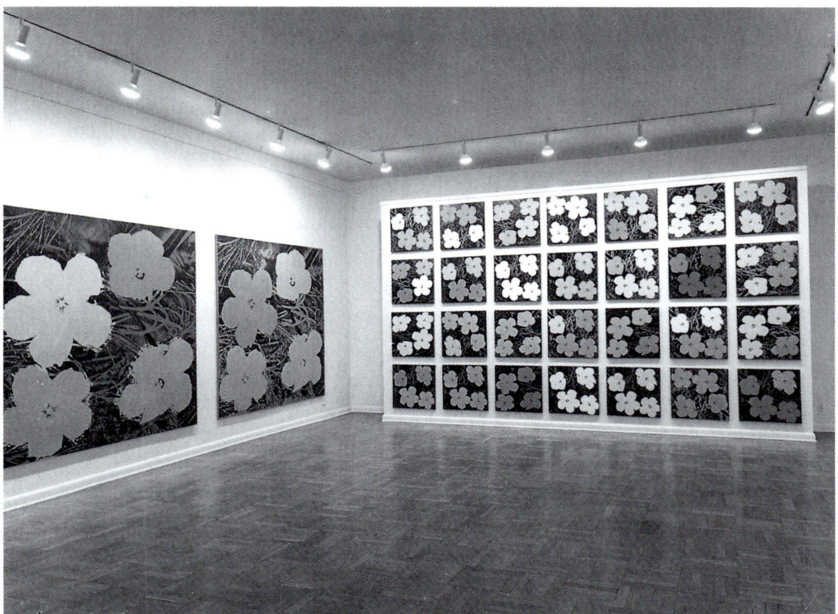

View of the exhibition "Andy Warhol," Leo Castelli Gallery, New York, 1964

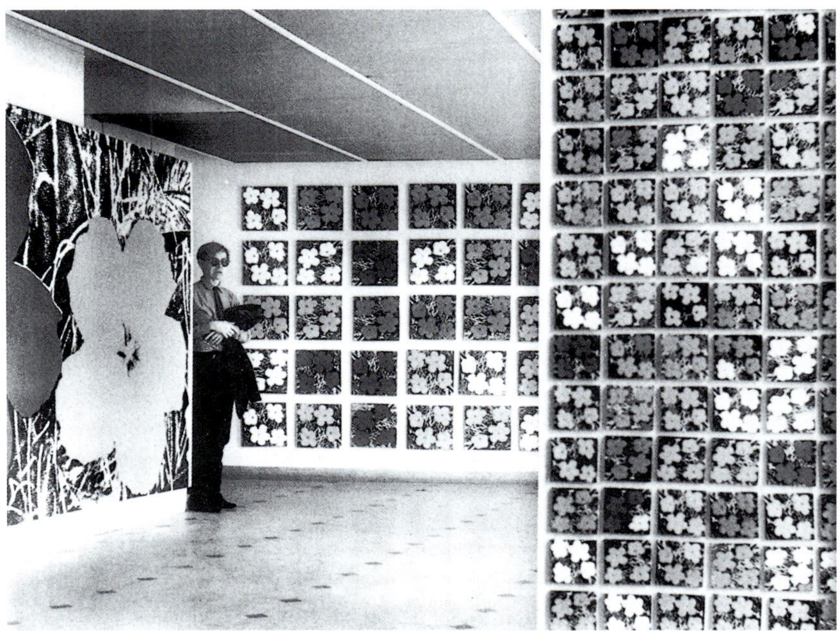

View of the exhibition "Andy Warhol," Galerie Ileana Sonnabend, Paris, 1965

View of the exhibition "Andy Warhol," Leo Castelli Gallery, New York, 1966

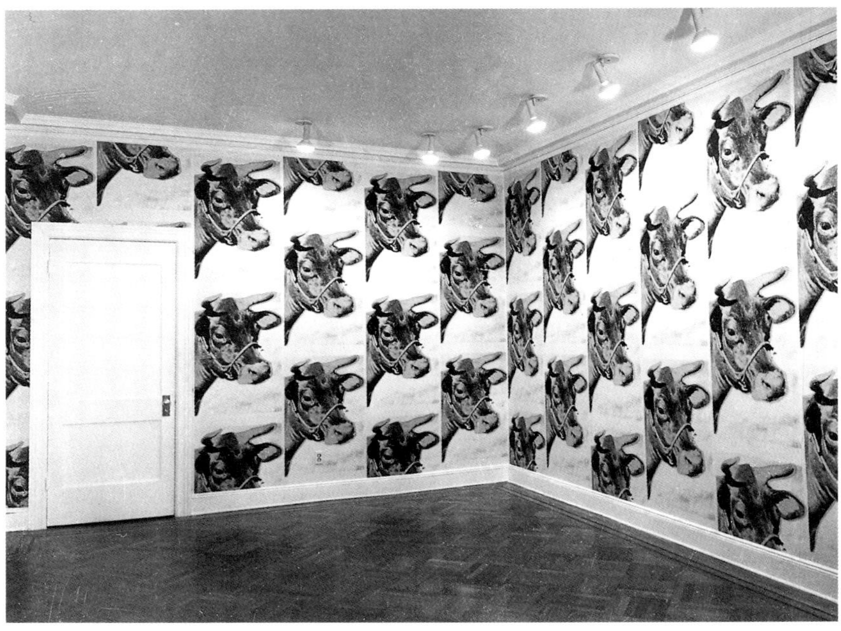

Left center: Merce Cunningham and an ensemble member in *Rain Forest*, 1968. Photo: James Klosty

Right center: *Silver Clouds* in the Leo Castelli Gallery, New York, 1966. Metallized polyester film with helium, each 39 x 59 x ca. 15"

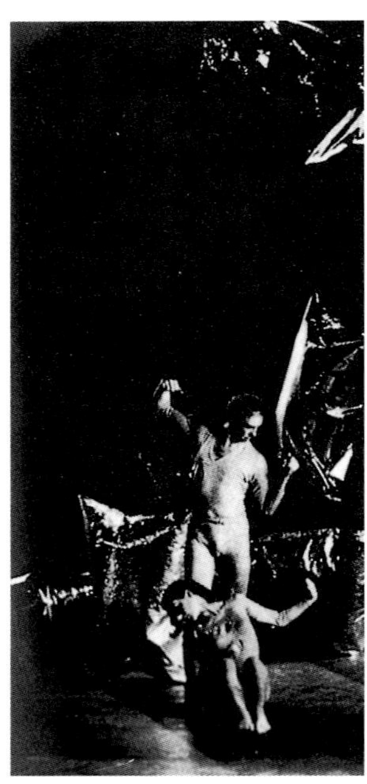

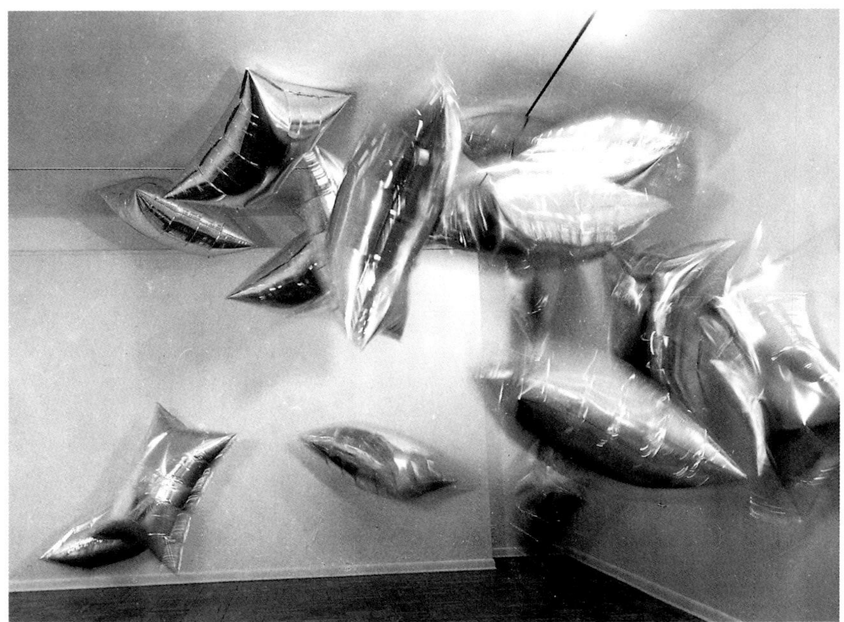

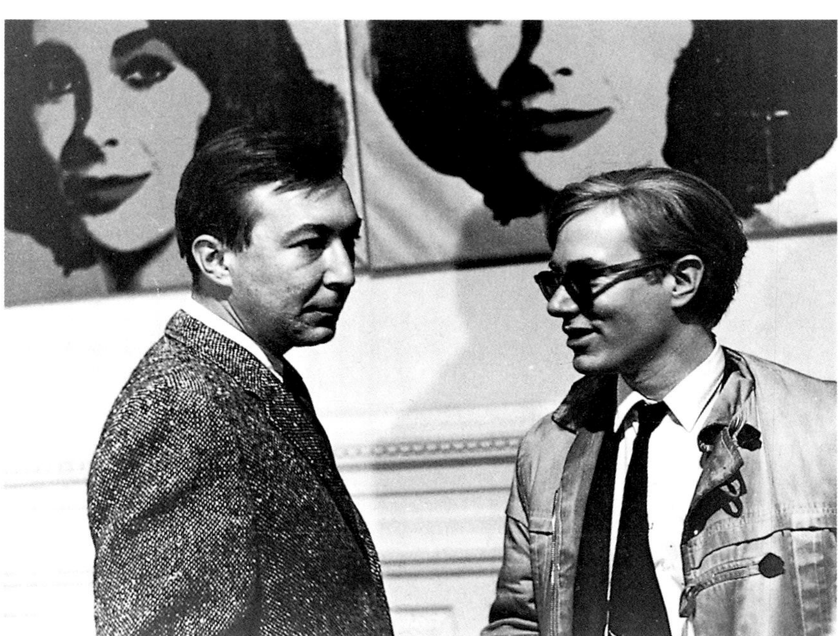

Left: Jasper Johns and Andy Warhol in the Factory, 1964. Photo: Billy Name

Right: Andy Warhol and Marisol, Stable Gallery, 1964. Photo: Billy Name

1965
In Paris, where his "Flower" paintings are on show at the Galerie Ileana Sonnabend, Warhol announces his intention to retire from painting and focus on filmmaking.

The first multicolored Campbell's Soup Can paintings. Designs a cover for *Time* magazine, using photographs taken in a photo booth.

Gerard Malanga introduces Warhol to filmmaker Paul Morrissey, who becomes vital to his film production at the Factory.

Lester Persky, a film producer, gives "The Fifty Most Beautiful People" party at the Factory. Judy Garland, Rudolf Nureyev, Tennessee Williams, Juliet Prowse, Allen Ginsberg, and Montgomery Clift, among others, attend.

One-man shows: "Andy Warhol," Galerie Ileana Sonnabend, Paris (Flowers); "Andy Warhol," Galeria Rubbers, Buenos Aires; Jerrold Morris International Gallery, Toronto; "Andy Warhol," Institute of Contemporary Art, University of Pennsylvania, Philadelphia; and "Warhol," Gian Enzo Sperone, Turin.

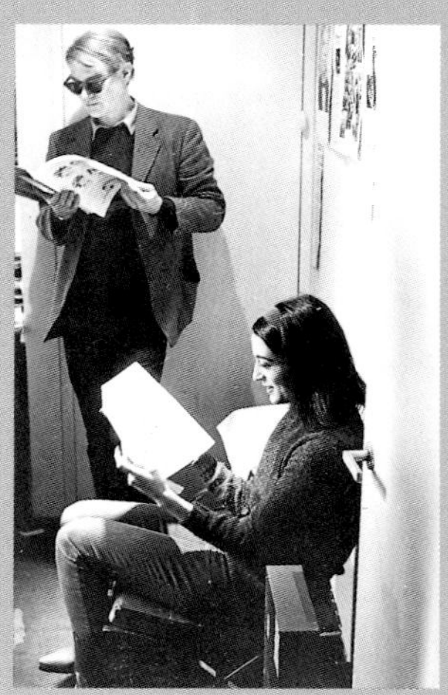

1966
At Castelli's, Warhol exhibits wallpaper with a cow pattern, and silver clouds filled with helium.
Begins to produce multimedia presentations called *The Erupting* (later changed to *Exploding*) *Plastic Inevitable*, featuring Nico and the Velvet Underground. The events include live music, dance, monologues by Factory performers, and bands performing against a background of Warhol's films.
Accompanies the Velvet Underground to various concerts.

One-man shows: "Warhol," Gian Enzo Sperone, Turin; "Andy Warhol," Leo Castelli Gallery, New York; "Andy Warhol Holy Cow! Silver Clouds!! Holy Cow!," Contemporary Arts Center, Cincinnati; "Andy Warhol," Institute of Contemporary Art, Boston; and Ferus Gallery, Los Angeles.

1967
"Electric Chairs." Continues making films. He produces the Velvet Underground's first album, for which he designs the famous

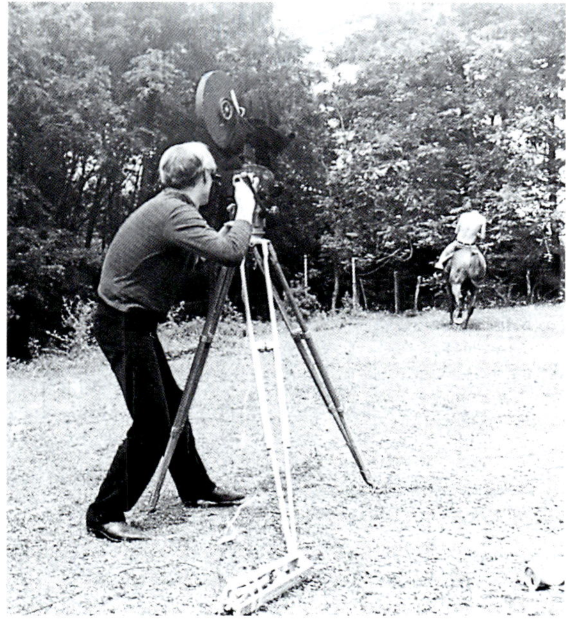

Left: Warhol filming in New York, 1964

Left center: Andy Warhol in the Factory in the early 1960s. Photo: Billy Name

Right center: The first issue of *Interview*, 1969

Lower left: Warhol in the Factory in front of his *Self-Portrait*. Photo: Billy Name

Lower center: From above, clockwise: Warhol with Nico's son on his lap, Lou Reed, Nico, John Cale, Maureen Tucker, Mary Woronov, Sterling Morrison, and Gerard Malanga

Lower right: Warhol filming in New York, 1964. Photo: Billy Name

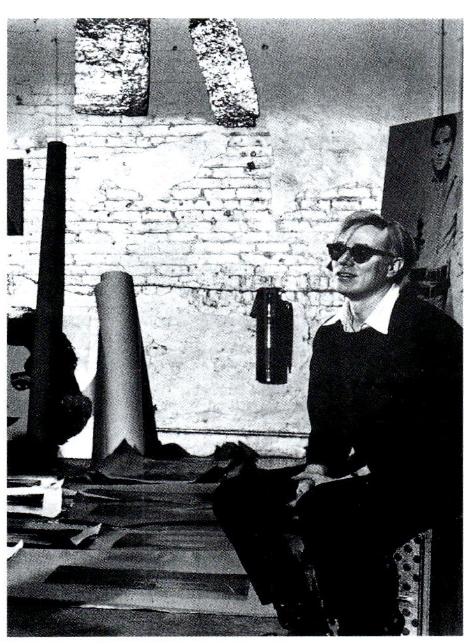

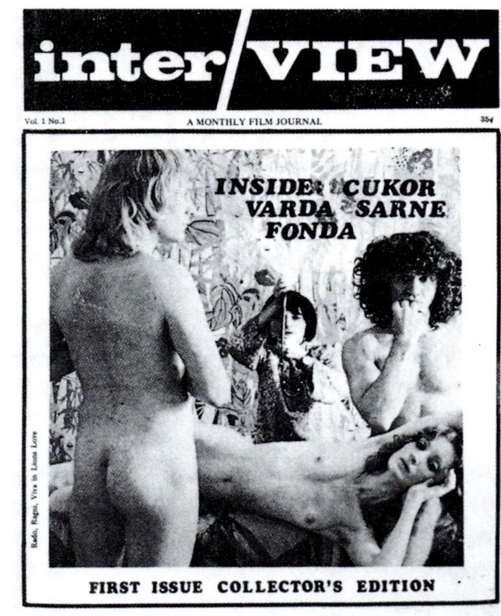

inter/VIEW

Vol. 1 No.1 A MONTHLY FILM JOURNAL 35¢

INSIDE: CUKOR VARDA SARNE FONDA

FIRST ISSUE COLLECTOR'S EDITION

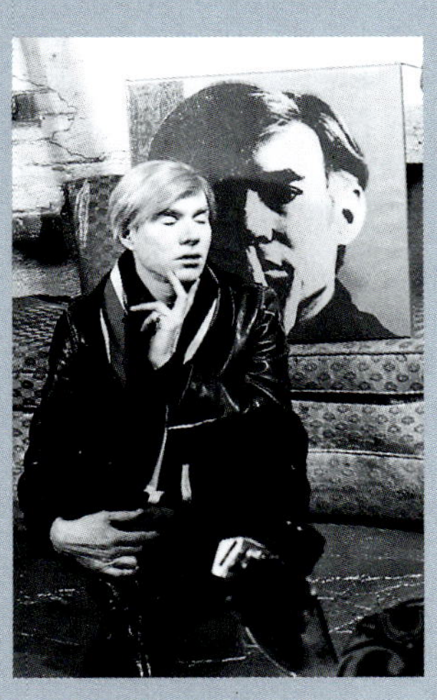

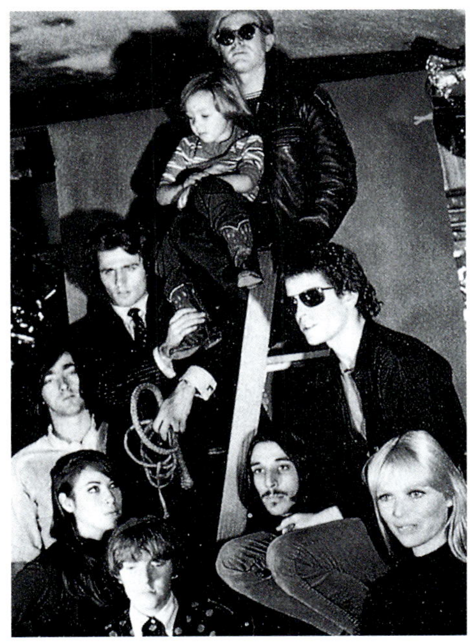

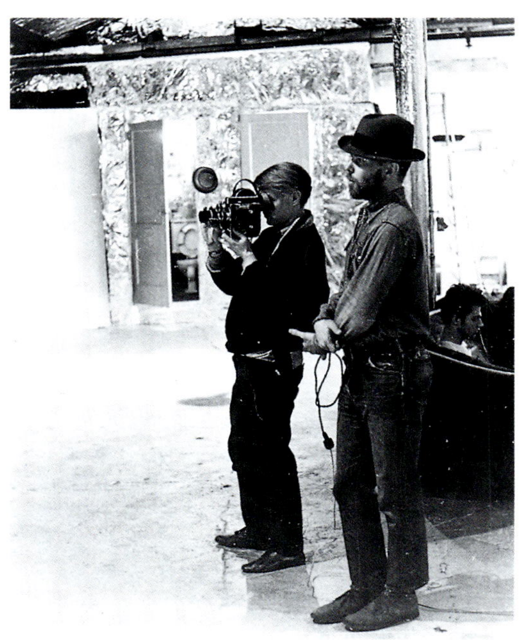

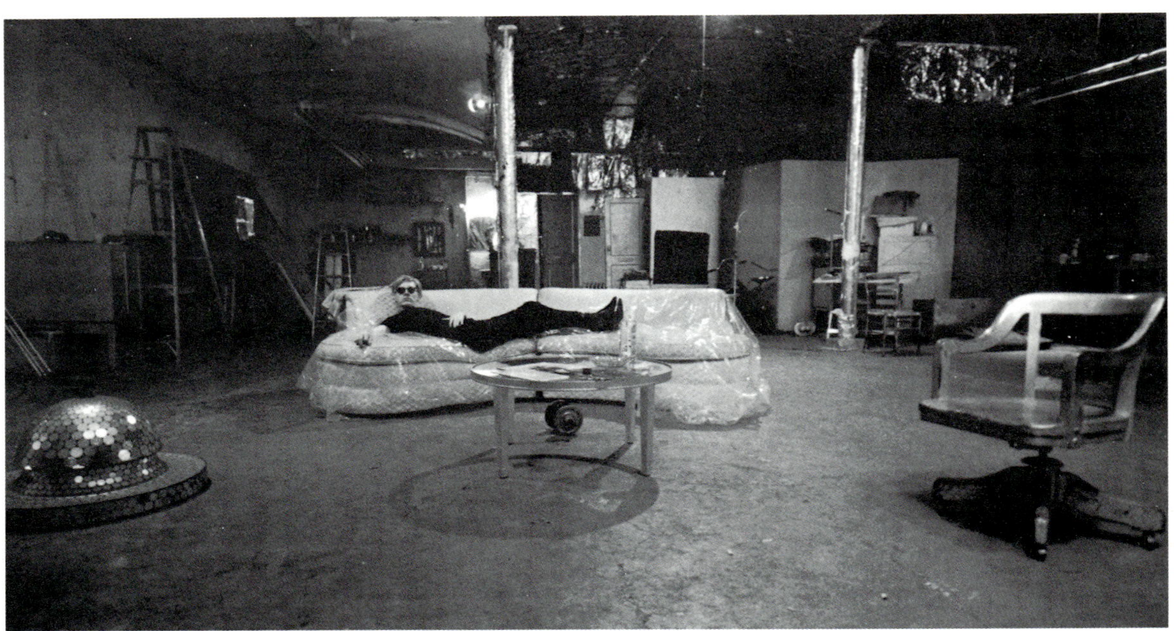

Andy Warhol, 1965. Photo: Stephen Shore

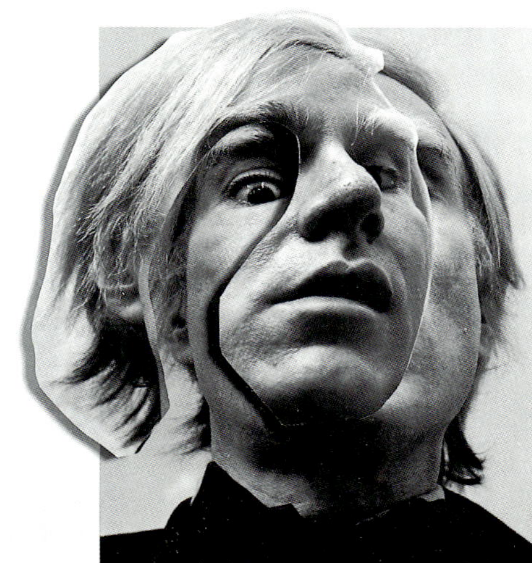

Right: Andy Warhol, 1973/74.
Photo collage: © Arnold Newman

Below: Maquettes for the portfolio *Mick Jagger*, 1975. Silkscreen on paper and acetate collaged foil on paper. Ten pieces, each 50 x 38½". Museum moderner Kunst, Vienna, lent by the Stiftung Ludwig, Austria

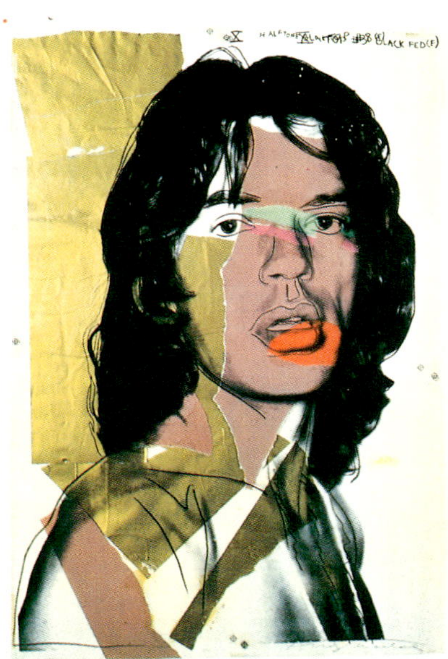

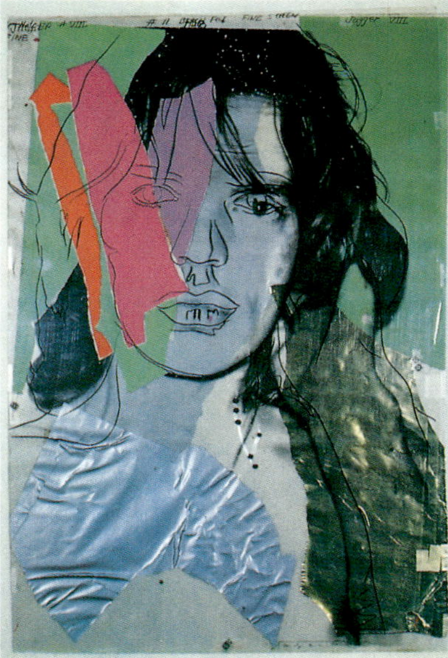

banana cover. At Expo '67 in Montreal, Warhol's "Self-Portraits" are exhibited in the U.S. pavilion. Meets Fred (Frederick) W. Hughes, who becomes his friend and business advisor.

One-man shows: "Kühe und Schwebende Kissen von Andy Warhol," Rudolf Zwirner Gallery, Cologne; "Andy Warhol Most Wanted," Rudolf Zwirner Gallery, Cologne; "Andy Warhol – The Thirteen Most Wanted Men," Galerie Ileana Sonnabend, Paris; Kunstkabinett Hans Neuendorf, Hamburg.

1968

Attends a retrospective of his works at the Moderna Museet in Stockholm.

In February, the Factory moves to 33 Union Square West. Grove Press publishes *A: A Novel*.

Helium-filled silver clouds are used as the set for *Rain Forest*, a ballet choreographed by Merce Cunningham.

June 3. Valerie Solanas, the founder and only member of S.C.U.M. (Society for Cutting Up Men), shoots and seriously wounds Warhol. In danger of his life, he undergoes an operation lasting several hours and remains in the hospital until June 28.

Prints small portraits of Mrs. Nelson A. Rockefeller.

Takes part in "documenta 4" in Kassel.

Morrissey takes a more active role in directing films at the Factory for the first time.

One-man shows: "Andy Warhol," Moderna Museet, Stockholm (followed by Stedelijk Museum, Amsterdam; Kunsthalle, Berne; and Kunsternes Hus, Oslo); "Andy Warhol," Rowan Gallery, London (Most Wanted Men, Marilyns).

1969
The film *Trash* is produced, directed by Paul Morrissey.
First issue of Warhol's monthly magazine, *Interview*.

One-man shows: "Andy Warhol," National Gallery and the Deutsche Gesellschaft für Bildende Kunst, Berlin; "Andy Warhol," Castelli/Whitney Graphics, New York (Campbell's Soup Can prints).

1970
Participates in Expo '70 in Osaka.
At the suggestion of John and Dominique de Menil, Warhol directs the exhibition "Raid the Icebox I with Andy Warhol" at the Rhode Island School of Design, in Providence, R. I. The exhibition shows objects in the school's collection.
The script of Warhol's *Blue Movie* is published by Grove Press.

One-man show: "Andy Warhol," Pasadena Art Museum (followed by Museum of Contemporary Art, Chicago; Stedelijk Van Abbe Museum, Eindhoven; Musée d'Art Moderne de la Ville de Paris; Tate Gallery, London; and Whitney Museum of American Art, New York).

1971
Warhol's play, *Pork*, is performed at LaMama Experimental Theater Club, New York, and at the Round House, London.

One-man shows: "Andy Warhol," Cenobio-Visualità, Madrid; "Andy Warhol: His Early Works, 1947-1959," Gotham Book Mart Gallery, New York; "Andy Warhol Graphik, 1964 bis 1970," Museum Haus Lange, Krefeld, Germany; "Andy Warhol," Musée d'Art Moderne de la Ville de Paris.

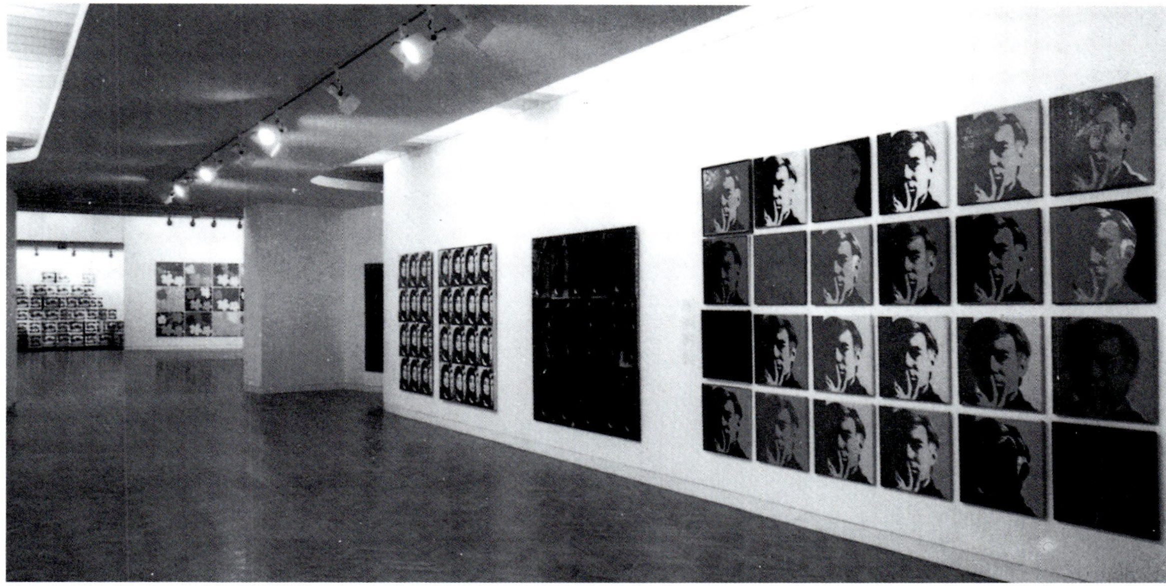

View of the exhibition "Andy Warhol," Pasadena Art Museum, 1970

View of the exhibition "Andy Warhol," Musée Galliera, Paris, 1974

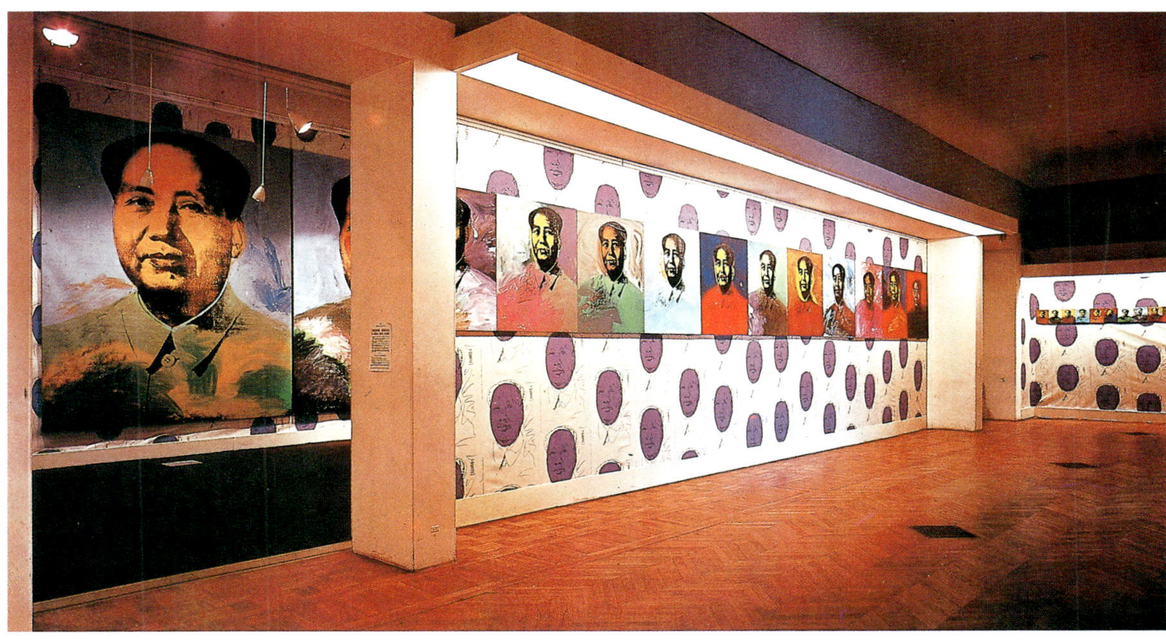

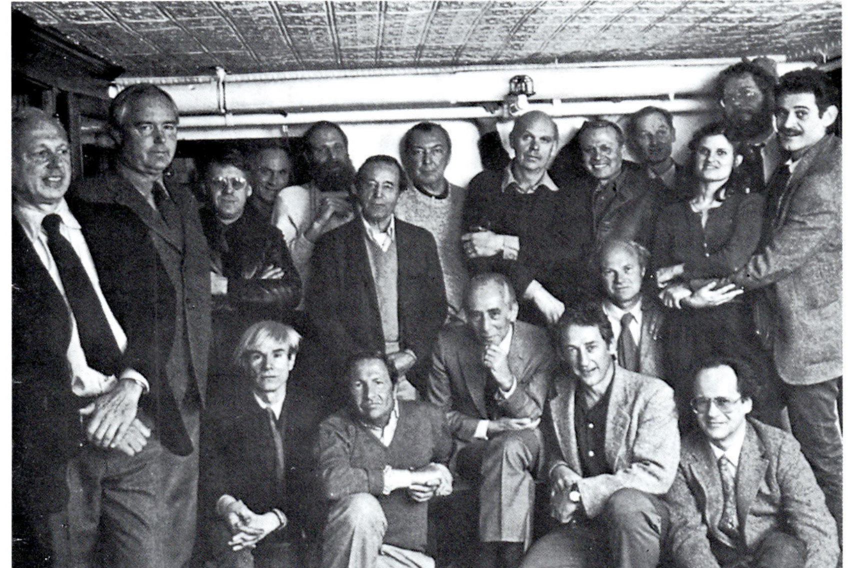

Leo Castelli's birthday party, September 19, 1982. Standing from left to right: Ellsworth Kelly, Dan Flavin, Joseph Kosuth, Richard Serra, Lawrence Weiner, Nassos Daphnis, Jasper Johns, Claes Oldenburg, Salvatore Scarpitta, Richard Artschwager, Mia Westerlund Roosen, Cletus Johnson, Keith Sonnier; seated from left to right: Andy Warhol, Robert Rauschenberg, Leo Castelli, Ed Ruscha, James Rosenquist, Robert Barry. Photo: Hans Namuth

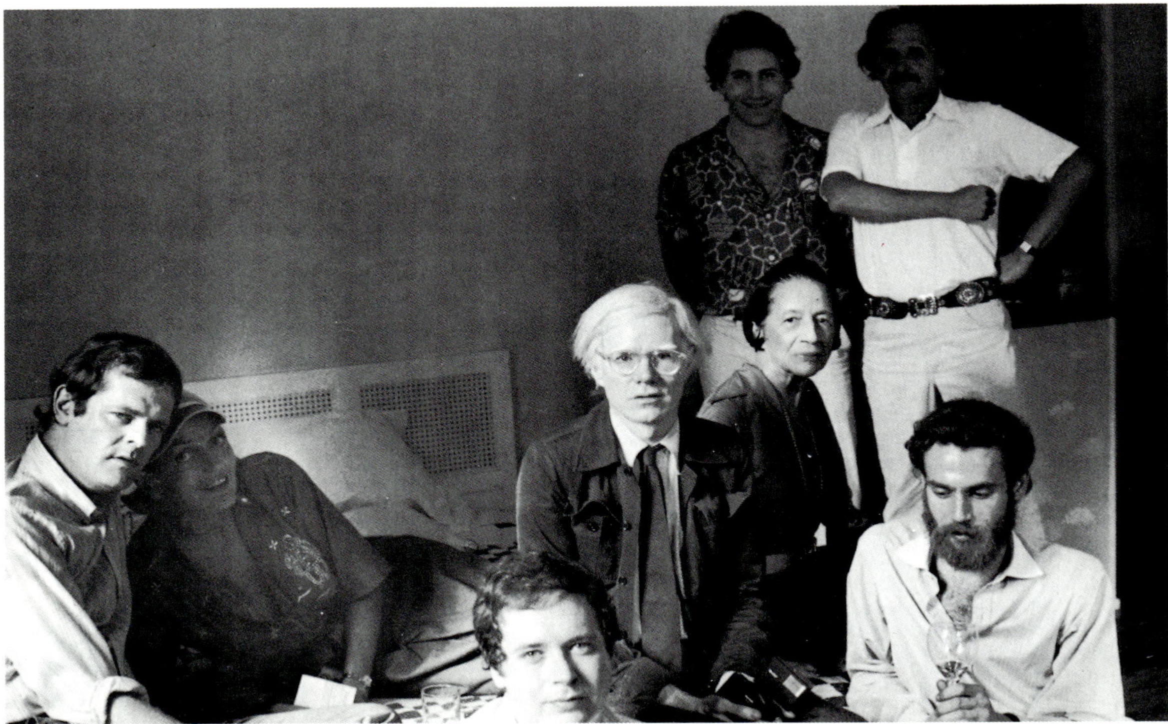

Paul Morrissey, Maxime McKendry, Alexander Hesketh, Warhol, Steven Paley, Diana Vreeland, Earl McGrath, and Jonathan Liebersohn, 1976. Photo: Camilla McGrath

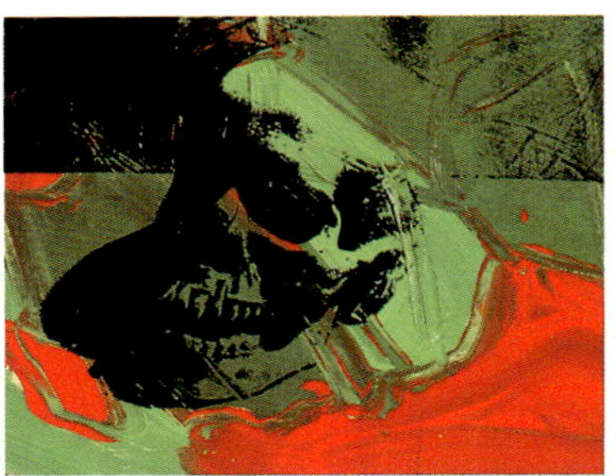
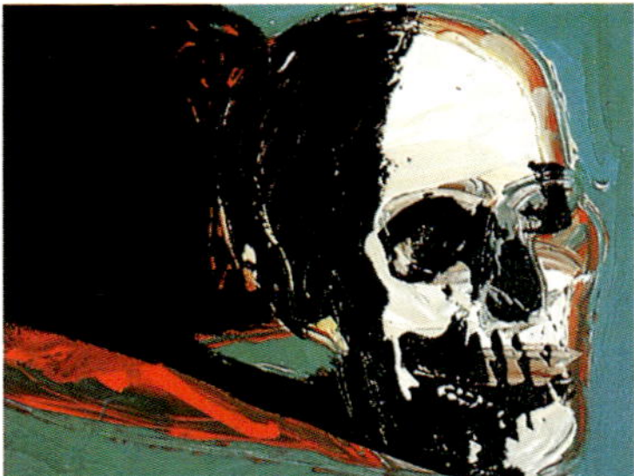
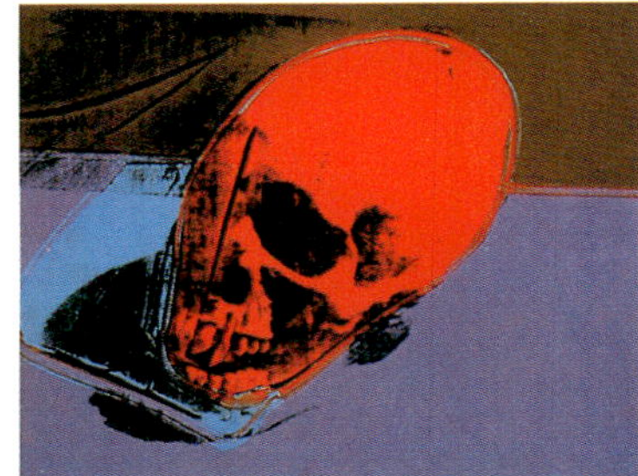
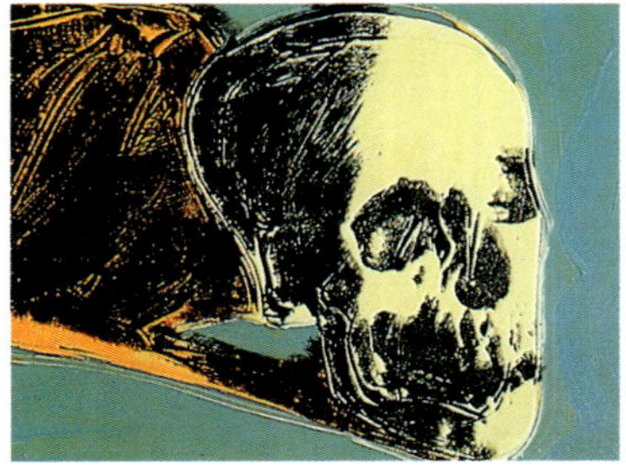
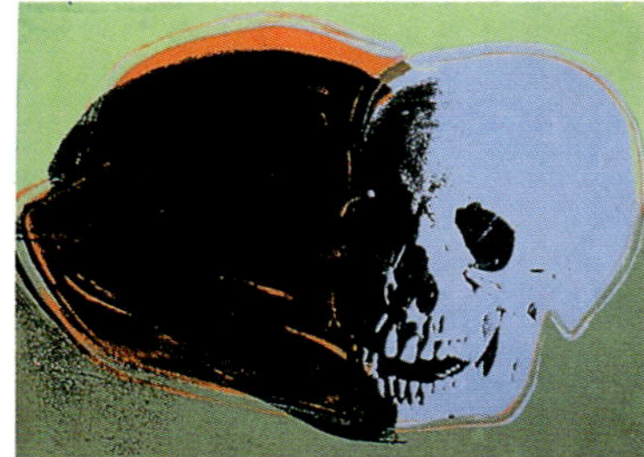
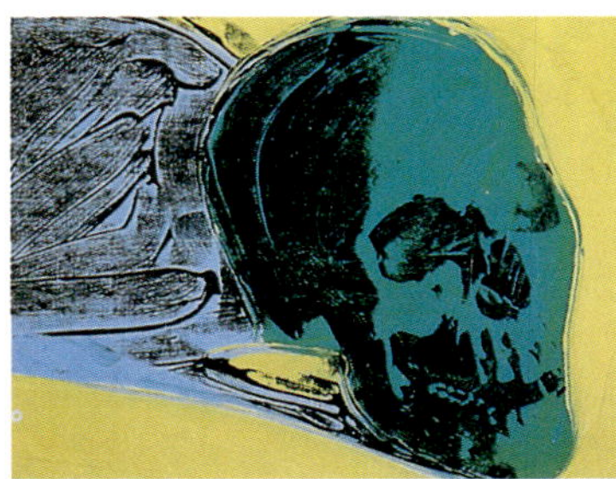

Six "Skulls," 1976. Acrylic and silkscreen on canvas, each 15 x 19". Andy Warhol Estate

Right: *Hammer and Sickle*, 1977. Acrylic and silkscreen on canvas, 72 x 86". Andy Warhol Estate

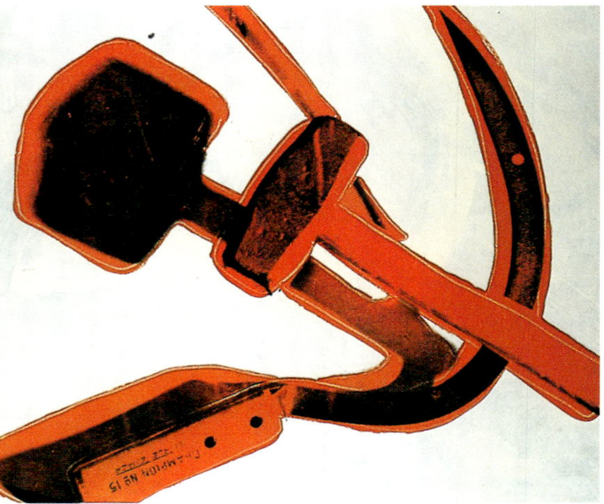

1972
Mao portraits, and films: *Heat* and *Women in Revolt*. Warhol starts to paint again; from now until his death he produces some fifty to a hundred commissioned portraits per year.

He paints portraits of Mick Jagger, the Shah of Iran, Princess Caroline, Michael Jackson, Chris Evert, Brigitte Bardot, and Sylvester Stallone, among others.

His mother Julia Warhola dies, aged 80, in Pittsburgh.

One-man shows: "Warhol Maos," Kunstmusem Basle; Modern Art Agency, Naples.

1973
Warhol produces the film *L'Amour*. Plays a part in a film with Elizabeth Taylor, *The Driver's Seat*.

One-man shows: John Berggruen Gallery, San Francisco; New Gallery, Cleveland; Irving Blum Gallery, Los Angeles.

1974
The films *Andy Warhol's Frankenstein*, and *Andy Warhol's Dracula* are produced.

Warhol experiments with creating an "invisible sculpture" consisting of motion detectors that set off alarms when the space they demarcate is violated.

The Factory moves to 860 Broadway.

One-man shows: "Andy Warhol," Musée Galliera, Paris (paintings of Mao); "Warhol," Milwaukee Art Museum; "Andy Warhol: Old Paintings, New Prints," Max Protetch Gallery, Washington, D.C.; "Andy Warhol," Museo de Arte Moderno, Bogotá; Galerie Ileana Sonnabend, Paris; Jared Sable Gallery, Toronto; and Mayor Gallery, London.

1975
The Philosophy of Andy Warhol (from A to B and Back Again) is published by Harcourt Brace Jovanovich.

One-man shows: "Andy Warhol: Paintings," Margo Leavin Gallery, Los Angeles; "Andy Warhol: Paintings 1962-1975," The Baltimore Museum of Art; Locksley Shea Gallery, Minneapolis; "Andy Warhol's Ladies and Gentlemen," Romani Adami, Rome; "Andy Warhol," Max Protetch Gallery, Washington, D.C.

1976
Produces Skull paintings.

One-man shows: "Andy Warhol: Das Zeichnerische Werk 1942-1975," Württembergischer Kunstverein, Stuttgart (followed by Städtische Kunsthalle, Düsseldorf; Kunsthalle Bremen; Städtische Galerie im Lenbachhaus, Munich; Haus am Waldsee, Berlin; Museum Moderner Kunst, Museum des 20. Jahrhunderts, Vienna; and Kunstmuseum, Lucerne); "Andy Warhol Animals," Arno Schefler, New York; "Andy Warhol and Jamie Wyeth: Portraits of Each Other," Coe Kerr Gallery, New York; "Cats and Dogs by Andy Warhol," Mayor Gallery, London; "Andy Warhol: 1974-1976," Centro Internationale di Sperimentazioni Artistiche Marie-Louise Jeanneret, Boissano, Italy.

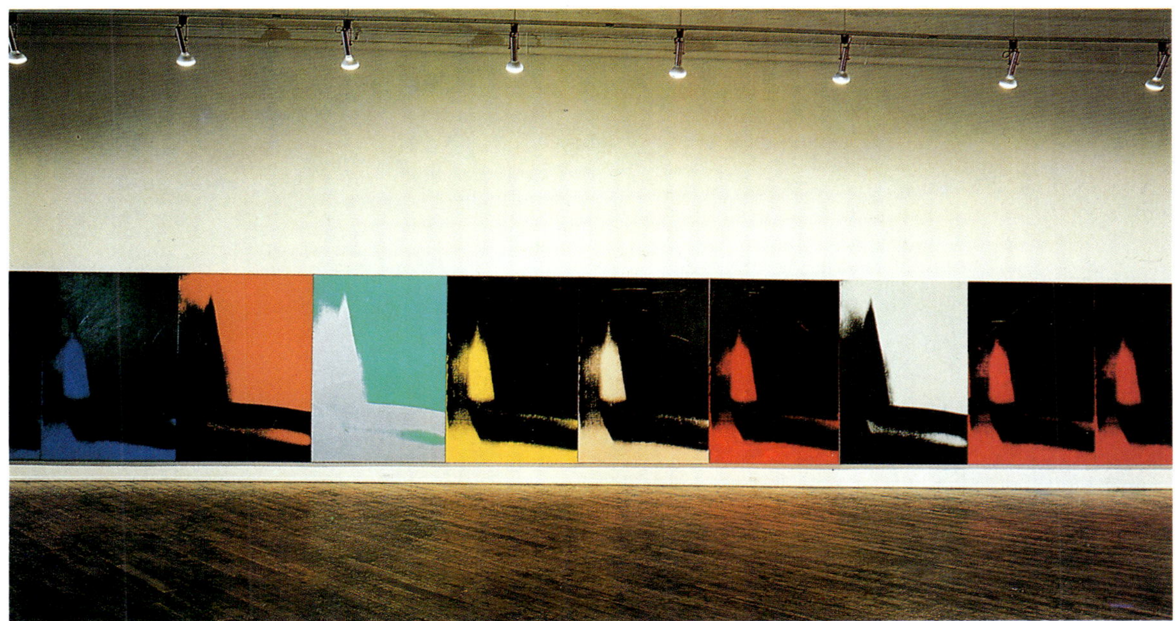

Shadows, 1978. Hanging at 393 West Broadway, New York, 1979. Acrylic and silkscreen on canvas. 102 pictures, each 76 x 52". Dia Art Foundation, New York

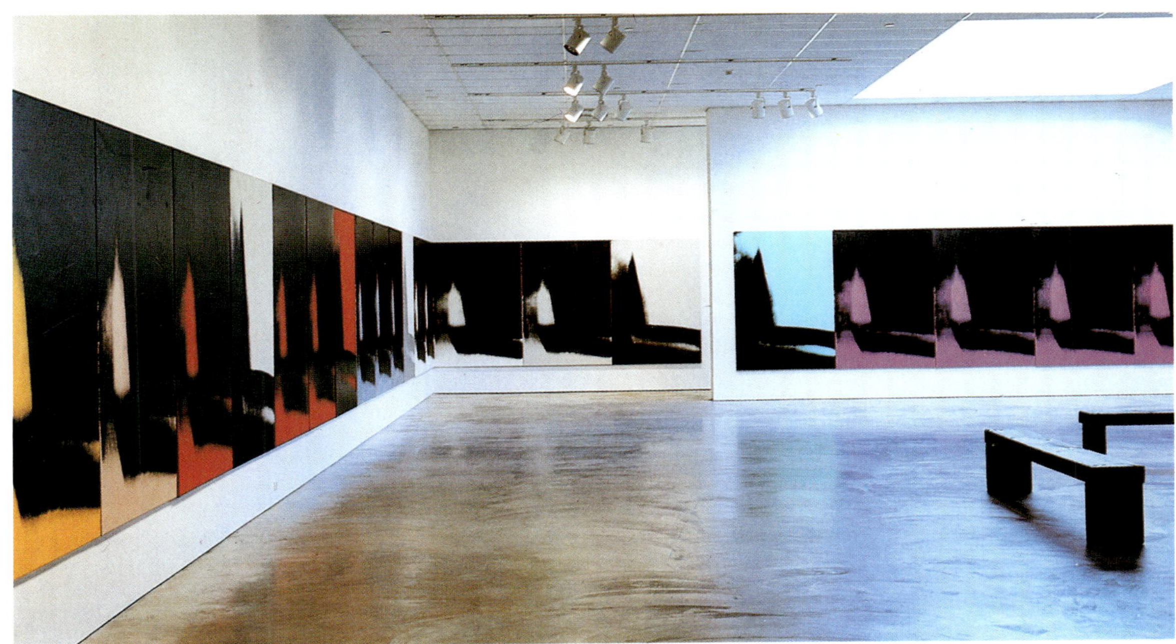

View of the exhibition "Warhol Shadows," Richmond Hall, The Menil Collection, Houston, 1987/88

Big Retrospective Painting (Reversal Series), 1979. Acrylic and silkscreen on canvas, 81 ½ x 425 ¼"

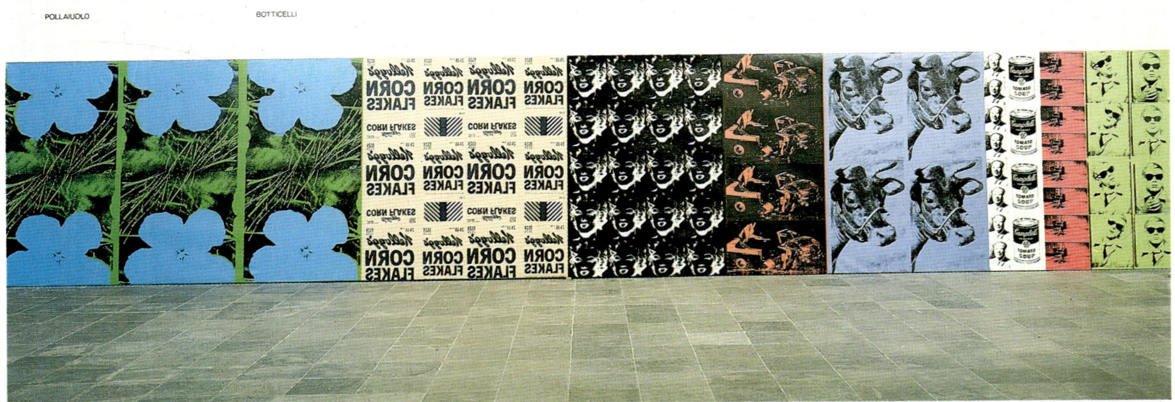

Warhol showing art dealers a Joseph Beuys portrait

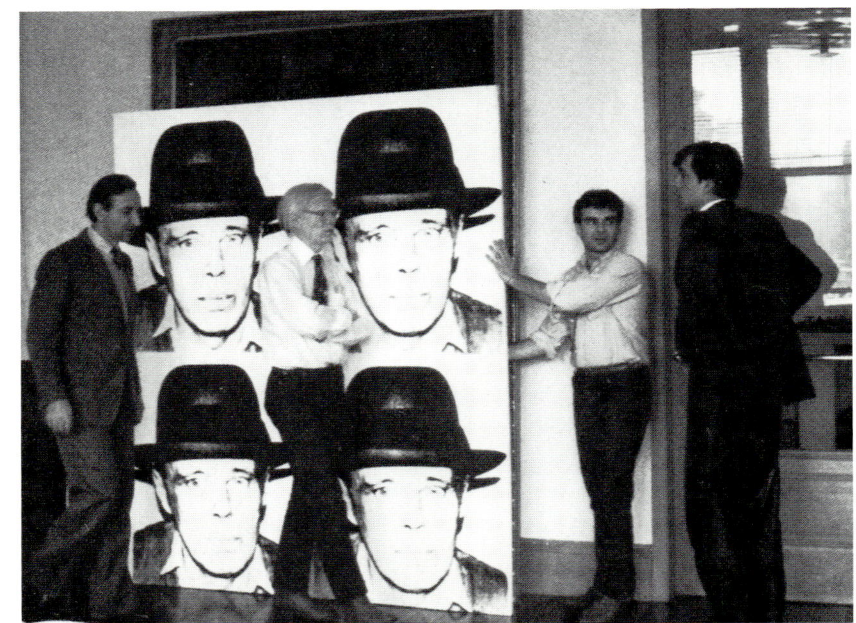

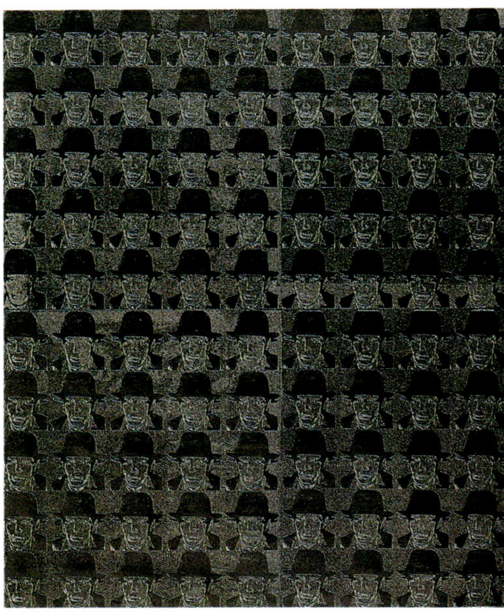

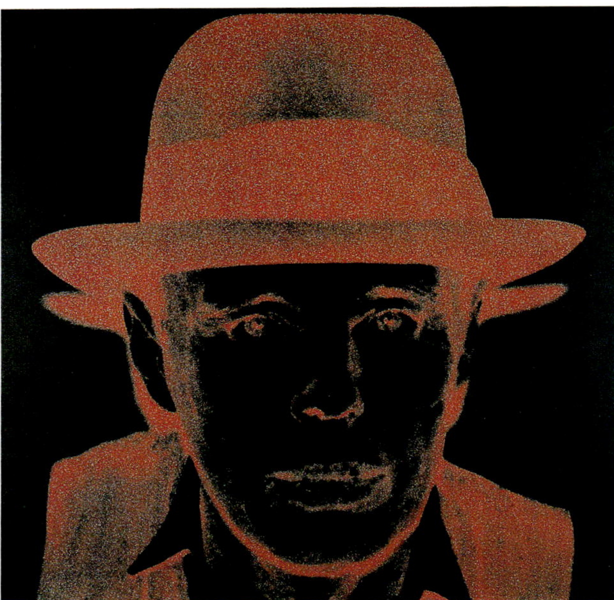

Left center: *Diamond Dust Joseph Beuys*, 1980. Acrylic, diamond dust, and silkscreen on canvas, 100x80". Andy Warhol Estate

Right center: *Diamond Dust Joseph Beuys*, 1980. Acrylic, diamond dust, and silkscreen on canvas. 40x40". Collection Francesco Pellizzi

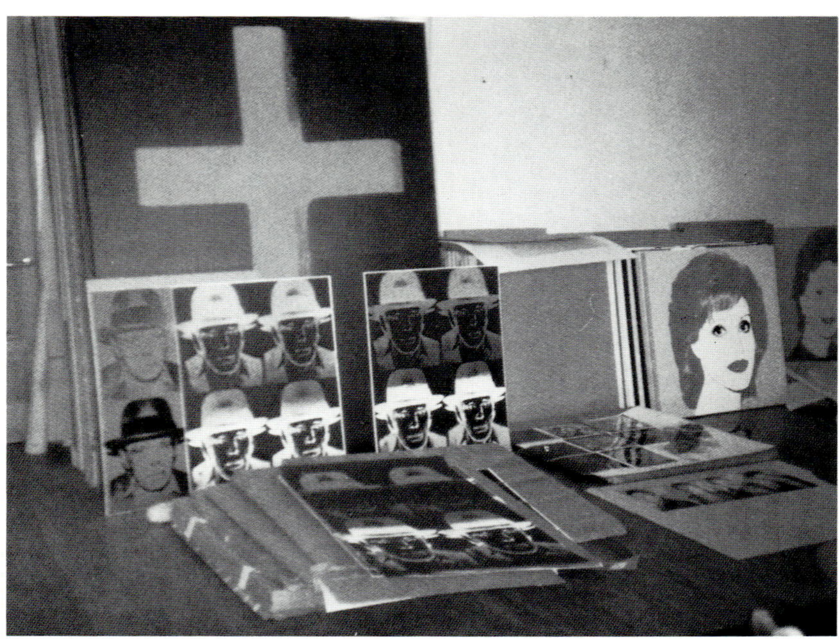

Warhol's art works in the Factory

1977

Series of Athletes, Hammer and Sickles, and Torsos. The film: *Andy Warhol's Bad* is produced. The Museum of American Folk Art, New York, shows an exhibition of Warhol's private collection of American folk art under the title "Andy Warhol's Folk and Funk."

One-man shows: "Retrospective Exhibition of Paintings by Andy Warhol from 1962-1976," Pyramid Galleries, Washington, D.C.; "Andy Warhol Hammer and Sickle," Galerie Daniel Templon, Paris; "Andy Warhol Flash, Electric Chair, Campbell's Soup Serigraphien," Museum Folkwang, Essen; "Andy Warhol: The American Indian," Musée d'Art et d'Histoire, Geneva; "Athletes by Andy Warhol," Coe Kerr Gallery, New York (followed by Sable-Castelli Gallery, Toronto; Galerie Heiner Friedrich, Cologne; and Leo Castelli Gallery, New York).

1978

Series of Oxidations and Shadows.

One-man shows: "Athletes by Andy Warhol," Virginia Museum of Fine Arts, Richmond; "Andy Warhol: Portraits," University Gallery, Meadows School of the Arts, Southern Methodist University, Dallas; "Andy Warhol," Kunsthaus, Zurich; "Andy Warhol Athletes," Institute of Contemporary Art, London; "Andy Warhol: Torsos," Ace Gallery, Venice, California; "Andy Warhol," Louisiana Museum, Humlebaek, Denmark; "Andy Warhol: Early Paintings," Blum Helman Gallery, New York.

1979
Series: Retrospectives and Reversals.
Publication of *Andy Warhol's Exposures* by Andy Warhol Books/Grosset & Dunlap.

One-man shows: "Andy Warhol: Shadows," Heiner Friedrich Gallery, New York; Massimo Valsecchi, Milan; "Andy Warhol: Torsos," Ace Gallery, Vancouver; "Andy Warhol," Wadsworth Atheneum, Hartford, Connecticut (followed by University Art Museum, University of California, Berkeley); "Andy Warhol, Multiple Images: Landscapes, City Spaces, Country Places," Arts Gallery, Baltimore; "Andy Warhol: Portraits of the 70s," Whitney Museum of American Art, New York.

1980
Diamond Dust Shoes; portraits of Joseph Beuys and of Jews of the 20th Century.
Travels to Düsseldorf, Paris, and Stuttgart. *POPism: the Warhol 60s*, by Warhol and Pat Hackett, is published by Harcourt Brace Jovanovich.

One-man shows: "Andy Warhol: American Indian Drawings," Boehm Gallery, Palomar College, San Marcos, California; "Joseph Beuys by Andy Warhol," Galleria Lucio Amelio, Naples; "Andy Warhol Reversals," Galerie Bruno Bischofberger, Zurich; "Joseph Beuys by Andy Warhol," Centre d'Art Contemporain, Geneva; "Andy Warhol: Fotografien," Museum Ludwig, Cologne; "Andy Warhol: Exposures," Stedelijk Museum, Amsterdam; "Andy Warhol: Ten Portraits of Jews of the Twentieth Century," Lowe Art Museum, University of Miami, Coral Gables, Florida; "Andy Warhol: Photographs," Lisson Gallery, London; "Portraits of Jews of the Twentieth

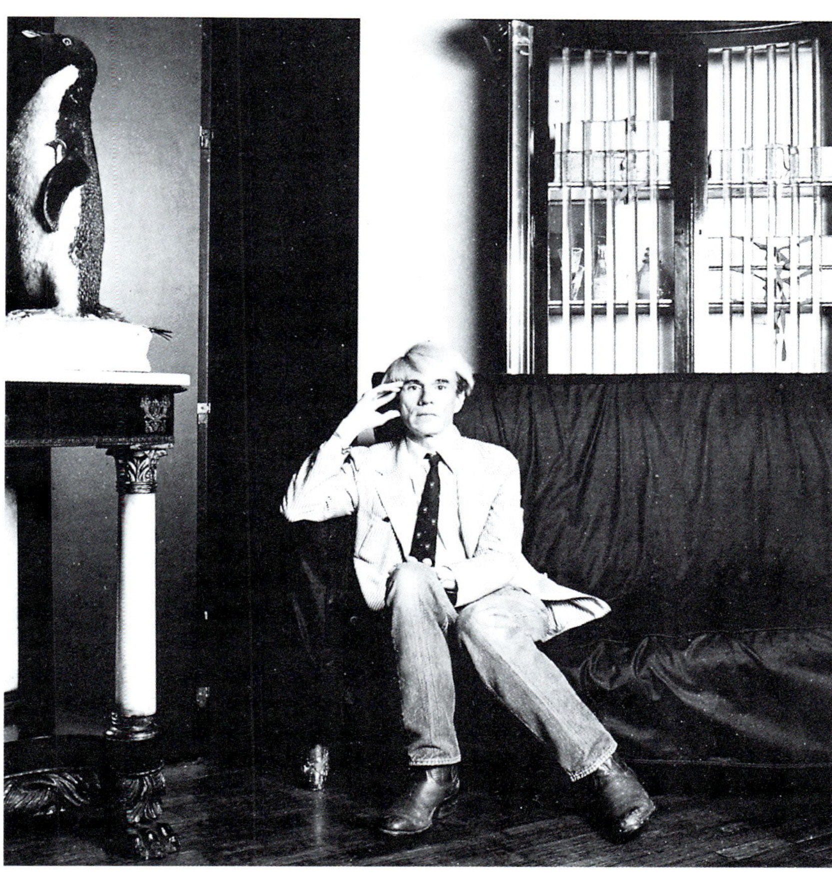

Andy Warhol in the Factory, 1981. Photo: Marcus Leatherdale

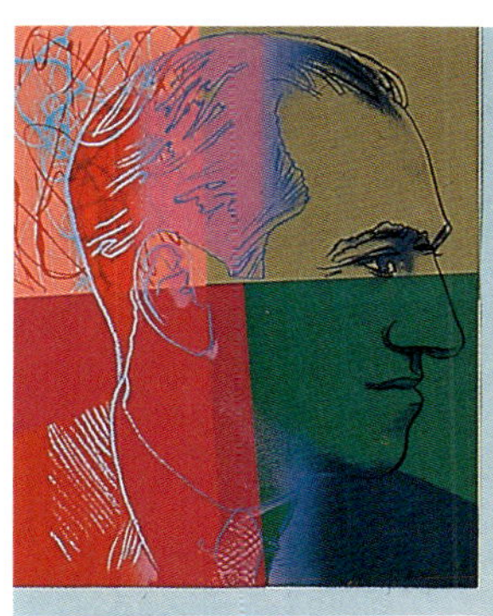
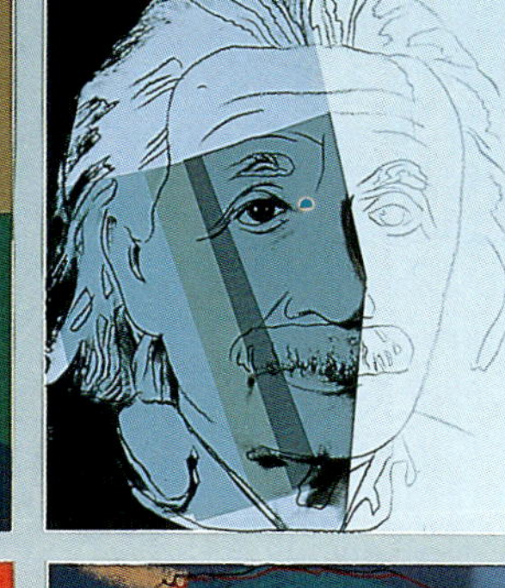
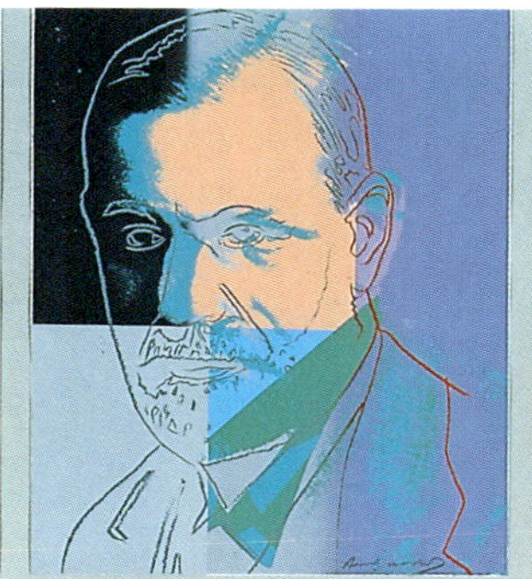
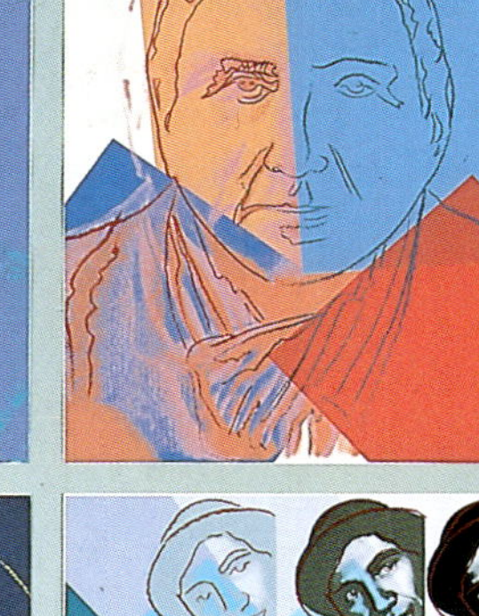
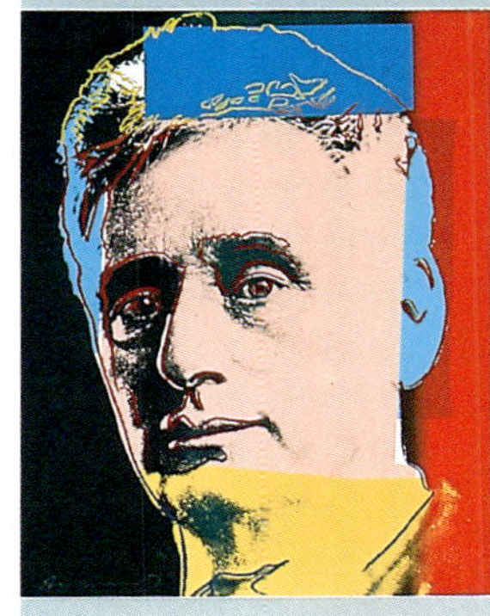
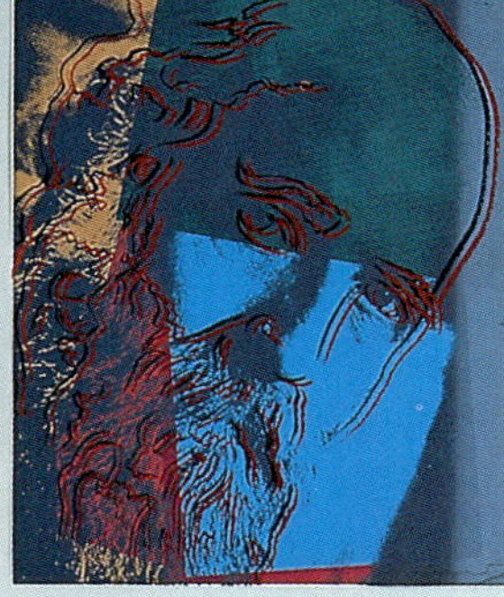
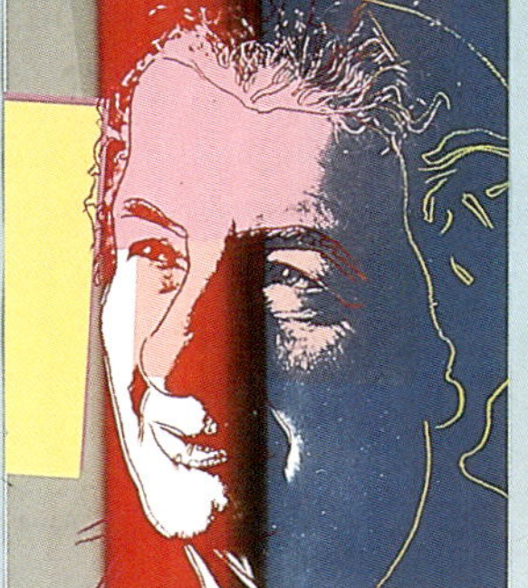
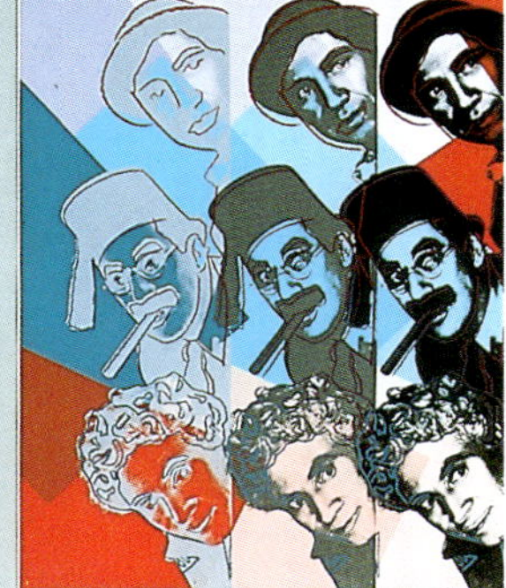
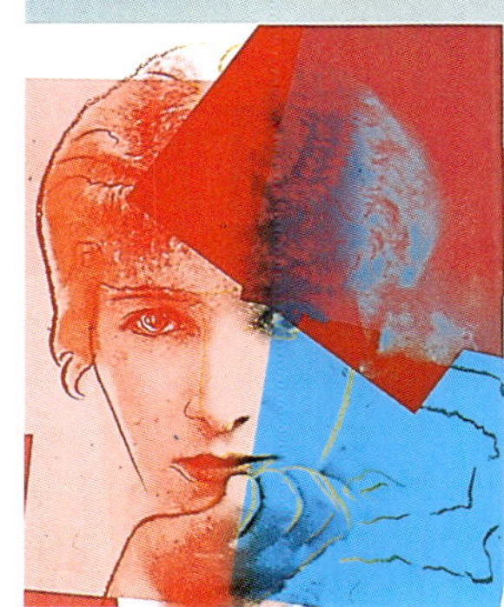
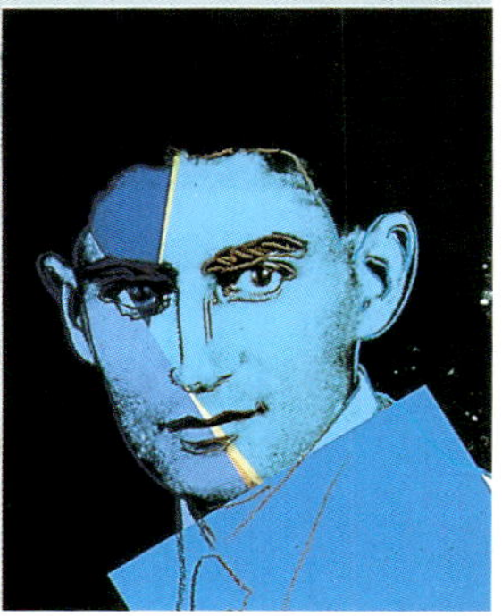

Ten Portraits of Jews of the Twentieth Century, 1980. Portfolio of ten prints, each 40 x 32"

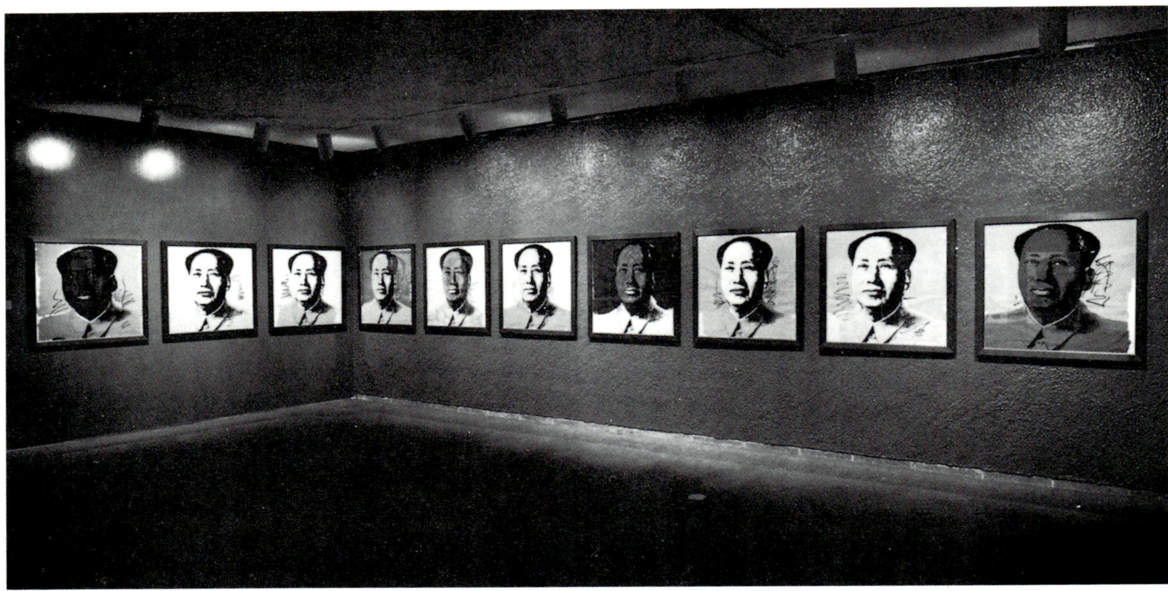

View of the exhibition "Andy Warhol: Portraits of the 70s," Whitney Museum of American Art, New York, 1979

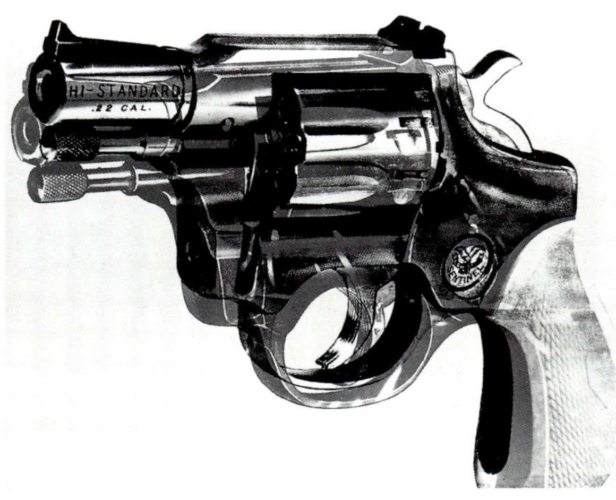

Gun, 1981. Acrylic and silkscreen on canvas, 70 x 90"

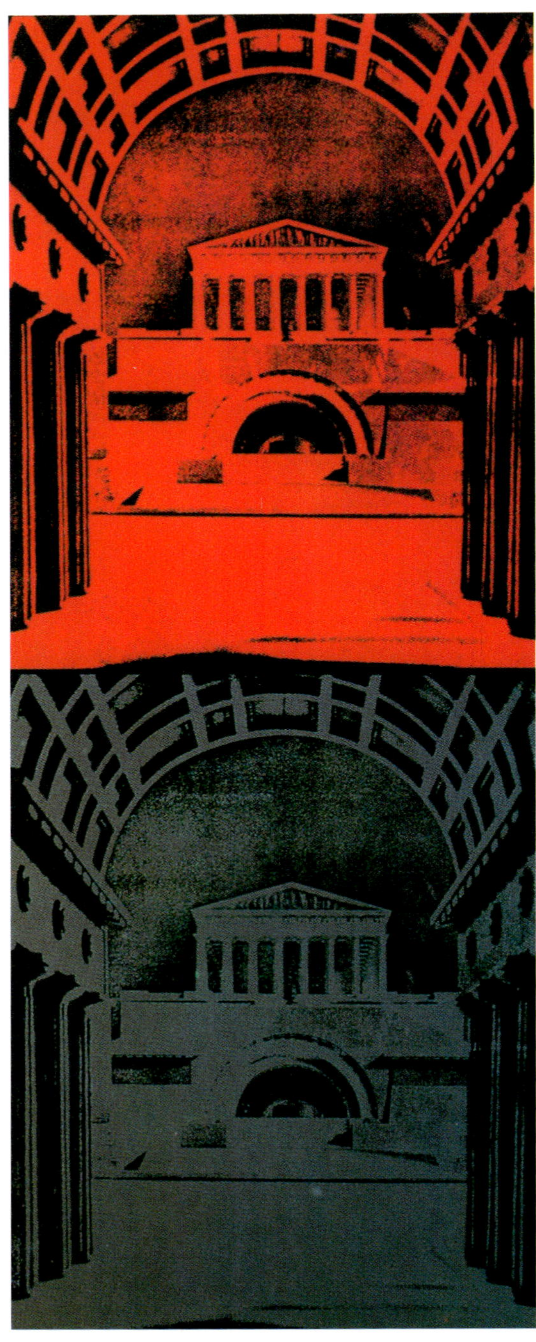

The Berlin Friedrich Monument I (Zeitgeist Series), 1982. Acrylic and silkscreen on canvas. 180 x 70"

Right: Andy Warhol at the opening of his exhibition in Vienna, 1981. Photo: Sabine Schmeller

Century," The Jewish Museum, New York (followed by Akron Art Museum); "Andy Warhol: Œuvres récentes, 'Reversal,' Galerie Daniel Templon, Paris; "Andy Warhol: Paintings and Prints," Portland Center for the Visual Arts, Portland, Oregon; "Andy Warhol's Portraits of Georgia O'Keefe" (*sic*), Gray Gaultney, New York; Schellmann & Klüser, Munich.

1981

Series: Dollar Signs, Guns, Knives, Myths, and Crosses. Travels to Munich, Bonn, Hannover, Vienna, and Paris.

One-man shows: "The Shoe Portfolio," Galerie Watari, Tokyo; "Warhol '80: Serie Reversal, "Museum Moderner Kunst, Museum des 20. Jahrhunderts, Vienna; "Andy Warhol at Colorado State University," Colorado State University, Fort Collins; "Andy Warhol Myths," Ronald Feldman Fine Arts, Inc., New York; "Andy Warhol: Bilder 1961 bis 1981," Kestner-Gesellschaft, Hannover (fol-

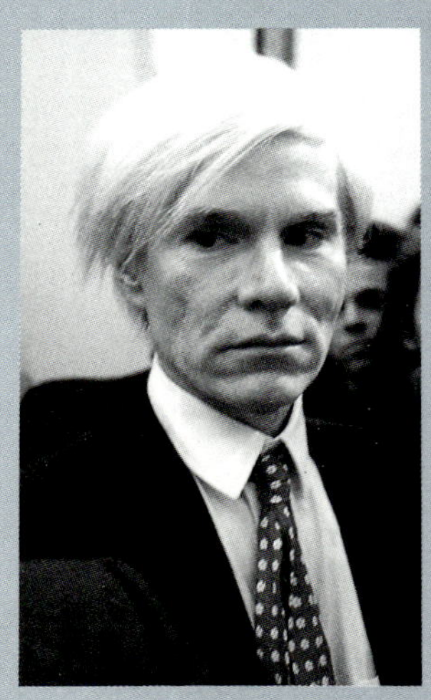

lowed by Städtische Galerie im Lenbachhaus, Munich); "Andy Warhol: A Print Retrospective," Castelli Graphics, New York; "Andy Warhol: Myths 1981," Thomas Segal Gallery, Boston; "LeRoy Neiman, Andy Warhol: An Exhibition of Sports Paintings," Los Angeles Institute of Contemporary Art.

1982
Portraits of Goethe and Stadiums. A cable television station in U.S. broadcasts a program of Warhol interviews, with many guests. Travels to Aspen, Colorado, Palm Beach, Beijing, Paris, and Zurich.

Produces posters for Fassbinder's film *Querelle*.

Participates in the Berlin exhibition "Zeitgeist" and in "documenta 7" in Kassel.

One-man shows: "Andy Warhol: Reversals," Leo Castelli Gallery (West Broadway), New York; "Andy Warhol: Dollar Signs," Leo Castelli (Greene Street), New York; "Andy Warhol: Myths," Marianne Deson Gallery, Chicago; "Andy Warhol: Dollar Signs," Galerie Daniel Templon, Paris; "Andy Warhol: Myths," Modernism, San Francisco; "Warhol au plus juste," Galerie des Ponchettes, Nice; "Andy Warhol: Dollar Signs/ Knives/Guns," Castelli/ Goodman/Solomon, East Hampton, New York; "Andy Warhol: Schweizer Portraits," Kunstsammlung der Stadt Thun, Switzerland; "Andy Warhol: Portrait Screenprints 1965-80," Dover Museum, Dover (followed by Wansbeck Square Gallery, Ashington; Usher Gallery, Lincoln; and Aberystwyth Arts Center, Aberystwyth, Wales); "Warhol verso de Chirico," Campidoglio, Rome; "Andy Warhol: Guns, Knives, & Crosses," Galeria Fernando Vijande, Madrid.

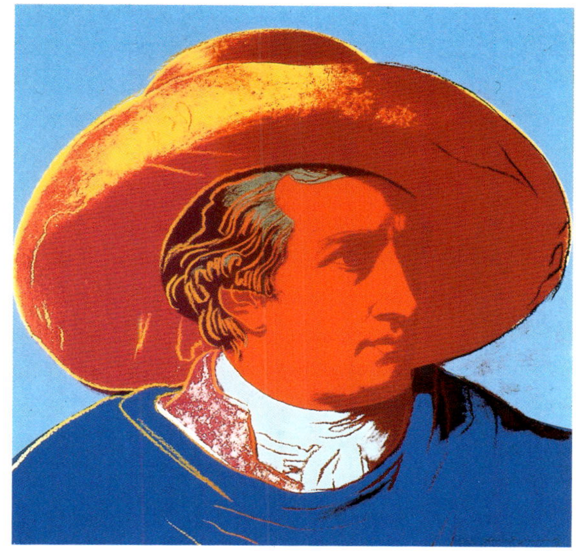

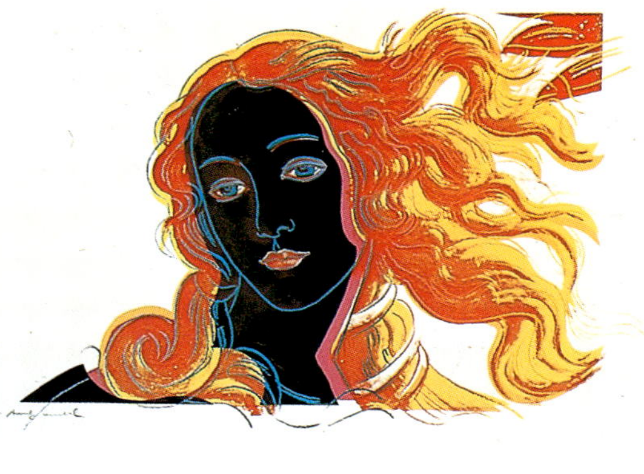

Upper left: *Goethe*, 1982. Serigraph on paper, portfolio with four prints, 38 x 38". Private collection

Upper right: *Details of Renaissance Paintings* (Sandro Botticelli, *Birth of Venus*, 1482), 1984. Serigraph on paper from a portfolio of four prints, 32 x 44"

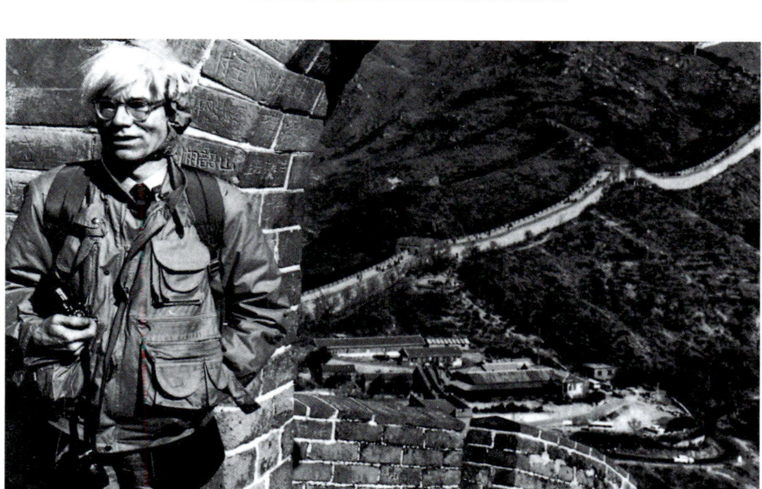

Center: Andy Warhol at the Great Wall, 1982. Photo: Christopher Makos

Below: *Myths*, 1981. Portfolio with ten prints, each 38 x 38"

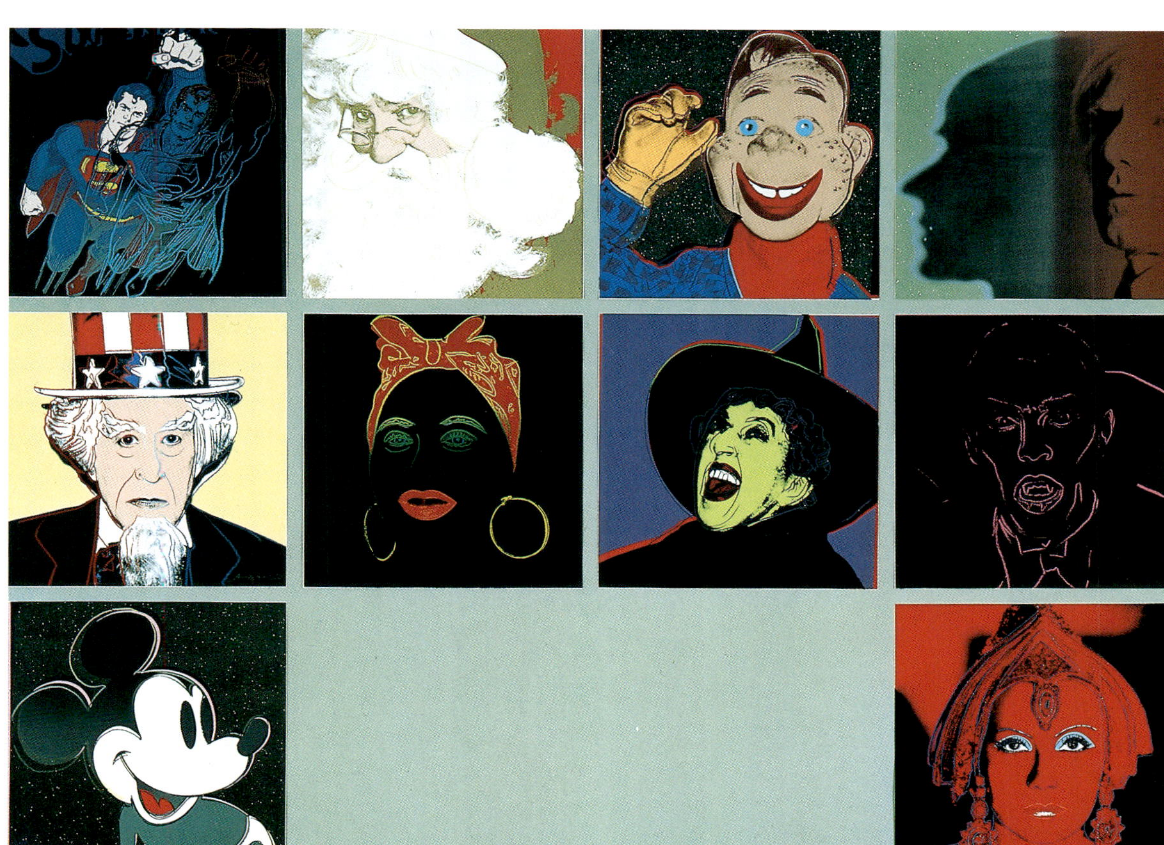

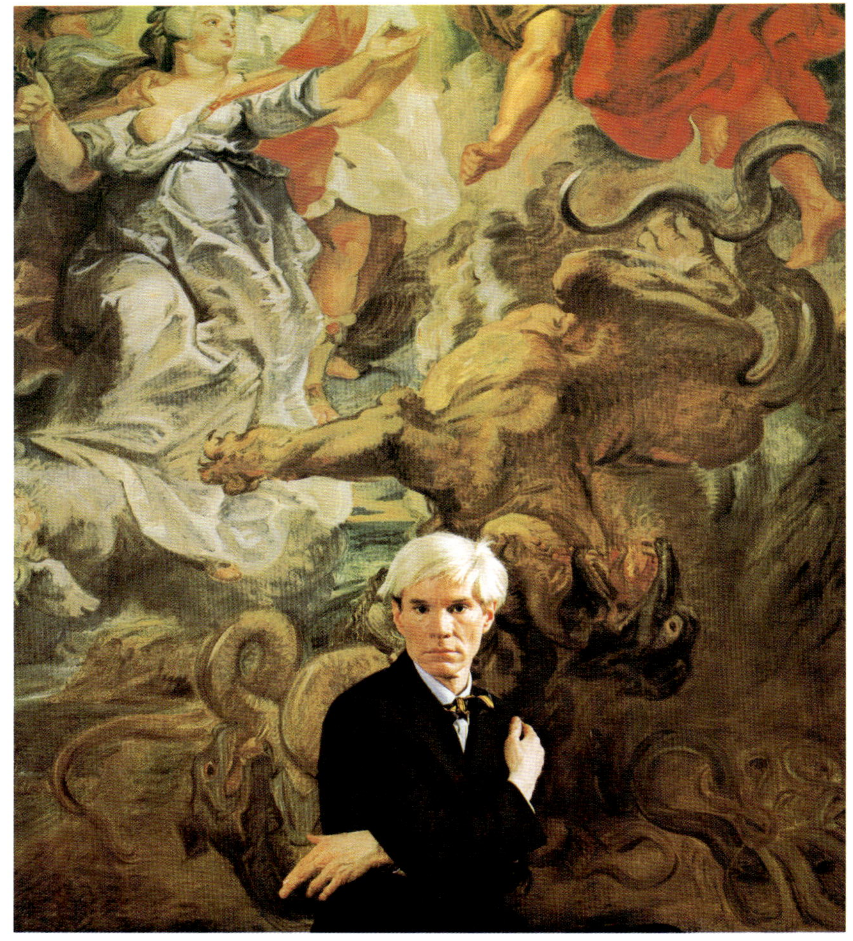

Andy Warhol, 1982.
Poster for the Leo Castelli Gallery, New York.
Photo: Hans Namuth

At the exhibition "Andy Warhol: Dollar Signs," Leo Castelli Gallery, New York, 1982

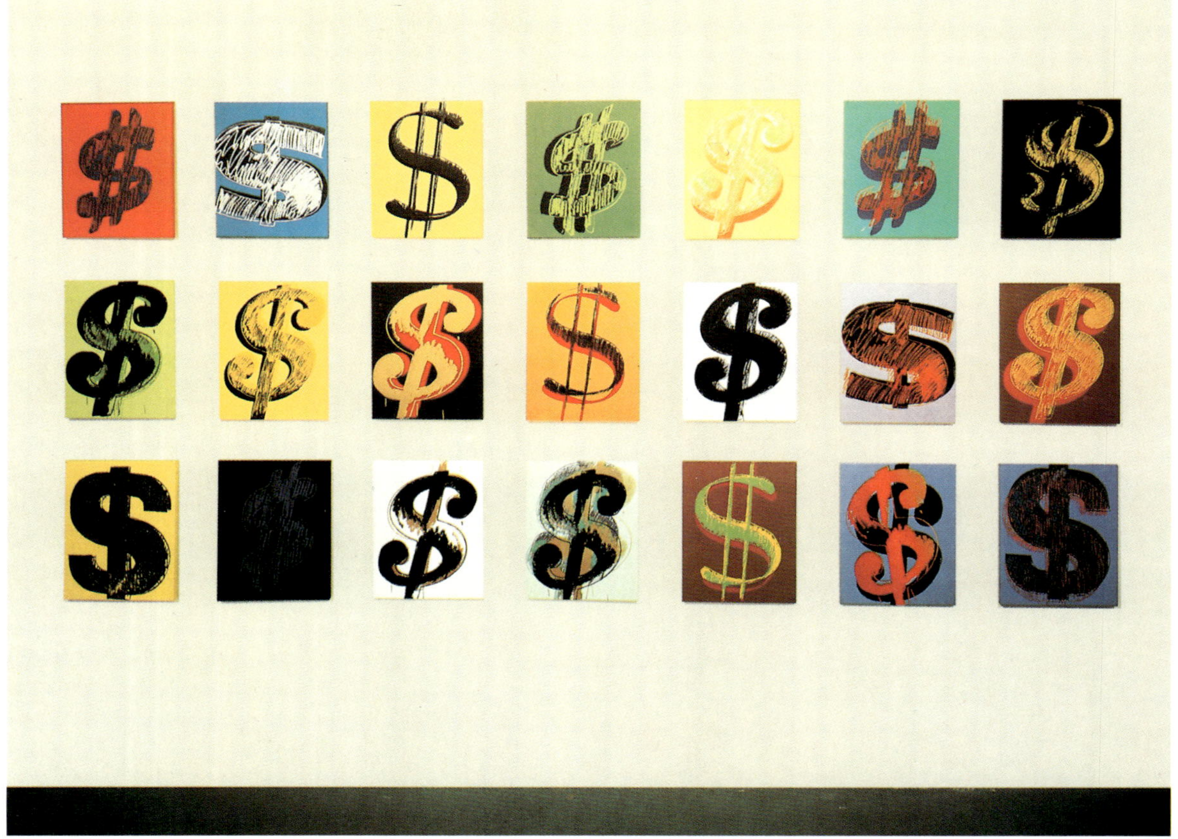

1983
Designs the posters for the centenary of the Brooklyn Bridge. Travels to Denver, Paris, Spain, and Zurich.

One-man shows: "Warhol's Animals: Species at Risk," American Museum of Natural History, New York; "Andy Warhol's Electric Chairs," Fraenkel Gallery, San Francisco; "Andy Warhol in the 1980s," Aldrich Museum of Contemporary Art, Ridgefield, Connecticut; "Paintings for Children," (also known as "Toy Paintings"), Galerie Bruno Bischofberger, Zurich.

1984
Series of detail paintings on the subject of the Renaissance, paintings after Munch, and Rorschach paintings. Works with Jean-Michel Basquiat and Keith Haring.

One-man shows: "Three Portraits of Ingrid Bergman," Galerie Börjeson, Malmö, Sweden; "Andy Warhol: Paintings and Prints," Delahunty, Dallas; "Andy Warhol: Renaissance Paintings," Waddington Graphics, London; "Collaborations: Jean-Michel Basquiat, Francesco Clemente, Andy Warhol," Galerie Bruno Bischofberger, Zurich; "Andy Warhol: Details of Renaissance Paintings," Editions Schellmann and Klüser, New York.

1985
Series: "Ads."
Harper and Row publish *Andy Warhol's America*.

One-man shows: "Ads," Amelie A. Wallace Gallery, State University of New York at Old Westbury; "Warhol verso de Chirico," Marisa del Re Gallery, New York; "Warhol, Basquiat Paintings," Tony Shafrazi Gallery, New York; "Andy Warhol: Reigning Queens 1985," Leo Castelli Gallery, New York; "The Silkscreens of Andy Warhol: 1962-1985," Lehmann College Art Gallery, Lehmann College, Bronx; "Andy Warhol: Paintings 1962-1985 and Early Prints," Galerie Paul Maenz, Cologne.

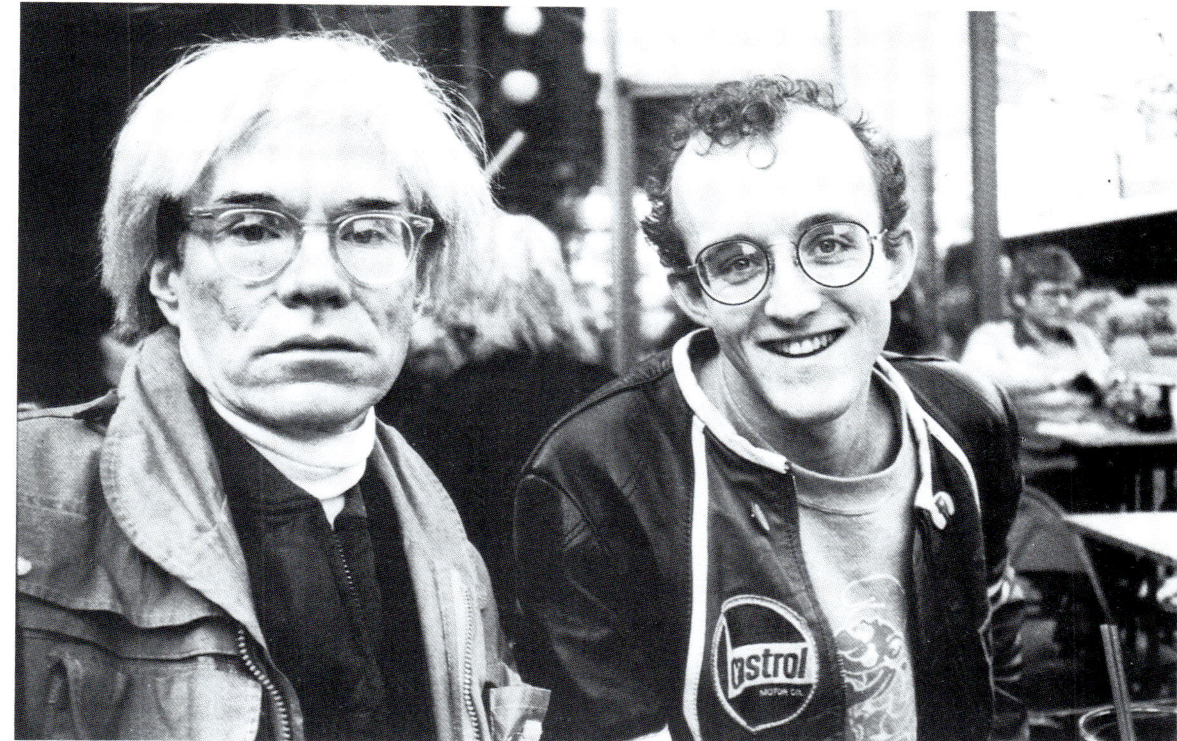

Andy Warhol and Keith Haring in New York City, 1983. Photo: Christopher Makos

Ingrid Bergman: Herself – The Nun – With Hat, 1985. Three silkscreen prints

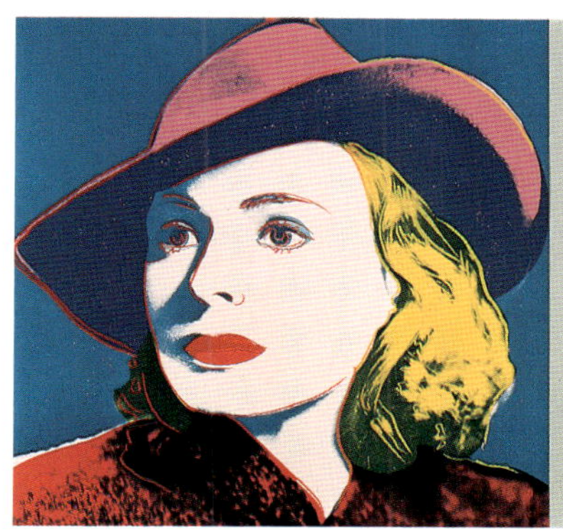
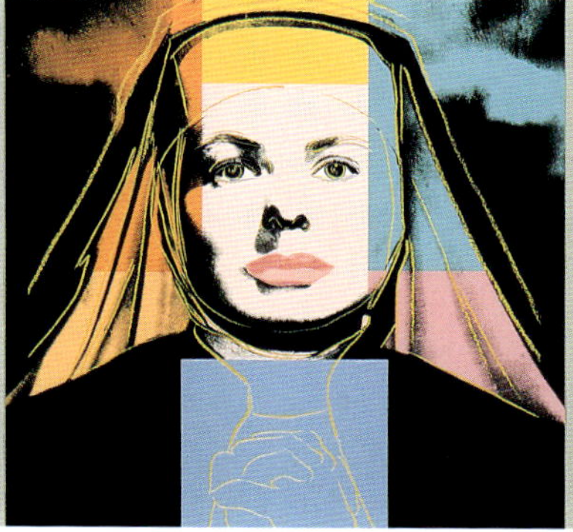
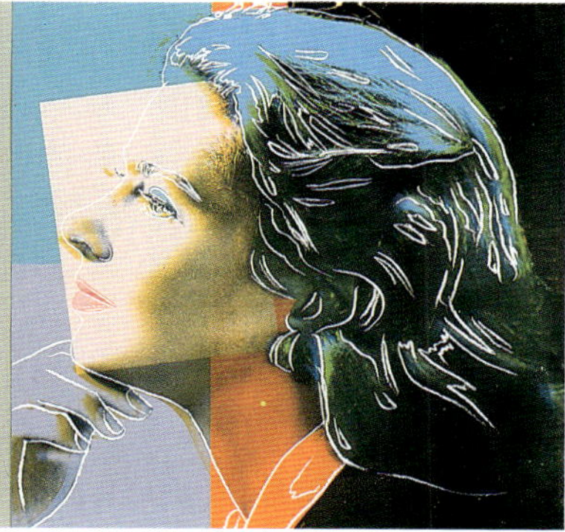

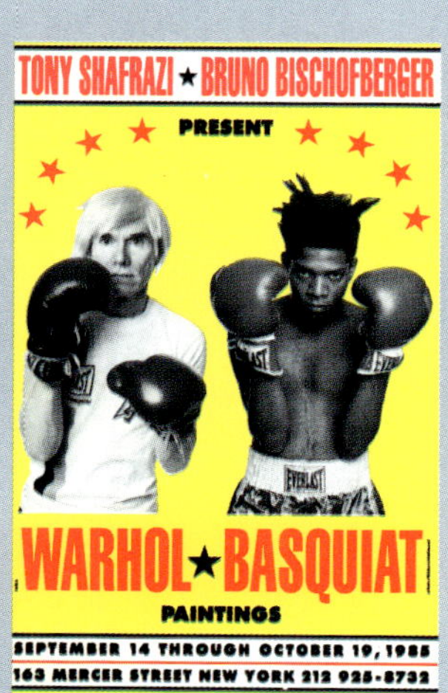

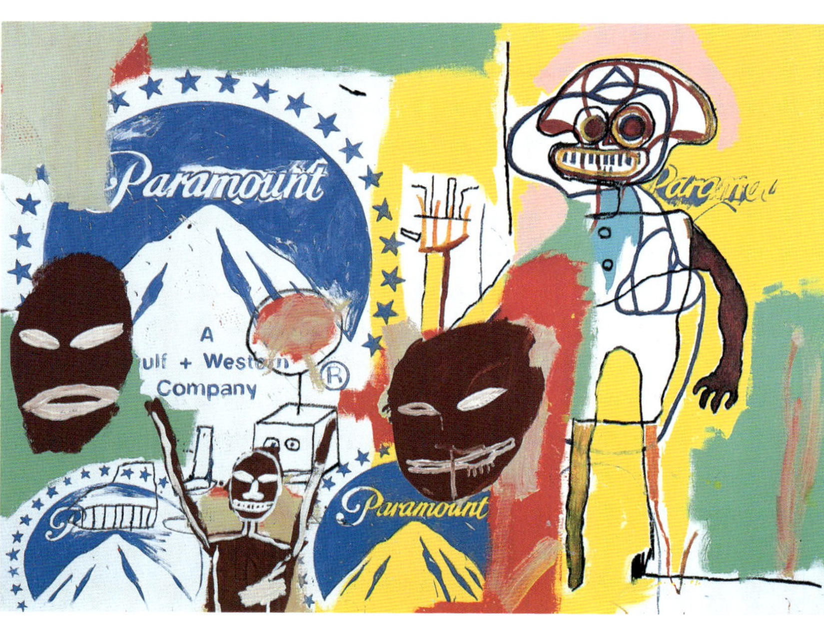

Lower right: Jean-Michel Basquiat and Andy Warhol, *Untitled*, 1984/85. Oil and acrylic on canvas, 75 x 103 ½"

Lower left: Poster for the Warhol and Basquiat exhibition, 1985

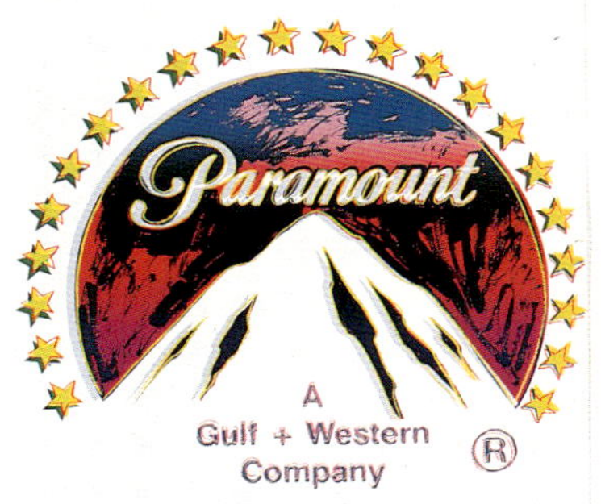

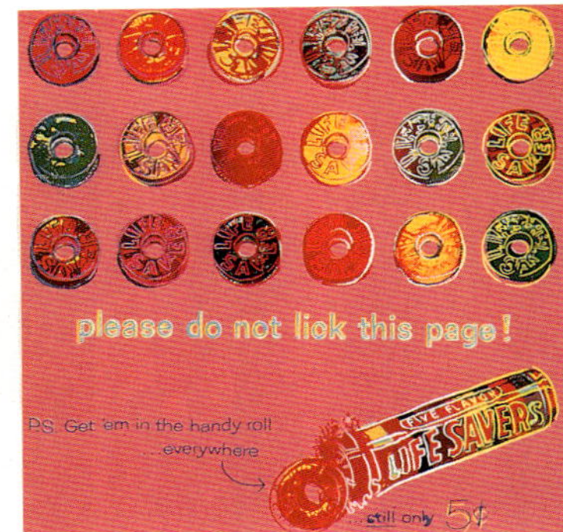

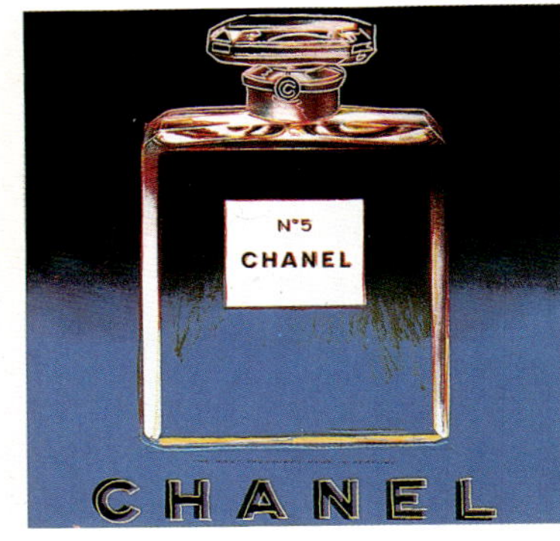

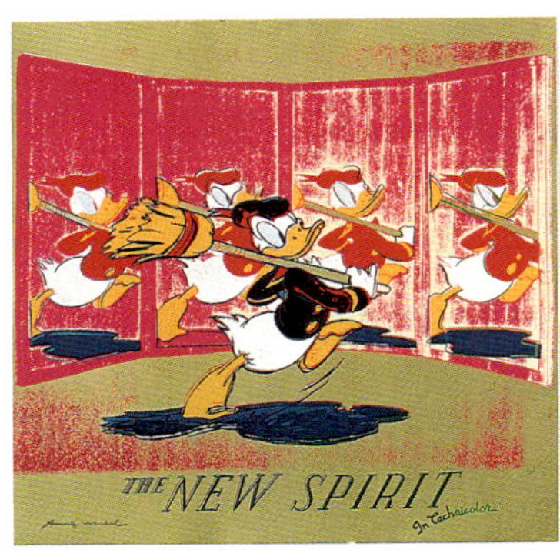

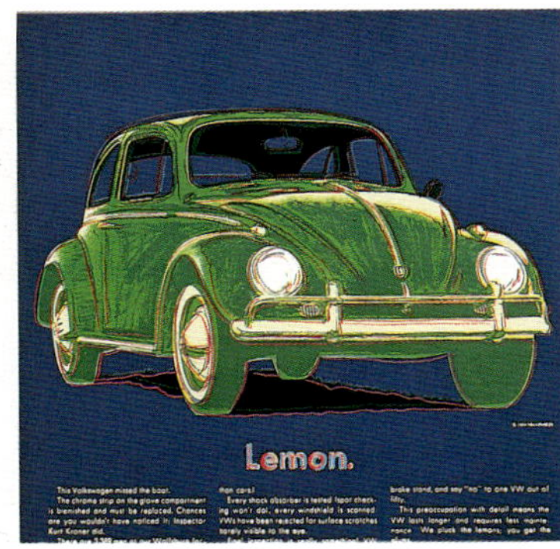

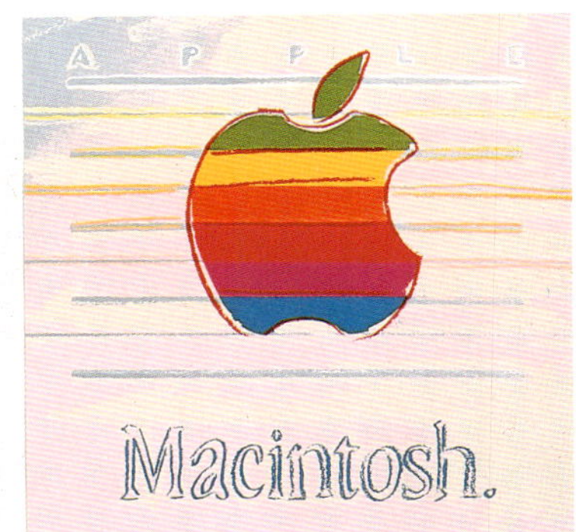

Ads, 1985. From a portfolio of ten silkscreen prints, each 38 x 38". Ronald Feldman Fine Arts, New York

Center: Andy Warhol and Giorgio de Chirico, New York City, ca. 1974. Photo: Gianfranco Gorgoni

Lower left: *The Disquieting Muses* (after De Chirico), 1982. Acrylic and silkscreen on canvas, 50 x 42". Andy Warhol Estate

Lower right: *The Two Sisters* (after De Chirico), 1982. Acrylic and silkscreen on canvas, 50 x 42". Andy Warhol Estate

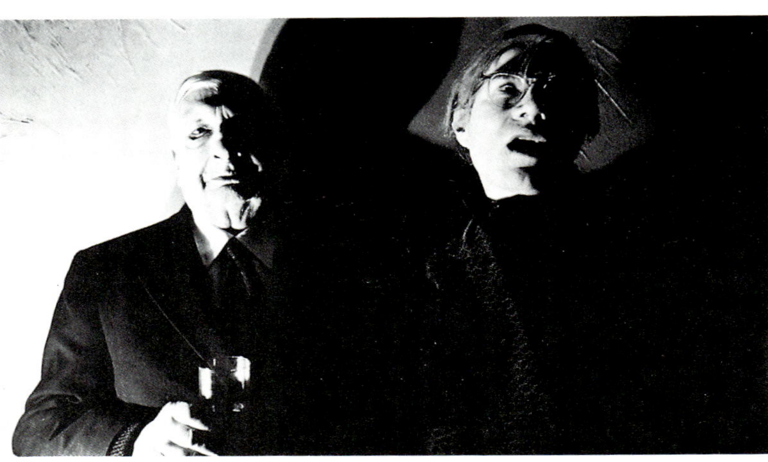

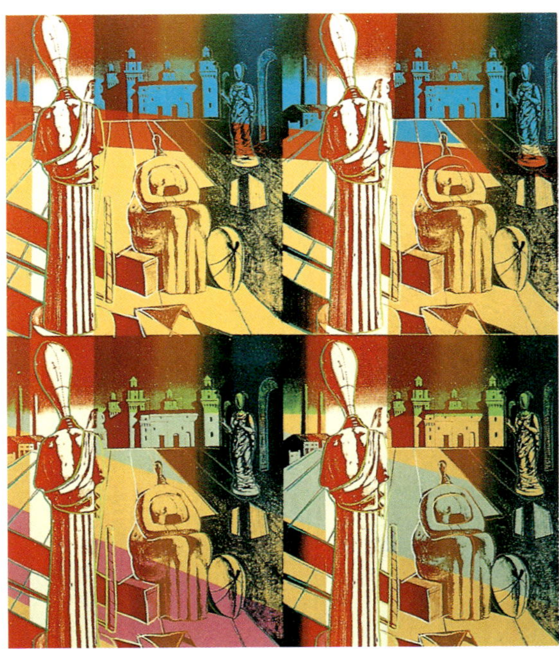

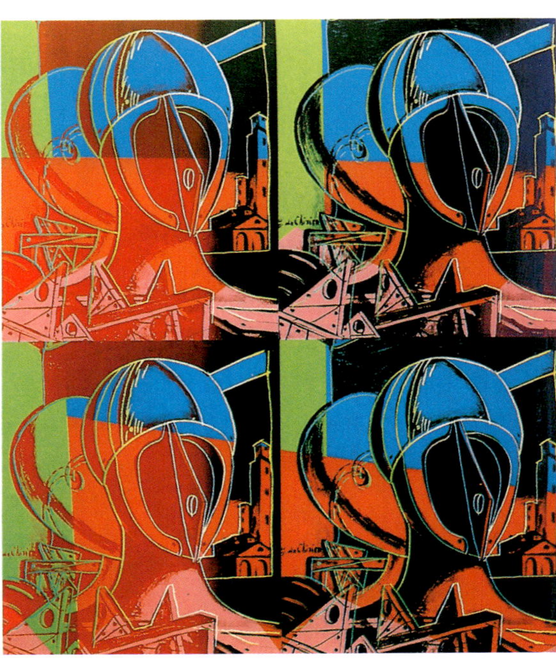

1986
Warhol produces Camouflages, Campbell's Soup Crates, Cars, Flowers, Self-Portraits, and Frederick the Great.

"Andy Warhol: Fifteen Minutes," a second series in which guests appear in very short segments, is shown on MTV cable television.

One-man shows: "Andy Warhol: Major Prints," Galerie Daniel Templon, Paris; "Andy Warhol Disaster Paintings 1963", Dia Art Foundation, New York; "Andy Warhol," Anthony d'Offay Gallery, London (Self-Portraits); "Hand-Painted Images, Andy Warhol 1960-1962," Dia Art Foundation, New York; "Oxidation Paintings," Larry Gagosian Gallery, New York.

1987
Portraits of Beethoven.
Begins work on a series entitled "History of American Television," and designs radio watches, as well as a watch for the Movado Company in New York.
Travels to Paris and Milan, where his "Last Supper" paintings are shown.
Dies February 22 after a gallbladder operation at New York Hospital – Cornell Medical Center, New York. He is buried in Pittsburgh, alongside his parents.
Following his wishes, the Andy Warhol Foundation for the Visual Arts is established in New York to support young artists, museums, exhibitions, and other cultural events in the plastic arts. Fred Hughes becomes president of the foundation.
On April 1, a memorial mass is held, with music by Mozart, Ravel, and Messiaen, at St. Patrick's Cathedral in New York.
Speakers at the memorial are John Richardson (the Picasso biographer and art historian), Yoko Ono, and Nicholas Love.

One-man show: "Andy Warhol Photographs," Robert Miller Gallery, New York.

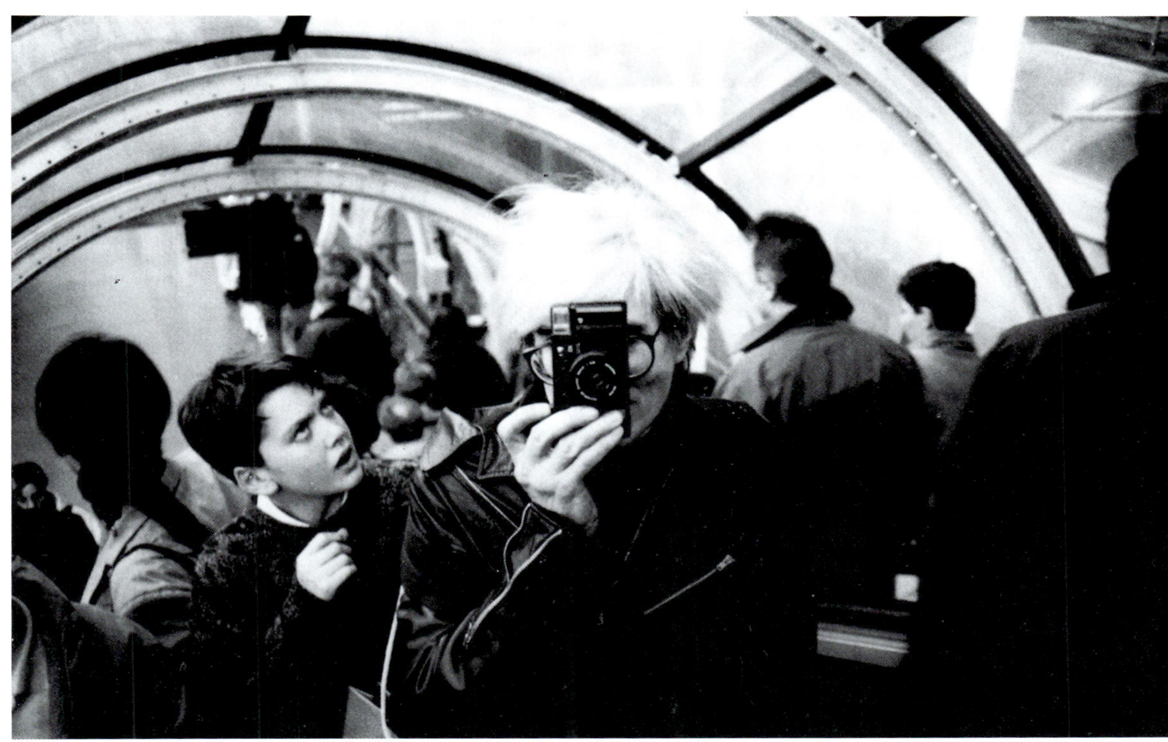

Andy Warhol at the Centre Pompidou, Paris, 1986. Photo: Christopher Makos

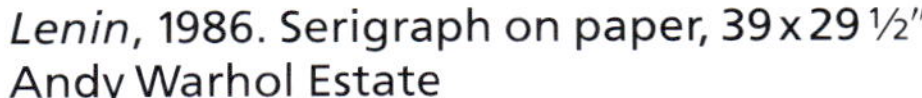

Lenin, 1986. Serigraph on paper, 39 x 29 ½". Andy Warhol Estate

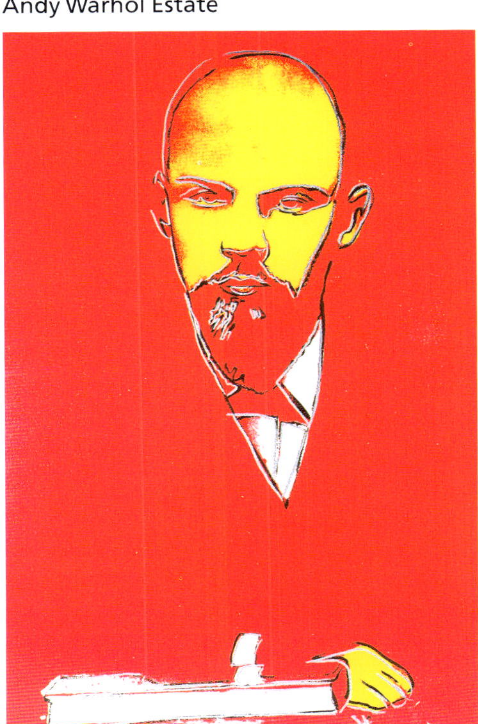

Beethoven, 1987. Acrylic and silkscreen on canvas, 40 x 40"

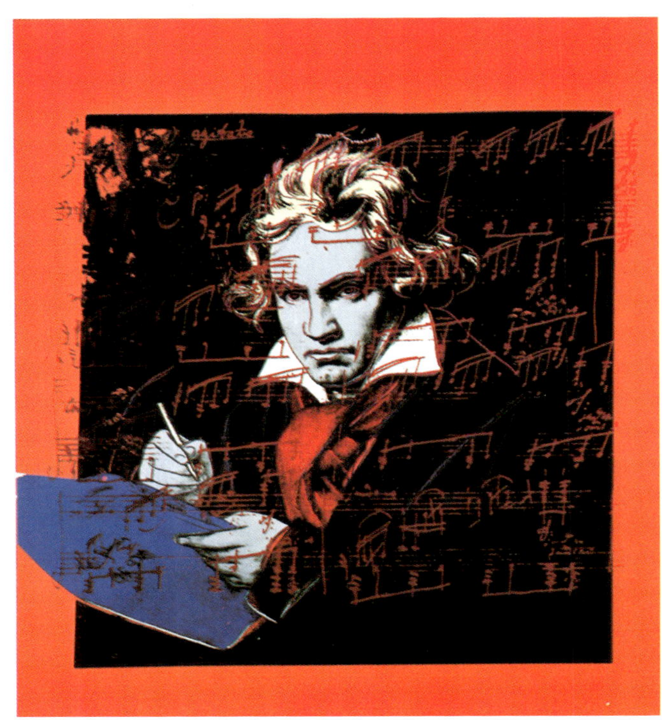

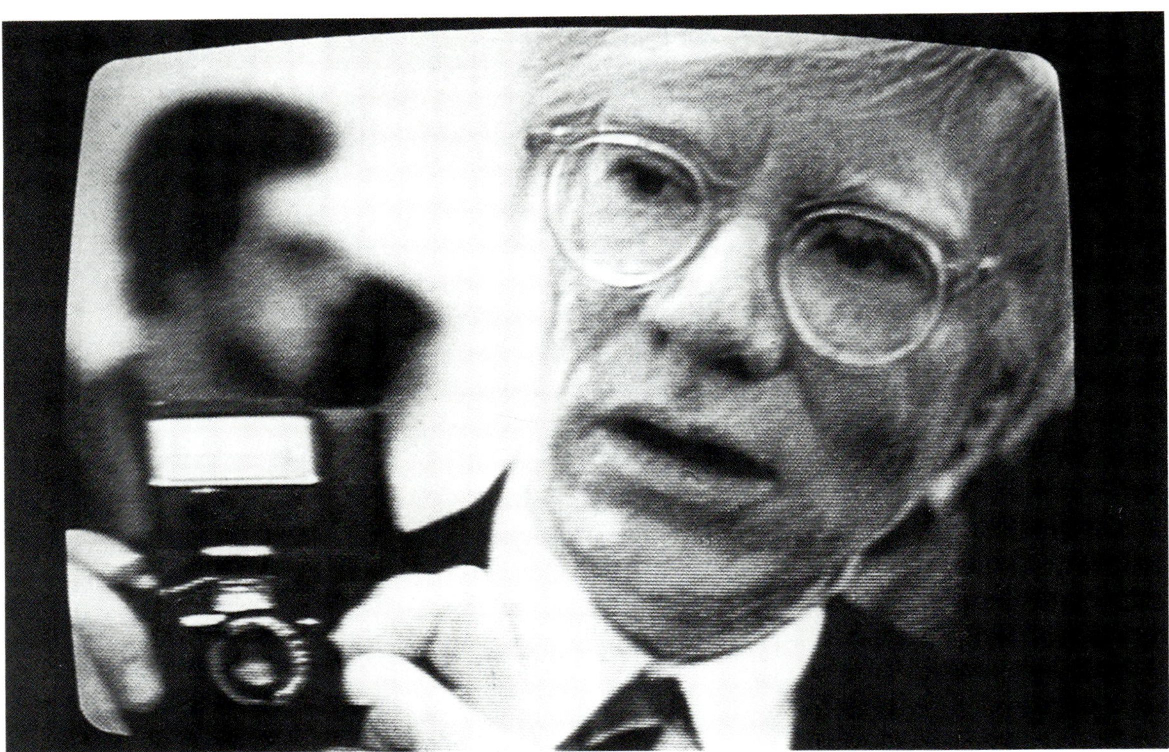

Andy Warhol shortly before his death, 1987. Photo: Christopher Makos

Auction of Andy Warhol's collection: cover of Sotheby's catalogue, New York, 1988

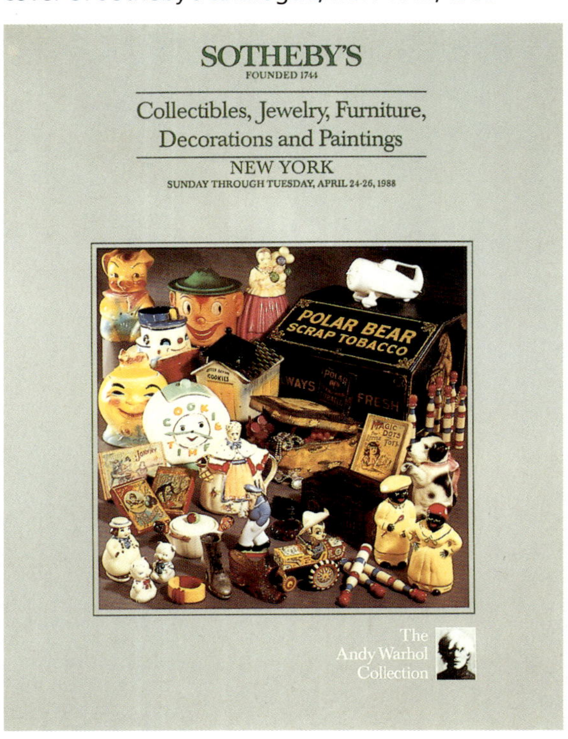

The kitchen in Warhol's house, Sotheby's catalogue, 1988

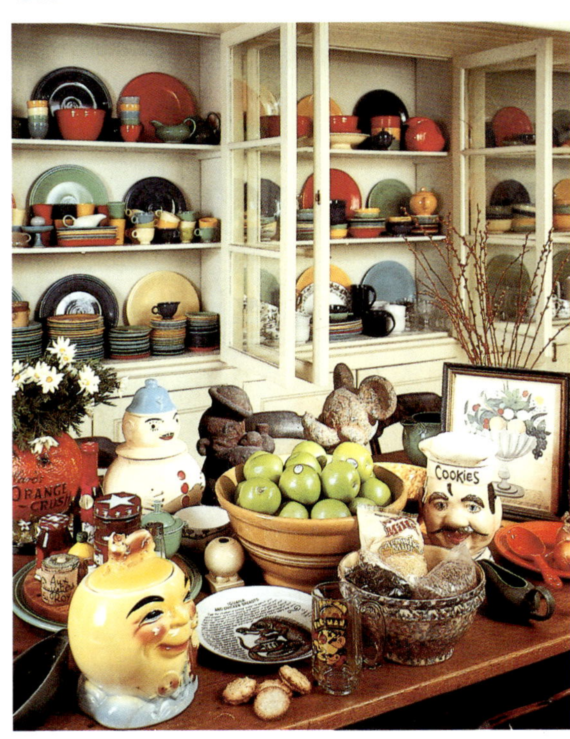

1988
The Andy Warhol Foundation for the Visual Arts, Inc. sells over 10,000 objects from Warhol's private collection of contemporary and modern art, Art Nouveau, Art Deco, American Indian art, jewelry, and furniture, at Sotheby's, New York. In December more jewelry and a collection of watches are auctioned at Sotheby's for the benefit of the Warhol Foundation.

1989
The Museum of Modern Art in New York organizes a major Warhol exhibition, under the direction of Kynaston McShine, Senior Curator of the Department of Painting and Sculpture at the museum. The exhibition travels to the Art Institute of Chicago; the Hayward Gallery, London; Museum Ludwig, Cologne; Palazzo Reale, Milan; and the Musée National d'Art Moderne, Centre Georges Pompidou, Paris.

Gene R. Swenson

Interview with Andy Warhol

Andy Warhol: Someone said that Brecht wanted everybody to think alike. I want everybody to think alike. But Brecht wanted to do it through Communism, in a way. Russia is doing it under government. It's happening here all by itself without being under a strict government; so if it's working without trying, why can't it work without being Communist? Everybody looks alike and acts alike, and we're getting more and more that way.

I think everybody should be a machine.

I think everybody should like everybody.

Gene R. Swenson: Is that what Pop Art is all about?

Yes. It's liking things.

And liking things is like being a machine?

Yes, because you do the same thing every time. You do it over and over again.

And you approve of that?

Yes, because it's all fantasy. It's hard to be creative and it's also hard not to think what you do is creative or hard not to be called creative because everybody is always talking about that and individuality. Everybody's always being creative. And it's so funny when you say things aren't, like the shoe I would draw for an advertisement was called a "creation" but the drawing of it was not. But I guess I believe in both ways. All these people who aren't very good should be really good. Everybody is too good now, really. Like, how many actors are there? There are millions of actors. They're all pretty good. And how many painters are there? Millions of painters and all pretty good. How can you say one style is better than another? You ought to be able to be an Abstract Expressionist next week, or a Pop artist, or a realist, without feeling you've given up something. I think the artists who aren't very good should become like everybody else so that people would like things that aren't very good. It's already happening. All you have to do is read the magazines and the catalogues. It's this style or that style, this or that image of man – but that really doesn't make any difference. Some artists get left out that way, and why should they?

Is Pop Art a fad?

Yes, it's a fad, but I don't see what difference it makes. I just heard a rumor that G. quit working, that she's given up art altogether. And everyone is saying how awful it is that A. gave up his style and is doing it in a different way. I don't think so at all. If an artist can't do any more, then he should just quit; and an artist ought to be able to change his style without feeling bad. I heard that Lichtenstein said he might not be painting comic strips a year or two from now – I think that would be so great, to be able to change styles. And I think that's what's going to happen, that's going to be the whole new scene. That's probably one reason I'm using silk screens now. I think somebody should be able to do all my paintings for me. I haven't been able to make every image clear and simple and the same as the first one. I think it would be so great if more people took up silk screens so that no one would know whether my picture was mine or somebody else's.

It would turn art history upside down?

Yes.

Is that your aim?

No. The reason I'm painting this way is that I want to be a machine, and I feel that whatever I do and do machine-like is what I want to do.

Was commercial art more machine-like?

No, it wasn't. I was getting paid for it, and did anything they told me to do. If they told me to draw a shoe, I'd do it, and if they told me to correct it, I would – I'd do anything they told me to do, correct it and do it right. I'd have to invent and now I don't; after all that "correction," those commercial drawings would have feelings, they would have a style. The attitude of those who hired me had feeling or something to it; they knew what they wanted, they insisted; sometimes they got very emotional. The process of doing work in commercial art was machine-like, but the attitude had feeling to it.

Why did you start painting soup cans?

Because I used to drink it. I used to have the same lunch every day, for twenty years, I guess, the same thing over and over again. Someone said my life has dominated me; I liked that idea. I used to want to live at the Waldorf Towers and have soup and a sandwich, like that scene in the restaurant in *Naked Lunch*....

We went to see *Dr No* at Forty-second Street. It's a fantastic movie, so cool. We walked outside and somebody threw a cherry bomb right in front of us, in this big crowd. And there was blood. I saw blood on people and all over. I felt like I was bleeding all over. I saw in the paper last week that there are more people throwing them – it's just part of the scene – and hurting people. My show in Paris is going to be called "Death in America." I'll show the electric-chair pictures and the dogs in Birmingham and car wrecks and some suicide pictures.

Why did you start these "Death" pictures?

I believe in it. Did you see the *Enquirer* this week? It had "The Wreck that Made Cops Cry" – a head cut in half, the arms and hands just lying there. It's sick, but I'm sure it happens all the time. I've met a lot of cops recently. They take pictures of everything, only it's almost impossible to get pictures from them.

When did you start with the "Death" series?

I guess it was the big plane crash picture, the front page of a newspaper: 129 DIE. I was also painting the "Marilyns." I realized that everything I was doing must have been Death. It was Christmas or Labor Day – a holiday – and every time you turned on the radio they said something like, "4 million are going to die." That started it. But when you see a gruesome picture over and over again, it doesn't really have any effect.

But you're still doing "Elizabeth Taylor" pictures.

I started those a long time ago, when she was so sick and everybody said she was going to die. Now I'm doing them all over, putting bright colors on her lips and eyes.

My next series will be pornographic pictures. They will look blank; when you turn on the black lights, then you see them – big breasts and... If a cop came in, you could just flick out the lights or turn to the regular lights – how could you say that was pornography? But I'm still just practising with these yet. Segal did a sculpture of two people making love, but he cut it all up, I guess because he thought it was too pornographic to be art. Actually it was very beautiful, perhaps a little too good, or he may feel a little protective about art. When you read Gênet you get all hot, and that makes some people say this is not art. The thing I like about it is that it makes you forget about style and that sort of thing; style isn't really important.

Is "Pop" a bad name?

The name sounds so awful. Dada must have something to do with Pop – it's so funny, the names are really synonyms. Does anyone know what they're supposed to mean or have to do with, those names? Johns and Rauschenberg – Neo-Dada for all these years, and everyone calling them derivative and unable to transform the things they use – are now called progenitors of Pop. It's funny the way things change. I think John Cage has been very influential, and Merce Cunningham, too, maybe. Did you see that article in the *Hudson Review* ["The End of the Renaissance?", Summer, 1963]? It was about Cage and that whole crowd, but with a lot of big words like radical empiricism and teleology. Who knows? Maybe Jap and Bob were Neo-Dada and aren't any more. History books are being rewritten all the time. It doesn't matter what you do. Everybody just goes on thinking the same thing, and every year it gets more and more alike. Those who talk about individuality the most are the ones who most object to deviation, and in a few years it may be the other way around. Some day everybody will think just what they want to think, and then everybody will probably be thinking alike; that seems to be what is happening.

First published in *Artnews* (New York), vol. 62, November 1963, pp. 60-63.

Pierre Restany

Andy Warhol: "Less is More"

Andy Warhol, that ageless son of the media world, and "America's most famous artist," just died of a burst gall bladder. He was not yet 59 years old. This text, written under the shock of this news, stems at one and the same time from analysis and remembrances. If I had to give it a title, I would willingly paraphrase Mies van der Rohe by saying: "Less is More."

Andy Warhol composed his style from a harmony of technical brainwaves, details from scripts and elements of strategy which are in themselves commonplace, and this very banality creates the effect of a super-presence: the man is dear to us because he is so close. In Warhol's case, there's no question of looking for the usual parameters that involve esthetic conviction, or even, if pushed to it, the elementary criteria of quality. The truth about Warhol lies in the sense of an immense and familiar presence conjured up in us by the repetitive use of all that goes to make up daily life. He made of this a direct language which concerns us all, that means those who don't like him, by the same token as those who adore him and consider him as a value-symbol for today's society.

Warhol is there before us, like an immanent presence. Should a publisher ask my advice regarding the cover illustration for a book on existentialist philosophy, I would suggest a self-portrait of Warhol. All the more so if it concerned one of Heidegger's works. For me, Warhol incarnates the "being there," the "*Da sein*," the ontological immanence, the quality of a presence having nothing to do with the astuteness of the discourse. Being there because one has elected to be there, with the simplest means of affirmation of the being. Warhol is the synonym of this essential simplicity.

I met Andy in New York in 1962 on the occasion of the exhibition I had organized with Sidney Janis, getting together simultaneously the European New Realists and those who were to become the Pop Art stars, Oldenburg, Lichtenstein, Rosenquist, Segal, and of course Warhol. I was staying in the Chelsea Hotel which at that time welcomed all the passing artists and writers from Europe. Warhol haunted the corridors, camera in hand, in search of benevolent actors for his first films. Back stage at the Chelsea he obviously had considerable possibilities for the taking. It happened to me, just like Geldzahler, to pose for one of his films. In *The Kiss* I gave what in fact was the longest kiss in the history of cinema: by repeating a one and a half minute sequence, Warhol produced a 55-minute film....

The setting of a situation within an action crystallized in its duration is characteristic of the first experimental films. The themes provided are simple, but very strong – illustrating the relativity of time: *The Kiss*, *Sleep*, or again Geldzahler filmed brushing his teeth the wrong way round!

Although Warhol had given up his career as publicity painter at Glamour and Vogue some years back, a lightning stroke suddenly won fame for him in 1962: the exhibition of the Campbell's Soups series at Stable Gallery, which affirmed the process of transferring negative photos onto canvas. Out of this typical publicity drawing process he made up his mind to invent a complete artistic language, and he succeeded beyond all hopes. Rauschenberg adopted the outcome on the spot.

The very banality of the subjects contributed to the success of the undertaking: by repeating umpteen times the can of soup, the packet of Brillo washing powder or the portrait of Marilyn, the artist appealed directly to the iconography of the dominant ideology, Pop ideology, recording the perfect metaphor of American consumerism of the sixties, in the most natural register: confirmation of cold facts.

Amongst the forerunners of Pop Art who were making a name for themselves at that time, Warhol already ranked as someone apart, even though he shared the views on the world as seen by people like Oldenburg, Lichtenstein or Wesselman. Warhol personally remained close to daily life in all its banality and with all its uncertainties. In a very short spell, the series-symbols of the consumer society were augmented by the "news in brief" chapter – "Disaster Paintings" depicting car accidents, the electric chair, lynchings, atomic bombs. The cold-bloodedness of this projection of current events as the objective increased the tragic note; brutal as they are, these images are basically nothing more than objects found in the ragtag and bobtail of the popular press, clichés already published and here reproduced on canvas. The "objectivation" of the process is complete. Compared to Pop's iconographic production, for Warhol everything is much simpler: there is nothing really sophisticated about it. And it's this "just as it is," that "factual" element that makes of Warhol the purest recording phenomenon of his period's daily tempo. Warhol's vision, derived from the image's ready-made Pop is every man's vision, without the slightest psychological or cultural transfer, easy to share with all and sundry. It goes without saying, Warhol substitutes his vision of things to ours: his "naturalness" is communicable at once. The less he adds on, the more the current flows back and forth: "Less is more."

His films, on which he began practically at the same moment as he found his path in the pictorial field, add practically nothing to the way he sees things. I already mentioned the duration. There is a highly significant element to be found in his full-length films such as *Chelsea Girls*: simultaneous use of different screens, first creating the flow of two parallel images, then mingling them on the rim, and even juxtaposing them at times. All this is the fruit of a series of brainwaves, producing an ensemble of relatively simple technical finds, which are registered directly in our memory and describe an extremely common mental process: the time lag between the emission of a clear thought and its brusque contamination by another idea coming to overlap it at the language level.

Of a current phenomenon alone, Warhol succeeded in producing a strong and concrete vision. The themes of his films are of secondary importance; for all that, they were declared to be shocking. They were no more nor less pornographic, sensual or provocative than the subjects of the underground literature then invading the new American cinema in the wake of Kenneth Anger. It is interesting to note that indeed the first films Warhol authored himself bear witness to a direct influence of the underground cinema. Moreover, Warhol never considered himself anything other than a chronicler of the air of the times: times he well knew, having explored them from A to Z with no mental restrictions. He knew how to take advantage of the wave of permissivity then flowing over the American consumer society and to live it to the full, with no complexes. His cinema was a cinema without complexes, as were his life and his painting.

He was surrounded by a bevy of friends and collaborators, rather fluid at the outset like a kind of nebula, but which subsequently condensed and became the technical top staff of the Factory.

In 1968, when he was specializing more and more in portraits of stars or members of the international jet set – Liz, Jackie, Elvis – the drama broke out. One of his former actresses, Valeria Solanis – frustrated not to have enjoyed the destiny of superstars like Ultra Violet or International Velvet – surprised him in his office, deep in conversation with the British art critic, Mario Amaya, and fired her revolver at the two celebrities. They were both hit, Amaya more superficially on the buttocks, whereas Warhol, who was facing the intruder, received two shots in the region of the breast and the pelvis. He miraculously recovered, adding a new aureola to his legend.

From that time on, a major evolution becomes patent in Warhol: the oeuvre transforms itself into destiny. The Warhol personnage transforms itself into the Warhol oeuvre, he commands it, he dominates it, and he is the parameter of reference. From then on he became renowned for his receptions, his spectacular appearances, his "carnet mondain" (social diary), the growing number of celebrities he frequented and whom he portrayed. He was the man of all the spectacular feats, the man one had to invite to dinner, a real "must," and at the same time he was the man who played less and less with his technique, setting up a production routine instead. In actual fact it was he who chose the themes and directed the production, but it was his assistants and sponsors who did the work itself.

After having created *Interview,* he imposed a type of journalism in his image: an ad hoc press model, when he was himself the product of this all-powerful press! The breathing space found in the large format was a program in itself, with the osmosis between a voluntarily restricted editorial content and a wide expanse of space for advertisements.

The liberties he took as regards his own technique, and his profound detachment from his own work helped him to stick more closely to current events. Some of his series, such as his portraits of Mao (1973), the Hammer and Sickle (1976), the Dollar Bills or the profile of the American Indian fitted quite naturally into our society's existential field, being precise allusions to major ideological, financial or racial problems of the moment. The dollar series appeared at the height of the American financial crisis, and everybody found it perfectly natural for Warhol to manipulate this money symbol at that particular time; as for the amerindian series, it was contemporary with Wounded Knee.... No one takes coincidences such as this to be pure hazard. Warhol gradually managed to eliminate this random dimension from his creation – that discretionary form of the problematical which had been the backbone of his first images.

His last two series dealt with two personages who were at one and the same time the superstars and the daily bread of two of the most powerful hagiographies in the world, Lenin and Christ – Leonardo's *The Last Supper*.

I was in Milan on January 22d, varnishing day of *The Last Supper*. Warhol's inauguration date coincided with the day when the prohibition for the public to visit the Chapel of Santa Maria delle Grazie – where Leonardo's original is to be found – came into effect. Warhol's series thus gave the impression of enabling the henceforth inaccessible message of this famous chef-d'oeuvre to pierce through the walls like a kind of relay, and at the same time, reactualizing an act where of all the symbolic value was enhanced on the white walls of the Palazzo delle Stelline – an ancient convent converted into a congress center, fifty yards as the crow flies from the Cenacolo. That day there, the winter sun of Lombardy shining bright and clear, imparted to Warhol's work an aura of quasi immaterial spirituality.

Warhol, very moving in his platinum state wig with a mauve sheen, making him look as if he were in half-mourning, seemed to be imbued with the importance of the moment. He greatly surprised me by saying: "Do you believe, Pierre, that the Italians are conscious of the respect I have for Leonardo?"

There was not the slightest trace of the tone of unemotional cynicism he adopted in all his public manifestations. Instead there was a reserve corresponding to the self-restraint he had exercised in his chromatic intervention on the transfer of the faces of Christ and his Apostles, whether to one side or the other.

This series of "L'Ultima Cena" bears witness to a more or less avowed desire to recuperate a great spiritual message. Whether consciously or not, it seems to me that Warhol betook himself there as the curator of a masterpiece of Christian culture, to maintain a tradition which was not his own. The crowd thronged to see Warhol rather than his version of La Cena. But despite the public's indifference, for me the works on the walls conserved all their aura, somewhat as if Warhol had wanted to transmit through them a message reaching beyond readymade visual effect. And I am convinced he achieved this.

That is the last memory Andy left me, and the retrospective glance I cast today on the man and his work is laden with unsuspected fondness. On reflection, I realize that this warmth of feeling is linked to a brusque recalling to the obvious. This man was close to me, as he was to millions of other men, precisely because he opted for the way of the majority. And this, going beyond all appearances of facility. His philosophy of the banal was his way of being human to the very backbone. Less is more.

Andy Warhol's disappearance will leave a great void. It will take a long time for the American media culture to fabricate a guru dandy of this caliber, or a Peter Pan with all that charm – sulfurous at times – yet knowing how to address, in all simplicity, the world of man, as a man of the world.

First published in *Galeries Magazine* (Paris), April/May 1987, pp. 80-87.

Paul Taylor

Andy Warhol: The Last Interview

Paul Taylor: You are going to be showing your *Last Supper* paintings in Milan this year.

Andy Warhol: Yes.

When did you make the paintings?

I was working on them all year. They were supposed to be shown in December, then January. Now I don't know when.

Are they painted?

I don't know. Some were painted, but they're not going to show the painted ones. We'll use the silkscreened ones.

On some of them you have camouflage over the top of the images. Why is that?

I had some leftover camouflage.

From the self-portraits?

Yeah.

Did you do any preparatory drawings from them?

Yeah I tried. I did about forty paintings.

They were all preparatory?

Yeah.

It's very odd to see images like this one doubled.

They're just the small ones.

The really big one is where there are images upsidedown and the right way up.

That's right.

It's odd because you normally see just one Jesus at a time.

Now there are two.

Like the two Popes.

The European Pope and the American Pope.

Did you see Dokoupil's show at Sonnabend Gallery?

Oh no I haven't gone there yet. I want to go on Saturday.

It might be the last day. There you will see two Jesuses on crucifixes, one beside the other.

Oh.

And he explained to me something like how it was transgressive to have two Jesuses in the same picture.

He took the words out of my mouth.

You're trying to be transgressive?

Yes.

In America, you could be almost as famous as Charles Manson. Is there any similarity between you at the Factory and Jesus at the *Last Supper*?

That's negative; to me it's negative. I don't want to talk about negative things.

Well, what about these happier days at the present Factory. Now you're a Corporation President.

It's the same.

Why did you do the *Last Supper*?

Because Iolas asked me to do the *Last Supper*.

He got a gallery in front of the other Last Supper, and he asked three or four people to do Last Suppers.

Does the Last Supper theme mean anything in particular to you?

It's a good picture.

What do you think of the subject matter?

It's something that you see all the time. You don't think about it.

What do you think about those books and articles, like Stephen Koch's *Stargazer* and a 1964 *Newsweek* piece called *"Saint Andre"* that bring up the subject of Catholicism?

I don't know. Stephen Koch's book was interesting because he was able to write a whole book about it. He has a new book out which I'm trying to buy to turn into a screenplay. I think it's called *The Bride's Bachelors* or some Duchampy title. Have you read it yet?

No, I read the review in the *New York Times Book Review*.

What did it say?

It was okay.

Yeah? What's it about?

Stephen Koch described it to me himself. He said it was about a heterosexual Rauschenberg figure in the '60s, a magnetic artist who has qualities of a lot of '60s artists. He has an entourage. I don't know the rest.

I've been meaning to call him and see if he can tell me the story and send me the book.

Who's making a screenplay?

We thought that we might be able to do it.

It's a great idea. Would you be able to get real people to play themselves in it?

I don't know. It might be good.

Do you have screenwriters here?

We just bought Tama Janowicz's book called *Slaves of New York*.

Does that mean you're going into movie production?

We're trying. But actually what we're working on is our video show which MTV is buying.

"Nothing Special"?

No it's called "Andy Warhol's Fifteen Minutes." It was on Thursday last week and it's showing again Monday and it'll be shown two more times. December and we're doing one for January.

Do you make them?

No, Vincent works on them, Vincent Fremont.

Do you look through the camera on these things at all?

No.

What's your role?

Just interviewing people.

If there was a movie made out of Stephen Koch's novel, what would be your role in it?

I don't know, I'd have to read it first.

It's not usual for business people to talk about these deals before they make them.

I don't care if anyone . . . there's always another book.

I saw Ileana today and asked her what I should ask you, and she said, "I don't know. For Andy everything is equal."

She's right.

How do you describe that point of view?

I don't know. If she said it she's right (laughs).

It sounds Zennish.

Zennish. What's that?

Like Zen.

Zennish. That's a good word. That's a good title for ... my new book.

What about your transformation from being a commercial artist to a real artist?

I'm still a commercial artist. I was always a commercial artist.

Then what's a commercial artist?

I don't know; someone who sells art.

So almost all artists are commercial artists, just to varying degrees.

I think so.

Is a better commercial artist one who sells more work?

I don't know. When I started out, art was going down the drain. The people who used to do magazine illustrations and the covers were being replaced by photographers. And when they started using photographers I started to show my work with galleries. Everybody also was doing window decoration. That led into more galleries. I had some paintings in a window, then in a gallery.

Is there a parallel situation now?

No, it just caught on so well that there's a new gallery open every day now. There are a lot more artists, which is real great.

What has happened to the idea of good art?

It's all good art.

Is that to say that it's all equal?

Yeah well, I don't know, I can't ...

You're not interested in making distinctions.

Well no, I just can't tell the difference. I don't see why one Jasper Johns sells for three million and one sells for, you know, like four hundred thousand. They were both good paintings.

The market for your works has changed a little in the last few years. To people my age – in their twenties – you were always more important than to the collecting group of people in their fifties and sixties.

Well I think the people who buy art now are these younger kids who have a lot of money.

And that's made a difference in your market.

Yeah, a little bit.

How important is it for you to maintain control?

I've been busy since I started – since I was a working artist. If I wasn't showing in New York I was doing work in Germany, or I was doing portraits.

What I mean is that as more and more artists come up, and as new galleries open every day, the whole idea of what an artist is changes. It's no longer so special, and maybe a more special artist is one who maintains more control of his or her work.

I don't know. It seems like every year there's one artist for that year. The people from twenty years ago are still around. I don't know why. The kids nowadays – there's just one a year. They stay around, they just don't ...

You were identified with a few artists a couple of years ago Kenny Scharf, Keith Haring.

We're still friends.

But I never see you with any of this season's flavors.

I don't know. They got so much press. It was great. I'm taking photographs now. I have a photography show at Robert Miller Gallery.

And there's going to be a retrospective of your films at the Whitney Museum.

Maybe, yes.

Are you excited about that?

No.

Why not?

They're better talked about than seen.

Your work as an artist has always been so plural, like Leonardo. You're a painter, a filmmaker, a publisher .... Do you think that's what an artist is?

No.

Can you define an artist for me?

I think an artist is anybody who does something well, like if you cook well.

What do you think about all the younger artists now in New York who are using Pop imagery?

Pretty good.

It is the same as when it happened in the '60s?

No, they have different reasons to do things. All these kids are so intellectual.

Did you like the punk era?

Well it's still around. I always think it's gone but it isn't. They still have their hard rock nights at the Ritz. Do you ever go there?

No. But punk, like Pop, might never go away.

I guess so.

How's *Interview* going?

It's not bad.

You're going to be audited soon for the Audit Bureau of Circulations.

Yeah, they're doing it now.

What difference will it make?

I don't know.

It will be better for advertising ...

Yeah.

What's the circulation now?

170,000. The magazine's getting bigger and bigger.

What magazines do you read?

I just read everything.

You look at everything. Do you read the art magazines?

Yeah. I look at the pictures.

You've been in trouble for using someone else's image as far back as 1964. What do you think about the legal situation of appropriated imagery, and the copyright situation?

I don't know. It's just like a Coca-Cola bottle when you buy it you always think that it's yours and you can do what ever

you like with it. Now it's sort of different because you pay a deposit on the bottle. We're having the same problem now with the John Wayne pictures. I don't want to get involved, it's too much trouble. I think that you buy a magazine, you pay for it, it's yours. I don't get mad when people take my things.

You don't do anything about it?

No. It got a little crazy when people were turning out paintings and signing my name.

What did you think about that?

Signing my name to it was wrong but other than that I don't care.

The whole appropriation epidemic comes down to who is responsible for art. If indeed anyone can manufacture the pictures of those flowers, the whole idea of the artist gets lost somewhere in the process.

Is that good or bad?

Well, first of all, do you agree with me?

Yes, if they take my name away. But when I used the flowers, the original photograph was huge and I just used one square inch of the photo and magnified it.

What do you ever see that makes you stop in your tracks?

A good display in a window ... I don't know ... a good looking face.

What's the feeling when you see a good window display or a good face?

You just take longer to look at it. I went to China. I didn't want to go, and I went to see the Great Wall. You know, you read about it for years. And actually it was great. It was really really really great.

Have you been working out lately?

I just did it.

How much are you lifting now?

105 lbs.

On the benchpress? That's strong.

No it's light. You're stronger than me, and fitter and handsomer and younger, and you wear better clothes.

Did you enjoy the opening party thrown by GFT at the Tunnel?

I had already been there before.

In the sixties you mean?

(Laughs) No – the manager or someone took me around it a few days ago.

It's a very convenient club for the Bridge and Tunnel people – they'll be able to come in on those tracks from New Jersey.

I don't know. I just worked hard. It's all fantasy, someone else's idea that I liked, but I think it's a good name.

And lots of people turned out for Claes Oldenburg's show.

He looked happy. A lot of people said he looked happy. I always liked Claes actually. You looked great the other night. I took lots of photos of you in your new jacket.

Yes? How did I turn out?

They haven't come back yet. Next time you come by I'll take some close-ups.

For the Upfront section of *Interview* perhaps? Except that I'm not accomplished enough.

You could sleep with the publisher.

If you were starting out now, would you do anything differently?

I dont know. I just worked hard. It's all fantasy.

Life is fantasy?

Yeah it is.

What's real?

Don't know.

Some people would.

Would they?

Do you really believe it, or tomorrow will you say the opposite?

I don't know. I like this idea that you can say the opposite.

But would wouldn't in this case?

No.

Is there any connection between fantasy and religious feeling?

Maybe, I don't know. Church is a fun place to go.

Do you go to Italy very often?

You know we use to make films there.

And didn't you have a studio in the country for a while?

Outside of Rome.

And did you go to the Vatican?

We passed by it every day.

I remeber a polaroid you took of the Pope.

Yeah.

Did you take that from very close up?

Yes. He walked past us.

And he blessed you?

I have a photo of him shaking Fred Hughes's hand. Someone wanted us to make a portrait of the Pope and they've been trying to get us together but we can't and by now the Pope has changed three times.

Fred said he used to feel like the Pope in the old Factory in Union Square. He used to go out on that balcony and wave at the passing masses underneath.

He has a balcony now.

Yes, but from the current Factory he can only see the reception area.

He can wave.

And sometimes it's just as busy as Union Square too.

This is the last interview with Andy Warhol, which took place just before the opening of *Il Cenacolo* (The Last Supper) exhibition in Milan.
First published in *Flash Art* (Milan), April 1987, pp. 41-44.

Selected Films by Andy Warhol

Sleep
By Andy Warhol. 1963. U.S.A. 42 min. B & W. Silent. 18 fps.* (excerpt)
The six-hour film *Sleep* shows poet John Giorno in various positions of sleep. Warhol elongated the "action," recorded on 100-foot rolls of film, by repeating filmed segments through loop printing. The concluding image is a frozen still.

Kiss
By Andy Warhol. 1963. U.S.A. 58 min. B & W. Silent. 18 fps.*
This film was originally shown as a serial. It features close-up sequences of couples kissing, each sequence lasting for one roll of film. It includes Warhol Factory regulars Naomi Levine, Gerard Malanga, Baby Jane Holzer, and John Palmer, as well as artist Marisol, art critic Pierre Restany, and poet Ed Sanders.

Eat
By Andy Warhol. 1963. U.S.A. 39 min. B & W. Silent. 18 fps.*
Eat shows artist Robert Indiana slowly eating one mushroom. Time figures strongly in this work; simple action is repeated and slowed down by loop printing, frozen frames, and a retarded projection speed.

Blow Job
By Andy Warhol. 1963. U.S.A. 35 min. B & W. Silent. 18 fps.*
The voyeuristic camera focuses in close-up on the face of a young man, the collar of his jacket just showing. The actor's head remains fixed within the frame, the eroticism suggested by his face as it signals the subtle rise and fall of his emotions. The sexual activity indicated by the title, if it does occur, takes place entirely off screen and is left to the imagination of the viewer.

Henry Geldzahler
By Andy Warhol. 1964. U.S.A. 90 min. B & W. Silent. 18 fps.*
The well-known curator and early champion of Warhol is seen smoking a large cigar. The slowing-down of the already minimal action foregrounds the textures and subtle values of the film record of the human face. This work certainly ranks with Warhol's canvas portraits in its insightful exploitation of the medium and an ability to highlight the distinctive features of the subject.

Empire
By Andy Warhol. 1964. U.S.A. 48 min. B &W. Silent. 18 fps.* (excerpt).
An excerpt from the eight-hour filming of the Empire State Building, shot from night to morning on June 25, 1964, from the forty-fourth floor of the Time-Life building. In Warhol's cinema, action is refined through a new sense of cinematic time – "real time" as a continuous presence. The 100-foot rolls of film that make up each title can be likened to Warhol's serial silkscreens, with their rough edges and acknowledgment of process and materials. In the films, each roll constitutes a piece of time separated by light flashes at the beginning and end. This dialectic between the camera and time reaches its apotheosis in *Empire.*

Vinyl
By Andy Warhol. 1965. U.S.A. 64 min. B & W. Sound.
The second phase of Warhol's filmmaking is more closely related to the theater and the establishment of "Superstars" whose actions form a series of exploration of sexual taboos. In *Vinyl*, as Gerard Malanga dances and performs with chains, Edie Sedgwick, sitting to the right of the frame, assumes the position of the viewer, while pseudo sado-masochistic torture takes place in the background. The action circulates within the confined space of the film frame; the scene becomes a tightly orchestrated play on the pathos of gesture, acted out within a space delineated by the camera.

Beauty #2
By Andy Warhol. 1965. U.S.A. 66 min. B & W. Sound.
Beauty #2 is set on a bed as we watch Edie Sedgwick and a young man carry on a conversation and banter between themselves and the off-screen voices of Chuck Wein and Gerard Malanga. Sedgwick becomes a magnetic presence whose strength and vulnerability are exposed in her improvisational interplay with the camera. The off-screen dialogue foregrounds the point of view of the camera and ourselves as voyeurs to the production process. *Beauty #2* establishes a compelling and moving mise-en-scene through Sedgwick's cool beauty and the elegant transparency of the filmmaking.

My Hustler
By Andy Warhol. 1965. U.S.A. 67 min. B & W. Sound.
In this film we see the emergence of a narrative articulated in scenes of everyday life. The negotiated gestures of grooming and seduction between men in a bathroom become a voyeuristic documentation of the intimacies of private ritual. The erotic power of the camera is acknowledged as it forms a transparent wall between us and the action, a position which is also held by the film's maker, Warhol.

The Life of Juanita Castro
By Andy Warhol. 1965. U.S.A. 65 min. B & W. Sound.
This film follows the theater of the absurd and camp sensibility of Jack Smith and Ronald Tavel. Its send-up of "South of the Border" B-movies shows Warhol's fascination with the Hollywood mystique and uses sexuality and theatricality as a

means to reflect back on and play with the models of popular culture. Thus *The Life of Juanita Castro* combines the outrageous characterizations of its transvestite stars with Warhol's desire to cross-over to the commercial cinema.

Chelsea Girls

By Andy Warhol. 1966. U.S.A. 210 min. Color & B & W. Sound.

Chelsea Girls presents a much larger narrative design than Warhol's other films. New York's Chelsea Hotel is the setting for a series of narratives, each acted out by the stars of the Warhol entourage. Each of the film's twelve reels constitutes a separate episode. The reels are not projected in a single linear sequence, but rather are divided into two parts that play off each other as pairs of reels are projected side by side on the screen. This work is a brilliant synthesis of the narrative and voyeuristic camera. *Note: The white scratch lines in reel #2 are part of the film.*

Nude Restaurant

By Andy Warhol. 1967. U.S.A. 95 min. Color. Sound.

In an outrageous spoof of the movies, *Nude Restaurant* offers an open-ended series of dialogues and monologues between Viva and Taylor Mead and various other denizens of the makeshift space of a restaurant. The film is noteworthy for its characterizations by Viva as the strident foil and catalyst for a scatological spoof of pornography.

Lonesome Cowboys

By Andy Warhol. 1967. U.S.A. 110 min. Color. Sound.

This is the last film Warhol directed and he gives full rein to the articulation of a camp sensibility operating within the conventions of melodramatic imagination. We observe the casual, carnal improvisations of actors Joe Dallesandro and Viva as they cavort, dressed and undressed, about the set of a Western town. Their actions mime and ironically expose the cliches of the Western genre. Thus *Lonesome Cowboys* directly acknowledges traditional genres of filmmaking and acting and lays the aesthetic foundation for the later feature-length films which Warhol produced and Paul Morrissey directed.

* Note: Warhol shot his silent films at 16 fps but since nearly all silent speed projectors operate at only 18 fps, we recommend that speed for the Warhol silent films. These films are available at the circulating library of the Museum of Modern Art in New York.

Selected Bibliography

Books by the Artist

With David Paul and Stephen Shore. *Andy Warhol's Index (Book)*. New York: Random House, 1967.
With Gerald Malanga. *Screen Tests: A Diary*. New York: Kulchur Press, 1967.
A: A Novel. New York: Grove Press, 1968.
Blue Movie: A Film. New York: Grove Press, 1970.
The Philosophy of Andy Warhol (From A to B and Back Again). New York: Harcourt Brace Jovanovich, 1975.
Andy Warhol's Exposures. New York: Andy Warhol Books/Grosset & Dunlap, 1979.
With Pat Hackett. *POPism: The Warhol '60s*. New York: Harcourt Brace Jovanovich, 1980.
America. New York: Harper & Row, 1985.
Andy Warhol's Party Book. New York: Crown, 1988.

Books Illustrated by the Artist

Vanderbilt, Amy. *Amy Vanderbilt's Complete Book of Etiquette*. Garden City, N.Y.: Doubleday, 1952. Illustrated by Warhol, Fred McCarroll, and Mary Suzuki. Reprints 1954-72.
A Is an Alphabet. (New York, 1953). "By Corkie and Andy." Texts by Ralph T. Ward.
Love Is a Pink Cake. (New York, 1953). "By Corkie and Andy." Texts by Ralph T. Ward.
25 Cats Name Sam and One Blue Pussy. (New York, 1954, printed by Seymour Berlin). Reprint (together with *Holy Cats by Andy Warhol's Mother*). New York: Panache Press at Random House, 1987. Texts by Charles Lisanby.
A La Recherche du Shoe Perdu. (New York, 1955). Poems by Ralph Pomeroy.
In the Bottom of My Garden. (New York, 1955).
A Gold Book. (New York, 1957).
Wild Raspberries. (New York, 1959). Texts by Suzie Frankfurt.
Andy Warhol's Children's Book. Küsnacht, Switzerland: Edition Galerie Bruno Bischofberger, 1983.
Bernischke, Kurt. *Vanishing Animals*. New York: Springer Verlag, 1986.

Books and Catalogues about the Artist

Abrahams, Anna. *Warhol Films*. Amsterdam: Wiederhall Editions, 1989.
Andy Warhol: Arbeiten/Works, 1962-1986. Salzburg: Galerie Thaddaeus Ropac, 1987.
Andy Warhol: Death and Disasters. Houston: Menil Collection and Houston Fine Arts Press, 1988.
Andy Warhol: Portrait Screenprints, 1965-80. London: Arts Council of Great Britain, 1981.
Andy Warhol. Andy Warhol, Kasper König, Pontus Hulten & Olle Granath, eds. Stockholm: Moderna Museet, 1968.
The Andy Warhol Collection: Sold for the Benefit of the Andy Warhol Foundation for the Visual Arts. New York: Sotheby's, 1988.
Andy Warhol in the 1980s. Ridgefield, Conn.: Aldrich Museum of Contemporary Art, 1983.
Andy Warhol in Venice. Milan: Mazzotta, 1988.
Baal-Teshuva, Jacob, guest curator. *Andy Warhol*. Tel Aviv: Tel Aviv Museum of Art, 1992.
Bailey, David. *Andy Warhol: Transcript of David Bailey's ATV Documentary*. London: Bailey Litchfield/Mathews Miller Dunbar Ltd., 1972.
Barthes, Roland. *Wilhelm von Gloeden: Interventi di Joseph Beuys, Michelangelo Pistoletto, Andy Warhol*. Naples: Amelio, 1978.
Billeter, Erika, ed. *Andy Warhol: Ein Buch zur Ausstellung 1978 im Kunsthaus Zürich*. Zurich: Kunsthaus, 1978.
Bockris, Victor. *The Life and Death of Andy Warhol*. New York: Bantam Books, 1989.
Bonuomo, Michele, ed. *Vesuvius by Warhol*. Naples: Electa Napoli, 1985.
Bourdon, David. *Warhol*. New York: Harry N. Abrams, Inc., 1989.
Bowman, Russell. *Warhol/Beuys/Polke*. Milwaukee: Milwaukee Art Museum, 1987.
Brant, Sandra, and Elissa Cullman. *Andy Warhol's "Folk and Funk."* New York: Museum of American Folk Art, 1977.
Brown, Andreas, compiler. *Andy Warhol: His Early Works, 1947-1959*. New York: Gotham Book Mart Gallery, 1971.
Colacello, Bob. *Holy Terror: Andy Warhol Close-Up*. New York: Harper-Collins, 1990.
Collaborations: Jean-Michel Basquiat, Francesco Clemente, Andy Warhol. Küsnacht, Switzerland: Edition Galerie Bruno Bischofberger, 1984.
Coplans, John. *Andy Warhol*. Greenwich, Conn.: New York Graphic Society, 1970.
Crone, Rainer. *Andy Warhol*. New York: Praeger, 1970.
–. *Das bildnerische Werk Andy Warhols*. Berlin: Kommissionsvertrieb Wasmuth, 1976.
–. *Andy Warhol: A Picture Show by the Artist*. New York: Rizzoli, 1987. Translation and elaboration of *Andy Warhol: Das zeichnerische Werk, 1942-1975*.
–, ed. *Andy Warhol: Die frühen Werke, 1942-62*. Stuttgart: Edition Cantz, 1987.
Dufresne, Isabelle C. *Famous for 15 Minutes: My Years with Andy Warhol*. New York: Harcourt Brace Jovanovich, 1988.
Feldman, Frayda, and Jörg Schellmann, eds. *Andy Warhol Prints: A Catalogue Raisonné*. New York: Ronald Feldman Fine Arts, Editions Schellmann, and Abbeville Press, 1985.
Finkelstein, Nat. *Andy Warhol: The Factory Years 1964-1967*. London: Sidgwick & Jackson, c. 1989.
Garrels, Gary, ed. *The Work of Andy Warhol*. Seattle: Bay Press, 1989.
Geldzahler, Henry. *Pop Art, 1955-70*. Sydney: International Cultural Corporation of Australia Ltd., 1985.
–. *Andy Warhol: A Memorial*. Bridgehampton, N.Y.: Dia Art Foundation, 1987.
–. *Andy Warhol*. Bogotá: Galeria Fernando Quintana, 1988.
Gidal, Peter. *Andy Warhol: Films and Paintings*. New York: Studio Vista, 1971.
Green, Samuel Adams. *Andy Warhol*. New York: Wittenborn, 1966. Reprint. New York, 1966.
Guiles, Fred L. *Loner at the Ball: The Life of Andy Warhol*. New York: Bantam Press, 1989.
Hahn, Otto. *Andy Warhol*. Paris: Galerie Ileana Sonnabend, 1965.
–. *Warhol*. Paris: Fernand Hazan Editeur, 1972.
Hanhardt, John G. and Jon Gartenberg. *The Films of Andy Warhol: An Introduction*. New York: Whitney Museum of American Art, 1988.
Honnef, Klaus. *Andy Warhol: 1928-87, Kunst als Kommerz*. Cologne: Benedikt Taschen, 1989.
Koch, Stephen. *Stargazer: Andy Warhol's World and His Films*. Second edition. New York: M. Boyars, 1985.
–. *Andy Warhol Photographs*. New York: Robert Miller Gallery, 1986.
Kornbluth, Jesse. *Pre-Pop Warhol*. New York: Panache Press at Random House, 1988.
Kramer, Margia. *Andy Warhol et al.: The FBI File on Andy Warhol*. New York: UnSub Press, 1988.
Levi, Marcello. *Andy Warhol: 1974-1976*. Boissano, Italy: Centro Internazionale di Sperimentazioni Artistiche Marie-Louise Jeanneret, 1976.
Makos, Christopher. *Warhol: A Personal Photographic Memoir*. London: W. H. Allen, 1988.
McShine, Kynaston, ed. *Andy Warhol: A Retrospective*. New York: Museum of Modern Art, 1989.
Morphet, Richard. *Warhol*. London: The Tate Gallery, 1971.
Obalk, Hector. *Andy Warhol n'est pas un grand artiste*. Paris: Edition Aubier, 1990.
Ostrow, Stephen E. *Raid the Icebox I with Andy Warhol: An Exhibition Selected from the Storage Vaults of the Museum of Art, Rhode Island School of Design*. Providence: Museum of Art, Rhode Island School of Design, 1969.
Paoletti, John. *Andy Warhol*. Hartford: Wadsworth Atheneum, 1979.
Ratcliff, Carter. *Andy Warhol*. New York: Abbeville Press, 1983.
Rosebush, Judson, ed. *Studies for Warhol's Marilyns, Beuys' Actions and Objects, Duchamp's Etc., Including Film*. Syracuse, N.Y.: Everson Museum of Art, 1973.
Schmidt, K. K. *Karl Ströher: Sammler und Sammlung*. Stuttgart, 1982.
Smith, Patrick S. *Andy Warhol's Art and Films*. Ann Arbor: UMI Research Press, 1986.
–. *Warhol: Conversations about the Artist*. Ann Arbor: UMI Research Press, 1986.
Solomon, Alan. *Andy Warhol*. Boston: Institute of Contemporary Art, 1966.
Spies, Werner. *Andy Warhol – Cars: Die letzten Bilder, 1986/1987*. Stuttgart: Gerd Hatje Verlag GmbH, 1988.
Thorpe, Lynn Teresa. *Andy Warhol: Critical Evaluation of His Images and Books*. Ph. D. dissertation, Cornell University, Ithaca, N.Y., 1980.
Warhol. Paris: Galerie Ileana Sonnabend, 1964.
Warhol. Milan: Galleria Il Fauno, 1974.
Warhol: Campbell's Soup Boxes. Van Nuys, Calif.: Martin Lawrence Limited Editions, 1986.
Whitney, David, ed. *Andy Warhol: Portraits of the 70s*. New York: Random House in association with the Whitney Museum of American Art, 1979.
Wilcock, John. *The Autobiography & Sex Life of Andy Warhol*. New York: Other Scenes, 1971.

Photographic Acknowledgments

Jan Abbot, courtesy The Menil Collection, Houston p. 121 (top)
Courtesy Galerie Bruno Bischofberger, Zurich pp. 64, 66/67, 121 (bottom), 124 (bottom right)
Rudolph Burckhardt p. 113 (center); courtesy Leo Castelli Gallery, New York p. 116 (top and right center)
Courtesy Leo Castelli Gallery, New York p. 115 (center)
D. James Dee, © 1993 Estate & Foundation of Andy Warhol / ARS, New York, courtesy Ronald Feldman Fine Arts, New York p. 123 (bottom), 125 (top left and right), 126 (bottom), 127 (center), 128 (top), 129 (bottom right)
Courtesy The Estate of Andy Warhol p. 109 (top right)
Gianfranco Gorgoni p. 128 (center)
Grey Art Gallery & Study Center, New York University Art Collection p. 108 (bottom left)
John M. Hall p. 112 (top right)
© Howard Halma p. 109 (left center)
Michael Halsband p. 127 (bottom left)
Robert Hausser GDL, Mannheim p. 114 (top left)
Paul Hester p. 121 (center)
Dennis Hopper, courtesy The Menil Collection, Houston p. 111 (right center)
Jacqueline Hyde, courtesy Leo Castelli Gallery, New York p. 119 (center)
James Klosty, courtesy Cunningham Dance Foundation, Inc. p. 116 (left center)
Marcus Leatherdale p. 123 (top)
Linich/Factory photo, New York p. 117 (left center)
© Christopher Makos pp. 2, 13, 125 (center), 127 (top), 129 (top), 130 (top)
Camilla McGrath p. 120 (top)
Courtesy The Menil Collection, Houston p. 109 (bottom)
© Duane Michals p. 109 (right center), 111 (top right)
Ugo Mulas p. 8
The Museum of Modern Art, New York pp. 110 (top), 117 (right center)
Courtesy The Museum of Modern Art, New York p. 112 (bottom right)
Billy Name, Krunk Kronk Truck Photo pp. 106, 114 (bottom left and center), 116 (bottom left and bottom right), 117 (top, bottom left, and bottom right)
Hans Namuth pp. 119 (bottom), 126 (top)
© Arnold Newman p. 118 (center)
Phillips/Schwab plates 56, 58-65, 67, 69, 71-79, 82-85; pp. 120 (bottom), 122 (left center), 128 (bottom left and bottom right), 129 (bottom left); courtesy Leo Castelli Gallery, New York p. 125 (bottom); courtesy Galerie Bernd Klüser, Munich p. 129 (bottom left); courtesy Tony Shafrazi Gallery, Bruno Bischofberger, New York p. 127 (bottom right)
Philip Pocock, courtesy The Estate of Andy Warhol pp. 109 (top left), 111 (top left)
Eric Pollitzer, Hempstead, New York p. 112 (left center); courtesy Sidney Janis Gallery, New York p. 112 (top left)
Courtesy John Richardson p. 108 (top left)
Seymour Rosen, Los Angeles p. 113 (bottom)
Jörg Schellmann p. 122 (top and bottom)
Sabine Schmeller, Vienna p. 124 (bottom right)
© Stephen Shore p. 118 (top)
© Harry Shunk pp. 113 (top), 115 (bottom), 124 (top)
Niklaus Stauss, Zurich p. 64 (top)
Glenn Steigelman Inc. Photography, New York, courtesy Leo Castelli Gallery, New York p. 124 (left center)
Jim Strong, Inc., Hempstead, New York plate 40
Frank J. Thomas p. 119 (top)
Bill Yoscary p. 110 (bottom left)